Christ-
Centered
Preaching

Christ-Centered Preaching

Redeeming the
EXPOSITORY SERMON

SECOND EDITION

Bryan Chapell

Baker Academic
Grand Rapids, Michigan

Published by Baker Academic
a division of Baker Publishing Group
P.O. Box 6287, Grand Rapids, MI 49516-6287
www.bakeracademic.com

Fifth printing, October 2008

Printed in the United States of America

Library of Congress Cataloging-in-Publication Data

Chapell, Bryan.
    Christ-centered preaching : redeeming the expository sermon / Bryan Chapell.—2nd ed.
        p.   cm.
    Includes bibliographical references and index.
    ISBN 978-0-8010-2798-7
    ISBN 0-8010-2798-5 (hardcover)
    1. Preaching. 2. Bible—Homiletical use. I. Title.
BV4211.3.C48 2005
251—dc22
                                            2004018671

To
my wife, Kathy,
for the love, family, home, and friendship
the Lord has graced us to share

Contents

Appendixes

Figures

9

Tables

Preface to the
Second Edition

I consider this second edition of *Christ-Centered Preaching* to be a collaborative effort. In the ten years since its first publication, many pastors, students, and colleagues have offered encouragement, suggestions, and clarifications that I have incorporated into this volume.

I am particularly thankful for the aid provided by fellow homiletics instructors who so thoughtfully responded to my requests for input on making this second edition better serve the next generation of preachers. A host of homiletics colleagues responded, and I want to express my gratitude in particular to the following: Ronald Allen, a thoughtful examiner of many preaching traditions; Edmund Clowney, esteemed father of the unfolding mystery of all Scripture; Steve Brown, an uncompromising pastor-teacher of grace; Zack Eswine, my colleague of great heart for God's Word; Sidney Greidanus, dean of redemptive preaching and its finest scholar; Bill Hogan, a fellow yokeman in preparing a generation of Reformed pastors; David Larsen, a great historian and advocate of faithful exposition; Calvin Miller, a master storyteller and imagination's spokesman; Haddon Robinson, expository preaching's senior statesman; Larry Roff, a faithful listener to the music of Scripture; Robert Smith, a zealot for keeping the heart with the mind of preaching; Timothy Warren, a pastor of preachers; and Paul Scott Wilson, an insightful scholar of homiletics' scope. Thank you, friends and colleagues, for your aid and encouragement.

I am also grateful for my students. Twenty-plus years of teaching you to preach, listening to your sermons, and thrilling in the ways that God is ministering through you have refined my thought, deepened my appreciation for God's Word, and made me a better preacher. I am especially thankful for those in class during 2003 and 2004 who helped me review and correct this manuscript. Your diligence and care ministered to me and will minister to many more through the publication of this book you helped me write.

A second edition offers the opportunity for clarification, addition, and even correction. In the ten years since the first publication, I have rethought some things, learned some things, and become more committed to preaching my Savior always. All of these aspects of discovery find expression here.

Clarifications

As to clarification, I have taken greater pains to indicate that the reason all Scripture has a Fallen Condition Focus (FCF) is so that it can expose God's redemptive purposes for his people in order to magnify his glory. Although the preeminent goal of God's glory was expressed in the first edition, recent discussions of need-based preaching caused some to read the Fallen Condition Focus as just an oblique way of speaking about human, felt needs. The main reason to ask why the Holy Spirit inspired any text is to expose what fallen aspect of the human condition needs to be addressed in order for God's glory to be properly recognized and honored. The FCF exposes the necessity of a divine solution to the human dilemma and necessarily makes God the hero of the text as he displays his redemptive provision for his people. God rescues his people from their broken nature and world by his grace alone in order for them to experience his goodness and express his glory.

Contemporary discussions about the proper motivation for Christian obedience have also led me to refine my discussion of this important aspect of preaching. "Gratitude" is a concept richly used in church history to reflect loving thankfulness for all aspects of God's redemption—past, present, and future. In some contemporary church contexts, however, the term *gratitude* has been abused, suggesting a debt for believers to repay in order to claim Christ's *past* redeeming work. Preachers may plead (or imply), "Can't you do this little act of obedience to pay back Jesus, since he did so much for you?" The creation of a "debtor's ethic" that calls for a believer's obedience primarily as a way of paying back God for his mercy fails to recognize the unconditional nature of his grace and the inadequacy of our best works to compensate God for his inestimable gift. Thus, I have sought to make plain that the historic sense of gratitude is used in this book and to make this term (as well as terms such as *thanksgiving, appreciation,* and *praise*) but one expression of the unfettered, freely offered, and compelling love by which the Spirit motivates believers to honor God because of their joy in all the dimensions of his matchless gift.

In numerous places of this edition, I have sought to clean up fuzzy wording, awkward phrasing, and misleading emphases. I have sought to indicate in clearer terms what may be right as well as what may be wrong with messages that encourage imitating a biblical character or practice. The "Deadly Be's" (i.e., messages that only exhort believers to be like a biblical character, to be good, or to be more disciplined) possess deadly stings if redemptive contexts are not included.

I have attempted to clarify the redemptive context of "Christ-centered" messages in two ways. First, by indicating that the term itself is a synecdoche—standing not only for reference to Christ's incarnation or death on the cross but for the entire matrix of God's redemptive work, which finds its culminating expression in Christ's person and work. Second, by indicating that a message is Christ-centered not because it makes creative mention of an aspect of Jesus' life or death but because it discloses an aspect of God's redeeming nature (evident in the text) that is ultimately understood, fulfilled, and/or accomplished in Christ. Messages on the atonement are certainly Christ-centered because Christ provided his sacrifice on our behalf. But messages on the establishment of the Old Testament kingdom and the new creation kingdom are also Christ-centered to the extent that they demonstrate that each is a provision of God's grace for his people in order to glorify himself in his Son. Grace may appear in "Old Testament clothes" or "new covenant robes," but it is always "Christ-centered" when a preacher makes it plain that God provides what his people could not and cannot provide for themselves.

Additions

In responding to numerous suggestions and requests, I have added more examples in the text: sample outlines, examples of structural do's and don'ts, and a sample sermon. For additional clarity, I have also added more information on how to move from an exegetical to a homiletical outline. A definition of expository preaching now appears in the first chapter in addition to the more refined definition in chapter 6.

In the ten years since *Christ-Centered Preaching* was first published, narrative and inductive approaches to preaching have received a great deal of attention. The impact of technology and mass communication has also made preachers question traditional approaches to preparing sermons. In this text, I interact more with these movements—endorsing some aspects and critiquing others. I remain convinced that an expository approach is the most fruitful as the mainstay of a pulpit ministry (and I rejoice in the recent spate of books that has endorsed this biblically committed approach), but we can always learn from other communication fields how people hear and how better to minister God's Word to them. There is not one right style of preaching any more than there is one right style of Scripture. The Word of God comes to us in propositions, poems, epistles, stories, and more. Discerning how these different expressions of God's truth are best related to God's people today is a dynamic task that is full of surprises and delight for those willing to learn how better to say what God says—the ultimate expository task.

In my own growth, I have discovered that though my writing emphasized discerning the place of each passage in the historical sweep of God's redemptive plan, my preaching has increasingly focused on the grace evident in particular passages. The more I have become aware that God's revelation of his redemptive character occurs at the micro- as well as the macro-level of Scripture, the more I have delighted to preach his redeeming character from virtually every page of the Bible. As a consequence, I have added significant sections to the final chapters that describe how God's grace is evident in "doctrinal statements" and "relational interaction" throughout Scripture. My sense is that, while academics more often write about redemptive-historical methods, those active in the pulpit frequently approach a text on its more immediate foundations. Thus, I have more fully explored how redemptive themes can be variously developed using the different periods and types of biblical literature.

My goal in further describing how the gold of grace can be mined from each passage is to have students worry less whether they have to preach Genesis to Revelation in every sermon and to have scholars debate less who has the right master metaphor for the science of biblical theology. The result may be that many more will experience the joy of preaching the myriad ways that God makes his redemption known and will encounter the fellowship with him that each text encourages and enables. While we cannot and should not ignore the cognitive dimensions of a text, we should remember the relational aims that are its purpose. By consistent adulation of the mercy of God in Christ, preachers fuel the love for the Savior that is his people's greatest motivation and power for glorifying him in all of life.

The ultimate aim of Christ-centered preaching is not to burden preachers with a new science of interpretation but to release them to preach the grace of all Scripture that secures and enables relationship with the Savior—making preaching a joy to our hearts and strength to God's people. The ultimate purpose of preaching is the promotion of this union with Christ, which is our hope, joy, strength, and peace. Through the truths of the text, God intends to bring forth the fruit of our union with him and with one another for his glory. To ensure that we do not think of our union only in personal terms, I have also taken greater care to underscore the community dimensions of preaching that unite believers with the Savior of the world.

Corrections

Of the making of edits there is no end. Although I have attempted to catch typos, tweak figures, and correct footnotes, I am sure that the updated material in this edition will contain enough glitches and bugs to torment me until there is a future edition. Our world remains fallen, and correction of the work of my hands will continue until that great day when the Savior comes and perfects all things. Until that day, I pray to live under the correction of God's Word so that I may continually know the necessity of all the mercies of his Book that are intended for my delight. May the apprehension of that joy be in me and in those who read this work such a fountain of blessing that we will boldly profess what convicts of sin and powerfully proclaim what convinces of grace with the authority of God's Word and for his glory.

Preface to the
First Edition

The two words around which the whole of this work could be wrapped are *authority* and *redemption*.

In our day, two opposing forces challenge the effective exposition of the Word of God. The first well-documented foe of the gospel is the erosion of authority. The philosophies of subjectivism have joined hands with the skeptics of transcendent truth to create a cultural climate antagonistic toward any authority. Yet as the apostle Paul saw long ago, this release from biblical standards inevitably makes persons slaves to their own passions and victims of one another's selfishness (Rom. 6:19–22).

Our culture and the church are desperate for dependable truths that address the brokenness of the world, which this loss of authority has made more acute. Not all answers the church supplies through its preachers herald good news. Some preachers simply have abandoned any hope of finding a source of eternal truth or of being able to communicate it to a diverse world. Others who sense our culture's antipathy for all who dare to contend that they have definite, value- and behavior-binding answers have chosen to preach without authority. Though they retain a desire to heal, such pastors too often settle for a mere repackaging of counseling or management theories in religious-sounding words. By offering the comfort of merely human answers that are due to change with the next wave of best-selling books, such preaching masks rather than heals the pain of the soul (1 Cor. 2:4–5; 1 Tim. 6:20; 2 Tim. 4:3).

Expository preaching that explains precisely what the Word of God says for the issues of our day, the concerns of our lives, and the destiny of our souls provides an alternative. In keeping with the mandates of Scripture, such preaching offers a voice of authority not of human origin and not subject to cultural vagaries (Isa. 40:8; 1 Thess. 2:13; Titus 2:15). As obvious as this solution may seem, its widespread adoption faces large challenges. Over the last two generations, the expository sermon has been stigmatized (not always unfairly) as a style of preaching that degenerates into dry recitations of biblical trivia or that arrogates into dogmatic defenses of doctrinal distinctives removed from ordinary life. This challenge has become even more acute as all forms of preaching have increasingly been accused of being anachronistic communication tools incapable of addressing the tastes and needs of a culture attuned to the aids and innovations of modern technology.

The time has come for redeeming the expository sermon—not only reclaiming a needed voice of biblical authority for our day but also rescuing the expository approach from practitioners unaware of (or unconcerned about) cultural forces, communication requirements, and biblical principles that cause their sermons to be disconnected from God's power and people. This book attempts to provide one approach to such a reclamation and rescue. Initially, this text offers practical instruction that binds the expository sermon to Scripture's truths while releasing it from tradition-bound attitudes and communication-naive practices that can needlessly deny both pulpit and pew the power and the hope of an accessible message from God's Word.

Along with practical instruction, this book also attempts to confront a second foe of the effective communication of the gospel. This foe too often arises as an unrecognized side effect of a well-intended quest for authority. Evangelical preachers reacting to the secularization of both culture and church can mistakenly make moral instruction or societal reform the *primary* focus of their messages. No one can blame these preachers for wanting to challenge the evils of the day. When sin closes in, faithful preachers have a desire, a right, and a responsibility to say, "Stop it!"

However, if these preachers' actual or perceived cure for sin's sickness is human behavior change, then they inadvertently present a message contrary to the gospel. The Bible does not tell us how *we* can improve ourselves to gain God's acceptance or reform our world (Gal. 2:15–20). Fundamentally and pervasively, the Scriptures teach the inadequacy of any purely human effort to achieve divine approval or purposes. We are entirely dependent on the mercy and power provided through our Savior to be what he desires and to do what he requires. Grace rules—as both the most powerful motivation and the only true means of Christian obedience!

However well-intended and biblically rooted a sermon's instruction may be, if the message does not incorporate the motivation and enablement inherent in proper apprehension of the redeeming work of Jesus Christ, the preacher proclaims mere Pharisaism. Preaching that is faithful to the whole of Scripture not only establishes God's requirements but also highlights the redemptive truths that make holiness possible. The task may seem impossible. How can we make all Scripture center on Christ's work when vast portions make no mention of him? The answer lies in learning to see all of God's Word as a unified message of human need and divine provision (Luke 24:27; Rom. 15:4).

By exploring how this gospel of redemption pervades all of Scripture, this book also establishes theological principles for redeeming the expository sermon from the well-intended but ill-conceived legalism that characterizes too much evangelical preaching. Christ-centered preaching replaces futile harangues for human striving with exhortations to obey God as a loving response to the redeeming work of Jesus Christ and in thankful dependence on the divine enablement of his Spirit. True holiness, loving obedience, spiritual strength, and lasting joy flow from this precise and powerful form of biblical exposition (1 Tim. 2:1; Titus 2:11–15).

Acknowledgments

I write this book with deep appreciation for those whose contributions to my own thought and life have been significant.

Thanks are especially owed to Robert G. Rayburn, my homiletics professor, who settled for nothing less than excellence while consistently teaching that God's glory has to be the sole focus of the preaching task, and to John Sanderson, professor of biblical theology, who opened my eyes to the necessity of Christ focus in all faithful exposition.

I am greatly indebted to the Rayburn family, especially LaVerne Rayburn and her son, Robert S. Rayburn, for allowing me access to Robert G. Rayburn's unpublished writings and notes. Being entrusted with sharing some of my mentor's insights is a great privilege.

Although the research and thought behind the two editions of this work have spanned three decades, I did most of the writing during sabbaticals provided by Covenant Theological Seminary. I want to express my thanks to the board of trustees for granting me these wonderful writing opportunities. Working at an institution governed by godly principles is a blessing for which I am daily thankful.

I am especially grateful to Paul Kooistra, who preceded me in the presidency of Covenant Seminary and whose encouragement, ministry, and many hours of conversation along our jogging path about the role of grace in preaching sharpened and strengthened my thought.

I am thankful for the ministry and friendship of James Meek, whose faithfulness as associate dean for academics at Covenant Seminary during my first writing sabbatical allowed me to complete the first edition of this work, and for Donald Guthrie and Wayne Copeland, who expanded their vice presidential duties so that I could write this second edition.

As always, I owe more than words can express to the untiring and joyful service of June Dare and Kathy Woodard, whose secretarial skills have made me look better than I have any right to expect.

Part 1

Principles
for Expository
Preaching

G O A L   O F   C H A P T E R   1

*To communicate how important preaching is and
what is really important in preaching*

1

Word and Witness

The Nobility of Preaching

I am "asking God to fill you with the knowledge of his will through all spiritual wisdom and understanding . . . in order that you may live a life worthy of the Lord and may please him in every way: bearing fruit in every good work, growing in the knowledge of God." The prayer of every preacher who loves God's Word and God's people echoes this prayer of the apostle Paul for the Colossian church (Col. 1:9–10). We pray that God will also use our preaching to produce such a knowledge of God's will that others will live to please him and will produce spiritual fruit, resulting in an ever growing knowledge of their God. These priorities indicate that the goal of preaching is not merely to impart information but to provide the means of transformation ordained by a sovereign God that will affect the lives and destinies of eternal souls committed to a preacher's spiritual care.

English preacher Ian Tait quips that those who study the Bible only to gain more information may believe their minds are expanding when, in fact, only their heads are swelling. Knowledge purely for knowledge's sake "puffeth up" (1 Cor. 8:1 KJV). The riches of God's Word are no one's private treasure, and when we share its wealth, we participate in its highest purposes. Whether your studies take place through a seminary, a Bible college, or a program of personal reading, they will be more rewarding when you realize how each element prepares you to preach with accuracy and authority for the sake of others' growth in grace. Every biblical discipline reaches a pinnacle purpose when we use it not merely to expand our minds but also to further the priorities of the gospel. That is why, for more than a quarter century, Robert G. Rayburn taught seminary students, "Christ is the only King of your studies, but homiletics is the queen."[1]

Elevating preaching to such a royal pedestal can intimidate even the most committed student of Scripture. Probably no conscientious preacher has failed to question whether this lofty task is greater than the lowly servant who dares to step behind a pulpit. When we face real people with eternal souls balanced between heaven and hell, the nobility of preaching both awes us and makes us more aware of our inadequacies (cf. 1 Cor. 2:3). We know our skills are insufficient for an activity with such vast consequences. We recognize that our hearts are too lacking in purity to lead others to holiness. Honest evaluation inevitably causes us to conclude that we do not have sufficient eloquence, wisdom, or character to be capable of turning others from spiritual death to eternal life. Such a realization can cause young preachers to run from their first preaching assignment and experienced pastors to despair in their pulpits.

The Power in the Word

What we require in the face of the limits of our personal effectiveness and in an age that increasingly questions the validity of preaching[2] is a reminder of God's design for spiritual transformation. Ultimately, preaching accomplishes its spiritual purposes not because of the skills or the wisdom of a preacher but because of the power of the Scripture proclaimed (1 Cor. 2:4–5). Preachers minister with greater zeal, confidence, and freedom when they realize that God has taken from their backs the monkey of spiritual manipulation. God is not relying on the sufficiency of our craft or character to accomplish his purposes (2 Cor. 3:5). God certainly can use eloquence and desires lives befitting the sanctity of our subject matter, but his Spirit uses the Word itself to fulfill his saving and sanctifying purposes. The human efforts of the greatest preachers are still too weak and sin-tainted to be responsible for others' eternal destinies. For this reason, God infuses his Word with his own spiritual power. The efficacy of the truths in God's message rather than any virtue in the messenger transforms hearts.

1. Robert G. Rayburn was the founding president of Covenant Theological Seminary and its primary homiletics professor from 1956 to 1984. The quotation is from his unpublished class notes.
2. David L. Larsen, *The Anatomy of Preaching: Identifying the Issues in Preaching Today* (Grand Rapids: Baker, 1989), 11–12; and Byron Val Johnson, "A Media Selection Model for Use with a Homiletical Taxonomy" (Ph.D. diss., Southern Illinois University at Carbondale, 1982), 215.

The Power of God Inherent in the Word

Precisely how the Holy Spirit uses scriptural truth to convert souls and change lives we cannot say, but we must sense the dynamics that give us hope when we preach God's Word. The Bible makes it clear that the Word is not merely powerful; it is without peer or dependence. The Word of God

creates: "God said, 'Let there be light,' and there was light" (Gen. 1:3). "For he spoke, and it came to be; he commanded, and it stood firm" (Ps. 33:9).

controls: "He sends his command to the earth; his word runs swiftly. He spreads the snow like wool and scatters the frost like ashes. He hurls down his hail like pebbles. . . . He sends his word and melts them" (Ps. 147:15–18).

convicts: "Let the one who has my word speak it faithfully . . ." declares the LORD. "Is not my word like fire," declares the LORD, "and like a hammer that breaks a rock in pieces?" (Jer. 23:28–29).

performs his purposes: "As the rain and the snow come down from heaven, and do not return to it without watering the earth . . . so is my word that goes out from my mouth: It will not return to me empty, but will accomplish what I desire and achieve the purpose for which I sent it" (Isa. 55:10–11).

overrides human weakness: While in prison the apostle Paul rejoiced that when others preach the Word with "false motives or true," the work of God still moves forward (Phil. 1:18).

Scripture's portrayal of its own potency challenges us always to remember that the Word preached, rather than the *preaching* of the Word, accomplishes heaven's purposes. Preaching that is true to Scripture converts, convicts, and eternally changes the souls of men and women because God's Word is the instrument of divine compulsion, not because preachers have any power in themselves to stimulate such godly transformations (although human powers can certainly bring about all kinds of worldly changes, including those that masquerade as the products of heaven).

The Power of the Word Manifested in Christ

God fully reveals the dynamic power of his Word in the New Testament, where he identifies his Son as the divine *Logos,* or Word (John 1:1). By identifying Jesus as his Word, God indicates that his message and his person are inseparable. The Word embodies him. This is not to say that the letters and the paper of a Bible are divine but that the truths Scripture holds are God's means of making his person and his presence real to his people.

God's Word is powerful because he chooses to exercise his power through it and to be present in it. By his word God brought the world into being (Gen. 1), and Jesus is the Word by whom "all things were made" (John 1:1–3; Col. 1:16) and who continues "sustaining all things by his powerful word" (Heb. 1:3). The Word uses his word to reveal his person and to carry out all his purposes.

Christ's redemptive power and the power of his Word coalesce in the New Testament, with *Logos* (the incarnation of God) and *logos* (the message about God) becoming so reflexive as to form a conceptual identity. As the work of the original creation comes through the spoken word of God, so the work of new creation (i.e., redemption) comes through the living Word of God. James says, "He [the Father] chose to give us birth through the word of truth" (James 1:18). The phrase "word of truth" reflects the message about salvation and the One who gives the new birth. The same play on words is used by Peter: "For you have been born again, not of perishable seed, but of imperishable, through the living and enduring word of God" (1 Pet. 1:23). In these passages, the message about Jesus and Christ himself are unified. Both are the "living and enduring [W]ord of God" by which we have been born again.

Thus, it is not merely prosaic to insist that a faithful preacher should serve the text.[3] Since the Word is the mediate presence of Christ, service is due. Paul rightly instructs the young pastor Timothy to be a workman "who correctly handles the word of truth" (2 Tim. 2:15) because the Word of God is "living and active" (Heb. 4:12). Scriptural truth is not a passive object for examination and presentation. The Word examines us. "It judges the thoughts and attitudes of the heart" (4:12). Christ remains active in his Word, performing divine tasks that one presenting the Word has no right or ability personally to assume.

These perspectives on the Word of God culminate in the ministry of the apostle Paul. The bookish missionary who was not known for his pulpit expertise nonetheless wrote, "I am not ashamed of the gospel, because it is the power of God for . . . everyone who believes" (Rom. 1:16). As students of elementary Greek soon learn, the word for "power" in this verse is *dunamis*, from which we get the English word *dynamite*. The gospel's force lies beyond the power of the preacher. Paul preaches without shame in his delivery skills because he trusts that the Spirit of God will use the Word the apostle proclaims to shatter the hardness of the human heart in ways no stage technique or philosophical construct can rival.

In some ways, the entire process seems ridiculous. Common sense rebels against claims that eternal destinies will change simply because we voice thoughts from an ancient text. When Paul commends the foolishness of

---

3. Herbert H. Farmer, *The Servant of the Word* (New York: Scribner's, 1942), 16–17.

preaching—not foolish preaching—he acknowledges the apparent senseless-
ness of trying to transform attitudes, lifestyles, philosophical perspectives,
and faith commitments with mere words about a once crucified rabbi (see
1 Cor. 1:21). Yet preaching endures and the gospel spreads because the Holy
Spirit uses puny human efforts as the conduit for the force of his own Word.
By the blessing of God's Spirit, the Word yet transforms (i.e., causes our
hearts to love God and our wills to seek his will).

Each year I recount for new seminary students a time when the reality
of the Word's power struck me with exceptional force. The Lord's work
overwhelmed me when I walked into a new members' class of our church.
Sitting together on the front row were three young women—all cousins.
Though they had promised to come to the class, the reality of their being
there still shook me.

In the previous year, each of these women had approached our church
for help with serious problems. I got acquainted with the first after she left
her husband because of his alcoholism. As an Easter-only member of our
church, he had previously expressed little use for "religion," but he came
seeking help when she left. He said he was willing to do anything to get her
to return. They came together for counseling. He dealt with his drinking.
They reunited, and now she wanted to become part of our faith family.

The second cousin also had fled her marriage and had come seeking help
at the first cousin's suggestion. She was the victim of spousal abuse and had
sought solace with another man outside her marriage. Although neither
man sought God, our ministry to this woman warmed her heart toward
Christ. Even after her husband turned to other women, she left her lover
and submitted her life to God's will.

The last cousin was also married, but she worked as a traveling salesper-
son and was living with several men as though each were her husband. An
accident that injured a young nephew brought our church into her life. As
she witnessed the care of Christians for the child and for her (despite her
initial hostility toward us), she found a love that her sexual encounters had
not supplied. Now she, too, came to be a part of the family of God.

The presence of these three cousins in a church membership class was a
miracle. How foolish it would be to think that mere words I had said—some
consonants and vowels pushed out of the mouth by a little burst of air—could
account for their decisions. No amount of human convincing could have
turned them from their selfish, pleasure-seeking, or self-destructive lifestyles
to an eternal commitment to Jesus Christ. Hearts hostile to God's Word
now wanted fellowship with him simply because Christians had lovingly
and faithfully expressed its truth.

God plucked three souls from a hellish swirl of family confusion, spousal
betrayal, and personal sin by the means of his Word. Yet as unlikely as these
events seem, they are readily explained. The Lord uses the truth of his Word

to change hearts. In the terms of Scripture, these cousins "turned to God from idols to serve the living and true God, and to wait for his Son from heaven" not because of any preacher's skills but because of the Word's own power (1 Thess. 1:9–10).

When preachers perceive the power that the Word holds, confidence in their calling grows even as pride in their performance withers. We need not fear our ineffectiveness when we speak truths God has empowered to perform his purposes. At the same time, acting as though our talents are responsible for spiritual change is like a messenger claiming credit for ending a war because he delivered the peace documents. The messenger has a noble task to perform, but he jeopardizes his mission and belittles the true victor with claims of personal achievement. Credit, honor, and glory for preaching's effects belong to Christ alone because his Word alone saves and transforms.

The Power of the Word Applied in Preaching

EXPOSITORY PREACHING PRESENTS THE POWER OF THE WORD

The fact that the power for spiritual change resides in God's Word argues the case for *expository* preaching. Expository preaching attempts to present and apply the truths of a specific biblical passage.[4] Other types of preaching that proclaim biblical truth are certainly valid and valuable, but for the beginning preacher and for a regular congregational diet, no preaching type is more important than expository.

Biblical exposition binds the preacher and the people to the only source of true spiritual change. Because hearts are transformed when people are confronted with the Word of God, expository preachers are committed to saying what God says.[5] The expository preacher opens the Bible before God's people and dares to say, "I will explain to you what this passage means." The words are not meant to convey one's own authority but rather humbly to confess that the preacher has no better word than God's Word. Thus, the preacher's mission and calling is to explain to God's people what the Bible means.

The most dependable way of explaining what the Bible means is to select a biblical text prayerfully, divide it according to its significant thoughts and features, and then explain the nature and implications of each. Explaining the text according to the intent of the author also requires that we not skip portions of the passage or neglect features of its context that must be un-

---

4. Haddon Robinson, *Biblical Preaching: The Development and Delivery of Expository Messages,* 2nd ed. (Grand Rapids: Baker, 2001), 21. See further the definition below and in chap. 6.

5. Sidney Greidanus, *The Modern Preacher and the Ancient Text: Interpreting and Preaching Biblical Literature* (Grand Rapids: Eerdmans, 1988), 15.

derstood in order for the principles the passage is teaching to be grasped. *An expository sermon may be defined as a message whose structure and thought are derived from a biblical text, that covers the scope of the text, and that explains the features and context of the text in order to disclose the enduring principles for faithful thinking, living, and worship intended by the Spirit, who inspired the text.* The expository sermon uses the features of the text and its context to explain what that portion of the Bible means.

As expository preachers, our ultimate goal is not to communicate the value of our opinions, others' philosophies, or speculative meditations but rather to show how God's Word discloses his will for those united to him through his Son. Truths of God proclaimed in such a way that people can see that the concepts derive from Scripture and apply to their lives preoccupy the expository preacher's efforts. Such preaching puts people in immediate contact with the power of the Word.

Expository Preaching Presents the Authority of the Word

Preaching addresses the perpetual human quest for authority and meaning. Though we live in an age hostile to authority, everyday struggles for significance, security, and acceptance force every individual to ask, "Who has the right to tell me what to do?" This question, typically posed as a challenge, is really a plea for help. Without an ultimate authority for truth, all human striving has no ultimate value, and life itself becomes futile. Modern trends in preaching that deny the authority of the Word[6] in the name of intellectual sophistication lead to a despairing subjectivism in which people do what is right in their own eyes—a state whose futility Scripture has clearly articulated (Judg. 21:25).

The answer to the radical relativism of our culture and its accompanying uncertainties is the Bible's claim of authority. Paul commended the Thessalonian Christians because they accepted his message "not as the word of men, but as it actually is, the word of God, which is at work in you who believe" (1 Thess. 2:13). The claim of Scripture and the premise of expository preaching is that God has spoken in his Word. Long ago Augustine simply summarized, "When the Bible speaks, God speaks." Thus, the expository preaching task is to communicate what God committed to Scripture in order to give God's people his truth for their time. Such effort is not blind adherence to fundamentalist dogma but rather a commitment to a source that both faith and reason confirm is the only basis of human hope—for without a source of transcendence and certitude, all foundations for society, identity, and sanity vanish.

---

6. David Buttrick, *Homiletic: Moves and Structures* (Philadelphia: Fortress, 1987), 408.

Without the authority of the Word, preaching becomes an endless search for topics, therapies, and techniques that will win approval, promote acceptance, advance a cause, or soothe worry. Human reason, social agendas, popular consensus, and personal moral convictions become the resources of preaching that lacks "the historic conviction that what Scripture says, God says."[7] The opinions and emotions that formulate the content of preaching that lacks biblical authority are the same forces that can deny the validity of those concepts in a changed culture, a subsequent generation, or a rebellious heart. Expository preaching avoids this shifting sand by committing a preacher to the foundation of God's Word.

When we preach, God is the true audience of our efforts. Just as true but perhaps more humbling and emboldening is the conviction that when we speak the truths of God's Word, God speaks (cf. Luke 10:16). The Second Helvetic Confession of the Protestant Reformation says, "The preaching of the Word of God is the Word of God." The idea that what comes out of our mouths is the word of God initially sounds arrogant if not blasphemous. Yet the humility implicit in such a confession is that we have nothing of importance, merit, or authority to say comparable to what God has said. When we speak, therefore, we design our messages to express the truths of the eternal Word so that the church may be the "mouth house" of God that Martin Luther described.

When preachers approach the Bible as God's very Word, questions about what we have a right to say vanish. God can tell his people what they should believe and do, and he has. Scripture obligates preachers to make sure others understand what God says. We have no biblical authority to say anything else. It is true that our expressions are culturally conditioned, but the transcendence of God's truth and the divine image-bearing privileges of our nature make it possible for us to receive and communicate his Word.

Only preachers committed to proclaiming what God says have the Bible's imprimatur on their preaching. Thus, expository preaching endeavors to discover and convey the precise meaning of the Word. Scripture determines what expositors preach because they unfold what it says. *The meaning of the passage is the message of the sermon.* The text governs the preacher. Expository preachers do not expect others to honor their opinions. Such ministers adhere to Scripture's truths and expect their listeners to heed the same.

Expository Preaching Presents the Work of the Spirit

The expectations of expository preachers are themselves based on the truths of the Bible. If no amount of eloquence and oratory can account for spiritual transformation, who alone can change hearts? Leaders of the Protestant Reformation answered, "The Holy Spirit working by and with

---

7. J. I. Packer, *God Speaks to Man: Revelation and the Bible* (Philadelphia: Westminster, 1965), 18.

the Word in our hearts."[8] The Word of God is the sword of the Spirit (Eph. 6:17; cf. Acts 10:44; Eph. 1:13). The extraordinary but regular means by which God transforms lives is through his Word, which is accompanied by the regenerating, convicting, and enabling power of his Spirit.

When we proclaim the Word, we bring the work of the Holy Spirit to bear on others' lives. No truth grants greater encouragement in our preaching and gives us more cause to expect results from our efforts. The work of the Spirit is as inextricably linked to preaching as heat is to the light a bulb emits. When we present the light of God's Word, his Spirit performs his purposes of warming, melting, and conforming hearts to his will.

The Holy Spirit uses our words, but his work, not ours, affects the hidden recesses of the human will. Paul wrote, "God . . . made his light shine in our hearts to give us the light of the knowledge of the glory of God in the face of Christ. But we have this treasure in jars of clay to show that this all-surpassing power is from God and not from us" (2 Cor. 4:6–7). The glory of preaching is that God accomplishes his will through it, but we are always humbled and occasionally comforted by the knowledge that he works beyond our human limitations. Ours is only the second sermon; the first and last are those of the Holy Spirit, who first gave his Word and quickens it in the hearts of hearers.

These truths challenge all preachers to approach their task with a deep sense of dependence on the Spirit of God. Public ministry true to God's purposes requires devoted private prayer. We should not expect our words to acquaint others with the power of the Spirit if we have not met with him. Faithful preachers plead for God to work as well as for their own accuracy, integrity, and skill in proclaiming his Word. Success in the pulpit can be the force that leads a preacher from prayerful dependence on the Spirit. Congregational accolades for pulpit excellence may tempt one to put too much confidence in personal gifts, acquired skills, or a particular method of preaching. Succumbing to such a temptation is evidenced not so much by a change in belief as by a change in practice. Neglect of prayer signals serious deficiencies in a ministry even if other signs of success have not diminished. We must always remember that popular acclaim is not necessarily the same as spiritual effectiveness.

The spiritual dimensions of preaching undercut much of what you may be tempted to believe about this book—that if you learn to speak well enough, you can be a great preacher. Not true! Do not let the necessary emphases of this book, the comments of others, or the desires of your own heart mislead you. Great gifts do not necessarily make for great preaching. The technical excellence of a message may rest on your skills, but the spiritual efficacy of your message resides with God.

8. Westminster Confession of Faith, 1.5.

The Effectiveness of Testimony

Faith in the working of God's Word and Spirit does not mean that you are without responsibility. Early American pastor John Shaw once preached at an ordination:

> It's true as one observes, God can work by what means He will; by a scandalous, domineering, self-seeking preacher, but it is not His usual way. Foxes and wolves are not nature's instrument to generate sheep. Whoever knew much good done to souls by any pastors but such as preached and lived in the power of love, working by a clear, convincing light, and both managed by a holy, lively seriousness? You must bring fire to kindle fire.[9]

There is no need to presume upon the goodness of God. Although the power inherent in the Word can work despite our weaknesses, there is no reason to put hurdles in its path. Good preaching in one sense involves getting out of the way so that the Word can do its work. Shaw's comments remind us what clearing the path usually means: preaching and living in such a way as to make the Word plain and credible.

Classical Distinctions

The apostle Paul taught of the inherent efficacy of the Word, but he also related his personal resolve to put no stumbling block to the gospel in anyone's path (2 Cor. 6:3). Aristotle's classic rhetorical distinctions, though not inspired, can help us understand the basic components of every message we preach so that we do not needlessly cause others to stumble over what or how we speak.

In classical rhetoric, three elements compose every persuasive message:

logos: the verbal content of the message, including its craft and logic

pathos: the emotive features of a message, including the passion, fervor, and feeling that a speaker conveys and the listeners experience

ethos: the perceived character of the speaker, determined most significantly by the concern expressed for the listeners' welfare. Aristotle's belief (confirmed in countless modern studies) was that *ethos* is the most powerful component of persuasion.

Listeners automatically evaluate each of these elements of persuasion in sermons in order to weigh the truths that the preacher presents. This realization should convince preachers who want to create clear access to the Word

---

9. John Shaw, "The Character of a Pastor according to God's Heart" (Ligonier, Pa.: Soli Deo Gloria Publications, 1992), 3–4.

to strive to make each aspect of their messages a door and not a barrier. For instance, it may be hard for men in this culture of John Wayne, Denzel Washington, and Aragorn heroes to express emotion when they preach. Yet failing to speak with conviction appropriate to one's subject and personality about the truths of eternity—to appear to be unmoved or unaffected by the joy of salvation or the plight of the lost—actually miscommunicates Scripture's meaning.

Paul reflects the importance of each of the components of persuasion in his first letter to the Thessalonians (see fig. 1.1). Although his terms are not Aristotle's, they echo features of the classic rhetor's categories and remind us that craft cannot make a message powerful if one's heart and character do not validate its truths. Paul makes it clear that though the Holy Spirit forges the path of the gospel, listeners advance to confrontation with the Word through doors the preacher opens with the message. Significantly, Paul cites his own life as affecting the reception of the message, thus giving scriptural credence to the notion that *ethos* is a powerful force in the ordinary process of spiritual persuasion.

Figure 1.1

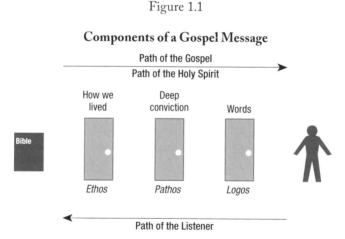

Components of a Gospel Message

"Our gospel came to you not simply with **words** [*logos*], but also **with power, and with deep conviction** [*pathos*]. You **know how we lived** [*ethos*] among you for your sake" (1 Thess. 1:5).

Paul cites his conduct and his compassion not only as evidences of his "deep conviction" but also as integral sources of his message's "power." Although this book of homiletical method necessarily focuses on the elements of *logos* and *pathos* in preaching, the Bible's own emphases remind us that pastoral character remains the foundation of ministry. Preaching's earthly glory may be eloquence, but its eternal heartbeat is faithfulness.

Phillips Brooks's oft-cited observation that preaching is "truth poured through personality" reflects biblical principle as well as common sense. Our fathers taught, "Your actions speak so loudly I can't hear what you say." Today's young people tell us, "Don't talk the talk if you don't walk the walk." Each maxim merely reflects a higher wisdom that urges Christian leaders to "conduct [themselves] in a manner worthy of the gospel" (Phil. 1:27). Our preaching should reflect the uniqueness of our personalities, but our lives should reflect Christ in order for his message to spread unhindered.

Scriptural Corroboration

There is no scarcity of Scripture passages that confirm the importance of *ethos* for effective proclamation. Beginning with the preeminent passages on pastoral theology, with emphases added, the following texts link the quality of preaching with the quality of a preacher's character and conduct.

1 Thessalonians 2:3–8 and 11–12

For the appeal we make does not spring from error or impure motives, nor are we trying to trick you. On the contrary, we speak as men approved by God to be entrusted with the gospel. We are not trying to please men but God, who tests our hearts. You know we never used flattery, nor did we put on a mask to cover up greed—God is our witness. We were not looking for praise from men, not from you or anyone else.

As apostles of Christ we could have been a burden to you, but we were gentle among you, like a mother caring for her little children. We loved you so much that *we were delighted to share with you not only the gospel of God but our lives as well,* because you had become so dear to us.

For you know that we dealt with each of you as a father deals with his own children, encouraging, comforting and urging you to live lives worthy of God, who calls you into his kingdom and glory.

2 Timothy 2:15–16 and 22–24

Do your best to present yourself to God as *one approved, a workman who does not need to be ashamed* and who correctly handles the word of truth. Avoid godless chatter, because those who indulge in it will become more and more ungodly.

Flee the evil desires of youth, and pursue righteousness, faith, love and peace, along with those who call on the Lord out of a pure heart. Don't have anything to do with foolish and stupid arguments, because you know they produce quarrels. And the Lord's servant must not quarrel; instead, he must be kind to everyone, able to teach, not resentful.

Titus 2:7–8

In everything set them an *example* by doing what is good. In your teaching show integrity, seriousness and soundness of speech that cannot be condemned.

2 Corinthians 6:3–4

We put no stumbling block in anyone's path, so that our ministry will not be discredited. Rather, as servants of God *we commend ourselves in every way.*

James 1:26–27

If anyone considers himself religious and yet does not keep a tight rein on his tongue, he deceives himself and his religion is worthless. Religion that God our Father accepts as pure and faultless is this: to look after orphans and widows in their distress and to keep oneself from being polluted by the world.

James 3:13

Who is wise and understanding among you? *Let him show it* by his good life, by deeds done in the humility that comes from wisdom.

Ethos *Implications*

Guard Your Character

The influence of a preacher's testimony on the acceptance of a sermon requires that one's life be under the rule of Scripture. With unblinking candor, John Wesley once explained to a struggling protégé why his ministry lacked power: "Your temper is uneven; you lack love for your neighbors. You grow angry too easily; your tongue is too sharp—thus, the people will not hear you."[10] Wesley's honesty reflects Scripture's admonition and challenges each of us to guard our character if we desire effectiveness with the Word.

True character cannot be hidden, although it can be temporarily masked. Character oozes out of us in our messages. Just as people reveal themselves in conversations by their words and mannerisms, we constantly reveal ourselves to others in our preaching. Over time our word choices, topics, examples, and tone unveil our hearts regardless of how well we think we have cordoned off deeper truths from public display. The inside is always on view. People sense more than they can prove by the way we present ourselves in the most inadvertent ways.

With the insight of many years of preaching experience, Haddon Robinson summarizes:

> As much as we might wish it otherwise, we cannot be separated from the message. Who has not heard some devout brother or sister pray in anticipa-

---

10. Quoted in James L. Golden, Goodwin F. Berquist, and William Coleman, *The Rhetoric of Western Thought,* 3rd ed. (Dubuque: Kendall-Hunt, 1978), 297.

tion of a sermon, "Hide our pastor behind the cross so that we may see not him but Jesus only." We commend the spirit of such a prayer. . . . Yet no place exists where a preacher may hide. Even a large pulpit cannot conceal us from view. . . . We affect our message. We may be mouthing a scriptural idea yet we can remain as impersonal as a telephone recording, as superficial as a radio commercial, or as manipulative as a con man. The audience does not hear a sermon, they hear a person—they hear you.[11]

No truth calls louder for pastoral holiness than the link between a preacher's character and a sermon's reception.

If I were to return to churches I have pastored, it is unlikely that people would remember many specifics from my previous sermons. They might remember a particularly vivid illustration, the way a verse had a telling effect at a crisis moment in their lives, or the impression a particular message left on their minds. Yet not one person would remember a dozen words of the thousands I spoke throughout the years. People may not remember what we say, but they will remember *us* and whether our lives gave credence to the message of Scripture. The impressions that others have of our lives are the videos they will replay in their minds to discern whether the truths of the gospel we proclaim are real for us—and therefore can be real for them.

Effective ministry corresponds so much with the character of a minister that theologian John Sanderson advised people to play softball with pastoral candidates interviewing for a position. "Then on a close play at second base," Sanderson said (with his tongue *mostly* in cheek), "call him out when he is really safe. Then see what happens!"[12]

Of course, no one reflects Christ's character as purely as he or she desires. That is why God does not make the effects of his Word dependent on our actions. But as the eighteenth-century minister George Campbell said, "When our practice conforms to our theory, our effectiveness trebles."[13] This does not deny the extraordinary power inherent in God's Word but affirms that it is the ordinary pattern of the Holy Spirit to affirm and further the purposes of his Word by the testimony of our lives. It is the joy of the Christian minister to serve God in this way. Yet it is also a comfort to recognize that if the Spirit must leapfrog over human frailty to reach the heart of others with the sufficiency of the Word, then he can certainly do so. In the course of our ministries, it will often be necessary for him to do so.

Perhaps most of us have experienced the influence of pastoral character on a sermon when we have visited a church at a friend's request to hear the preacher's "marvelous messages" and have heard mediocrity instead. Our friend's love and trust of the pastor generated regard for the sermon and

11. Robinson, *Biblical Preaching,* 25–26.
12. From classroom lecture notes at Covenant Seminary, St. Louis, 1978.
13. Golden, Berquist, and Coleman, *Rhetoric of Western Thought,* 295.

obscured its weaknesses. The character and compassion of a minister more than the characteristics of the message preached determine the quality of the message heard.

Love Grace

Emphasis on the character of a preacher is futile and errant without underscoring the grace that molds one's character and message according to God's will. Human effort is engaged in holy living but does not itself produce holiness. Selfless righteousness and sacrificial love are never self-induced. Attempts to conform our character to God's requirements by the sufficiency of our actions are as arrogant as efforts to save souls by our talents. Powerful preachers must become well-acquainted with the grace their character requires.

Emphasis on the power of *ethos* without dependence on God's mercy has the potential to drive preachers either to arrogance or to despair. While it is certainly true that a life of consistently hidden or unrepentant sin makes a poor vehicle for the gospel, it is equally true that pride in one's moral superiority is damaging to the communication of faith in Christ alone. In contrast, some preachers are so conscience-stricken by their inability to live faultlessly that they cannot enter the pulpit without stumbling over mountains of self-accusation. By such over-conscientiousness, which parades in the soul as spiritual zeal, many preachers actually deny to themselves and others a deep and authentic understanding of the efficacy and sufficiency of Christ's blood.

You must know grace to preach it. No matter how great your skill or accolades, you are unlikely to lead others closer to God if your heart does not reflect the continuing work of the Savior in your life. A testimony that reinforces the message of the gospel is not merely a matter of public conduct. It is a product of consistent private meditation on the gospel that character daily requires.

Grace-focused ministers recognize the daily repentance that private prayers must include, confess to others the divine aid that grants them the strength of their resolutions, obey God in loving thankfulness for the forgiveness and future Christ supplies, model the humility appropriate for a fellow sinner, express the courage and authority of one confident of the Savior's provision, exude the joy of salvation by faith alone, reflect the love that claims their souls, and perform their service without any claim of personal merit.[14]

Preaching without a grace focus concentrates on means of earning divine acceptance, proofs of personal righteousness, and contrasts with those less holy. Preaching with a grace focus concentrates on responding to God's

14. Michael Fabarez, *Preaching That Changes Lives* (Nashville: Thomas Nelson, 2002), 130–35.

mercy with loving thankfulness, joyful worship, humble service, and a caring witness to the Savior's love.

The necessity of grace in balanced preaching inevitably points both preacher and parishioner to the work of Christ as the only proper center of a sermon. Christ-centered preaching is not merely evangelistic, nor is it confined to a few gospel accounts. It perceives the whole of Scripture as revelatory of God's redemptive plan and sees every passage within this context—a pattern Jesus himself introduced (Luke 24:27). More will be said about this later. What is critical at this point as we begin to consider the structural components of a sermon is to understand that our union with Christ is the end and the means of all biblical obedience (Rom. 6:1–14; Phil. 2:1–5). Thus, the Bible requires that we construct our messages in such a way as to reveal the grace that is the ultimate foundation of every text, the ultimate enablement for every instruction, and the only source of true holiness.

Without understanding our daily dependence on grace, we have little hope of reflecting the character that endorses the integrity of our messages. Discovering the redemptive context of every text allows us to use the entire Bible to discern the grace we need to preach and to live so as to lead others to closer fellowship with the Lord. Joseph Ruggles Wilson, a nineteenth-century Presbyterian minister and the father of Woodrow Wilson, advised, "Become what you preach and then preach Christ in you."[15] His words remind us that the sanctifying Redeemer who unites and conforms us to himself to endorse his message cannot be neglected in our sermons. Word and witness are inextricably linked in preaching worthy of Christ's gospel.

Without a redemptive focus, we may believe we have exegeted Scripture when in fact we have simply translated its parts and parsed its pieces without reference to the role they have in God's eternal plan. John Calvin said, "God has ordained his Word as the instrument by which Jesus Christ, with all His graces, is dispensed to us."[16] No such process occurs when passages of the Word are ripped from their redemptive context and are seen as mere moral examples and behavioral guidelines. Grace keeps our character true to God, our messages true to Scripture, and our efforts true to Christ's will. Reliance on this grace results in sermons that are empowered by God (despite our knowledge of our sin and inadequacy), for he alone is responsible for the holiness and truth that fuel preaching's spiritual force.

15. Joseph Ruggles Wilson, "In What Sense Are Preachers to Preach Themselves?" *Southern Presbyterian Review* 25 (1874): 360.

16. Quoted in Larsen, *Anatomy of Preaching*, 19. Compare John Calvin's *Institutes of the Christian Religion*, 2.9.1; 4.1.6.

BE A GREAT PREACHER

Consciousness of God's enablement should encourage all preachers (including beginning preachers) to throw themselves wholeheartedly into their calling. Although the degree of homiletical skill will vary, God promises to perform his purposes through all who faithfully proclaim his truth. Even if your words barely crawl over the edge of the pulpit, love of God's Word and his people ensures an effective spiritual ministry. You may never hear the applause of the world or pastor a church of thousands, but a life of godliness combined with clear explanations of Scripture's saving and sanctifying grace will engage the power of the Spirit for the glory of God.

If your goal is Christ's honor, you *can* be a great preacher through faithfulness to him and his message. Paul offers this same encouragement to Timothy with promises that yet apply to you:

> Don't let anyone look down on you because you are young, but set an example for the believers in speech, in life, in love, in faith and in purity. Until I come, devote yourself to the public reading of Scripture, to preaching and to teaching. . . .
>
> Be diligent in these matters; give yourself wholly to them, so that everyone may see your progress. Watch your life and doctrine closely. Persevere in them, because if you do, you will save both yourself and your hearers.
>
> 1 Timothy 4:12–13, 15–16

Questions for Review and Discussion

1. Why are expository preachers committed to making the meaning of the passage the message of the sermon?
2. Who or what alone has the power to change hearts eternally?
3. What are *logos, pathos,* and *ethos*? Which most affects the persuasiveness of a message?
4. Why should every sermon have a redemptive focus?
5. On what does great preaching most depend?

Exercises

1. Locate and comment on biblical passages that confirm the inherent power of the Word.
2. Locate and comment on biblical passages that link the character of the messenger to the effects of the message.

Goal of Chapter 2

To identify the commitments a preacher assumes
in developing a well-constructed sermon

2

Obligations of the Sermon

Truth Is Not a Sermon

Why would a message organized around the following statements probably not go in the annals of preaching's greatest sermons?

1. The walls of Babylon were as much as 350 feet high and 80 feet wide.
2. The Gnostic heresy at Colosse contained elements of extreme hedonism and asceticism.
3. The Greek word for the "emptying" concept of Philippians 2:7 is *kenosis.*

The statements are clear, true, and biblical. Why do they not form a sermon?

First, the statements lack unity. No obvious thread holds these statements together. Without a unifying theme, listeners have no means of grasping a sermon's many thoughts.

Second, the statements seem to have no purpose. They are simply disparate facts pried from the biblical moorings that communicate their cause and import. Without a clear purpose in view, listeners have no apparent reason to listen to a sermon.

Finally, the statements beacon no application. They have no apparent relevance to the lives of those addressed. Without application, a sermon offers people no incentive to heed a message. Most will reasonably question why they should waste time giving attention to something that even the preacher does not seem to be able to relate to their lives.

Statements of truth, even biblical truth, do not automatically make a message for the pulpit. Well-constructed sermons require unity, purpose, and application.

Unity

Key concept: How many things is a sermon about? One!

Sermons of any significant length contain theological concepts, illustrative materials, and corroborative facts. These many components, however, do not imply that a sermon is about many things. Each feature of a well-wrought message reflects, refines, and/or develops one major idea. This major idea, or theme, glues the message together and makes its features stick in a listener's mind. All the features of a sermon should support the concept that unifies the whole.

The Reasons for Unity

Constructing a message so that all its features support a main idea requires discipline. Boiling out extraneous thoughts and crystallizing ideas so that the entire message functions as a unit have tested many a preacher. Some yield to the pressure and indiscriminately dispense their ideas using whatever sequence, emphasis, and structure most easily spring to mind. Others argue that they cannot say all they want about a text if they must relate particulars to a single theme. So why strive for unity?

SPEAKERS NEED FOCUS

The words of an old hymn too often apply to sermons as well as to our spiritual lives. We are "prone to wander." Preaching without the discipline of unity typically results in a preacher simply roaming from one stray thought to another. Such messages rarely communicate well. Listeners quickly tire of chasing ideas and anecdotes across the theological landscape in an effort to discover where their pastor is going.

We need unity to funnel the infinite exegetical possibilities into a manageable message. Quite literally, hundreds if not thousands of pages of commentary and grammatical analysis could be written on any biblical text (and in many cases have been). The depth of the Word provides us with inspiration for a lifetime of sermons, even as it challenges us to find a means to keep our listeners and ourselves from drowning in its intricacies. Unity may seem binding at first, but it actually frees preachers from entrapment in the endless labyrinth of language and explanation possibilities. The priorities of unity allow preachers to consider prayerfully and in good conscience what *not* to say as well as what *to* say.

Listeners Need Focus

Sermons are for listeners, not readers. The degree of detail and excursus acceptable for an essay or a novel cannot be handled in an aural environment by listeners who cannot turn back a page, reread a paragraph, slow down, or ask the speaker to pause while they catch up. Listeners simply have less inclination and opportunity to decipher a sermon than readers do a textbook or a commentary. If the parts of a sermon do not obviously relate to a clear theme that gives the message's pieces form and purpose, then listeners are not likely to focus their attention on the contents for long.

All good communication requires a theme. If a preacher does not provide a unifying concept for a message, listeners will. They instinctively will supply a thought peg on which to hang the preacher's ideas, knowing that if they do not, they will retain nothing. In the process of determining what thought peg to supply, listeners can drop thoughts the preacher has already distributed. Neither is there any guarantee that the pegs listeners choose will support the additional ideas the preacher wants to offer. When a wife asks her husband at Sunday lunch what the morning sermon was about, the answer "Something about prayer" is too generic to have real-life significance. As a result, response to the message will probably be more ho-hum than the preacher or the parishioner desired.

Listeners more readily grasp ideas that have been formed and pulled together. It is easier to catch a baseball than a handful of sand even if the two weigh about the same amount. The fact that a preacher's words are weighty does not mean that listeners will respond to them, especially when the speaker has not managed to bond the ideas together. Since even Paul prayed that he would speak "as [he] should" (Col. 4:4), we are not wrong to consider how we form our words or to learn from those who can teach us how to do this well (cf. v. 6).

The Nature of Unity

As we have already discovered, in expository preaching the meaning of a passage provides the message of a sermon. This means that the unifying concept of a sermon should come from the text itself. Haddon Robinson suggests that preachers determine the "big idea" of a message by first asking, "What is the author [of the passage] talking about?" and then "What is he saying about what he is talking about?"[1] These are the foundational questions of an expository sermon. They force us to examine the various

---

1. Haddon Robinson, *Biblical Preaching: The Development and Delivery of Expository Messages,* 2nd ed. (Grand Rapids: Baker, 2001), 43–46.

features of a passage and discern how the biblical writer employs them for his purpose(s).[2] Only in this way will we know how to unify the particulars of a text in accordance with the perspective and priorities of the author.

In expository preaching, unity occurs when a preacher demonstrates that the elements of a passage support a single major idea, which serves as the theme of the sermon. We want this theme to be the Bible's theme. This does not mean that only the *major* theme of a passage can serve as the theme of an expository sermon. A sermon on a minor theme of a passage may also be expository as long as there is sufficient exegetical material in the passage to support the theme *and* the theme accurately reflects the passage's truth in context. A sermon on God's love for a prodigal child may be legitimately drawn from Luke 15, even though the parables contained there are primarily directed to those who reflect the attitudes of the elder brother (cf. Luke 15:1–2, 28–32). If minor themes were not legitimate foci of individual sermons, preachers would ultimately be forced to preach on only whole books at a time.

Sermons must capture the theme, purpose, or focus of a biblical writer and put it into service in order for God's truth to rule our efforts. Our commitment to the sole efficacy of Scripture means that we need to say what the Bible says. The features of a sermon must all contribute to the theme derived from the text. Rarely do biblical writers simply dish out a smorgasbord of unrelated ideas (and when it seems they do, there is a larger purpose that the discerning interpreter can uncover). The components of a passage all contribute to the author's point. This is the way sermons should function. Although many ideas and features comprise a sermon, they should all contribute to one theme. A sermon is about one thing.

The Process of Unity

Once a preacher determines the importance of unity, the next question that arises is, How do I achieve it? The process is not complicated, but it can take hard work. The fruit of this labor, however, will save a preacher much additional labor and listeners much confusion. Follow these simple steps to obtain unity in a sermon:

I. Read and digest the passage to determine:
   A. the main idea the writer communicates through the text's nature, details, and features (i.e., discern what large concept the aspects of the text support or develop),[3] or

---

2. Jay E. Adams, *Preaching with Purpose: A Comprehensive Textbook on Biblical Preaching* (Grand Rapids: Baker, 1982), 31–33.

3. Daniel M. Doriani, *Getting the Message: A Plan for Interpreting and Applying the Bible* (Phillipsburg, N.J.: Presbyterian & Reformed, 1996), 155–67.

    B. an idea that is supported by sufficient material in the text and
        can be developed into the main subject of a message
  II. Melt down this idea and develop it into one concise statement.

You will have unity when you can demonstrate that the elements of the
passage support the theme of your message *and* you can state that theme in
a form simple enough to pass the "3 A.M. test." The 3:00 A.M. test requires
you to imagine a spouse, a roommate, or a parishioner waking you from a
deep slumber with this simple question: "What's the sermon about today,
Preacher?" If you cannot give a crisp answer, the sermon is probably half-
baked. Thoughts you cannot gather at 3:00 A.M. are not likely to be caught
by others at 11:00 A.M.

At 3:00 A.M. you know the following will not work as a theme:

> When the sinful nation of Israel went into exile, its messianic hope and
> vision were mistakenly and faithlessly diminished because pre-Ezran and
> pre-Nehemiahic proofs of God's sovereign plan, purpose, and intentions for
> his people were obscured in Babylonian circumstances of incarceration and
> oppression that would not be relieved until the Persian emancipation and
> further covenantal revelations in advancing redemptive history.

This will:

> God remains faithful to faithless people.

When we can crystallize the thought of a passage, then the focus, organization, and application of the message become clear for preacher and
listener. Preachers who develop concise and accurate theme statements can
speak with much greater detail without losing a congregation in a fog of
specifics. In Western preaching cultures, this theme is traditionally stated as
a proposition near the beginning of a sermon and developed with deductive
arguments as the message progresses. Other traditions (and some newer
homiletic approaches) lead listeners inductively to the sermon's theme in a
conclusion or define the main idea by circling it with wrong alternatives or
spiraling into it with ideas and stories that progressively near the mark. Yet
while approaches to defining the core idea may vary, the necessity of forming
a clear and concise statement of a sermon's unifying idea does not.

The Goal of Unity

Unity strives for the communication of biblical truth, not merely for its
discovery or statement. Unity organizes a message for a single thrust rather
than a shower of disconnected thoughts. One sermon cannot be about the
source of Samson's strength, how to determine God's will, and the proper

mode of baptism. Seminarians often stumble in their early preaching attempts when they try to load everything they are learning into a single sermon. More experienced preachers recognize that they have this week, and the next, and the next to communicate God's truths. It is better to convey one thought that can be held than a dozen that will slip from grasp.

When a sermon has unity, a preacher has the ability to focus on a subject in depth. Scripture truths fragment without unity, and as a result, their transforming force splinters. Preachers are particularly susceptible to following tangential thoughts and straying down so-called rabbit trails of incidental facts while explaining the main points of a message because the outlines of sermons are frequently more organized than their developmental features.[4] Even subordinate ideas should contribute to the overall theme since the main points they support form the message's coordinated thrust.

A well-constructed message may have three points (or more, or less), but it is not about three things. A sermon whose main points allege that (1) God is loving, (2) God is just, and (3) God is sovereign is not ready to be preached until the preacher determines that the sermon's subject is not these three things but rather "the nature of God." The single idea will hold the rest and, by illuminating their purpose, will deepen their impact.

A maxim reminds us, "The main thing is to keep the main thing the main thing." Preachers whose messages make the greatest impact have taken it to heart.

Purpose

Key concept: The Fallen Condition Focus (FCF) reveals a text's and a sermon's purpose.

Considering the FCF

Determining a sermon's subject is half done when a preacher has discerned what the biblical writer was saying. We do not fully understand the subject until we have also determined its purpose. It is too easy to preach on a doctrinal topic or an exegetical insight without considering the spiritual burden of the text for real people in the daily struggles of life. In doing so, preachers relieve themselves of having to deal with the messiness and pain of human existence. The greater intellectual and spiritual task is to discern the human concern that caused the Holy Spirit to inspire this aspect of Scripture so that God would be properly glorified by his people. Consideration of a passage's purpose ultimately forces us to ask, Why are these concerns addressed? What caused this account, these facts, or the recording of these

---

4. We will consider how to organize main points and subpoints in subsequent chapters.

ideas? What was the intent of the author? For what purpose did the Holy Spirit include these words in Scripture? Such questions force us to exegete the cause of a passage as well as its contents and to connect both to the lives of the people God calls us to shepherd with his truth.

Until we have determined a passage's purpose, we are not ready to preach its truths, even if we know many true facts about the text. Yet as obvious as this advice is, it is frequently neglected. Preachers often think they are ready to preach when they see a doctrinal subject reflected in a passage, though they have not yet determined the text's specific purpose. For example, simply recognizing that a passage contains features that support the doctrine of justification by faith alone does not adequately prepare a pastor to preach. A sermon is not just a systematics lesson. Why did the biblical writer bring up the subject of justification at this point? What were the struggles, concerns, or frailties of the persons to whom the text was originally addressed? Were the people claiming salvation based on their accomplishments, were they doubting the sufficiency of grace, or were they afraid of God's rejection because of some sin? We must determine the purpose (or burden) of a passage before we really know the subject of a sermon.[5]

We do not have to guess whether there is a purpose for a particular text. The Bible assures us that every passage has a purpose, and it clearly tells us the basic nature of this purpose. The apostle Paul writes, "All Scripture is God-breathed and is useful for teaching, rebuking, correcting and training in righteousness, so that the man of God may be thoroughly equipped for every good work" (2 Tim. 3:16–17). The Greek terms that Paul uses to express our need to be thoroughly equipped convey the idea of bringing to completion. God intends for his Word to "complete" us so that we can serve his good purposes.[6] That is why the translators of the King James Version interpreted verse 17 of the passage as "that the man of God may be *perfect*." God intends for every portion of his Word (i.e., "all Scripture") to make us more like him so that his glory is reflected in us.[7]

Since God designed the Bible to complete us for the purposes of his glory, the necessary implication is that in some sense we are incomplete. We lack the equipment required for every good work. Our lack of wholeness is a consequence of the fallen condition in which we live. Aspects of this fallenness that are reflected in our sinfulness and in our world's brokenness prompt

---

5. Adams, *Preaching with Purpose,* 27.

6. See the Greek term *artios* (complete) in v. 17.

7. Some exegetes understand the "man of God" in 2 Timothy 3:16 to refer to the Christian minister, in which case the "work" for which the Word equips refers to *ministry* rather than the *sanctification* of believers. This interpretation does not undermine the conclusion that God intends "all Scripture" to "complete" believers, since a minister's duties of "teaching, rebuking, correcting and training in righteousness" from "all Scripture" will convey God's perspective on the hearers' inherent need of the scope of biblical truth.

Scripture's instruction and construction.[8] Paul writes, "Everything that was written in the past was written to teach us, so that through endurance and the encouragement of the Scriptures we might have hope" (Rom. 15:4).

The corrupted state of our world and our beings cries for God's aid. He responds with the truths of Scripture and gives us hope by focusing his grace on a facet of our fallen condition in every portion of his Word. No text was written merely for those in the past; God intends for each passage to give us the "endurance and the encouragement" we need today (cf. 1 Cor. 10:13). Preaching that is true to these purposes (1) focuses on the fallen condition that necessitated the writing of the passage and (2) uses the text's features to explain how the Holy Spirit addresses that concern then and now. *The Fallen Condition Focus (FCF) is the mutual human condition that contemporary believers share with those to or about whom the text was written that requires the grace of the passage for God's people to glorify and enjoy him.*

By assuring us that all Scripture has a Fallen Condition Focus (FCF), God indicates his abiding care and underscores his preeminent status in preaching. The FCF present in every text demonstrates God's refusal to leave his frail and sinful children without guide or defense in a world antagonistic to their spiritual well-being. However, an FCF not only provides the human context needed for a passage's explanation but also indicates that biblical solutions must be divine and not merely human. Since fallen creatures cannot correct or remove their own fallenness, identification of an FCF forces a sermon to honor God as the only source of hope rather than merely promoting human fix-its or behavior change. In technical terms, though an FCF requires a sermon to deal honestly and directly with the human concerns of the text, this focus simultaneously keeps the sermon from being anthropocentric. The acknowledgment of human fallenness that undergirds the text's explanation and the sermon's development automatically requires the preacher to acknowledge the bankruptcy of merely human efforts and to honor the wonders of divine provision.

Because an FCF is a human problem or burden addressed by specific aspects of a scriptural text, informed preaching strives to unveil this purpose in order to explain each passage properly. Obviously, there may be more than one way of stating the purpose for a text since the biblical writer had various mechanisms for stating or implying his purpose. There may also be a variety of purposes within a specific text. Still, a sermon's unity requires a preacher to be selective and ordinarily to concentrate on a Scripture passage's main purpose. An FCF determines the real subject of a message by revealing the Holy Spirit's purpose(s) in inspiring a passage.[9] *Ultimately, a sermon is*

---

8. Haddon Robinson refers to this as the "depravity factor" in "The Heresy of Application," *Leadership Journal* 18, no. 4 (Fall 1997): 24.

9. Sidney Greidanus, *The Modern Preacher and the Ancient Text: Interpreting and Preaching Biblical Literature* (Grand Rapids: Eerdmans, 1988), 128–29.

about how a text says we are to respond biblically to the FCF as it is experienced in our lives—identifying the gracious means that God provides for us to deal with the human brokenness that deprives us of the full experience and expression of his glory.

Various subdivisions and dimensions of the FCF may be developed as a sermon unfolds, but the main theme should remain clear. This agenda makes sense when we remember that a text's contents are God's response to and provision for an aspect of our fallenness. The FCF sets the tone, determines the approach, and organizes the information in a sermon to reveal this divine provision and direct our response to it. Thus, the FCF is usually directly stated or strongly implied in the introductory portion of a sermon.

Determining the FCF

Proper understanding of a passage and formation of a sermon require a clear FCF. If we do not determine an FCF of a text, we do not really know what the passage is about, even if we know many true facts about it.[10] An FCF reveals the Spirit's own purpose for the passage, and we should not presume to preach unless we have identified his will for his Word. We must ask, What is an FCF that required the writing of this text? before we can accurately expound its meaning. This FCF will enable us to interpret the passage properly, communicate its contents, and give the congregation the Holy Spirit's own reason for listening.

The more specific the statement of the FCF early in the sermon, the more powerful and poignant the message will be. An FCF of "not being faithful to God" is not nearly as riveting as "How can I maintain my integrity when my boss has none?" A message directed to "the prayerless patterns of society" will not prick the conscience or ignite resolve nearly as effectively as a sermon on "why we struggle to pray when family stresses make prayer most necessary." Generic statements of an FCF give the preacher little guidance for the organization of the sermon and the congregation little reason for listening. Specificity tends to breed interest and power by demonstrating that Scripture speaks to the real concerns of individual lives.

Specific sins such as unforgiveness, lying, and racism are frequently the FCF of a passage, but a sin does not always have to be the FCF of a sermon. Grief, illness, longing for the Lord's return, the need to know how to share the gospel, and the desire to be a better parent are not sins, but they are needs that our fallen condition imposes and that Scripture addresses. Just as greed, rebellion, lust, irresponsibility, poor stewardship, and pride are proper subjects of a sermon, so also are the difficulties of raising godly children, determining God's will, and understanding one's gifts. *An FCF*

10. Ibid., 173.

need not be something for which we are guilty or culpable. It simply needs to be an aspect or problem of the human condition that requires the instruction, admonition, and/or comfort of Scripture. Thus, an FCF is always phrased in negative terms. It is something wrong (though not necessarily a moral evil) that needs correction or encouragement from Scripture.

The personality of the preacher, the circumstances of the congregation, and the emphases of a particular sermon can cause the statement of the FCF to vary greatly. A passage whose central focus is learning to trust in God's providence may equally well address the need to lean on God in hard times, the responsibility to teach others about God's abiding care, or the sin of doubting God's provision. There is more than one proper way of wording a passage's FCF for statement in a sermon. This is why preachers can preach remarkably different sermons on the same passage that are all faithful to the text. A preacher must be able to demonstrate that the text addresses the FCF as it is formulated for this particular sermon, not that this sermon's phrasing of the FCF is the only way of reflecting on this text. The truth of the text does not vary, but the significance of that truth can vary greatly and be stated in many different ways that are appropriate for difficult situations.

Since the FCF can vary greatly from text to text and from sermon to sermon preached on the same text, a preacher needs to make sure the purpose of a sermon remains evident in the passage. An FCF will remain faithful to a text and identify powerful purposes in a sermon if a preacher uses these three successive questions to develop the FCF:

1. What does the text say?
2. What spiritual concern(s) did the text address (in its context)?
3. What spiritual concerns do listeners share in common with those to (or about) whom the text was written?

By identifying listeners' mutual condition with the biblical writer, subject, and/or audience, we determine why the text was written, not just for biblical times but also for our time. We should realize, however, that the Holy Spirit does not introduce an FCF simply to inform us of a problem. Paul told Timothy that God inspires all Scripture to equip us for his work (see 2 Tim. 3:16–17). God expects us to act on the problems his Spirit reveals.

Application

Key concept: Without the "so what?" we preach to a "who cares?"

No passage relates neutral commentary on our fallenness. No text communicates facts for information alone. The Bible itself tells us that its message is intended to instruct, reprove, and correct (see 2 Tim. 3:16; 4:2). God expects scriptural truths to transform his people. Faithful preaching does the same. The preacher who identifies a passage's FCF for a congregation automatically moves the people to consider the Bible's solutions and instructions for contemporary life. Therefore, biblical preaching that brings an FCF to the surface also recognizes the need for application.

Memorable in my own homiletics training was the Air Force colonel turned seminary professor who challenged students, no matter where they preached in future years, to imagine him sitting at the back of the sanctuary. With a benign scowl the professor growled, "In your mind's eye look at me whenever you have said your concluding word. My arms are folded, my face holds a frown, and this question hangs on my lips: 'So what? What do you want me to do or believe?' If you cannot answer, you have not preached."

People have a right to ask, "Why did you tell me that? What am I supposed to do with that information? All right, I understand what you say is true—so what?" The healthiest preaching does not assume listeners will automatically see how to apply God's truths to their lives; it supplies the application people need.[11] If even the preacher cannot tell (or has not bothered to determine) how the sermon's truths relate to life, then people not only are unlikely to make the connection but also will wonder why they bothered to listen.

The Need for Application

The Bible's instruction and pattern indicate the importance of application in preaching. When Paul told Titus, "You must teach what is in accord with sound doctrine" (Titus 2:1), the Bible students of that day probably echoed the chorus of enthusiastic "Amens" today's seminarians voice at such a statement. But Paul did not mean that Titus was simply to teach theological propositions.[12] In the next sentence, the apostle begins to unfold what preachers should teach that "is in accord with sound doctrine":

> Teach the older men to be temperate, worthy of respect, self-controlled, and sound in faith, in love and in endurance.
> Likewise, teach the older women to be reverent in the way they live, not to be slanderers or addicted to much wine, but to teach what is good. Then they can train the younger women to love their husbands and children, to be

11. See chap. 8 for a full discussion of application in preaching.
12. Michael Fabarez offers this additional insight: "It can be demonstrated that the common usage of the word 'doctrine' today is more narrow than in biblical usage. The words *lequach*, *shemu'ah*, and *mucar* in the Old Testament, and *didaskalia* and *didache* in the New Testament (all of which are translated 'doctrine' in various English translations) represent both abstract propositions and practical directives" (*Preaching That Changes Lives* [Nashville: Thomas Nelson, 2002], 215–26).

self-controlled and pure, to be busy at home, to be kind, and to be subject to their husbands, so that no one will malign the word of God.

Similarly, encourage the young men to be self-controlled.

Titus 2:2–6

Paul expects Titus's "doctrine" to give the people of his congregation specific guidance for their everyday lives. Such instruction does not merely characterize this one passage; it reflects the pattern of Paul's epistles (cf. Rom. 1–15; Eph. 1–6). The apostle typically begins each letter with a greeting, moves to doctrinal instruction, and then applies the doctrine to a variety of circumstances. Paul refuses to leave biblical truth in the stratosphere of theological abstraction. He earths his message in the concerns of the people he addresses.[13] Preaching that is true to the pattern of Scripture should do the same.

Biblical preaching moves from exegetical commentary and doctrinal exposition to life instruction. Such preaching exhorts as well as expounds because it recognizes that Scripture's own goal is not merely to share information about God but to conform his people to the likeness of Jesus Christ. Preaching without application may serve the mind, but preaching with application results in service to Christ. Application makes Jesus the source and the objective of a sermon's exhortation as well as the focus of its explanation.

Clear articulation of an FCF drives a message's application and ensures the Christ-centeredness of a sermon. The FCF marshals a sermon's features toward a specific purpose and therefore helps a preacher see how to apply the information in the text. At the same time, the fact that a message is focused on an aspect of our fallenness precludes simplistic, human-centered solutions. If we could fix the problem with our own efforts in our own strength, then we would not be truly fallen. Application that addresses an FCF clearly rooted in the textual situation necessarily directs people to the presence and power of the Savior as they seek to serve him.

Early statements of an FCF in a sermon may open the door to application in a number of ways. A preacher may open a spiritual or an emotional wound in order to provide biblical healing, identify a grief in order to offer God's comfort, demonstrate a danger in order to warrant a scriptural command, or condemn a sin in order to offer cleansing to a sinner. In each case, the statement of the FCF creates a listener's longing for the Word and its solutions by identifying the biblical needs that the passage addresses.[14] The surfacing of these scriptural priorities compels a preacher to tell others

13. John R. W. Stott, *Between Two Worlds: The Art of Preaching in the Twentieth Century* (Grand Rapids: Eerdmans, 1988), 140.

14. A "biblical need" may or may not be a "felt need." In recent years, much criticism has been offered of preaching that focuses on felt needs in order to make the gospel appealing (see Terry Muck,

how and why to do something about them. This compulsion becomes the spiritual imperative that leads a preacher to discern the text's answers and instructions. When these crystallize, applications that are true to the text's purpose, focus, and context naturally develop.

The Consequences of Nonapplication

However well selected is the meat of a sermon, the message remains uncooked without thoughtful, true-to-the-text application. This rare meat is not at all rare in evangelical preaching, as Walter Liefeld attests:

> In earlier years (I hope no longer) I often did exegesis in the pulpit, in large measure because I was conscious of the deep and wide-spread hunger for teaching from God's Word. I finally realized that one can teach, but fail to feed or inspire. I think (and again hope) that my sermons today are no less informative but much more helpful.
>
> Expository preaching is not simply a running commentary. By this I mean a loosely connected string of thoughts, occasionally tied to the passage, which lacks homiletical structure or appropriate application. . . .
>
> Expository preaching is not a captioned survey of a passage. By this I mean the typical: "1. Saul's Contention, 2. Saul's Conversion, 3. Saul's Commission" (Acts 9:1–19). In my own circles I think I have heard more sermons of this type than any other. They sound very biblical because they are based on a passage of Scripture. But their basic failure is that they tend to be descriptive rather than pastoral. They lack a clear goal or practical application. The congregation may be left without any true insights as to what the passage is really about, and without having received any clear teaching about God or themselves.[15]

A grammar lesson is not a sermon. A sermon is not a textual commentary, a systematics discourse, or a history lecture. Mere lectures are *pre-sermons* because they dispense information about a text without relevant application from the text that helps listeners understand their obligations to Christ and his ministry to them.[16]

"The Danger of Preaching to Needs," cassette [Jackson, Miss.: Reformed Theological Seminary, 1986], responding to such works as Charles H. Kraft's *Communicating the Gospel God's Way* [Pasadena: William Carey Library, 1979]). Such criticism rightly assumes that a steady diet of preaching focused on felt needs can make faith and worship purely matters of self-concern. At the same time, the gospel often helps people to see their biblical needs through felt needs (John 4:4–26; Acts 17:22–23). Preachers should not be afraid to help others see their biblical needs in order for such persons to discern their biblical obligations.

15. Walter L. Liefeld, *New Testament Exposition: From Text to Sermon* (Grand Rapids: Zondervan, 1984), 20–21.

16. Adams, *Preaching with Purpose*, 51; and reiterated with even more force by the same author in *Truth Applied: Application in Preaching* (Grand Rapids: Zondervan, 1990), 33–39. See also Jonathan

A message remains a pre-sermon until a preacher organizes its ideas and the text's features to apply to a single, major FCF. We might represent the concept this way:

textual information (pre-sermon material) → addressing a textually rooted FCF + relevant textual application = sermon

A message that merely establishes "God is good" is not a sermon. However, when the same discourse deals with the doubt we may have about whether God is good when we face trials and demonstrates from the text how to handle our doubt with the truths of God's goodness, then the preacher has a sermon. A pre-sermon message merely describes the text. Such a "speech" may be accurate, biblically based, and erudite, but the congregation will know it falls short of a sermon even if the preacher does not.

A former student recently telephoned me for assistance because his congregation seemed to be growing less and less responsive to his preaching. "Last Sunday during the sermon," he said, "they just looked at me like they were lumps on a log. I got no feedback whatsoever. What am I doing wrong?"

I asked him to describe his sermon to me. He responded by giving me the main points of his outline:

Noah was wise.
Noah was fearless.
Noah was faithful.

"I understand," I said. "Now, why did you tell them that?"

There was a long pause on the other end of the phone line. Then he groaned. "Oh yeah. I forgot!"

Information without application yields frustration. This old adage rings true for preachers as well as for parishioners. Preachers who cannot answer "so what?" will preach to a "who cares?" Later in this book we will see that one way to help keep the Bible's truths from seeming disconnected from life today is to state main points and subpoints as universal principles rather than simply as descriptions or recitations of the facts in a text (such as "Noah was wise"). The reason is that only when we can demonstrate that the facts of Scripture were recorded for a purpose and have practical application for the lives of God's people today do our sermons warrant a hearing. This is not simply because people have no reason to listen to what has no apparent relevance to their lives—though this is certainly true. We must also recognize

---

Edwards, *Religious Affections*, in *The Works of Jonathan Edwards*, ed. Perry Miller, vol. 2, ed. John E. Smith (New Haven: Yale University Press, 1959), 115–16.

that sermons that do not spell out the purposes and applications for which they were written fail to fulfill God's stated will for his Word.

We are not simply ministers of information; we are ministers of Christ's transformation. He intends to restore his people with his Word and is not greatly served by preachers who do not discern the transformation Scripture requires or communicate the means it offers. In future chapters, we will discuss how a preacher remains true to Scripture and accomplishes these exegetical and communication tasks. Essential for the moment is the conclusion that unity, purpose, and application will help keep preachers faithful to their divine calling and to the Word's design.

Questions for Review and Discussion

1. How many things is a sermon about? Why?
2. What is the Fallen Condition Focus (FCF) of a sermon?
3. Ultimately, what is a sermon about?
4. What are three steps for determining an FCF of a sermon?
5. What are indications that a message is a "pre-sermon"?

Exercises

1. What are possible unifying themes for each of the following groups of main points?

   God is good.   Parents should discipline.
   God is faithful.   Parents should sacrifice.
   God is sovereign.   Parents should love.

   Sin always contradicts God's will.
   Sin sometimes veils God's will.
   Sin never thwarts God's will.

2. List five specific sins that might be the FCF of a sermon. List five specific "non-sins" that might be the FCF of a sermon.

CONTENTS OF CHAPTER 3

GOAL OF CHAPTER 3

To explain basic tools and rules for selecting and interpreting texts

3

The Priority of the Text

Begin Here

A nature trail that my family enjoys meanders through woods, parallels a stream, and circles a lake as it leads us to trees and rocks identified with placards that explain each landmark's significance. The explanations help us understand and enjoy features of the forest around us. But as interesting as the placards are, no trail sign is more important to us than the one at the outset, where several identical-looking paths jut away from the parking lot into dense woods. The placard displays an arrow and these simple words: Begin Here. Knowing where to begin takes us to the explanations we need.

The same is true in preaching. Knowing the landmarks that characterize good preaching will not automatically guide us to excellence. We must first start down the right path. Expository preaching points preachers to the biblical text with the instruction "begin here." This does not mean that preachers have not thought about the trail before or that they have no idea what they want to see. We often begin sermon preparation by looking for what the Bible has to say about a particular concern or topic. Still, the text itself is the source of the truths we ultimately present. In the pulpit, we are expositors, not authors. Sermons explain what the Bible says. This means that a preacher's first expository task is to choose a portion of Scripture from which to preach.

Considerations for Selecting a Passage

Passage Length

Although it may not be the first consideration in selecting a passage, what a preacher can cover in the time allotted for the sermon must affect the decision. When I was trained to preach, instructors used the term *expository unit* for the Scripture portion an expository sermon covered.[1] The term has strengths and liabilities.

On the plus side, the concept of a unit encourages preachers to see scriptural passages as collections of unified thought packets rather than arrays of disconnected verses.[2] The concept works especially well when we preach from didactic passages (epistles, biblical sermons, prophetic literature, etc.) that can be analyzed paragraph by paragraph. A paragraph of thought in such passages typically covers five to ten verses, contains a major idea with supporting concepts, and readily lends itself to expository development in a reasonably timed sermon.

The concept of an expository unit also has advantages over the idea of preaching paragraphs of Scripture because sometimes an expository sermon covers passages much longer or much shorter than a paragraph. *Distilling* the essence of a long passage or *exploding* the implications of a single phrase are both legitimate homiletical tasks.

The unit concept encourages a preacher not to feel constrained by the paragraph or verse divisions of a particular translation. Most text divisions within the books of modern Bibles have simply been added for readability. Therefore, a preacher does not need to address a passage in precisely the way it has been divided by translators if the thought being developed overlaps the translation's divisions. Prudence cautions preachers not to ignore completely the paragraph and verse divisions in the Bible. Scholars have usually indicated the divisions on the basis of transitions of thought observed in the text. Still, the divisions are not divine and should not force a preacher to break down a passage in precisely the same way.

On the negative side, expository unit terminology may limit a preacher's vision if it simply becomes synonymous with "a paragraph of thought." A few years ago I preached at the church of a friend who had attended seminary with me. I preached on one of the Gospel narratives that was many paragraphs long. Afterward my friend confided that he rarely preached from such narratives because we had been trained to preach only from expository

1. See how Andrew Blackwood prepared for the terminology in *The Fine Art of Preaching* (New York: Macmillan, 1943), 34–35; see also Robert G. Rayburn, *Expository Preaching* (a textbook begun by Rayburn prior to his death), available at Covenant Seminary in the files of the president's office.

2. Jay E. Adams, *Preaching with Purpose: A Comprehensive Textbook on Biblical Preaching* (Grand Rapids: Baker, 1982), 26.

units. By this he meant that he almost always preached from a paragraph or two at a time. He had missed the nuance of the term. *An expository unit is a large or a small portion of Scripture from which a preacher can demonstrate a single spiritual truth with adequate supporting facts or concepts arising within the scope of the text.*

Preachers can hardly communicate important truths from narratives such as the flood or the prodigal son if they do not cover the entire account.[3] Messages from the poetic portions of Scripture must sometimes deal with themes that are echoed or developed many lines apart. A biblical writer may deal with a subject and lay it aside for parenthetical discussion before picking up the original thought again several sentences or even several chapters later. Some sermons must cover several chapters at once to relate a biblical concept; others should strive to capture the meaning of an entire book (e.g., Job or Ruth) or extract a truth running in the grain of a family of books (e.g., remnant or kingdom).[4] While beginning preachers are best advised to learn their expository craft by preaching from a paragraph or two of Scripture, they are well advised to consider how they may ultimately expound passages of varying lengths since biblical truths are related through a great variety of literary means and lengths.[5]

Sermon Length

The amount of time a preacher has to present a message also affects the selection of a passage. I was raised in a tradition in which the preaching started at roughly 9:00 A.M. on Sunday morning, broke for a noon meal, and then continued into the early afternoon. Needless to say, this practice gave the preachers quite a bit of latitude in choosing their texts and forming their explanations. However, now it is almost impossible for most North American Christians to fathom sermons of such length and congregations of such patience. As we surf through the channels on our televisions with fingers poised on remote controls in order to relieve the slightest hint of boredom, the thought of listening to a sermon for hours practically paralyzes.

Cultural, ecclesiastical, and congregational differences cause sermon lengths to vary greatly. In parts of Africa and the Caribbean, a preacher who quits before an hour has passed is considered to have shortchanged the congregation. In many English and American churches in which the authority of the Word has deteriorated, a ten-minute homily on a cultural

---

3. Gordon D. Fee and Douglas Stuart, *How to Read the Bible for All Its Worth* (Grand Rapids: Zondervan, 1982), 77.

4. In the section of chap. 9 on Scripture introductions, we will discuss how a preacher can present and expound lengthy portions of Scripture.

5. David L. Larsen, *The Anatomy of Preaching: Identifying the Issues in Preaching Today* (Grand Rapids: Baker, 1989), 90–91.

topic has replaced even cursory explanations of "thus saith the Lord." At the same time, proponents of the church-growth movement in the United States often advocate eighteen- to twenty-minute sermons as a means of reaching unchurched ears in our rapidly paced culture. Sermon length is not an automatic measure of orthodoxy, yet sermons long enough to explain what a passage means and short enough to keep interested persons listening indicate much about the vitality of a congregation and the wisdom of the pastor.

For reasons both right and wrong, the churches I have attended as an adult tend to expect sermons to be twenty-five to thirty minutes long.[6] This appears to be something of an evangelical norm in North America, though there are exceptions on both sides of the stopwatch. Well-schooled and biblically literate congregations can generally feast on the Word longer than others, but overfeeding is always possible, and force-feeding remains the mark of either inexperienced or insensitive preachers. John R. W. Stott neatly sidesteps the issue of how long a sermon should be by saying, "Every sermon should 'seem like twenty minutes,' even if it is much longer."[7]

Whatever the norm of a particular congregation, however, a preacher must have the wisdom to choose passages of such length and/or substance that they can be expounded within the allotted time. The occasion, the makeup of the congregation, a church's ministry and mission goals, worship service parameters, and changes the church experiences in age, educational levels, and spiritual maturity can greatly affect appropriate passage and message length. Pastors should consider each of these factors when determining how long to preach and should press expectations only with care and patience.

There is always another verse that can be covered and another word that can be said, but ministers are best advised to select passages that allow them to quit before the congregation does. The well-prepared pastor always has more to say than time to say it. Part of the torture of sermon preparation is the discipline of setting aside for another occasion what there is not time to

6. George Sweazey offers this neat synopsis: "In the circles with which I am most familiar, a fifteen-minute message seems miniature, twenty minutes is short, twenty-five minutes is usual, and thirty minutes is long" (*Preaching the Good News* [Englewood Cliffs, N.J.: Prentice-Hall, 1976], 145). However, it is probably fair to say that in the time since Sweazey wrote those words, the length of sermons in the mainline churches with which he is most familiar has continued to shorten. John R. W. Stott does not debate Sweazey's basic analysis, writing, "No hard and fast rules can be laid down about the length of sermons, except perhaps that ten minutes are too short and forty minutes too long" (*Between Two Worlds: The Art of Preaching in the Twentieth Century* [Grand Rapids: Eerdmans, 1988], 294).

7. Stott, *Between Two Worlds*, 294. For additional corroboration of this impression, see Lori Carrell, *The Great American Sermon Survey* (Wheaton: Mainstay Church Resources, 2000), 111–15, 135–36. For an interesting historical perspective on the length of sermons, see the 1645 *Directory for the Publick [sic] Worship of God* prepared by the Westminster Assembly. In the section titled "Of Publick Reading of Holy Scripture," preachers are advised that "regard is always to be had unto the time so as preaching will not be rendered tedious."

say in this message. We simply will say more that is heard if we preach less than all we know. In the pulpit, less can often mean more. Still, we should never despair over the meat we have trimmed to make a message digestible. Faithful preparation outlasts the preaching moment and will serve the preacher and the congregation in future sermons, character formation, and counseling sessions, which are all part of the extended ministry of the Word.

Perhaps the length of a passage and the corresponding length of the message are best determined when preachers remember the ultimate object of each sermon: enabling people to honor Christ. Messages should not be so short as to make God's Word seem incidental nor so long as to make worship a burden. Either extreme robs Christ of the glory he deserves and the sweet prick his Word should provide the human conscience.

Concerns

Preaching on passages that are of particular meaning or interest to you is a great way to learn to expound texts. What excites or moves you is much more likely to elicit the passion from you that will excite and move others. Even experienced expositors frequently choose texts because they address a particular personal concern.[8] Messages fired by a pastor's burning conviction tend to spark congregational interest as well as pastoral enthusiasm. However, preachers who choose texts to address their personal concerns need to be cautioned in at least two ways. First, make sure you do not impose your concern on the text. Solid exposition should demonstrate that the passage really speaks to the issue you want to address and that your passion to address a particular subject has not abused the original author's intent. Second, be aware that a ministry that addresses only the preacher's personal concerns can become too limited in perspective for the needs of a congregation. The pastor may end up riding hobby horses or unconsciously concentrating on personal struggles, thereby neglecting other important truths needed for a fully informed and mature congregation.

Congregational concerns should also influence what pastors choose to preach. Preachers will be regarded as out of touch and/or insensitive if they press forward with their sermon programs while ignoring a community's employment dilemma, the death of a pillar in the church, a local disaster, a building program, a young person's decision to enter the mission field, moral issues that the young encounter, health concerns that the elderly face, or a host of similar matters of significance in the life of the church. The world

---

8. Haddon Robinson calls this "topical exposition" (*Biblical Preaching: The Development and Delivery of Expository Messages,* 2nd ed. [Grand Rapids: Baker, 2001], 56–57).

should not set the agenda for our preaching, but ministry that ignores the world that a congregation confronts is a sanctimonious sham.

Experienced preachers typically set aside a portion of each year to look backward and forward—backward at what the preaching has covered and what the congregation has encountered, and forward to what the preaching should cover in light of what the congregation needs to know or will likely experience. Efforts to educate and prepare a congregation for the scope of life's spiritual challenges lead the pastor to a wide variety of topics and away from sermon ruts.

Many preachers try to use the slower summer months to plan the upcoming church year's preaching program, knowing that the quality of each sermon will greatly increase if they know well ahead of time what passages and topics they will address. Planning ahead enables a preacher to establish a pre-sermon file that keeps sermon preparation from degenerating into a Friday-afternoon flurry or a Saturday-night fever whose results distress preacher and congregation alike.

A folder set aside for each upcoming sermon acts as a magnet, drawing ideas from general reading and everyday experience. Flashes of insight, relevant quotations, newspaper clippings, exegetical discoveries, illustrations, and outlines can be dropped into the file over several weeks and will grant you vast resources for preparing a sermon the week it will be preached.[9] Even if you do not use all the information in the file, its presence will take much of the pressure out of weekly sermon preparation. You will not have to spend precious hours scanning books, magazines, and commentaries looking for that quotation you read months ago that you know fits perfectly in this message—but that you cannot quite remember. Pastors without pre-sermon files typically fall back on clichés because they do not have time to find memorable insights in the few hours each week they can devote to sermon preparation.

Many young pastors fear they will run out of preaching topics after a few months, but once they begin to know a congregation well enough to sense the depth and the number of its needs, doubts, griefs, sins, and challenges, concern quickly shifts to how so much can be addressed given the time allotted to preaching. Broad doctrinal principles that grant people the perspectives they need to handle a variety of problems need to be preached. In addition, preachers need to address particular concerns with specific instructions from Scripture. At the same time, they need to be careful that their pulpits are not simply captured by the currents of congregational desires. A ministry can be as warped by lending too much of an ear to what people

---

9. For additional ideas on preparing pre-sermon files, see Bryan Chapell, *Using Illustrations to Preach with Power*, rev. ed. (Wheaton: Crossway, 2001), 169–70.

want to hear as it can by giving too much weight to what the preacher wants to preach (2 Tim. 4:3).

Different church traditions have used various means to round out the emphases of preaching in a local setting. Roman Catholic, Orthodox, Lutheran, and mainline churches in the United States often use a lectionary tied to the liturgical calendar that leads ministers to cover a variety of preselected texts each year. Reformed churches have typically resisted lectionary usage for a variety of reasons: (1) the principle of *sola scriptura,* which teaches that Scripture alone should dictate what is preached; (2) the practice of *lectio continua* as opposed to *lectio selecta,* that is, presenting lessons from texts in consecutive sequence (e.g., preaching through a book in a series, also known as "consecutive preaching")[10] instead of choosing diverse selections week to week, since this was felt to lead to inappropriate human emphases; (3) the tradition of holding no day above another in reaction to Roman Catholic holy day observances that were seen as integral to sacramentalism; and (4) the regard given to the autonomy of the local pulpit on the assumption that the Holy Spirit will grant a local preacher unction (i.e., spiritual power) and insight for the task at hand.

Distance from the battles of the Reformation and a growing awareness of the need to speak directly to culture have made Reformed churches more willing to address seasonal matters but not more willing to mandate a liturgical calendar. Baptist, charismatic, and many independent church traditions have taken similar courses in recent decades. All these traditions recognize that congregational health cannot be maintained without a ministerial commitment to preach "the whole will of God" (Acts 20:20, 27). Whether a lectionary, a personal agenda, a worship committee, a book sequence, or community pressures influence the texts you select, you must take care to prepare people for the matters they want you to address *and* those they would never choose to face. Both congregational and pastoral appetites may need to be curbed and refined in order to meet this goal, lest a steady diet of what one considers chocolate cake malnourish everyone.

Catalysts

Series

What will help keep your text selection well-rounded? Honored practices and fresh approaches. Among the most honored practices is preaching text series. The consecutive preaching method provides significant benefits for a pastor preaching in sequence through a chapter or a book because of the following:

---

10. John A. Broadus refers to this as "continuous exposition" (*On the Preparation and Delivery of Sermons,* ed. J. B. Weatherspoon [New York: Harper & Row, 1944], 146–47).

- Matters in the text force the preacher to address a greater number of issues than what readily springs to mind.
- Sensitive matters can be addressed without the appearance of pointing a finger at persons or problems in the church (the matters simply appear next in the text sequence, and avoiding them would be even more obvious).
- Much time can be saved because the preacher does not have to go through the often time-consuming rigor of deciding what to preach on each week—the next section of the text is the obvious choice.
- Much research time can be saved (especially for the young pastor) because each new sermon does not require a new study of the book's or the passage's author, background, context, and cause.
- The congregation will learn to see the organizing themes and schemes of the Bible instead of perceiving it as an impenetrable mishmash of maxims, morals, and stories.
- The congregation and the pastor can monitor the progress of both their journey through a book and their exposure to important biblical and doctrinal topics. This is especially important as pastor and congregation consider what matters future preaching should address.[11]

Series preaching shows its greatest liabilities when preachers fail to make adequate or appropriate progress. D. Martyn Lloyd-Jones may have preached on Romans for fourteen years, but without his exceptional abilities, this extraordinary practice is likely to kill congregational interest and enthusiasm. The longtime practice of limiting Sunday school lessons to twelve-week sessions says much about the need people have for change. Recent studies that have convinced many publishers to package inductive Bible studies in seven- to eight-week sessions say yet more about the tolerance even committed Christians in our culture have for the routine. Although master expositors make exceptions, it is usually best for sermon series to last a few months at a maximum. People want to study their Bibles in depth, but like vacationers wanting more than one view of the Grand Canyon, they generally like to move along. When a preacher announces for the fifth week in a row, "Turn with me in your Bibles for our continuing series on Ecclesiastes 2:15d," the groans may not be audible, but the snores will be.

Series also cause problems if a preacher makes each sermon dependent on previous messages. Many times a topic or a passage will be better handled in

---

11. Stott advises a "partnership" between the pastor and the parishioners in determining what and how matters should be addressed (*Between Two Worlds*, 198–200). By this he does not advocate that preachers abdicate their divine calling but that they use committees and conversations with leaders and others in the church to discern the type and dosage of scriptural medicine needing to be administered. A pastor who does not arrange to take the pulse of the congregation is a poor physician of souls.

a series of sermons, but each sermon should be decipherable without a code dispensed in previous messages. Too many references to "As we discovered last week . . ." or "Three weeks ago we saw that . . ." will make those who were present for the earlier messages sense failure if they cannot remember the reference and will make those who were not present feel they cannot get the full impact of the current message because they were not around for the preview. Those new to the congregation may feel they will never catch up to a series that has gone on for six months and promises to continue for three months more if the pastor does not make most of each sermon stand on its own feet rather than on the shoulders of previous messages.

Series greatly aid a pastor's preparation and subject scope. Still, series generally work best when their duration is reasonable, their sermons are not too dependent on one another, and their subjects and/or approaches differ from those of recent series. Preaching through Philippians will stimulate many fine expository messages. A series on the Christian family or the marks of a healthy church can also lead a pastor to a sequence of texts in different books that can be handled expositionally.

CONTEXTS

If the sequence of a series does not itself determine the choice of a text, other considerations from a preacher's life, church, and culture can naturally help a pastor decide on what to preach.

Personal abilities. Even though you want your knowledge and skills to grow, there is no good reason to jump into an expository series on Ezekiel or Revelation if you do not yet have the background to handle accurately its contents. Tackle what you know best as you develop skills that will help you wrestle through and prepare for more challenging passages.

The calendar. In most churches, preachers can get away with not talking about fathers on Father's Day, but many will find that a failure to mention mothers on Mother's Day can cause significant upset. No mention of the resurrection on Easter will be a greater mystery than the empty tomb to those in the pew, and Christmas without the Christ child abuses most hearts. While some preachers in the Reformed tradition maintain the commitment to hold no day above another (see discussion above), connecting the events of Scripture to the times of our world can make both the Bible and the preacher seem aware of and sensitive to present concerns.

The situation. At times we flow through the mirrored hallways of Scripture, identifying issues to consider that address the context of our daily lives. Other times situations force us to safari through the Bible with our own concerns poised as nets to capture the text that will address our needs. Yet whether we reflect on how a text speaks to our context or go searching for a text to address a particular concern, we rightly bring our situation into the consideration of what we should address. Community concern over substance abuse in the local high school, a strike at a major employer, a tragedy, or a triumph all may prod a preacher to find relevant Scripture passages. Congregational concern about officer selection, vandalism, outreach, and a host of other issues will also stimulate the selection of passages.

The most frequently addressed subjects should be those that reflect the everyday situations people in the pew are facing or are likely to face. A pastor who lives among the people will know those struggling with a harsh boss, a prodigal son, guilt, depression, an unsaved relative, intolerant in-laws, an impossible spouse, irresponsible ambitions, unrestrained passions, and many similar concerns. Subjects such as these should be the FCFs addressed in many sermons and will serve as the guides to many suitable texts. Life-situation topics and texts help people know how to live faithfully in ordinary moments so that they will be prepared to act faithfully in extraordinary situations.

Current events. Christians also need biblical guidance to address the societal issues they do or should confront: poverty, abortion, disasters, dissent, military crises, political issues, epidemics, economics, health care, and so on. Evangelicals may believe that the advice to prepare sermons with the Bible in one hand and a newspaper in the other reflects a contemporary social agenda.[12] However, great preachers such as Charles Spurgeon have also urged this practice, which makes the preacher and the people integrate the eternal truths of Scripture into the daily patterns of their lives and thoughts.[13]

Current events tend to get pastors in trouble when sermons begin to argue for specific political agendas, candidates, or programs. Although there are moments for exceptions, a preacher's commitments and expertise are usually best limited to relating the biblical principles responsible Christians should employ as they bring God's Word to bear on their professional callings and ethical judgments. Of course, where there are clear biblical standards about an issue, preachers should speak with courage and clarity. A pastor who is perceived as a political animal, however, usually loses spiritual authority.

Hymnals. The hymnody of the church reveals much of what is dear to a congregation and a church's tradition. Both are ripe fields from which to harvest text suggestions.

Confessions, catechisms, and creeds. The doctrinal statements of a church need biblical explication in order for a congregation to know that its beliefs are more than traditional opinions. Pastors may find it difficult to preach uplifting messages on their church's approach to baptism, biblical discipline, hell, the Trinity, or the inspiration of Scripture, but texts on these subjects need to be explored, thus fully informing and preparing a congregation for the spiritual challenges all face.

12. Arthur Michael Ramsey and Leon-Joseph Suenens, *The Future of the Christian Church* (London: SCM, 1971), 13–14.

13. Charles Haddon Spurgeon, *Lectures to My Students* (Grand Rapids: Zondervan, 1980), 54.

Others' messages. Sermons you hear and materials you read can be wonderful catalysts for your own sermons. Learn from past and present greats, glean from the novel, and use the significant thoughts of others to generate ideas for what you can or should say to your own congregation. Give credit if you borrow the work of others. The availability of sermon tapes and websites has made plagiarism a serious problem and has shipwrecked numerous ministries.[14] Yet at the same time, recognize that the greatest preachers always keep eyes and ears open to harvest ideas, quotations, illustrations, outlines, exegetical insights, memorable wording, and topics from fellow laborers in the ministry.[15] No preaching rubric should require you to be the originator of all the truth parishioners receive. A file for storing articles of interest and ideas from others for future sermons is a must for most preachers.

The Holy Spirit. No catalyst for selecting a text is more important than sensitivity to the leading of God's Spirit. Prayer with godly concern for the good of others and the glory of Christ should lead you through the choices you must make among the catalysts for selecting a sermon's focus. Preaching in the power of the Spirit is the culmination of a process that has been Spirit-led. The conviction that the Holy Spirit gave the Word should yield a commitment to seek his leading and the courage to speak what he wants said rather than what we or our congregations fancy. In the heart in which the Spirit burns glows the fire that refines questions about what texts we should preach and lights the way our thoughts should turn.

Cautions

In my earliest years of ministry, I most valued mining obscure texts. I thought the effort showed how serious I was about all of Scripture. I also believed that handling such passages well would show how qualified I was to preach. Preaching difficult and little-known texts was like showing my diploma. I later learned to love shedding light on important texts or bringing new life to familiar texts. Concentrating on the Bible's "fine print" gave people the impression they could not read their Bibles without me. My pride may have appreciated this perception, but it was poor pastoring. The Bible became an opaque book full of grammatical mazes and logical knots that I had to untangle each week. Thus, by consistently choosing texts in the Bible's densest forests, I denied people the sunlight it more regularly offers and made them less willing to approach its paths. Some people may have thought much of my abilities to handle the Word, but more lost confidence in their ability to do the same.

14. For further advice on using the work of others without sacrificing personal integrity, see chap. 8.
15. Stott, *Between Two Worlds,* 219.

We are obligated to handle the hard passages from time to time, but we also should remember the example of Christ's ministry. He preached about the familiar: David and the consecrated bread, Jonah and the great fish, birds and flowers, the proverbs and prayer. The apostle Paul, while dealing with some complex subjects, was not ashamed to talk about Adam and Eve, the marketplace, a soldier's armor, and even how seeds grow. The importance of introducing people to the reality of the Word in terms they know cautions us to remember basic guidelines in choosing texts for our sermons.

Do not avoid familiar texts. Biblical passages that are familiar typically are well known because they have been of great value to the church throughout the ages. Consistently denying a congregation these passages is to deprive them of some of Scripture's richest treasure. Spurgeon, the prince of preachers, spoke over and over about Zacchaeus, Joshua, and the prodigal son. John Wesley loved to preach on Jesus Christ as our "wisdom, and righteousness, and sanctification, and redemption" (1 Cor. 1:30 KJV). Paul simply said, "I have not hesitated to preach anything that would be helpful to you" (Acts 20:20).

Do not search for texts obscure in meaning. There is great warrant for expounding texts many misunderstand and for clarifying difficult passages that unfold naturally in an expository series, but there is little value in explaining for the sake of explaining. Preaching should edify, not showcase erudition. Even if you know the meaning of "the baptism of the dead" and the names of all the sons of Pahathmoab, consider whether there are more vital matters that sin-sick and life-battered people need this Sunday. Obscure texts occasionally preached may enable a preacher to highlight an issue made evident by the peculiar twists or the unusual features of such passages, but we should not confuse a congregation's appreciation of an occasional taste of the exotic with a need for a diet of the same.

Do not purposely avoid any text. We should distinguish between wisely passing over some texts and purposely avoiding others. When Paul told the Ephesian elders, "I have not hesitated to proclaim to you the whole will of God" (Acts 20:27), his words revealed the courage and the integrity such conscientious proclamation requires. Wisdom and tact should guide the presentation of issues difficult for a particular congregation to face, but if a church never faces its faults and frailties, its pastor has failed to preach everything it needs to hear.

Do not use spurious texts. Concern for what a congregation needs to hear should never lead a pastor to proclaim as authoritative any words or texts that the Holy Spirit did not inspire. Scribal comments and errors that have mistakenly been included in some translations[16] should not be presented as the Word of God. Where there is the rare question about whether a particular

---

16. In the King James Version, 1 John 5:7 is a prime example, and Mark 16:18 is a sad one (given the way some groups have employed it as a test of spirituality).

passage is spurious, it is wise to see if the same truth can be preached from a more certain passage or to provide the congregation with your reasons for using the text (since the marginal notes in the most trustworthy translations in the laps of listeners will question the passage's authenticity).

Faith that the Holy Spirit knew what he was doing when he inspired the Word without the spurious texts will keep us confident of Scripture's sufficiency. We can help the people to whom we preach remain confident of the Bible's authority by reminding them how rare such questions are when they do arise in the ordinary course of preaching. Bible-believing scholars question the textual validity of less than one word in a thousand in the best translations.[17] As a result, there is little question concerning what statements appeared in the original manuscripts. The evangelical debate with modern theologies concentrates not on what Scripture says but on whether to believe and obey what it says. The Holy Spirit's divine inspiration and providential preservation of Scripture are continuing miracles of God's spiritual care for our souls. A good study Bible prepared by scholars who accept the Bible's full authority will give us ample warning of a questionable text and will grant us confidence that we are preaching in accord with the Spirit's imprimatur.

Tools for Interpreting a Passage

Once a passage is chosen, we want to be sure we are interpreting it properly. A host of good tools is available to help grant pastors confidence that they are preaching what the Holy Spirit intends. None of these is a substitute for a solid biblical education, but even those with extensive training depend on study tools to confirm, deepen, and brighten their interpretations. Listed below are tools that preachers commonly employ to help them interpret texts (the order of this list indicates a sequence of tools that preachers frequently use when preparing sermons).[18]

Study Bibles. No tool is more accessible and cost-effective than a good study Bible. Many preachers may not even think of the Bible they use as

---

17. J. I. Packer, "Text Criticism and Inerrancy," *Christianity Today* 46, no. 11 (October 7, 2002): 102.

18. Although many of its entries are now dated, Cyril J. Barber's *The Minister's Library,* 2 vols. (Neptune, N.J.: Loizeaux, 1974–89), remains an excellent, basic guide for determining the types of tools you need for scriptural research and pastoral work. For an updated guide to books for a minister's library, see Cyril J. Barber, *Best Books for Your Bible Study Library* (Neptune, N.J.: Loizeaux, 2000). Cyril J. Barber and Robert M. Krauss Jr. offer a more in-depth approach to reference works for theological scholarship in *An Introduction to Theological Research* (Lanham, Md.: University Press of America, 2000). See also David S. Dockery, K. A. Matthews, and Robert B. Sloan, eds., "Foundations for Biblical Interpretation: A Complete Library of Tools and Resources," *The Master's Seminary Journal* 6, no. 2 (Fall 1995): 244–47; and James Stitzinger, "850 Books for Biblical Expositors," http://www.tms.edu/750books.asp.

being a study tool since they use its resources so regularly and instinctively. A good study Bible with verse cross-references, book synopses, glossaries, concordances, explanatory notes, maps, Bible character summaries, charts, time lines, and other helps provides a succinct library of information in a preacher's palm (see select examples in table 1 in appendix 9). Other tools examine the Bible's details in greater depth, but nothing is handier or more dependable than a good study Bible for quickly informing a preacher whether an interpretation is on track.

Lexicons, grammatical aids, and analytical aids. Preachers who are committed to translating passages (or their key portions) to determine precise meaning in the original languages keep lexicons close at hand. Lexicons explain the meanings of the words behind the English translations. Complete lexicons provide definitions of a word along with various uses of the word, its root meanings, examples of where it occurs, and possible guidance as to how its grammatical variations can affect its meaning (see select examples in table 2 in appendix 9).

Grammatical aids help a preacher see how a particular word's tense, case, number, usage, or context affects its meaning. Examples and explanations of each of the grammatical features with extensive indexes characterize the best grammars (see select examples in table 3 in appendix 9).

Exegetical (i.e., language analysis) aids help a preacher analyze a word's tense, case, and number so that its specific grammatical features can be identified or researched in a grammatical aid or lexicon. Students in schools that encourage study in the original languages are familiar with the aids currently on the market (see select examples in tables 2 and 4 in appendix 9). Many have been incorporated into computer software at reasonable prices. Pastors who have grown distant from language training may find that these tools can reacquaint them with this valuable line of study. In addition, a host of new tools has found a home in the original-language study market. These computerized and print tools parse the verbs in every verse, identify the number and case of every noun, and reveal the root of each word. For advice on which tools will best suit your purposes, consult the guides to lexical aids listed in footnotes 21, 28, and 30 below.

Concordances. Once you start working within a text, you may wonder how some of its words are used elsewhere in Scripture, or you may recall a text in which a similar word or idea occurs that you could use to drive home a point, but you cannot remember its reference. Concordances help you find references by listing all the places where a particular word is found in the Bible (see select examples in table 4 in appendix 9). Modern concordances also guide you to the original-language meanings and uses of biblical words. A number of these tools now have numerical systems that cross-reference words to other reference sources. Some computerized concordances also have the capacity to provide exegetical information.

Topical Bibles. Sometimes pastors use concordances simply to find where a topic is covered in the Bible by looking up references for key words relating to that subject. Topical Bibles shorten this process by listing the verses and/or passages pertaining to a topic under alphabetized topic headings.[19] Pastors who want to preach on a particular subject often use topical Bibles to scan passages quickly and decide which deals best with the topic as they want to address it.

Bible translations. Often preachers can discern nuances in the original text by comparing how the experts have variously translated the text.[20] One old saying goes, "The King James Version is translated in the language of Pilgrim times, the New International Version is translated in the language of our times, and the New American Standard Bible is translated in the language of no time"—a line that is unfair because it fails to recognize the strengths of each version.

People love the King James Version (KJV) for the beauty of its language. That language now sounds archaic to most ears, but the translators were biblically sound and aided our understanding greatly by translating passages that echo one another theologically or terminologically in such a way that the reverberations remain clear in both Testaments. The New International Version (NIV), which now sells more than any other, is the most accurate translation that strives for easy reading by translating original phrases into their "dynamic equivalent" in our idiom. The New American Standard Bible (NASB) sacrifices readability for a more strictly equivalent translation, which continues to make it satisfying to many serious Bible students. The newer English Standard Version (ESV) maintains much of the majesty of style of the older Revised Standard Version (RSV) but was edited by Bible-believing scholars who made the ESV translation one of the most insightful and dependable currently available.

The Living Bible and other paraphrases can help preachers scan a large body of material in order to pick up its gist; the Amplified Bible and J. B. Phillips's translation concentrate more on communicating the nuances behind specific statements. Most of the popular translations that are committed to the authority of Scripture have strengths and can be employed once you discern the purpose of a particular translation.

Bible dictionaries, encyclopedias, and handbooks. Several major publishers offer reference works containing definitions, explanations, backgrounds, time lines, and/or descriptions of key Bible characters, terms, concepts, places, or

---

19. *Nave's Topical Bible* is the best-known example.

20. Leland Ryken, *The Word of God in English: Criteria for Excellence in Bible Translation* (Wheaton: Crossway, 2002), 123–241. Several works in the print and computer markets carry multiple translations so that a preacher can compare translations line by line (e.g., *The Layman's Parallel Bible* and *Comparative Study Bible,* both published by Zondervan; and the various computer concordance programs listed in appendix 9 that typically allow multiple-translation searches).

practices. Versions vary from single volumes to many tomes, but competition among these books, which can save a preacher many hours of numbing research, has driven the lower-quality sources from the stores. Evaluate your pocketbook and your probable purposes, and buy a recent edition from a major evangelical publisher (see select examples in table 5 in appendix 9).

Commentaries. The best commentators use all the tools already described plus more to help preachers determine what a particular passage says. Commentaries are usually devoted to a single book of the Bible, but there are also good single-volume commentaries on the entire Bible whose abbreviated entries alert preachers to major concerns. Especially in the early stages of ministry, no well-prepared preacher considers sermon preparation complete without consultation of an up-to-date commentary.

Bible commentaries vary greatly in their length, quality, type, and price. Publishers frequently offer commentaries in large sets covering the entire Old or New Testament. Sets are often the most economical and convenient way of obtaining the resources you need to cover an entire Testament, but those who have time to research their purchases may want to consult resources that evaluate the quality of each volume in a set.[21] You can usually construct the highest quality commentary library by selecting the best volumes out of a variety of sets.

The expertise that commentaries bring to bear on a particular passage is at one moment their greatest benefit and their greatest danger. The mixed blessing is evident in the two types of pastors who will never make great preachers: The first will not listen to what others say; the other will say only what others say. A preacher who refuses to pay attention to what gifted scholars have discovered mistakes personal arrogance for erudition. God does not give all his insights to any one person. At the same time, a preacher who says only what a commentator concludes is trying to preach by proxy.

You must think through what Scripture says in order to be able to expound adequately and apply meaningfully what commentators say. No commentator has room to write down all the implications, insights, and truths given in a text. No distant educator or long-dead scholar knows your situation or your congregation's concerns. It is not wise habitually to run to commentaries as the first step of sermon preparation, lest your thoughts start running in a groove carved by one not in touch with what you need to address.[22]

21. In addition to the works by Fee and Stuart cited in footnote 28 below, consult Tremper Longman III, *Old Testament Commentary Survey*, 3rd ed. (Grand Rapids: Baker, 2003); Donald Carson, *New Testament Commentary Survey* (Grand Rapids: Baker, 2001); and Douglas Stuart, *A Guide to Selecting and Using Bible Commentaries*, 5th ed. (Dallas: Word, 1990). A number of seminary faculties have also written guides to help their students build good personal preaching libraries. I am aware of such guides at Covenant Theological Seminary, Dallas Theological Seminary, Trinity Evangelical Divinity School, and Westminster Theological Seminary.

22. Edward F. Marquart, *Quest for Better Preaching* (Minneapolis: Augsburg, 1985), 101, 106.

Commentaries are better used as a check than as a guide.[23] Develop your exposition and tentative outline based on work with the basic tools and then consult commentaries to flesh out, refine, and, if necessary, revise your ideas. Try not to preach a dead or a distant person's sermon. Spurgeon advised, "The closet [i.e., the place of personal meditation] is the best study. The commentators are good instructors but the author himself is far better."[24] God called *you* to this situation. He wanted no one other than you to prepare this message for this moment. Joseph Ruggles Wilson reminds us how unique is each preacher's challenge:

> In other words, preaching is not an imitative exercise. Every preacher is to regard himself as an original exhibitor and enforcer of the terms of human salvation; a channel of gracious speech, markedly different from every other.
>   . . . Turn it which way we will, the conclusion is always before us, the preacher's preaching is just another form of himself; i.e., if he does his own thinking; exhibits no emotions that he does not actually feel; and presents divine truth, not as a bundle of opinions which orthodoxy has agreed upon, but as so much vital blood that has been made to course in his veins, and therefore takes the form of his own Christian life. It is these live men whom God supremely calls; men who have eaten the word, as a prophet did, and into whom it has passed to become a perpetual throb in their hearts; so that when it comes forth again, it will proceed upon its errand, bearing the warmth of their innermost experiences; those experiences wherein are traced the musings which continued until they could find vent only in fire; the fire that burns quickly into other souls, melts where it burns, and remoulds where it melts.[25]

Let the Holy Spirit work in your heart and mind to develop a message a commentator would approve, not design. Concern for precision should not so overwhelm you as to deny you or your listeners the insights God will grant you in his Word.

Principles for Interpreting a Passage

Concern to use good tools for interpreting biblical passages reflects a basic commitment to be true to the Bible. Expository preaching solemnly binds a preacher to the task of representing the precise meaning of a text as intended by the original author or as illumined by another inspired source within the Bible. As matter-of-fact as such a rubric may seem, homiletical history indicates how mutable such a standard is and how carefully it

23. Arndt L. Halvorson, *Authentic Preaching* (Minneapolis: Augsburg, 1982), 52.
24. Cited in Helmut Thielicke, *Encounter with Spurgeon* (Grand Rapids: Baker, 1977), 116.
25. Joseph Ruggles Wilson, "In What Sense Are Preachers to Preach Themselves?" *Southern Presbyterian Review* 25 (1874): 355–57.

must be guarded. Early church and medieval escapades into allegorical interpretation led ancient preachers to the conviction that the "literal interpretation" of a text was the least rewarding to preach.[26] Modern resurrections of the allegorical method regularly occur when preachers assume that the Holy Spirit will enable them to discern in a text something more than or different from what was meant by the biblical writer or what they can demonstrate that the divine Author makes evident within the canon of Scripture.[27] Preachers' interpretations remain consistent with Scripture when they follow long-honored and proven interpretive procedures that expose the Bible's original intent.

Preachers must consider the context as part of any text. Context limits and imparts an author's intended meaning. We cannot maintain the integrity of any biblical statement without considering its surroundings. Our first task as expositors is to use the best tools available to determine what a biblical author's statements mean in their context.[28]

Use the Grammatical-Historical Method

Discovering the "literal meaning" does not mean that we disregard the figurative, poetic, colloquial, metaphorical, or spiritual ways in which the biblical writers sometimes communicate. Literal interpretation occurs when we explain what a biblical writer meant, not what his words may connote

---

26. Moisés Silva, *Has the Church Misread the Bible? The History of Interpretation in the Light of Current Issues*, vol. 1, Foundations of Contemporary Interpretation (Grand Rapids: Zondervan, 1987), 41; and Bernard Ramm, *Protestant Biblical Interpretation*, 3rd rev. ed. (Grand Rapids: Baker, 1970), 38.

27. Although the concept of the *sensus plenior* remains controversial in conservative circles, preachers regularly make interpretations based on matters such as how frequently a word is used throughout Scripture, which would not always have been evident to the original writers. The Bible sometimes also demands that we interpret texts on the basis of how a later biblical writer uses an earlier statement of Scripture with only loose connections to its original context meaning. The potential and limits of the *sensus plenior* concept need much fuller explication. See Richard L. Pratt Jr., *He Gave Us Stories: The Bible Student's Guide to Interpreting Old Testament Narratives* (Phillipsburg, N.J.: Presbyterian & Reformed, 1990), 109–28; Edmund Clowney, *The Unfolding Mystery: Discovering Christ in the Old Testament* (Phillipsburg, N.J.: Presbyterian & Reformed, 1988), 155–63; and Dan McCartney and Charles Clayton, *Let the Reader Understand: A Guide to Interpreting and Applying the Bible* (Wheaton: Victor, 1994), 153–60; compared to Walter C. Kaiser Jr., *The Messiah in the Old Testament* (Grand Rapids: Zondervan, 1995), 13–35.

28. Excellent models of how to conduct exegetical research on a biblical passage include Fee and Stuart, *How to Read the Bible for All Its Worth;* Douglas Stuart, *Old Testament Exegesis: A Primer for Students and Pastors,* 2nd ed. (Philadelphia: Westminster, 1984); the companion work, Gordon D. Fee, *New Testament Exegesis: A Handbook for Students and Pastors* (Philadelphia: Westminster, 1983); Walter L. Liefeld, *New Testament Exposition: From Text to Sermon* (Grand Rapids: Zondervan, 1984); Donald Carson, *Exegetical Fallacies* (Grand Rapids: Baker, 1984); Pratt, *He Gave Us Stories;* William Klein, Craig Blomberg, and Robert Hubbard, *Introduction to Bible Interpretation* (Waco: Word, 1993); and Daniel M. Doriani, *Getting the Message: A Plan for Interpreting and Applying the Bible* (Phillipsburg, N.J.: Presbyterian & Reformed, 1996), 14–106.

outside their context. Original intent is sometimes called the "discourse meaning" of a text.[29] Such a designation helps us realize that we do not have to interpret a biblical reference to a sunrise as literally meaning the earth jumped from its orbit so that the sun could pass over it. We interpret the words in their linguistic context as we would if we were listening to someone talk today. Sometimes we use figurative, metaphorical, or colloquial terms to communicate, and so did the biblical writers.

Our task as preachers is to discern what the original writers meant by analyzing the background and grammatical features of what they said. Using grammar and history to discern a text's original meaning is called the grammatical-historical method.[30] This method allows Scripture to speak for itself instead of having an interpreter apply meaning to a text. Sometimes the latter does not seem dangerous when a preacher is committed to the historic truths of the faith. In such cases, we may hardly blink when told that the water from the rock Moses struck represents the water of baptism or that the worm at which Jonah railed is the sin that eats at a believer's heart. Despite the absence of biblical statements confirming these interpretations, they sound reasonable because they reflect biblical imagery and truths appearing elsewhere.

However, if anything in Scripture can mean whatever our imaginations suggest rather than what Scripture determines, then our opinions become as authoritative as the statements of God and we can make the Bible say anything we want. If we allow our imaginations to determine biblical meanings, then the water from the rock could represent baptism, or the water from Christ's side, or the water on which Peter walked by faith, or the crystal sea on which the saved will gather, or the fountain that should go in the new sanctuary's foyer. If Scripture does not determine meaning, ultimately Scripture has no meaning.

Occasionally, there may be a thin line between "it means" and "it may mean," but biblically bound preachers must recognize the difference. We may conjecture that the water and the blood that flowed from Christ's side represent New Testament baptism and communion, but we had best not command such observances on such a basis. We should never bind scriptural obligations to personal speculations.

The Protestant Reformers used the principle of the "analogy of faith" (sometimes identified as "the analogy of Scripture") to guide their interpre-

29. Peter Cotterell and Max Turner, *Linguistics and Biblical Interpretation* (Downers Grove, Ill.: InterVarsity, 1989), 69.

30. See Walter C. Kaiser Jr., *Toward an Exegetical Theology: Biblical Exegesis for Preaching and Teaching* (Grand Rapids: Baker, 1981), 87–88; William J. Larkin, *Culture and Biblical Hermeneutics: Interpreting and Applying the Authoritative Word in a Relativistic Age* (Grand Rapids: Baker, 1988), 115; and Leland Ryken, *Words of Delight: A Literary Introduction to the Bible* (Grand Rapids: Baker, 1987), 11–27. See also Leland Ryken, *How to Read the Bible as Literature* (Grand Rapids: Zondervan, 1985).

tations, and it should guide ours as well.[31] This standard requires preachers to use Scripture alone as the basis for their exhortations. Nothing but what Scripture itself attests should be the focus of our preaching. Expository preachers determine the biblical truths intended for the people addressed by a text and then identify similarities in our present condition that require the application of the same truths. This means applications may vary, but interpretations of a text's core ideas should not. The meaning of a text may be significant in many ways, but this should not imply that there is no definite meaning. For instance, Paul's command to "look not only to your own interests, but also to the interests of others" in Philippians 2:4 may be applied to concerns about disregard for the needs of others, divisive ambitions, or disrespect for the gifts of others, but the root idea of "selflessness based on Christ's example" must be maintained if the preaching is to be faithful to the original intent of the text.

Observe the Historical, Cultural, and Literary Context

Accurate interpretations require us not only to determine what particular words say but also to see how they function in their broader contexts. The reason "every heretic has his verse" is because Scripture can be twisted to say almost anything if interpreters ignore contexts. Attention to *historical* and *cultural* contexts helps explain the "offense" of the cross (Gal. 5:11) and reveals that certain healed lepers were not necessarily more thankful because they went to the temple before they went home (Luke 17:14). We determine *literary* contexts both by analyzing the concepts that surround a biblical statement *and* by identifying the type of literature in which the statement occurs.

Preachers should examine what chapters and verses surrounding a passage say in order to determine what a biblical writer intended to communicate through particular words. Without reading Romans 14 for its conceptual context, you are likely to determine that those called "weak" in Romans 15 are precisely the opposite of what Paul intended. Although John and James often use the word *believe,* contexts indicate that they are communicating quite different concepts (cf. John 3:16; James 2:19).

The temptation to lift verses from their contexts is perhaps best evident in the way popular Christian culture uses Scripture with scant regard for original intent. An early twentieth-century temperance hymn quotes "Touch not; taste not; handle not" (Col. 2:21 KJV) to condemn alcohol use. However, in the biblical context, the apostle condemns those who use these words to prohibit the permissible. In some wedding ceremonies, beaming brides recite to grateful grooms, "Where you go I will go, and where you stay I will stay.

---

31. Ramm, *Protestant Biblical Interpretation,* 55.

Your people will be my people and your God my God" (Ruth 1:16), yet the words were originally said by a woman to her mother-in-law. Friendship rings, pendants, and refrigerator magnets warmly exude, "May the LORD keep watch between you and me when we are away from each other" (Gen. 31:49), which in context was Laban's perpetual threat to harm Jacob if he ever returned to his uncle's territory.

Study of a passage's context also requires preachers to identify the genre, or type of literature, in which a biblical statement occurs. Many an error has been made by interpreting proverbs as promises, prophecy as history, parables as facts, and poetry as science.

For example, proverbs are truisms, statements so tending to be true that the wise take them to heart. A modern proverb on child rearing says, "As the twig is bent so grows the branch." The ancient equivalent is, "Train a child in the way he should go, and when he is old he will not turn from it" (Prov. 22:6). Both statements tend to be true, but neither is always true. This is the nature of proverbs. Proverbs are prescriptive, not predictive. God requires his people to heed his proverbs, not to interpret them as promises of what will always happen. Though the Bible says that a gentle word turns away wrath (Prov. 15:1), God does not promise that people will never get angry at us if we speak softly. He indicates that it is usually not wise for peacefully inclined people to answer fire with fire, but he does not promise that soft answers will always extinguish the rage of others (Matt. 26:62–68). Great damage is done to the intent of Scripture as well as to the consciences of Christians when preachers confuse these distinctions between promises and proverbs.

By contrast, prophecies are predictive and need to be interpreted with this perspective in mind. If we do not indicate the future basis of Israel's "comfort" in Isaiah 40, we diminish Christ's ministry. Additional damage can be done if we use details intended only to give a parable form (such as the physical abyss between Lazarus and the rich man in Luke 16) as the basis of a doctrinal formulation (such as heaven and hell being separated by physical barriers). If we use poetic language describing the wings of God (Ps. 91:4) as a scriptural argument for God's actual form, our theology will quickly decay. Prophecies, parables, and poetry, as well as other types of biblical literature, have their own unique uses in Scripture, and each genre should be interpreted according to the specific nature and purposes intended by its author and context.

Determine the Redemptive Context

Preachers determine the meaning of a passage by seeing not only how words are used in the context of a book or its passages but also how the passage functions in the entire scope of Scripture. An accurate interpretation requires preachers to ask, How does this text disclose the meaning or the need of redemption? Failure to ask and to answer this question leads to preaching that is highly moralistic or legalistic because it focuses on the behaviors a particular passage teaches without disclosing how the biblical writer was relating those behaviors to the work of the Savior.[32]

Regard for context requires preachers to consider a text in the light of its purpose in the redemptive message that unfolds throughout all of Scripture. Consider how the instructions of the apostle Paul honored the Christ-centrality of the entire Word. Paul preached about marital relationships, child rearing, qualifications for church officers, stewardship, handling anger, on-the-job conduct, regard for government authorities, and many other practical concerns, and at the same time he wrote, "But we preach Christ crucified: a stumbling block to Jews and foolishness to Gentiles. . . . For I resolved to know nothing while I was with you except Jesus Christ and him crucified" (1 Cor. 1:23; 2:2).

Somehow, though Paul addressed many issues of daily living, he believed he was always preaching about the person and work of Jesus. This must be the goal of expository preaching. The particulars of a passage need to be related to the overall purpose of Scripture.

In the latter portions of this book, we will devote much time to discovering how expository preachers can mine gospel gold from every biblical passage without adding matter to the text that is not already there. This discussion is important because preaching without an awareness of redemptive contexts is a great weakness in current evangelical circles. For the moment, it is sufficient to note that preachers need to interpret biblical texts in the light of Scripture's whole. This will inevitably force us to consider how a particular passage functions in revealing, preparing for, or reacting to the person and work of Christ, which is the ultimate message of the scope of Scripture.

Questions for Review and Discussion

1. What are the benefits and the liabilities of selecting texts for preaching that address personal and/or congregational concerns?
2. What are benefits and cautions associated with preaching a series?
3. What cautions does a preacher need to observe when approaching spurious texts?
4. Why should a preacher be cautious about turning to a commentary as a first step in sermon preparation?
5. How does an allegorical method of interpretation differ from an expository method?

---

32. Reasons for and means of determining the redemptive context are discussed more fully in chaps. 10 and 11.

6. In what ways can context (cultural, historical, literary, and redemptive) affect the interpretation of a text?

Exercises

1. Use research tools to determine what Greek word John and James use for "believe" in John 3:16 and James 2:19. Indicate the various ways in which they use the word.
2. Use your understanding of a proverb to explain Proverbs 15:1 and Proverbs 26:4–5.
3. Use context to determine who the "weak" are in Romans 15.

CONTENTS OF CHAPTER 4

GOAL OF CHAPTER 4

To identify the historical, homiletical, and attitudinal components of expository messages

4

Components of Exposition

The Goal

After the cruelty and selfishness of a thirty-seven-year-old man had forced his wife and children from his home, he called in desperation, wanting my aid in getting them to return. I said I would try to help if he agreed to get counseling for his problems. He agreed and came to the church office several days later. He brought a Bible with him. I could not help but notice how strange it was to see this abusive man with a Bible under his arm. I had seen him many times before. He even attended our church occasionally, but I had never seen him with a Bible. Yet here in the darkest hour of his life, he thought he would find wisdom and aid in a book written thousands of years ago. No doubt his thinking was colored by a desire to impress me, and he undoubtedly had little actual knowledge about how to discern what the Bible required of him. Still, I found it striking that I, and all expository preachers, shared something profoundly spiritual with this desperate man—an instinctive faith that the Bible has something to say about the deepest needs of our lives and can truly provide for them.

Expository preachers and the people who sit before them each week are convinced that Scripture can be mined to extract God's wisdom and power for daily living. Poor preaching may cause some occasional doubt, but preaching that truly reveals what the Bible means has kept this conviction alive for a hundred generations. Our goal as expository preachers is to keep this faith alive by demonstrating week after week what the Word of God says about the daily concerns we and our listeners face.

This goal reminds us that most people do not want or need a lecture that simply recounts Bible facts. They want and need a sermon that demonstrates how the information in the Bible applies to their lives. Expository preaching does not merely obligate preachers to explain what the Bible says; it obligates them to explain what the Bible means in the lives of people today.[1] Application is as necessary for sound exposition as is explication. In fact, the real meaning of a text remains hidden until we discern how its truths affect our lives.[2] This means that full exposition cannot be limited to a presentation of biblical information. A preacher should frame every explanatory detail of a sermon so that its impact on the lives of listeners is evident.

Such a perspective on the true nature of exposition challenges the notion some have of expository preaching. So much of the criticism expository preaching receives results from the assumption of some preachers that a sermon's primary goal is to expose listeners to more information about the Bible. Preachers whose primary purpose is simply to disseminate information may seem intelligent (and can garner great respect), but they will also seem out of touch, irrelevant, and even uncaring. Pastors, however, who organize textual information so as to minister to congregational concerns remain fully biblical while also expressing personal sensitivity in keeping

Figure 4.1

An Information-Priority Message

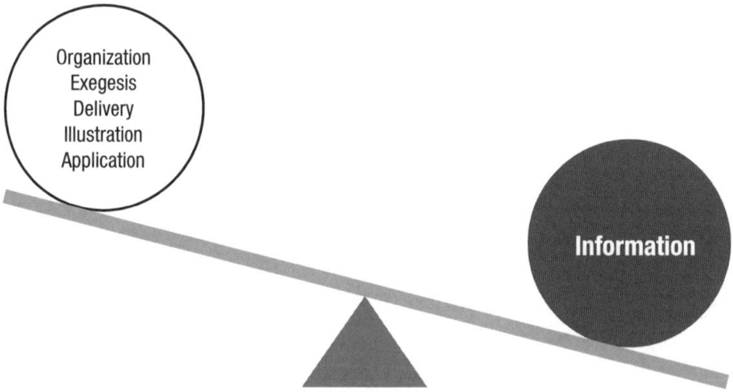

1. John R. W. Stott, *Between Two Worlds: The Art of Preaching in the Twentieth Century* (Grand Rapids: Eerdmans, 1988), 141, 145–50.

2. D. Martyn Lloyd-Jones, *Darkness and Light: An Exposition of Ephesians 4:17–5:17* (Grand Rapids: Baker, 1982), 200–201; see also John Frame, *Doctrine of the Knowledge of God* (Phillipsburg, N.J.: Presbyterian & Reformed, 1987), 93–98.

with their full obligations. Preaching a sermon is an act of shepherding that requires a minister to consider every aspect of structure, exegesis, and delivery as a potential tool for spiritual nurture, admonition, and healing.

When thinking of the object of a sermon as a large stone to be moved, some think of an expository sermon as using its resources and features as leverage to move information into the minds of listeners. Such a sermon model would look like figure 4.1.

A true expository message, however, uses all its resources to move application.[3] The sermon's features become the leverage to impel biblical understanding and action into the life circumstances of listeners based on sound exposition of the textual information (see fig. 4.2).

Figure 4.2

An Exposition-Priority Message

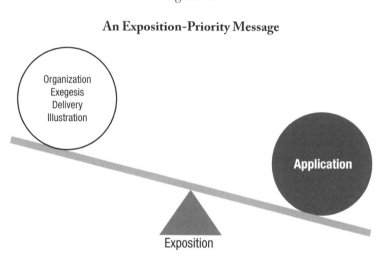

Figure 4.2 is more in keeping with the understanding of John A. Broadus, the father of modern expository preaching. In his classic *On the Preparation and Delivery of Sermons,* this master teacher and preacher concludes that in an expository sermon, "the application of the sermon is not merely an appendage to the discussion or a subordinate part of it, but is the main thing to be done."[4] For Broadus, the primary duty of the expositor is to exhort the people of God to apply the truths revealed in Scripture because this is the intent of God's Word.

3. David L. Larsen, *The Anatomy of Preaching: Identifying the Issues in Preaching Today* (Grand Rapids: Baker, 1989), 96.
4. John A. Broadus, *On the Preparation and Delivery of Sermons,* ed. J. B. Weatherspoon (New York: Harper & Row, 1944), 210.

The Pattern

Indications of preaching's obligations emerge in the Bible's descriptions of Christ's words as he accompanied the two disciples on the road to Emmaus. Luke records, "And beginning with Moses and all the Prophets, he explained to them what was said in all the Scriptures concerning himself" (24:27). The word translated "explained" means "to unfold the meaning of something" or "to interpret."[5] Later the two disciples offered commentary on Christ's words, saying, "Were not our hearts burning within us while he talked with us on the road and opened the Scriptures to us?" (Luke 24:32). This opening of Scripture expresses the concept of revealing the full implications of something (as in opening a door wide to show what is inside).[6]

Unfolding and *opening* the meaning of the Word of God characterize the expositor's task, not merely on the basis of Christ's example but also on the basis of ancient biblical precedent, which further defines exposition's essentials. Probably the best description of ancient exposition occurs in Nehemiah's account of Israel's reacquaintance with the Word of God after the people returned from exile in Babylon, where they had forgotten God's law and the language in which it had been given:

> Ezra opened the book. All the people could see him because he was standing above them; and as he opened it, the people all stood up. Ezra praised the LORD, the great God; and all the people lifted their hands and responded, "Amen! Amen!" Then they bowed down and worshiped the LORD with their faces to the ground.
>
> The Levites—Jeshua, Bani, Sherebiah, Jamin, Akkub, Shabbethai, Hodiah, Maaseiah, Kelita, Azariah, Jozabad, Hanan and Pelaiah—instructed the people in the Law while the people were standing there. They read from the Book of the Law of God, making it clear and giving the meaning so that the people could understand what was being read.
>
> Nehemiah 8:5–8

The exposition of the Word involved three elements: presentation of the Word (it was read), explanation of the Word (making it clear and giving its meaning),[7] and exhortation based on the Word (the priests caused the people to understand in such a way that they could use the information that was imparted).[8] Presentation of the Word itself, explanation of

---

5. Greek, *diermeneuo.*

6. Greek, *dianoigo.*

7. From *bin:* Hiphil participle masc. plural = "causing to understand" (v. 7); and from *parash:* Pual participle masc. singular = "made distinct or clear" (v. 8).

8. From *sekel* with the verb *sum* = "they gave the sense" (v. 8); and from *bin:* Consecutive with Qal imperfect, third person, masc. plural = "so that they understood" (v. 8). C. F. Keil comments, "It is more

its content, and exhortation to apply its truths composed the pattern of proclamation.

These three elements in this Old Testament proclamation consistently reappear in New Testament practice.[9] Luke records that when Jesus first explained his ministry in the synagogue, he read the Scripture out loud (4:18–19), explained the import of what was read (4:21), and then made the implications clear—though it was not to his listeners' liking that the obvious application meant yielding honor to Jesus (4:23–29). Word presentation, explanation, and exhortation are also present in the following Pauline instructions to a young preacher:

1 Timothy 4:13

"Devote yourself to the public reading of Scripture,	**Word Presentation**
to preaching [the actual term is *paraklesei,* meaning 'to exhort or entreat.' It comes from the same root as *Paraclete,* the name Jesus gave the Spirit, who comes as our counselor, advocate, or comforter]	**Word Exhortation**
and to teaching."	**Word Explanation**

2 Timothy 4:2

"Preach the Word; . . . [here the word for preach is *kerusso,* which means 'to proclaim or publish']	**Word Presentation**
correct, rebuke and encourage—with great patience	**Word Exhortation**
and careful instruction."	**Word Explanation**

---

correct to suppose a paraphrastic exposition and application of the law . . . not a distinct recitation according to appointed rules" (C. F. Keil and F. Delitzsch, *I and II Kings, I and II Chronicles, Ezra, Nehemiah, Esther,* vol. 3, trans. Sophia Taylor, Commentary on the Old Testament (Grand Rapids: Eerdmans, 1976), 230.

9. After the exile (although some claim the essential form dated to Moses), these elements constituted the usual (but not exclusive) synagogue pattern for preaching, which in God's providence prepared the New Testament church to institutionalize this highly effective means of protecting and promulgating God's Word. Cf. Alfred Edersheim, *The Life and Times of Jesus the Messiah,* 3rd ed. (Grand Rapids: Eerdmans, 1971), 443–46; and W. White Jr., "Synagogue," in *The Zondervan Pictorial Encyclopedia of the Bible,* vol. 5, ed. Merrill C. Tenney (Grand Rapids: Zondervan, 1975), 565–66.

Paul's practice was consistent with his instructions (see Acts 17:1–4). At Thessalonica, the apostle went into the synagogue and reasoned with the Jews "from the Scriptures." Paul first presented the Word to the people. Then Paul "explained and proved" from the Word "that the Christ had to suffer and rise from the dead." With this explanation came at least an implied if not an overt exhortation to commitment. Acts next records, "Some of the Jews were persuaded and joined Paul and Silas, as did a large number of God-fearing Greeks and not a few prominent women."

These features of exposition do not form the only observable pattern in the biblical preaching record, nor is every feature always equally evident. These features are consistent enough, however, to challenge today's preachers to consider whether their exposition of Scripture faithfully reflects these biblical elements: presentation of an aspect of the Word itself, explanation of what that portion of the Word means, and exhortation to act on the basis of what the explanation reveals. Such a pattern of unfolding and opening the Word not only reflects a simple logic for preaching but also conforms to Christ's instructions for proclamation. Surely it is noteworthy that the parting words of our Lord in the Gospels command his messengers to proclaim his ministry in the expositional pattern of the prophets and apostles:

Matthew 28:19–20a

"Therefore go and make disciples of all
   nations . . .
      teaching them   **Word Explanation**
      to obey   **Word Exhortation**
      everything I have commanded you."   **Word Presentation**

Though a normative order does not appear in Scripture, the features of exposition occur with enough frequency to suggest a common approach to expounding God's truth: present the Word, explain what it says, and exhort based on what it means. This is expository preaching.

The Components

Exposition does not merely involve the transmission of biblical information. It also demands establishment of the biblical basis for an action or a belief that God requires of his people. Relating the tense of a verb, the tribe of a person, or history of a battle does not adequately unfold the intended meaning of a text. God has revealed these matters for the purpose of telling his people who he is and how they should relate to him and one another. Until people can see how the truths of a text operate in their lives, the exposition remains incomplete. This is why explanation, illustration, and application should act as the proof, demonstration, and specification of the exhortation a preacher makes and the transformation God requires.[10]

This full-orbed understanding of exposition's content reduces the danger of an expository sermon degenerating into an exegetical paper, a systematics lecture, or a history lesson. Jerry Vines describes the danger:

> Some have understood an expository sermon to be a lifeless, meaningless, pointless, recounting of a Bible story. I can still remember a very fine man deliver such a sermon from John 10. He told us all the particular details about a sheepfold. We were given a complete explanation of the characteristics of sheep. We were informed about the methods of an Oriental shepherd. When the message ended we were still on the shepherd fields of Israel. We knew absolutely nothing about what John 10 had to say to the needs of our lives today. That is not expository preaching.[11]

Expository preaching aims to make the Bible useful as well as informative. Addressing a clear FCF as one researches and develops a sermon will keep the sermon on track biblically and practically. This practice keeps the goal of expository preachers and the intention of the writers of Scripture the same: to "take captive every thought to make it obedient to Christ" (2 Cor. 10:5). We want thought about God's Word to result in obedience to Christ.

Homileticians once divided sermons into three basic components: exposition (the explanations of and arguments for what a text says), illustration (demonstrations of what a text says), and application (the behavioral or attitudinal implications of what a text means).[12] These are helpful distinctions for teaching students to dissect others' sermons and to build their own. I will use these distinctions later in this book.[13] However, these traditional categories can damage expository preaching if preachers do not see that explanation, illustration, and application are all essential components of *opening* and *unfolding* the meaning of a text. Explanation answers the question, What does this text say? Illustration responds to, Show me what the text says. Application answers, What does the text mean to me? Ordinarily, each component has a vital role in establishing listeners' full understanding of a text.[14]

10. Farris D. Whitesell, *Power in Expository Preaching* (Old Tappan, N.J.: Revell, 1963), xi; and Jay E. Adams, *Truth Applied: Application in Preaching* (Grand Rapids: Zondervan, 1990), 42.

11. Jerry Vines, *A Practical Guide to Sermon Preparation* (Chicago: Moody, 1985), 5.

12. Cf. Broadus, who divides exposition into the categories of explanation and argument separate from illustration and application (*On the Preparation and Delivery of Sermons,* 144, 155); and Andrew Blackwood, *The Fine Art of Preaching* (New York: Macmillan, 1943), 113.

13. Note, however, that I do not limit "exposition" to the details and the arguments of a text's explanation but rather subsume explanation, illustration, and application under the larger heading of exposition. All are key in disclosing the meaning of a text.

14. Broadus, *On the Preparation and Delivery of Sermons,* 155.

We should not limit a sermon to technical explanations simply because it is expository. Biblical truths that a preacher cannot illustrate can hardly be considered apparent, and scriptural details that a preacher does not apply do not readily further obedience.[15] To expound Scripture fully means to unfold the meaning of a text in such a way that listeners can confront, understand, and act on its truths.[16] The more you preach, the more you will discover that this unfolding of biblical truth makes the components of exposition interdependent and, at times, indistinguishable.[17] Illustration sometimes offers the best explanation; explanation focused on an FCF may sound much like application; and application may offer the opportunity for both illustration and explanation (see James 3:2–12). As your expertise grows, the components of exposition will blend and bond to drive the truths of God's Word deep into the hearts of his people.[18]

In a traditional expository message, each component of exposition occurs in each main point of the sermon because it makes no sense to explain something that can be neither demonstrated nor applied.[19] There are, however, good reasons to make exceptions to this traditional expectation: Sometimes a preacher uses a series of explanations to build to an application or to veil implications for a later, more powerful impact. However, a beginning preacher will find that listeners usually pay closer attention to a message whose demonstrations and applications of truth occur regularly and frequently. Today's cultural influences make it unreasonable for a preacher to expect a congregation to stay with a message for twenty-five minutes with the hope that something relevant will be said in the last five minutes. Congregational needs and capabilities make the old rule of including explanation, illustration, and application in each main point a reasonable guideline, even if one does not follow it every time.

The Balance

A Generic Approach

The finest expository preachers prepare each message by imagining their listeners are present and asking themselves the following question: What

15. Larsen, *Anatomy of Preaching*, 96, 138–43.

16. Sidney Greidanus, *The Modern Preacher and the Ancient Text: Interpreting and Preaching Biblical Literature* (Grand Rapids: Eerdmans, 1988), 182–84.

17. Daniel M. Doriani, *Putting the Truth to Work: The Theory and Practice of Biblical Application* (Phillipsburg, N.J.: Presbyterian & Reformed, 2001), 20–27.

18. Broadus, *On the Preparation and Delivery of Sermons*, 155. See a later summary in Broadus, 4th ed. (San Francisco: Harper & Row, 1979), 58–59. See also Ian Pitt-Watson, *A Primer for Preachers* (Grand Rapids: Baker, 1986), 101; and Greidanus, *Modern Preacher and the Ancient Text*, 182–84.

19. Broadus, *On the Preparation and Delivery of Sermons*, 211; Greidanus, *Modern Preacher and the Ancient Text*, 182; D. Martyn Lloyd-Jones, *Preaching and Preachers* (Grand Rapids: Baker, 1971), 77; and Vines, *Practical Guide to Sermon Preparation*, 133.

may I, with the authority of God's Word, require of you as a result of what we discern this text means? Recognition that listeners have a need personally to discern a text's meaning for their lives, rather than simply accepting the assertions or the dictates of a preacher, forces pastors to evaluate whether their messages are accessible as well as informative, and applicable as well as erudite.

Figure 4.3

Balanced Exposition Double Helix

Explanation

Illustration

Application

Concern for the biblical needs of listeners as well as the biblical information to be conveyed should affect the balance of the components of a message. As we have already seen, the pattern of exposition can vary. The most common order in which exposition's components appear, however, is explanation, illustration, and application.[20] This allows a preacher to establish a truth, demonstrate and clarify its implications, and then apply it. If each of these components is given equal time within the development of a message, the form of the message can be pictured as a balanced double helix (see fig. 4.3). There is something for everyone in roughly equal proportions.

A Customized Approach

It is helpful for student preachers to prepare sermons that give equal attention to each of the sermon components so that they learn to use all the homiletical tools. Differences among congregations, however, require pastors to vary the proportions of the expositional components. The following descriptions border on being caricatures, but they do help demonstrate the ways in which preachers may vary the composition of their messages.

Youth pastors typically swell the illustrative component of their sermons and drive application home behind a few well-chosen explanatory points (see fig. 4.4, example A). Blue-collar congregations often desire solid explanation whose relevance is spelled out more fully in down-to-earth application (see fig. 4.4, example B). When professionals and management types dominate a congregation, the pastor may want to hit application lightly since these persons are often most motivated by what they determine to do and are not accustomed to having others make decisions for them. In such a congregation, it may be important to package explanation in such a way that application becomes largely self-evident (see fig. 4.4, example C).

Each of these congregational characterizations is almost sinfully stereotypical and should not rule common sense. My own experience has been

---

20. Later chapters will explain how and why this order should vary, but note for now this logical progression that is most common in expository preaching.

Figure 4.4

Exposition Component Variations

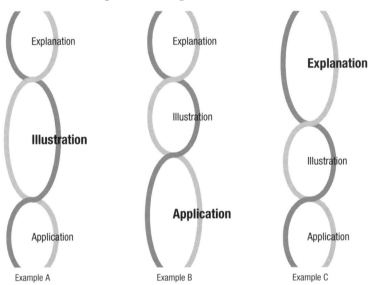

that sermons that provide a healthy combination of all the expositional components can be preached with impact almost anywhere with only minor adjustments. This is not simply because congregations typically have a mix of people in them but because we are each a mix. Our minds need explanations of what the Bible says so that we know we have grasped the thoughts and standards of our God. Our hearts need the illustrations that so often touch our emotions or fire our imaginations to convince us that God is not a cold collection of abstract ideas. We need application so that we have either the confidence that we are acting in accord with the will of God or the conviction that we must adjust our ways.

A Healthy Approach

Even though the relationships are not exclusive of one another, it is often helpful to think that explanations prepare the mind, illustrations prepare the heart, and applications prepare the will to obey God. This approach cautions preachers to avoid messages that do not offer adequate servings of explanation, illustration, and application. For example, a sermon that is three-quarters explanation, one-quarter illustration, and one sentence application (the classic seminary sermon) or the sermon that has one sentence of explanation, is three-quarters illustration, and is one-quarter application (the popular media message) is unbalanced.

A balanced expositional meal carries each component in sufficient proportion to nourish the whole person. In addition, an expositional meal placed before the entire family of God should feed the different ages, learning styles, and personalities present so as not to slight the needs and values of any.[21]

No strict rules determine the proportion these expository components should take in any specific sermon. The text, the topic, the purpose, the gifts of the preacher, the target audience, the situation, the makeup of the congregation, the time that may be required to express an idea, the persuasive or the structural advantages of placing one component over another, and the relative strengths of individual components of exposition in a particular sermon all have a role in determining how a preacher should distribute explanation, illustration, and application.

This does not mean that the composition of every sermon is completely up for grabs. I have observed a consensus—maybe a spiritual instinct Christians share—that guides me as I consider how to communicate Scripture. Balanced Christians disdain messages whose illustrations dominate to the point of entertainment, whose applications extend to the level of diatribes, or whose explanations enlarge to ponderous displays of academic erudition. Each extreme reveals a preacher preoccupied with special or personal interests over congregational health. Preachers once posted this reduction of the preaching task in their studies:

Preach
reach
each

Such a reduction still has great value.[22] It advises us to resist the emphases of our academic training, popular preaching, or a congregation's extremists who tempt us to preach without the balance that will nourish all the people at various levels of their being and understanding. The leaders of the Reformation encouraged pastors to preach to the "necessities and capacities of the hearer."[23] This wise advice reminds us not to speak only so as to please ourselves or further our reputations. The spiritual needs of God's people are too important for us to dispense with tools that will most effectively communicate to them the challenges and encouragements of God's Word.

---

21. See Roger E. Van Harn, *Pew Rights for People Who Listen to Sermons* (Grand Rapids: Eerdmans, 1992), 23–29; and compare to categories of hearers in William Perkins, *The Art of Prophesying* (1606; repr., Edinburgh: Banner of Truth Trust, 1996), 56–63.

22. Robert G. Rayburn's lecture notes indicate that he taught this reduction with its simple poignancy for more than twenty-five years at Covenant Theological Seminary.

23. Westminster Larger Catechism, 159.

Yet lest we think that such concerns require us to pander to interests less refined than our own, we should remember the common features of our humanity. Congregations simply need to hear what most preachers want to hear: solid explanation vividly illustrated and powerfully applied.

The Attitudes

A Divine Authority

The way in which divine authority is expressed in the pulpit needs to be discussed before we examine, in subsequent chapters, how to use each component of exposition. We have already examined why the expository sermon enables us to preach with authority. When we say what God says, we have his authority. This realization should caution us against peppering our sermons with expressions such as "I believe this means . . . ," "I feel we should understand . . . ," or even, "I think . . ." Quite frankly, except for peripheral matters, biblically astute congregations are not interested in what the preacher *thinks*. David Larsen chides us, "There is no place in the pulpit for a preacher who stutters, 'Everyone outside of Christ is going to hell, I think.'"[24] People sit in the pews to hear what God confirms in his Word. If you cannot say, "The Bible says . . ." about the core truths of the message, then the congregation owes no more regard to your conclusions than it does to any philosopher's speculations.

In obedience to biblical imperatives, an expositor must preach "as one speaking the very words of God" (1 Pet. 4:11). Preaching that lacks authority leaves a congregation longing for the divine voice. Lives sickened by sin, confused by culture, and crushed by tragedy desire no "uncertain sound." Still, we need to understand that this authority resides in the truth of the Word rather than in a particular tone we bring to our messages. We need to distinguish carefully between preaching with authority and merely sounding authoritarian.[25]

A pastor confident of the Bible's truth is able to preach with great force or with great gentleness and still speak with authority. Preaching with authority relates more to the confidence and the integrity with which a preacher

24. Larsen, *Anatomy of Preaching*, 81.
25. I am grateful for the analysis of my homiletics colleague, Zack Eswine, who writes, "The reasons why preachers struggle with expressing a proper voice of authority include: (1) a desire to emulate a respected preacher; (2) a caricature in the mind of how an old hero of the faith would have sounded; (3) a desire to compensate for an absence in the church—for example, internally concluding, 'Since sin isn't talked about much these days, I must take it upon myself to let the world know about it in every sermon'; (4) familial abuse or relational patterns of brokenness that have shaped the forms used for expressing anger, conviction, or challenge and that move the preacher to an exaggerated voice" (personal correspondence, September 30, 2003).

expresses God's truth than to a specific tone or posture a preacher assumes. The authority of the Word enables us to say the most challenging things to any person without apology, but that same authority lets us speak tenderly without compromising strength. Too often expository preachers get stuck in one gear, believing that preaching with authority means they must inject a certain hardness into their sermons. They sound as though they are trying by their efforts to make the Word authoritative rather than trusting its innate power to touch the soul. Preachers most trusting of the power of God's Word simply and boldly allow their manner to conform to the content of what they say so that the meaning of Scripture is unambiguous and the work of the Spirit is unhindered. The example of Christ and the instruction of the apostles should remind us that the truth of the Bible comes with various attitudes toward hearers depending on their situation and that this truth is undercut by a manner of proclamation milder or bolder than the text indicates is appropriate (see 1 Thess. 5:14).

A Biblical Manner

The same principles of exposition that require us to reflect the intent of a biblical author should direct us to speak in a manner appropriate for the truth being presented and the situation being addressed. The great variety of terms in the original languages that relate to preachers and their tasks confirm how manifold our expressions may need to be (see tables 4.1 and 4.2).

Table 4.1

Key Old Testament Terms

Term	Meaning	Reference (example)
parash	to distinguish or specify clearly (possibly, to translate)	Neh. 8:7–8
sekel	to give the sense or meaning	Neh. 8:7–8
bin	to cause to understand (to separate mentally for use)	Neh. 8:7–8
nabi	one who pours forth or announces under the divine impulse (a prophet)	Deut. 13:1; 18:20; Jer. 23:21; cf. Num. 11:25–29
hozeh	one who glows or grows warm (a seer or a prophet)	Amos 7:12
roeh	one who sees (a prophet)	1 Chron. 29:29; Isa. 30:10
qohelet	a caller or a preacher	Eccles. 1:1
qara	to call out	Isa. 61:1
basar	to announce glad tidings	Ps. 40:9; Isa. 61:1

Term	Meaning	Reference (example)
nataph	to drip, to pour out words	Ezek. 20:46; Amos 7:16; Mic. 2:6, 11

Table 4.2

Key New Testament Terms

Term	Meaning	Reference (example)
kerusso	to proclaim as a herald concerning a king or his decrees	Rom. 10:14–15; 1 Cor. 1:21–23; 2 Tim. 4:2 (more than seventy times in all)
euangelizo	to announce joyful news	Luke 4:18; cf. Acts 8:4 (more than forty times)
diermeneuo	to unfold the meaning of, to expound	Luke 24:27–32
dianoigo	to open up, to thoroughly disclose	Luke 24:27–32
dialegomai	to reason, to discuss, to converse	Acts 17:2–3
paratithemi	to allege, to place alongside (used to describe Jesus' use of parables)	Matt. 13:31
logos	a word or a saying	Matt. 13:19–23
rhema	a word or a message	Rom. 10:17; 1 Pet. 1:25
diangello	to declare	Luke 9:60
katangello	to proclaim	Acts 4:2; 13:5
parresiazomai	to preach, to speak boldly	Acts 9:27–29
elencho	to expose, to correct, to convict, to reprove	2 Tim. 4:2; Titus 1:9; 2:15
epitimao	to rebuke or warn seriously	2 Tim. 4:2
parakaleo	to encourage, to comfort, to defend (lit., to call to one's side as an advocate)	2 Tim. 4:2; cf. Acts 14:22
paramuthia	comfort, cheer, consolation	1 Cor. 14:3
martureo	to give a witness	Acts 20:21; cf. 1 John 4:14
homologeo	to say the same thing, to agree with, to profess or confess the truth of	1 Tim. 6:12
homileo	to converse, to talk with, to engage in conversation (this is the Greek word from which we derive the term *homiletics*)	Acts 20:11

Term	Meaning	Reference (example)
laleo	to speak	Mark 2:2; cf. 1 Cor. 2:6–7
didasko	to teach	Acts 5:42
epilusis	unloosing or untying; an explanation of what is obscure or difficult to understand	2 Pet. 1:20
suzeteo	to examine together, to discuss, to dispute	Acts 9:29
apologia	a verbal defense	Acts 22:1; Phil. 1:7, 16; 2 Tim. 4:16; 1 Pet. 3:15
metadidomi	to share the gospel as a gift	1 Thess. 2:8; cf. Rom. 1:11; Eph. 4:28

These lists of the biblical terms related to preaching are not exhaustive, but they do indicate the diverse tasks of faithful preachers. Sometimes we must proclaim the joys of the gospel to the unsaved. Other times we must rebuke the regenerate. Still other times we must comfort the broken.

A Humble Boldness

Just as no one word captures all the dimensions of biblical preaching, so no one style can reflect its many facets.[26] This is all the more true because different personalities express authority differently. For some, the most confident expression is spoken with an intense gaze and a level voice. Others use animated and forceful expressions to convey authority. Probably most of us vary the way we express authority based on the persons, circumstances, and issues faced.

These observations seem to elude many expository preachers who use an authoritarian style on every occasion, having the false impression that their tone will reflect their lack of biblical compromise. Unfortunately, a consistent authoritarian demeanor reflects a lack of biblical understanding:

> There is something inherently horrid about human beings who claim and attempt to wield personal authority they do not possess. It is particularly inappropriate in the pulpit. When a preacher pontificates like a tinpot demagogue, or boasts of his power and glory as Nebuchadnezzar did on the roof of his royal palace in Babylon (Dan. 4:28, 29), he deserves the judgment which fell on that dictator. . . .
>
> The authority with which we preach inheres neither in us as individuals, nor primarily in our office as clergy or preachers, nor even in the church whose members and accredited pastors we may be, but supremely in the Word of God which we expound.[27]

26. For material on "A Philosophy of Style," see appendix 2.
27. Stott, *Between Two Worlds,* 58.

We do not need to pump our authority into the Word to make it effective. Confidence in God's authority over the whole of life will grant us the courage to speak his Word whenever and however appropriate. This holy boldness is not so much a particular manner as a commitment to speak the truth in love out of a conviction that God's Word provides wisdom for every challenge, issue, and need that humankind confronts (Eph. 4:15; 1 Pet. 3:15; 2 Pet. 1:3).

No one approach, attitude, or tone will suit all occasions. The same apostle who advised one young preacher to "rebuke with all authority" (Titus 2:15) advised another that "those who oppose him he must gently instruct, in the hope that God will grant them repentance" (2 Tim. 2:25). In the passages in which Paul commands both of these young pastors to rebuke with authority, he also tells them to use the same authority to encourage (2 Tim. 4:2; Titus 2:15). Our struggles to know which manner to assert in different situations will make us no less qualified to preach the Word if our struggles make us more aware of the spiritual guidance we ourselves require. Writes Herbert Farmer:

> How may we have within ourselves that which shall impart to our preaching the right sort of authority, the conviction and confidence which lacks neither a proper respect for the hearer nor the humility of a sinful man, which is neither overridingly dogmatic nor weakly diffident? I suppose in the end the secret lies in the quality of our own spiritual life and the extent to which we are ourselves walking humbly with God in Christ.[28]

Our own relationship with Christ teaches us that we must treat people with compassion as well as confront them with the authority of the Word. As we need a stern hand in some moments and a loving embrace at others, so too do the people we face from the pulpit. The soul made sensitive by the recognition of its own sin, the awareness of God's sovereignty, and the miracle of the Savior's love is the one best suited to guide the tongue in the sanctuary as well as in the circumstances of life. Consistently aggressive or combative preachers ill disguise the spiritually resistant recesses of their own hearts.

Life is too complex, the obligations of preaching too myriad, and the message of Scripture too rich for preachers to impoverish their ministries with one style of sermonizing. Only in the worst caricatures do preachers speak with the same tone before a grieving family, wedding celebrants, a skeptical college crowd, a crisis-bound community, a rebellious congregation, a battered church, anxious leaders, or seeking sinners. Only the

28. Herbert H. Farmer, *The Servant of the Word* (New York: Scribner's, 1942), 63.

most limited preacher would try to comfort, convict, challenge, correct, encourage, and command with the same manner. Scripture's authority grants us the right to say what it says. Scripture's wisdom advises us to speak as prudently and diversely as it does. Our manner should reflect Scripture's content. Because we convey meaning not merely by what we say but also by how we speak, accurate exposition requires us to reflect a text's tone as well as define its terms. Sometimes this requires a voice reminiscent of the thunder on Sinai, and other times it requires the still small voice heard at Horeb.

A Christlikeness

Our tone should always resonate with the humility of one who speaks with authority under the authority of another (2 Tim. 4:2). Ultimately, our awareness of the divine activity that empowers our words defines our preaching. As the Spirit of God uses our words to communicate his truth, we speak for God.[29] Despite the frailties and the foibles of our expressions, the Spirit burns away the dross of our preaching to refine Christ's very words in others' hearts. Martin Luther pictured this more vividly than we may find it comfortable to consider: "Now let me and everyone who speaks the word of Christ freely boast that *our mouths are the mouths of Christ.* I am certain indeed that my word is not mine, but the word of Christ. So must my mouth be the mouth of him who utters it."[30] This powerful image should caution us never to speak with a tone that compromises Christ's authority or contradicts his care. We represent him. Therefore, we must consider how he would speak were he to address our listeners with the truths committed to our care. If the words we are saying came from Christ's mouth, how would he say them? Our words must reflect his character as well as his truth if our preaching is to remain true to him.

Questions for Review and Discussion

1. What three elements of exposition consistently appear in examples of Old and New Testament preaching? What does the consistency of these elements say about the nature of exposition?
2. What three components of exposition usually occur in each main point? Why are all three important?

29. Westminster Shorter Catechism, 89.

30. As cited in Edward F. Marquart, *Quest for Better Preaching* (Minneapolis: Augsburg, 1985), 83–84. Calvin wrote similarly in his *Institutes of the Christian Religion* (4.1.5): "Among the many excellent gifts with which God has adorned the human race, it is a singular privilege that he deigns to consecrate to himself the mouths and tongues of men in order that his voice may resound in them."

3. How may the proportion of the components of exposition vary according to the nature of a congregation? Why are all the components still important for all congregations?
4. What does the diversity of biblical terms related to preaching indicate about the tone and the manner of expository preaching? What, ultimately, should govern the tone of our sermons?

Exercises

1. Indicate how explanation, illustration, and application are used in Jesus' Sermon on the Mount (Matt. 5–7) and Stephen's speech to the Sanhedrin (Acts 7:2–53).
2. Determine how and why the tone of the gospel varies between Matthew 23 and Acts 17:16–31.

PART 2

Preparation of Expository Sermons

GOAL OF CHAPTER 5

To explain how to prepare and present the explanation component of a sermon

5

The Process of Explanation

The Labyrinth

The conviction that people are spiritually transformed only through personal confrontation with the truths of the Word of God complicates the task of preaching. For most people in our culture, the Bible is an opaque book whose truths are hidden in an endless maze of difficult words, unfamiliar history, unpronounceable names, and impenetrable mysticism. This situation and a preacher's calling obligate every expositor to lead people through this labyrinth so that they confront God's words for their lives. The best preachers, however, guide in such a way that their listeners discover that the labyrinth is a myth.

There are no dark passageways through twisted mazes of logic to biblical truth that require the expertise of the spiritually elite.[1] There is only a well-worn path that anyone can follow if a preacher sheds some ordinary light along the way. Expository preaching sheds ordinary light on the path that leads to understanding a text. An expositor not only must follow the path to shine this light personally but also must learn when the light used to lead others glows too dimly, creates a blinding glare, or merely displays the preacher. The right amount of light not only exposes the path but also helps those on the path find their own way in the future. We will navigate

1. John A. Broadus, *On the Preparation and Delivery of Sermons*, ed. J. B. Weatherspoon (New York: Harper & Row, 1944), 157.

this path first by outlining the steps a preacher follows in preparing an expository message and then by describing how to shed light on the path while presenting the message. Later chapters concentrate on illustration and application; the remainder of this chapter focuses on the path that explanation follows.

The Path of Preparation

Six Critical Questions

Before we begin to blaze the trail of exposition, we have to determine where we are going. An expositor's course can be charted by determining what questions need to be answered in preparing a particular message. These questions provide a bird's-eye view of the path. Ultimately, they determine what path explanation will follow and the steps a pastor should take to lead others along the way. At first glance, the questions may appear so obvious and/or intuitive as to need no identification. Unfortunately, however, significant questions on this list are often not asked or answered in sermon preparation.

This list is not meant to lock a preacher into a rigid pattern of preparation. The questions are listed in a logical order, but individual preachers may skip and jump along the way so that various questions blend together or change sequence. The greatest concern of the careful expositor is not the order in which the questions are asked but the necessity that all be answered.

The first three questions relate to a preacher's research of a text's meaning:

1. What does the text mean?
2. How do I know what the text means?
3. What concerns caused the text to be written?

The reasoning for the first question is the most obvious: Preachers need to do enough research to determine what the scope and the particulars of a text mean. The second question begins to orient preachers to their listeners. In a sense, this question forces preachers to retrace the steps that led them to their conclusions in order to identify significant landmarks that others will be able to follow. It is not at all uncommon for preachers to feel fairly confident about a text's meaning without being able to specify in their own minds what led them to their conclusion. Solid explanations—and the second question—require preachers to identify what establishes a text's meaning. The third question requires preachers to determine the cause of a text. This question is related to the first two (and usually is integral to how they are answered), but it is listed separately because its answer is vital to the ultimate development of a sermon and the answers to the remaining questions.

The next three questions determine how a preacher relates a text's meaning:

4. What do we share in common with those to (or about) whom the text was written and/or the one by whom the text was written?
5. How should people now respond to the truths of the text?
6. What is the most effective way I can communicate the meaning of the text?

Prior to answering these questions, a preacher has information only about a text, not a sermon. Although many preachers may feel that when they have done enough research to determine a text's meaning they are ready to preach, they are mistaken. To this point they are only like "the little engine that could," chugging up the expositor's mountain saying, "I think I can preach. I think I can." Answering these remaining questions actually pushes a preacher over the crest of the mountain, converting a textual commentary or an exegetical lecture into a sermon.[2]

The fourth question takes us back to the principles of a Fallen Condition Focus (FCF).[3] By identifying what we share with the people of Scripture, we bring the truths of the text into immediate contact with the lives of people today. Not to do so simply steals from Scripture the impact God intends. I tried to demonstrate this to a student who once phrased a main point this way: "The Judaizers believed they could earn salvation with good works." The statement was true but was poorly designed as the main point of a sermon. It left listeners asking, "So what? What does that have to do with me?"

I asked the student to try to frame the main point in such a way that it would deal with what we have in common with the people in the text. He replied, "But I don't have anything in common with those people. I don't believe my works will gain my salvation." "Oh!?" I replied. "I do. I don't believe in my head that my works will save me, but I sometimes feel and even behave that way. I am always tempted to believe that when I am good God will love me more." So is everyone else. We all have moments, or even years, when an aspect of us lives the Judaizers' theology. We all have vestiges of Babel with us—as a consequence of our fallen nature, we are all trying to climb our ladders to heaven and claim responsibility for the grace that saves us. Our pride wars against the admission that there is no good in us. Our sinful condition forever struggles with our total dependence on grace.

---

2. Jay E. Adams, *Preaching with Purpose: A Comprehensive Textbook on Biblical Preaching* (Grand Rapids: Baker, 1982), 51–52.

3. See chap. 2 for the development of the FCF concept.

Only when we can identify the humanness that unites us with the struggles of those whom Paul had to warn about the Judaizers do we really know why he wrote and what we are to preach.

Preaching does not point primarily at what happened to others—it points to us. Preachers identify principles of spiritual truth evident in the biblical situation that are also present in ours.[4] This forces us to look deep into our hearts and into the hearts of those around us to discover what Scripture is addressing at the level of our common humanity. Truth assumes living power when its original meaning is understood in the context of the present reality for which it was inscripturated. In some sense, we all share David's guilt, Thomas's doubt, and Peter's denial (1 Cor. 10:13). Therefore, a solid explanation of a text does not merely display the facts in the text or describe how they defend a doctrine. A full explanation of a text's meaning identifies how its FCF touches and characterizes our lives.

The fifth question of explanation may not appear to be part of explanation at all. Determining how we should respond to the truths of Scripture may sound much more like application than explanation. However, this question must be asked as part of the explanation process. If it is not, it is impossible to determine what we are explaining. Any text of Scripture has near limitless explanation avenues and possibilities. Only when we determine what the text requires of us as a consequence of the FCF the sermon addresses do we know how to focus, phrase, and organize the explanation of the text. Determining for listeners what a text means for them is as central to the process of explanation as is the researching of grammar and history.

These last questions indicate that a sermon is not merely an outlined description of a text. *A sermon is an explanation of the continuing truth principles evident in the Bible that indicate how contemporary persons should respond to a mutual condition we share with those who were the original subjects or recipients of the text in the light of God's response to or provision for their situation.* Since a sermon ultimately answers for listeners, What does this text mean to me? the explanation has to be framed in such a way that it maximizes meaning for listeners. Thus, adequate explanation requires accurate understanding of both the text and the audience. We must exegete our listeners as well as the text to construct a sermon that most powerfully and accurately explains what the text means. It is, after all, quite possible to say many true things about a text and yet communicate a highly inadequate or an entirely false meaning by not taking into consideration a congregation's background and situation.[5] What can be heard as well as what should be said demand attention as a preacher lays the path of explanation.

4. Walter C. Kaiser Jr., *Toward an Exegetical Theology: Biblical Exegesis for Preaching and Teaching* (Grand Rapids: Baker, 1981), 152.

5. Ian Pitt-Watson, *A Primer for Preachers* (Grand Rapids: Baker, 1986), 23–24.

Four Necessary Steps

Preachers provide answers to the critical questions that define the path of explanation by following four steps in their sermon preparation. Each step reflects a skill that preachers must exercise as they interpret a passage for a congregation's use. Preachers must learn to observe and interrogate the features of a text as well as to relate and organize their conclusions about the text's meaning. These four steps are discussed in their logical order, but the sequence often varies and the steps frequently blend in the process of preparing an expository message.

OBSERVE

A preacher uses the faculties of observation to determine what is present. The method is simple: read, read, and reread the text. Read broadly enough to see the context. Read closely enough to identify important or unique phrasing. Reread until the flow of thought begins to surface. Look up unknown words, names, and places so that you are sure you are reading with understanding. Make sure you are familiar with the features of the text even if you do not yet grasp its full meaning. Gazing deeply and carefully into a text is no cursory matter. As simplistic as it may sound to insist that a preacher read a text carefully, the instruction cannot be overemphasized. Charles Spurgeon's oft-quoted advice bears repeating, not because of its great insight but because of its frequent neglect: "Get saturated with the Gospel. I always find that I can preach best when I can manage to lie asoak in my text. I like to get a text, and find out its meanings and bearings, and so on, and then, after I have bathed in it, I delight to lie down in it, and let it soak into me."[6]

Listen to the text, absorb it, wrestle with it, digest it, immerse in it, breathe it in as God's breath for your life, pray over it. The greatest danger you will face is that you will focus too narrowly or too quickly on certain features of the text and, by neglecting surrounding details, will misinterpret the whole. I confess that at times I have discovered, only moments before preaching a sermon, an aspect of a text that eluded my attention (and undercut my conclusions) because I had focused too exclusively on the part of the text that interested me. I would love to spare you the horror of a similar realization in like circumstances.

Careful and complete reading of a text ordinarily leads to good conclusions about its meaning. Still, we must be careful to keep these initial impressions subject to the discoveries of further research. Research should substantiate the validity of conclusions derived from a thorough reading of a text and usually

6. Charles Haddon Spurgeon, *All Round Ministry: Addresses to Ministers and Students* (Carlisle, Pa.: Banner of Truth, 1960), 124.

will provide us with more details that broaden and deepen our insights. Occasionally, however, research will indicate that our initial conclusions need revision. Exposition of depth and accuracy requires thorough preparation as well as the willingness and the humility to adjust initial impressions.

INTERROGATE

A preacher will most readily discern the key questions that need to be asked of a text by keeping in view the goals of the preaching task during all phases of sermon preparation. John R. W. Stott helps us discern the goals of the expository preacher by writing, "To expound a Scripture is to bring out of the text what is there and expose it to view. . . . The opposite of exposition is 'imposition,' which is to impose on the text what is not there."[7] The expository obligation requires you to do two things accurately and concisely in the pulpit: State what the text means, and show how you know what it means. These obligations impose definite procedures during sermon preparation. In the reading stage, preachers primarily ask, What's here? This question, however, quickly leads to more penetrating questions: What does it mean? and Why is it here? Often these questions lead to additional discoveries of what's here. Preachers interrogate the text in this way, knowing that they must eventually discern the faith principles and exhortations the text supports as well as state the conclusions that are established by the information in the text.

Expository preachers prepare to explain a text by asking the questions their listeners would ask if they wanted to discover what it means. Most homiletics texts allude to the journalist's five W's and an H that we intuitively use to get the facts: who, what, when, where, why, and how. These questions, however, describe what a preacher is trying to discover rather than how to get there. The preparation of explanation leads preachers down a well-worn path that they travel in stages that involve exegesis, outlining, backgrounding, and spotlighting. No stage is independent of any other, and often one stage will shed more light on the discoveries of other stages (even those previously traversed). The nature of the passage, the purpose of the sermon, or the expertise of the preacher will also signal appropriate shortcuts or sequence variations in these stages. Still, although years of experience allow most preachers to ramble and roam unconsciously through these stages of preparation in ways best suited to their styles, expository sermons require the insights of each stage.

Exegete the Passage (What Does It Say?)

To know what a passage means, we have to know what its words mean and how they are used. Exegesis is the process by which preachers discover

---

7. John R. W. Stott, *Between Two Worlds: The Art of Preaching in the Twentieth Century* (Grand Rapids: Eerdmans, 1988), 125–26.

the precise definitions, grammatical distinctions, and literary character of the words and phrases in a text. Preachers with Greek and Hebrew expertise translate passages, recognizing that even the best English translations of the Bible cannot communicate fully the nuances of the words in the original languages. Even pastors without the language skills or the time to translate an entire passage can use the language tools described in chapter 3 of this book to conduct profitable "pinpoint exegesis."

With pinpoint exegesis, a preacher looks up unknown words or examines more fully words that, by their placement, tense, structural role, repetition, rarity, function, or relationships to other words in the passage (or related passages), demonstrate a key role in determining the text's meaning. For instance, many people refer to the "fruits of the Spirit." It is significant that the passage from which this phrase is taken does not make the word *fruit* plural (Gal. 5:22–23). The grammar indicates that the Spirit brings to bear in some measure all the characteristics listed in these two verses. One cannot say, "I do not have to be kind because the kindness listed in this passage is not one of the fruits the Spirit has granted me." The Spirit's fruit is of one variety. While the characteristics of the fruit may vary in degree, none of the distinguishing features of the fruit of the Spirit is lacking in what truly is of him. Such exegesis allows a preacher to require kindness of all who claim the presence of the Spirit.

Not always mentioned in discussions of exegesis is the importance of comparison. Comparing the number of times or the differing ways specific words are used (or are not used) in related verses or comparing the way specific words are variously translated can indicate where preachers should focus their pinpoint exegesis or concentrate their translation efforts. Cross- and chain-reference Bibles, concordances, commentaries, comparison versions of the Bible, and good observation skills lead a preacher to significant interpretive insights on the basis of comparison exegesis.

The importance of original-language exegesis should not discourage preachers from using careful analysis of the text in English as a primary exegetical tool. One of the graces of the Spirit is the general clarity of Scripture.[8] While original-language study adds richness to exposition, the Bible does not intend to hide its truths in language mazes. Certainly, there are difficult passages of Scripture. We do not expect the depth of the riches of the wisdom and knowledge of God always to be expressed in the terms of first-grade readers. But neither do we expect God to delight in hiding the bread of life from those hungry for its nourishment. Careful attention to grammar, syntax, word relationships, and logic development in a Bible version translated by scholars committed to biblical authority will provide you with the vast majority of your exegetical insights in terms that will be

8. Westminster Confession of Faith, 1.5.

apparent to your listeners.[9] We should not convince our listeners or ourselves that only those with twenty years of Greek and Hebrew can *really* understand the Bible. God does not grant deep understanding of his Word only to persons with seminary degrees, and those who pretend otherwise feed their egos at the expense of those whose faith needs nourishment. Excellent preaching makes people confident that biblical truth lies within their reach, not beyond their grasp.

Outline the Passage (How Does It Fit Together?)

The thought of a biblical writer typically shines more clearly when an expositor creates a study outline of a passage. Outlines visually exegete the thought flow of a text and enable a preacher to see the chief features of its development. The length and nature of the passage under consideration determine which of the following three types of exegetical outlines will best aid a pastor's study.[10]

Grammatical outlines (or sentence diagrams) show the relationships of words in sentences. By identifying the subject, verb, object, and modifiers, complex thoughts can often be deciphered and misinterpretations avoided. A typical grammatical outline diagrams sentences according to standard grammatical conventions whether in an original language or in English (see fig. 5.1).

Figure 5.1

Examples of Grammatical Outlines

Grammatical Outline
Example 1:

Grammatical Outline
Example 2:

| Jesus | died | | Lord | heard | cry |

for ungodly   *the*   *my*

the

By displaying the grammatical relationships of the words, a grammatical outline highlights the development of thought within a sentence and often helps clarify how specific words relate to one another.

Mechanical layouts help a preacher see how entire phrases or sentences relate to one another. Whereas a grammatical outline diagrams word relationships within sentences, a mechanical layout attempts to diagram the

---

9. See chap. 3 for a discussion of the strengths of various English versions.

10. These first two types of exegetical outlines receive helpful discussion and instruction in Haddon Robinson, *Biblical Preaching: The Development and Delivery of Expository Messages*, 2nd ed. (Grand Rapids: Baker, 2001), 67–68, 240–42; see also the example in the first edition of Robinson's work (1980), 216; and J. Robertson McQuilkin, *Understanding and Applying the Bible* (Chicago: Moody, 1983), 108–21.

relationships among sentences and phrases. A single mechanical outline can cover an entire passage or major portions of it.

Typically, a mechanical layout identifies independent clauses (or main ideas) and then places dependent clauses (or developmental ideas) in subordinate positions under them. There are no strict conventions to determine how to construct a mechanical layout. The idea is to place phrases and concepts in such a way that you are able to see how they correspond. Major ideas are usually listed to the left with subordinate phrases and conjunctions indented to indicate their relationships to the main clauses, but many variations work (see figs. 5.2, 5.3).

Figure 5.2

Traditional Mechanical Layout of 2 Timothy 4:1–2

```
(v. 1)    In the presence of
          God
          and
          Christ Jesus
                  who will judge
                          the living
                          and
                          the dead
                  and
          in view of his appearing
          I give you this charge:
(v. 2)    Preach the Word;
          be prepared
                  in season
                  and
                  out of season
          correct, rebuke, and encourage
                  with great patience
                  and
                  (with) careful instruction
```

Figure 5.3

Alternative Mechanical Layout of 2 Timothy 4:2

```
be prepared  →  ( preach the word )  →  correct, rebuke, and encourage
 in season                                 with
  and                                    great patience
 out of season                             and
                                         careful instruction
```

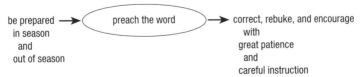

A mechanical layout often takes less linguistic expertise than a grammatical outline but still forces a preacher to ask questions about the structure of a passage and to determine the text's thought development. J. Robertson McQuilkin says that a mechanical layout "will keep [the interpreter] from assuming he understands the flow of thought before he has actually studied each part of the sentence and paragraph."[11]

There is no need to segregate the outlining alternatives. Often a preacher will apply a mechanical layout to a larger Scripture portion but will do a grammatical diagram of a particularly complex sentence within the passage. The mechanical layout can actually help spotlight areas that need closer grammatical examination. Mechanical layouts are applied to larger expository units, while grammatical outlines aid the microscopic analysis of smaller portions. Neither alternative works well, however, when the expository unit is extremely large.

Conceptual outlines best serve the preparation of sermons covering many verses or even multiple chapters. When narratives or other Scripture portions require a preacher to analyze lengthy passages, an outline that captures the broad features of the text best serves sermon preparation. Again there are multiple ways to construct such an outline. The goal remains to place supporting thoughts in subordinate positions to main ideas. However, in a conceptual outline, ideas (or the characters and events that represent them rather than precise phrases from the text) usually form the exegetical outline.[12] A statement listed in a conceptual outline may summarize many sentences:

2 Samuel 11–12:23

   I. David disobeyed
      A. Committed adultery (11:1–5)
      B. Committed murder (11:6–26)
   II. God convicted
      A. Sent a prophetic word (12:1–6)
      B. Identified the king's sin (12:7–12)
      C. Specified the king's punishment (12:11–12, 14)
  III. David repented
      A. Confessed sin (12:13)
      B. Expressed sorrow (12:15–17)
      C. Accepted discipline (12:18–23)
      D. Renewed obedience (12:20)

11. McQuilkin, *Understanding and Applying the Bible*, 116.

12. A conceptual outline sometimes does work well using the precise phrases of an epistle when the paragraph nature of the writer's thought allows a preacher to identify major ideas and supporting concepts in the words of the text.

Each of these three types of exegetical outlines has distinct advantages depending on the length of the passage and the nature of the pastor's questions about the text. The larger the expository unit, the more advantageous are the latter styles of study outlines. However, multiple approaches may well serve any single sermon preparation. Note also that outlines covering large portions of Scripture often paraphrase an author's thoughts rather than quote the text directly. In such cases, outlining—in addition to describing the text's contents—requires a pastor to make interpretive decisions that will greatly aid the construction of the sermon.

It is almost always important to use the space around an exegetical outline to make notes of textual insights that you discover in your study tools or that come to mind as your sermon research advances. Write the insights near that portion of the outline representing the section of the text to which the insights apply. Keeping verse numbers visible in the outline makes this type of notation easier and helps preachers quickly find information in the exegetical outline that they will need when later organizing all the sermon material (illustrations, applications, transitions, etc.) into a *homiletical outline* for the actual construction of the message.

Background the Text (Where Does It Fit?)

Careful reading, exegeting, and outlining of a text will automatically force a preacher to look up unfamiliar words, characters, quotations, events, references, or places, but the interrogation of a text is not complete until the preacher uncovers the background of the text. Determining the background of a text locates the passage in its historical, logical-doctrinal, and literary setting. The goal of this preparation step is simply to make sure that a preacher interprets a text in context. Since matters of context were discussed in chapter 3, I will not reiterate their importance here except to note that the preparation of explanation requires context research.

A preacher determines the *historical context* by reading about and researching the culture, concerns, and events that surrounded and stimulated the writing of a text.[13] Understanding the historical situation will cause a preacher to look at the chronology of events, the biography of the people, and the details of the culture at the time of the passage's writing and the place of the passage in the development of God's redemptive plan. Reading broadly enough to see the development of the biblical writer's argument or concerns in this and other relevant Scripture passages will reveal the *logical-doctrinal context* of the passage through the truths God is expessing by direct statements or interactive relationships. Surrounding passages, the literary form (or genre) of the passage, the intended use of the text,

---

13. Daniel M. Doriani, *Getting the Message: A Plan for Interpreting and Applying the Bible* (Phillipsburg, N.J.: Presbyterian & Reformed, 1996), 29–42.

the narrative voice, the role of this portion in the broader book or scope of Scripture, figures of speech, parallel passages, echoes and quotations of other references, or rhetorical patterns expose the *literary context* of the passage.[14]

Backgrounding cannot be isolated from the other preparation steps. Usually a preacher begins to collect background information when examining the context of a passage and gains much information about the role of the text in its setting when researching the passage's details. Study Bibles, commentaries, Bible handbooks, Bible dictionaries and encyclopedias, as well as the resources used in exegesis illuminate the background of a passage. In recent years, a number of books and book series have put particular emphases on revealing where specific texts fit in the context of redemptive history or doctrinal development.[15] Most preachers make notes of important background details at appropriate places in the exegetical outline where it can be readily accessed for writing the sermon.

RELATE

Simply collecting information about grammar, thought flow, and background does not prepare a pastor to preach on a text. Preachers cannot determine how to organize their explanations or how to state their discoveries meaningfully until they consider the impact the information should have on the congregation. While researching a text, the best preachers are always asking themselves questions on their listeners' behalf. Questions such as, Who needs to hear this? What will make this sink in? What are we facing that is similar to this biblical situation? and How are we like these people

---

14. Leland Ryken, *Words of Life: A Literary Introduction to the New Testament* (Grand Rapids: Baker, 1987), 21ff.; and ibid., 29–42.

15. Edmund P. Clowney, *Preaching Christ in All of Scripture* (Wheaton: Crossway, 2003); idem, *The Unfolding Mystery: Discovering Christ in the Old Testament* (Phillipsburg, N.J.: Presbyterian & Reformed, 1988); Ian M. Duguid, *Hero of Heroes: Seeing Christ in the Beatitudes* (Phillipsburg, N.J.: Presbyterian & Reformed, 2001); idem, *Living in the Gap between Promise and Reality: The Gospel according to Abraham* (Phillipsburg, N.J.: Presbyterian & Reformed, 1999); Raymond B. Dillard, *Faith in the Face of Apostasy: The Gospel according to Elijah and Elisha* (Phillipsburg, N.J.: Presbyterian & Reformed, 1999); Graeme Goldsworthy, *Gospel and Kingdom: A Christian Interpretation of the Old Testament* (Carlisle, U.K.: Paternoster, 1994); idem, *Preaching the Whole Bible as Christian Scripture* (Grand Rapids: Eerdmans, 2000); Sidney Greidanus, *Preaching Christ from the Old Testament* (Grand Rapids: Eerdmans, 1999); Dennis E. Johnson, *The Message of Acts in the History of Redemption* (Phillipsburg, N.J.: Presbyterian & Reformed, 1997); Vern S. Poythress, *God-Centered Biblical Interpretation* (Phillipsburg, N.J.: Presbyterian & Reformed, 1999); idem, *The Shadow of Christ in the Law of Moses* (Phillipsburg, N.J.: Presbyterian & Reformed, 1991); C. Trimp, *Preaching and the History of Salvation: Continuing an Unfinished Discussion,* trans. Nelson D. Kloosterman (Scarsdale, N.Y.: Westminster Discount Book Service, 1996); Gerard Van Groningen, *Messianic Revelation in the Old Testament* (Grand Rapids: Baker, 1990); and Michael J. Williams, *The Prophet and His Message: Reading Old Testament Prophecy Today* (Phillipsburg, N.J.: Presbyterian & Reformed, 2003).

in the Bible? help preachers determine which features of their explanatory insights to highlight.

Although these questions may sound as if they are oriented more to the preparation of application than to explanation, sound exposition requires us to ask these questions at this stage in sermon preparation. Jerry Vines explains:

> I have found it very helpful to visualize certain members of my congregation as I study through a Scripture passage. I am constantly asking myself, What does this passage have to say to John Smith? Or Pam Jones? Or Billy Foster? Horne mentions a helpful practice followed by Alexander Maclaren. As Maclaren studied the Scriptures during his sermon preparation he placed across from his desk an empty chair. He imagined a person sitting in the chair as he prepared his sermons. He carried on a dialogue between himself and the imaginary person. Such a practice would be helpful at all times in keeping us aware at all times that we are preparing our message for real people.[16]

Note that these premier evangelical preachers do not wait until their Scripture research is done to start thinking about people. Explanation prepared in the abstract is irrelevant. When each word and every statement of a message are intimately related to the concerns of the people who must apply the biblical truths to their lives, then explanation assumes sermonic form and power.

The goal of a preacher's exegesis is to be able to state (usually in the main points and subpoints) the universal truths established by a text for the congregation. The accompanying explanation supports these points of truth principle and is furthered by illustration and application. The danger, of course, is that contemporary concerns will sway a preacher's interpretation. A preacher must remain aware of the temptation to soften, recast, or change a passage's truths in light of a congregation's situation or sensitivities. Still, though the danger to abandon scriptural truth in the light of congregational pressures is great, we must also remain careful not to abort biblical truth by delivering words and stating conclusions that have not breathed the air of our listeners in the sermon's preparation.

Discerning the human background and the persuasive focus of a passage prepares pastors to relate the explanatory material to similar concerns faced by a present congregation and provides direction for a message's organization. Without relating explanations of a text to the concerns of a congregation, there are no fences to corral the thousands of explanatory alternatives, other than time constraints and a preacher's personal interests. Neither of these is more holy than the desire to explain matters in such a way that they can and will be heard.

---

16. Jerry Vines, *A Practical Guide to Sermon Preparation* (Chicago: Moody, 1985), 98.

ORGANIZE

Although the next chapter covers the process of outlining a sermon in much greater detail, here we note that preachers need general principles for organizing their research so that their preparation proceeds smoothly. An expositor's explanations must cover an entire text efficiently. This requirement obligates a preacher to order the explanatory material, exhaust the scope of the text, and subordinate incidental facts to critical information.

Sequence and Order

Putting textual information in a logical order is a common first step. It is also important to understand why the exegetical outline of a passage does not automatically determine the sequence in which a preacher makes explanations: (1) An exegetical outline describes the immediate text; however, an exegetical outline does not contain context and background information. Aspects of a biblical person's biography outside the immediate text, the usage of a word in parallel texts, the previous argument of an apostle, and many other aspects of a passage may need additional attention in an order not supplied by the text for a pastor to explain the text fully and accurately. (2) An exegetical outline also does not indicate the pastoral emphasis that the minister knows should be given to the various components of the passage in light of the issues or concerns facing a particular congregation. A preacher must incorporate these features and concerns, which are not supplied by an exegetical outline, into the sermon. Thus, insights from the exegetical outline, the passage's background, and the present level of a congregation's knowledge about these matters must all funnel into a *homiletical outline* in order for a competent sermon to take shape. Although the two may echo one another closely, *an exegetical outline ordinarily is not a homiletical outline.* An exegetical outline establishes what a text says. A homiletical outline establishes how a text's meaning is best communicated to a congregation.

The movement from text description to sermon construction occurs as a preacher demonstrates and, if necessary, proves that the principles for life and belief that are stated as the sermon's main points are substantiated by the details of the text—and that the situation of the text is sufficiently parallel to our situation so that the principles are applicable to our lives. Thus, a preacher must analyze a text and the congregation to convert an exegetical outline to a homiletical outline. In an expository sermon, the homiletical outline is worded in principles derived from and supported by features of the text in its context. The preacher demonstrates how the text supports these principles and then applies them to the contemporary context of the listeners. Note that by demonstrating how a text supports the principles of the exposition, a preacher automatically and simultaneously shows how the principles explain the meaning of the text.

The most common (and usually the most helpful) expository approach is to advance through the explanation of a text in the order of its ideas. Exceptions may occur, however, for various reasons. Sometimes the sequence of thought in a text does not allow a preacher to introduce background information efficiently. For instance, a key word in an epistle or a snatch of dialogue in a narrative may reappear several times in a passage, and a preacher will need to explain the verbal connection by racing forward or reflecting backward through the passage. The pattern of a text in its written form may also not communicate well in the oral medium of the sermon. Hebrew poetry may include a refrain that occurs many times in a passage (e.g., "His love endures forever"). An apostle may offer a parenthetical thought for ten verses before returning to the original idea. Such biblical patterns of organization are appropriate for their original purposes but need not always be presented in lockstep order to communicate the truth of the passage. *An expository sermon obligates a preacher to present the truths of a text but not necessarily the pattern of the passage.*

Maintaining a rigid and wooden mirroring of the sequence of a text may actually misrepresent the truth of the text.[17] For example, a *writer* most often says significant things first and then develops them (e.g., Eph. 1; Heb. 1). Listeners, however, usually hear as most significant what a *speaker* says last. Therefore, for preachers to represent most accurately the weight of a truth that a biblical writer wants to emphasize, they may need to advance the later truths of the biblical writer to an earlier phase of the sermon. Adequate explanation of some major portions of the Bible may also require a preacher to keep more than sequential order before listeners. The early speeches of Job's friends will almost certainly convey wrong ideas to modern listeners if a preacher offers no simultaneous reflection on the lessons of the last chapters of the book.

A text may also reflect a written pattern that for readers is understandable but for listeners is too complex.[18] For example, some psalms are patterned after the entire Hebrew alphabet and have multiple verses applied to each letter. In such cases, preachers exercise sound judgment when they reorganize the information so that modern hearers can grasp the writer's thought. Haddon Robinson says:

> Sometimes the arrangement of ideas in the passage will have to be altered in the [sermon] outline. The biblical writer did not have your audience in mind. He may have followed an inductive order; but because of your hearers, you may select a deductive plan. Sermons from the epistles more easily fit into outlines than do poems, parables, or narratives. Unless you remain flexible in the ways you communicate passages, you will find it impossible to accomplish the purposes of some passages with your audience.[19]

17. Adams, *Preaching with Purpose*, 56–58.
18. Sidney Greidanus, *The Modern Preacher and the Ancient Text: Interpreting and Preaching Biblical Literature* (Grand Rapids: Eerdmans, 1988), 19.
19. Robinson, *Biblical Preaching*, 132.

These cautions should not blind us to the usual advantages of explaining a text's features in the order they occur. The pattern of a text tends to reflect the pattern of the biblical writer's thought, and listeners can more easily follow the structure of a sermon that moves in a straightforward way through the text. Such straightforwardness can support the credibility and the authority of a preacher's explanations and can give listeners confidence that they can read the text easily. Because of these advantages, it is usually best and the most common expository practice to follow the sequence of a passage in its explanation. Still, the advantages of following the pattern of a text are overturned when doing so would overcomplicate the organization of the sermon, miss key thoughts in the text, or misrepresent the text's purpose.

The more the pattern of a passage governs the truth that the biblical writer wanted to convey, the greater the obligation of the expositor to make listeners aware of that pattern. Still, a preacher has a greater obligation to make sure that listeners understand and apply the truths of the passage than to cover the passage in sentence or verse order.

Exhaust and Cover

Expositors cover the scope of a text. An expository sermon obligates a preacher to base main points and subpoints of the sermon's explanation on the text and not to skip important features of the passage.[20] A clear exegetical outline points to the material a preacher needs to mine to construct a homiletical outline and allows the preacher to see if the sermon inadvertently ignores significant aspects of the text.

When a preacher has mined each feature of the exegetical outline and has applied its truth to the homiletical outline, then the text has been "exhausted." Exhausting the text is a distinction of expository preaching that obligates a preacher to deal with the entire passage.[21] This trait of expository preaching does not mean that a preacher must (or could) exhaust all the truth the passage contains. Rather, it indicates that a preacher has explained all the key sections of the text. Expository preachers implicitly say to their listeners, "Let me tell you what this text means." If the preachers then fail to *cover the territory* of the text, they have not met their obligation to explain what lies there.[22]

20. David L. Larsen, *The Anatomy of Preaching: Identifying the Issues in Preaching Today* (Grand Rapids: Baker, 1989), 32. Robert G. Rayburn makes this distinction both in his personal lecture notes and in his unfinished volume on expository preaching.

21. Rayburn popularized this wording in his lectures on expository preaching. The terminology actually originates in Broadus, *On the Preparation and Delivery of Sermons*, 114–15, though there the concept relates more to covering fully the subject proposed for the sermon rather than the passage itself.

22. A helpful way of making sure you have covered the territory of a didactic passage is simply to see if you have referred to all the verses of the text in the sermon. Checking to see if you have mentioned the major characters or events that determine the conceptual development of a narrative passage accomplishes the same. Neither procedure will guarantee that you have dealt with everything needed to explain a passage, but at least you will not have skipped entire portions of the text.

Yet not everything has to be covered in equal detail. To cover the territory, a preacher will undoubtedly group some aspects of the text while minutely examining others. For example, a cursory comment may cover the content of three verses, or ten minutes may be spent on one word. The FCF and the relative clarity of different portions of a passage dictate how a preacher organizes the material. Still, a preacher must in some way deal with the entire text, taking special care not to neglect those features that pose problems or raise questions for listeners. People should be able to walk away with a reasonable understanding of the entire passage.

Pastoral judgment, congregational sensitivity, and preaching experience help a preacher develop a sense for what needs to be explained and what amount of explanation is required, but until these instincts develop, a good exegetical outline provides a healthy check for sermon preparation. The relationships among words and ideas in an exegetical outline bring to the surface major ideas and signal those portions of the text that need attention.

Highlight and Subordinate

Because there is never enough time to cover every textual feature or every pastoral insight, a preacher must highlight certain ideas and subordinate others.[23] We make choices on the basis of what will best represent a text's instruction regarding the FCF of the sermon. Stott writes:

> We have to be ruthless in discarding the irrelevant. This is easier said than done. During our hours of meditation numerous blessed thoughts and scintillating ideas may have occurred to us and been dutifully jotted down. It is tempting to drag them all in somehow. Resist the temptation! Irrelevant material will weaken the sermon's effect. It will come in handy some other time. We need the strength of mind to keep it till then.
>
> Positively, we have to subordinate our material to our theme in such a way as to illumine and enforce it.[24]

A homiletical outline reflects a preacher's judgment of what takes a little explanation and what takes much. We must advance what addresses the FCF, elevate what reinforces our exhortation, eliminate what clouds the exposition, and rebut what seems to challenge our explanations.

As a rule of thumb, *expositors owe no more to explanation than what is necessary to make their points clear but owe no less than what is necessary to prove their points.* Crystallize your thought as much as possible. Divide what is too lengthy. Group what is too numerous. Make the complex simple (and not vice versa). Clarify the obscure. Then frame the whole in a structure that makes the scriptural basis of your exhortation as clear and memorable as possible.[25]

---

23. Arndt L. Halvorson, *Authentic Preaching* (Minneapolis: Augsburg, 1982), 179.
24. Stott, *Between Two Worlds*, 228.
25. Chap. 6 details outline structures and procedures.

The Light of Presentation

Preparing explanations does not always equip a preacher to present them. Too much information and too much complexity can lead to confusion or paralysis. Although there are many valid approaches to presenting material to a congregation, preachers are usually on sure ground when they follow three simple steps:

1. State the truth.
2. Place the truth.
3. Prove the truth.

By stating what truth a text establishes (with a main point or subpoint statement), showing in the text where that truth originates (i.e., "placing" or locating in the text where the truth originates), and proving how the text backs the truth, preachers present the discoveries of their textual study in a highly comprehensible form. These steps presume that the thought divisions of the explanation components form the principal outline of the message; that is, main point and subpoint statements summarize what a preacher believes a text means. Illustrations and applications support and develop these statements but are *not* the main divisions of the formal outline.[26]

The state-place-prove order of these steps can vary. Sometimes we want to prove a truth before we formally state it. Other times it will be advantageous to delay pointing out where the text supports the truth statement until it has been fully explained. For the expositor, the order of the steps is not as crucial as the need to take each one. There are, of course, other valid ways of structuring sermons, but this state-place-prove pattern is the most natural way of constructing an expository message and typifies the approach of most who are learning to preach.

State and Place

If you follow the most typical pattern of presentation, you will first state what the text means. This statement of a truth principle supported by the text may be either a main point or a subpoint. Next, place (or locate) where in the text you derived that idea. If you are preaching on a didactic portion of Scripture (an epistle, a prophecy, a proverb, or a psalm), you will probably say, "The Bible makes this plain to us in verse 6," or more simply, "Look where Paul says this in verse 9." Then read the verse (or the portion of it) that supports the statement you just made. Taking the eyes of the

---

26. In other words, an illustration may clarify a main point, "Prepare because Christ will come," but the main point is not the illustration itself. Cf. Hugh Litchfield, "Outlining the Sermon," in *Handbook of Contemporary Preaching*, ed. Michael Duduit (Nashville: Broadman, 1992), 173.

congregation to the biblical text grants authority to your words, assuring listeners that your statements directly reflect what God says and are not merely your opinion.

Sometimes a statement of a truth is based on information from several verses (or from the context). In this case, you must exercise good judgment about how you locate the textual evidence that supports your conclusion. It hardly makes sense to say, "Look at how sorrowful Jesus appears in verses 9 through 12 and 16 through 36." In the few moments you can allow, no one can scan that much material to confirm what you said. Still, you can often summarize the content of a few verses: "Peter offers a doxology in verses 2 through 4." Or you can point out a feature that reappears in several verses: "Look how the word *joy* occurs three times in verse 3 and two more times in verse 6."

When preaching on narrative passages, we have less obligation to cite precise verses that support our statements. Since our conclusions are often based on events in the scriptural narrative that an earlier reading firmly etched on the mind, listeners do not always need to see the verse that repeats what everyone already knows. We do not gain much by saying, "Verse 49 says Goliath fell down!" if everyone already knows he hit the ground. Yet where precise wording affects interpretation, we should continue to cite specific verses. The goal is to back our statements with Scripture's authority. Whether sight or memory of a text confirms our words, we meet that goal.

Prove

Once you state a truth and locate where the text confirms that truth, it is necessary to prove that the text means what you said it means. Homiletics texts at this point usually offer a myriad of formal proofs and forms of argument that preachers may employ to establish a biblical basis for their conclusions. Before diving into these, however, it is important to remember that the Bible was originally written in the language of common folk and will be best interpreted when we understand that most of its meaning is in plain sight. If you listen closely to the best expositors, you will notice that, after they make a declarative statement of what a text means, they most often simply repeat or restate the portion of the text that supports their statement and thus establishes its truth.

RESTATEMENT

If simply quoting a text or rewording it in a clearer form establishes the truth of your words, by all means conclude the explanation there. After all, what does it mean to "pray and not give up" (Luke 18:1) except that we should pray and not give up? We could say, "What this verse means is that we should pray and keep on praying." Yet whether we repeat or reword the verse, its meaning is clear without a great deal of further explanation because the verse itself is clear. Though homiletics texts spend much time discussing other forms of explanation that are frequently needed, simple restatement of a text is the form of explanation expositors use most of the time. We make a declarative statement of the truth principle that discloses a text's meaning and then cite the scriptural portion that supports that statement as the obvious and sufficient proof.

Restatement uses the principles of focus and redundancy to make a point clear. Until a preacher restates (by quoting or rewording) the portion of a text that supports a declarative statement of meaning, the words of the text tend to blend together in listeners' minds. By narrowing attention to a single phrase or verse, a preacher makes that portion of the passage jump out at listeners, and its meaning becomes obvious. The highlighted portion of the verse is also a restatement of what the preacher just said. This repetition engraves more meaning on the minds of listeners. Such repetition would seem simplistic and redundant in a written document, but experienced preachers recognize that *repetition is one of the most powerful oral communication tools.*[27] Since listeners (unlike readers) cannot review what has come before, repetition underlines what a preacher wants most to impress on their minds. As a result, major ideas stated in crisp phrases often echo through a sermon like a refrain to signal key thoughts.[28]

NARRATION

Retelling the story of what is happening in a passage is another way of explaining its meaning. This is really a broader form of restatement. Preachers may paint the background of the account, remind listeners of a biographical incident, recount a parable using contemporary words or modern comparisons, underscore dramatic aspects of the event, re-create dialogue, or add interest and clarity to the passage by fleshing out the setting, the action, or the personalities in vivid detail.

A healthy imagination greatly aids the narration process. Portraying the facts of a passage with energy and sensory details makes the Bible interesting, clear, and real to listeners.[29] A word of caution must be added, however. Preachers must be sure that their narration explains what is recorded in the account (or is a necessary implication of the account) and does not present as fact what the passage does not. It is possible for storytelling to get too imaginative and too exuberant. If you end up basing a point of your sermon on an imaginary detail, then your narration is no longer exposition but imposition. We should recognize, however, that imposition occurs not only

---

27. Vines, *Practical Guide to Sermon Preparation,* 78; and Ralph L. Lewis, with Gregg Lewis, *Inductive Preaching: Helping People Listen* (Westchester, Ill.: Crossway, 1983), 202.

28. Robinson, *Biblical Preaching,* 75–77, 140–42.

29. See further discussion of sensory dynamics and reason in chap. 7.

when we present ideas that the Bible does not but also when we distract from the message of the Bible. Biblically minded congregations want clarity and accuracy more than high drama. Enthusiastic, creative, and powerful delivery is important, but we must recognize the sometimes thin line between striving to create understanding of a passage and trying to dazzle listeners with personal skills (see chaps. 6 and 7 for more discussion of storytelling distinctions and techniques).

DESCRIPTION AND DEFINITION

Closely related to narration is description. With this form of explanation, a preacher describes a word, a scene, a character, or a situation in such a way that listeners are better able to understand a text. For example, throughout the course of many sermons, a preacher could describe the Passover service, an ephod, the geography of Palestine, a Roman coin, ancient fishing boats, the continuous action of the present tense in Greek, or a host of other unfamiliar biblical details, all of which can greatly aid a congregation's understanding of various biblical passages.

Frequently, listeners do not need description but definition. Our age, in which biblical literacy is low, obligates preachers to explain the words of a passage as well as to describe its features. The terms *justification, election, remnant, Sabbath, holiness,* and *sin* are so obvious to preachers that we forget that many people around us find the words mysterious or obtuse. A pastor who encourages parishioners to use the word *apologetics* when presenting their faith should not be surprised when most listeners feel they have been encouraged to apologize for the gospel.

Definitions contained in a sermon are usually not of the same length or complexity as the same definitions in the pages of textbooks. Definitions given in sermons need to be accurate but also clear and concise. This means we usually cannot provide a definition that will encompass every nuance of meaning to all people in all places. We are merely trying to define terms in such a way that they make sense for this sermon. Often we will contrast or compare a term to other terms to provide a meaning (e.g., *agape* versus *eros* versus *philia*). We may list synonyms for a term (e.g., Sin is any wrongdoing or non-doing of what God requires) or set it against common misconceptions (e.g., One doesn't have to be Hitler, Genghis Khan, or Charles Manson to be guilty of sin). We want to provide people with handles that enable them to grasp enough meaning to understand the information in a particular sermon. Whether difficult words originate in the text itself or in our explanations of the text, we must define our terms simply. Many volumes could be written on the meaning of *faith*, but in many messages, Phillips Brooks's acronym **F**orsaking **A**ll **I** **T**ake **H**im will suffice. Excellence in preaching is more often displayed by this kind of sermon-specific clarity than by academic complexity.

EXEGESIS

Preachers who have the ability to study the Word of God in the original languages have a wonderful privilege of being able to plumb the depths of the Bible, and it is natural and appropriate to share the insights of their exegetical studies with their listeners. Most expository sermons make reference to exegetical insights in order to expose the subsurface meaning of a text. Still, preachers must take care not to flaunt their education. Exegesis should help explain what a text means. It should not merely cloud meaning in a fog of Hebrew words, parsing notes, and grammatical terms unfamiliar to anyone without a seminary degree.[30] If no one will remember two seconds later that *metadidomi* means "share," why should we bother to mention the Greek term? If no one knows what the *aorist* is, we should not pretend that the mention of it clarifies the meaning of the text.

Preaching should never be an excuse to display our erudition at the expense of convincing listeners that they can never really understand what Scripture says because they read only English. We are obligated to explain exegetical insights in such a way that they make the meaning of a text more obvious, not more remote. Robert G. Rayburn explains:

> Nothing is more wearisome to the average layperson than to hear a preacher explaining the cases of nouns and the tenses of verbs or the other grammatical matters in Greek or Hebrew. Well educated preachers are expected to know the languages of the Bible but the layman who has no knowledge of them is not impressed when grammatical observations are made using the original words in the text. He is interested only in knowing the true meaning of the text, not the mechanics of the method by which that meaning was determined.[31]

Young preachers often think that heaping exegetical intricacies on their explanations will expand their credibility, when in fact this practice may damage it. Such academic exercises may demonstrate that a preacher does not know or does not care about listeners' capacities. By all means use your translation tools and preach important exegetical insights, but do so in plain terms.[32] Share the fruit, not the sweat, of your exegetical labor.

When your exegetical conclusions differ in some degree with the translation most of your listeners have in their laps, handle the differences carefully.

30. Edward F. Marquart, *Quest for Better Preaching* (Minneapolis: Augsburg, 1985), 105.

31. Robert G. Rayburn, "Exposition," uncompleted ms., 7.

32. The Westminster divines admonished, "They that are called to labour in the ministry of the word, are to preach sound doctrine, diligently, in season and out of season; *plainly*, not in the enticing words of man's wisdom, but in the demonstration of the Spirit, and of power; faithfully, making known the whole counsel of God; wisely, *applying themselves to the necessities and capacities of the hearers*" (Westminster Larger Catechism, 159, emphasis added). John Calvin wrote, "I have always studied to be simple" (as quoted in Stott, *Between Two Worlds*, 128).

A preacher who in essence asserts, "I know what your Bibles say, but I know better" may sound arrogant. An even greater danger is that a preacher may convince people that their Bibles are untrustworthy. Translations by scholars committed to scriptural truth generally need the support of preachers who want their listeners to respect the authority of the Word. It is usually far better to claim, "We gain an even richer understanding of the meaning of this verse by noting . . ." than to say, "The translators of the version of the Bible we are reading made a mistake here." Who can help wondering in the wake of such a statement what other "mistakes" the Bible contains?

ARGUMENT

Presenting an argument that supports your explanation rarely justifies being argumentative. Nonetheless, we often need to present the facts, the testimony of authorities, causal relationships, and logic that confirm the accuracy of our explanations. Sermons are usually prepared for a mixed group of people, including those who are informed and those who are not, those who are able to reason well and those who are not, those who are ready to accept a preacher's pronouncements and those who are not. Each of these factors must be considered as preachers prepare to support, develop, and, when necessary, defend an exposition (1 Pet. 3:15).

It is beyond the scope of this book to discuss all the types of formal argument a preacher may use.[33] If preachers keep challenging themselves to prove their argument as they make declarative statements of truth principles supported by the text, then natural arguments tend to take shape in fairly good order. Yet some cautions must be considered. First, not all things need to be proven—many are obvious. Second, few things need all the proofs you can muster. Choose what is most powerful and most concise. Third, some things cannot be proven. Rayburn writes, "The preacher should never attempt to explain what he himself does not really understand nor should he ever attempt to explain a doctrine which is incomprehensible such as the doctrine of the Trinity. In an attempt to explain things which cannot be explained, gross error will often be introduced."[34] Rayburn does not mean that we should abandon trying to gain an understanding of what is unclear to us or that we should avoid explaining what we do know about biblical truths that have incomprehensible aspects. Still, we should be ready to bow before the omniscience of God when our understanding reaches its finite limits. There is no shame in doing this or in teaching listeners to do the same.

Whatever arguments we settle on, we must resolve to present them as interestingly and simply as possible. Many inexperienced preachers make

---

33. For some traditional distinctions among the types of formal argumentation, see Broadus, *On the Preparation and Delivery of Sermons,* 167–95.

34. Rayburn, "Exposition," 5.

the mistake of confusing complexity with seriousness and tedium with orthodoxy. As a caution for this rather common error, homiletics instructors often present the so-called KISS principle (i.e., *Keep It Simple Stupid*). This principle is misleading. Neither you nor your listeners are stupid. Your tools and your mind will provide you with wonderful proofs of the rich truths in God's Word. You should delight to proclaim truth as expansively and powerfully as God grants you the gifts to do so. All preachers simply need to make sure that what they preach communicates rather than complicates the truths of God. Doing so will require you to apply all the resources of your mind and heart. Although it is relatively easy to express what you know in the jargon of theological textbooks and commentaries, the real challenge of preaching is to say the same things in the language of ordinary people who are intelligent but are not as familiar with the Bible or the lexical tools used in the preparation of the sermon. For this reason, keeping matters simple is *smart*. Saying profound things obscurely or saying simple things cleverly requires relatively little thought, but saying profound things simply is the true mark of pastoral genius.

More Light

By stating what a text means, placing that truth where it originates in the text, and proving how the text establishes that truth, you fulfill the fundamental obligations of an expositor: State what you know and show how you know. By meeting these obligations, we illuminate a path to a text's meaning so that others can see the truth of Scripture, follow it to the source, and confirm its authority over their lives. This confirmation is critical because though we may at times wish that our words alone would persuade others to act in a certain way, "it is a serious mistake to appeal for a response to an argument when the listener does not understand the Biblical basis for the truth that is at the heart of the appeal."[35] The church's greatest mistakes occur when the people of God honor what a leader says without examining that instruction in the light of Scripture.

In one of the key debates during the formulation of the Westminster Confession of Faith, one scholar spoke with great skill and persuasiveness for a position that would have mired the church in political debates for many years. As the man spoke, George Gillespie prepared a rebuttal in the same room. As they watched him write furiously on a tablet, all in the assembly knew the pressure on the young man to organize a response while the scholar delivered one telling argument after another. Yet when Gillespie rose, his words were filled with such power and scriptural persuasion that the haste of his preparation was not discernible. Gillespie's message so im-

35. Ibid., 5.

pressed those assembled as the wisdom of God that the opposing scholar conceded that a lifetime of study had just been undone by the younger man's presentation. When the matter was decided, the friends of Gillespie snatched from his desk the tablet on which he had so hastily collected his thoughts. They expected to find a brilliant summary of the words so masterfully just delivered. Instead, they found only one phrase written over and over again: *Da lucem, Domine* (Give light, O Lord).

Over and over Gillespie had prayed for more light from God. Instead of the genius of his own thought, this valiant Reformer wanted more of the mind of God. His humble prayer for God to shed more light on the Word is the goal of every expositor. We pray that God will shed more light on his Word through us. We know that what we say must be biblically apparent, logically consistent, and unquestionably clear if we are to be the faithful guides God requires. It is not enough for our words to be true or our intentions to be good. To the extent that our words obscure his Word, we fail in our task. To the degree that our words illuminate the pages of Scripture, God answers our and our listeners' prayers.

Questions for Review and Discussion

1. What are the critical questions that preachers must answer in order to convert mere lectures to sermons?
2. Why is an exegetical outline by itself usually insufficient as a homiletical outline?
3. Why are preachers not necessarily obligated to present the pattern of a text as the structure of a sermon? Why is it most often advisable to follow the pattern of a text?
4. What advantages does an expositor have in following the state, place, and prove steps? Do these advantages require these steps in this order?
5. How many proofs should a preacher present in regard to a particular concept in a sermon? Which proofs of a particular concept should a preacher present?
6. What cautions should a preacher exercise in presenting exegetical insights in a sermon?
7. Why is profound truth in simple language a mark of pastoral genius?

Exercises

1. Create a mechanical layout of Philippians 4:4–7.
2. Create a conceptual outline of Matthew 14:22–32.

CONTENTS OF CHAPTER 6

GOAL OF CHAPTER 6

*To present the rationale for, the features of, and
an instructional system for good outlining*

6

Outlining and Structure

Outlines for Exposition

Why do biblical sermons on the same passage often sound so different? Just as architects using identical resources can create many different structures, so preachers handling truths developed in the preparation of a text's explanation can construct many different sermons. Design varies with purpose. If preachers were interested only in describing a text, then messages on identical passages might sound similar, since all would follow nearly identical *exegetical* outlines. Preachers, however, have greater obligations than simply reporting a text's features. To expound a passage, a preacher must explain context, establish meaning, and demonstrate implications in a way that a specific group of listeners will find interesting, understandable, and applicable. To accomplish these goals, an expositor designs a *homiletical* outline to create a sermon faithful to the truths of a text and relevant to the needs of a congregation. An exegetical outline displays a passage's thought flow; a homiletical outline organizes a preacher's explanation, development, application, and communication of a passage's truths.

The first key to organizing a sermon is to determine the type of message you want to present.[1] In traditional homiletics, a *topical sermon* takes its topic (i.e., the theme or the main subject) from a passage; the sermon is organized according to the subject's nature rather than according to the text's distinctions.

---

1. Helpful discussions of the classifications of messages are offered in David L. Larsen, *The Anatomy of Preaching: Identifying the Issues in Preaching Today* (Grand Rapids: Baker, 1989), 32; Ian Pitt-Watson,

A Topical Message Outline regarding Care for the Poor
Based on Psalm 82:3–4

I. The history of caring for the poor in the church
II. The history of caring for the poor in this nation
III. The necessity of caring for the poor today

Note: Though derived from the text, the topic is divided according to the nature of the subject the preacher chooses to address rather than according to divisions of the text.

For a *textual message*, preachers glean the topic of a sermon *and* its main points from ideas in a text. A textual message reflects some of the text's particulars in the statement of its main ideas, but the development of those main ideas comes from sources outside the immediate text.

A Textual Message regarding Resisting Worldliness
Based on 1 John 2:16 KJV

I. We should resist the lust of the flesh (v. 16a)
   A. The lust of the flesh is materialism
   B. The lust of the flesh eroded David's faith
II. We should resist the lust of the eyes (v. 16b)
   A. The lust of the eyes is sensuality
   B. The lust of the eyes damaged David's purity
III. We should resist the pride of life (v. 16c)
   A. The pride of life is arrogance
   B. The pride of life destroyed David's humility

Note: The topic and main points are derived from the text being explained, but the developmental features (i.e., subpoints) come from other passages or sources.

Both topical and textual sermons have esteemed positions in the history of the church, and both have distinct advantages for certain situations and subjects. If a preacher wants to preach comprehensively on a particular subject such as baptism, Christian responsibility in society, divorce, or perseverance, a topical or a textual approach often is best. Most of the sermons recorded in church history are topical or textual developments of a particular theme or doctrine. Settings in which listeners are unlikely to have a Bible (e.g., weddings, funerals, community gatherings) often call for messages of a textual or a topical nature.

A Primer for Preachers (Grand Rapids: Baker, 1986), 23; Edward F. Marquart, *Quest for Better Preaching* (Minneapolis: Augsburg, 1985), 103, 105; and Sidney Greidanus, *The Modern Preacher and the Ancient Text: Interpreting and Preaching Biblical Literature* (Grand Rapids: Eerdmans, 1988), 15.

An *expository sermon* is designed for the study of the specific details, context, and development of a biblical passage in order to encourage and enable listeners to love God and to help them understand how to apply the truths of his Word to their lives. An expository sermon takes its topic, main points, *and* subpoints from a text.[2] In an expository message, a preacher makes a commitment to explain what a particular text means by using the spiritual principles it supports as the points of the message. References to other passages should occur only as the preacher attempts to confirm, corroborate, or elaborate principles that are evident in the immediate text. Unless other passages clarify what the immediate passage says, referencing numerous other texts can distract and confuse listeners—and possibly misrepresent the primary text.

An Expository Outline regarding Assurance of God's Love
Based on Romans 8:31–39

I. God's love is greater than sin
   A. Greater than past sin (vv. 31–33)
   B. Greater than present sin (v. 34)
II. God's love is greater than circumstances
   A. Circumstances challenge God's love (vv. 35–36)
   B. Circumstances cannot undo God's love (vv. 32, 37)
III. God's love is greater than Satan
   A. God's love is greater than spiritual powers (v. 38)
   B. God's love is greater than Satan's strength (v. 39)

Note: The topic, main points, and subpoints come directly from the text being explained in this expository outline.

Merely because an idea is true, because it has a biblical foundation, or because it comes to a preacher's mind does not mean it has a place in an expository message. The main idea of an expository sermon (the topic), the divisions of that idea (the main points), and the development of those divisions (the subpoints) all come from truths the text itself contains. No significant portion of the text is ignored. In other words, expositors willingly stay within the boundaries of a text (and its relevant context) and do not leave until they have surveyed its entirety with their listeners.[3]

A sermon is not expository simply because it addresses a subject in the Bible.[4] Neither does quoting numerous Scripture references in a sermon

2. I am indebted to Robert G. Rayburn, whose personal lecture notes contain the most articulate and refined statements of these distinctions that I have seen.

3. See the previous discussion on the expository sermon distinctive of exhausting the text in chap. 5.

4. An expository message's general aim (i.e., "to bring out of the text what is there and expose it to view" [John R. W. Stott, *Between Two Worlds: The Art of Preaching in the Twentieth Century* (Grand Rapids: Eerd-

make a preacher an expositor. "It is one thing to quote a Bible passage. It is quite another to explain accurately what the passage really says, and what it actually means, especially in our contemporary circumstances."[5] A sermon that explores a biblical concept is in the broadest sense "expository," but *the technical definition of an expository sermon requires that it expound Scripture by deriving from a specific text main points and subpoints that disclose the thought of the author, cover the scope of the passage, and are applied to the lives of listeners.*[6]

During the past 150 years, expository preaching has gained prominence in conservative Western churches for at least two reasons: (1) the evangelical search for a means to stem the erosion of commitment to biblical authority and (2) the nearly universal access to biblical material.[7] Evangelical pastors and scholars alike have responded to our culture's skepticism of all authority and to our society's loss of biblical knowledge by challenging parishioners to see the Bible for themselves.[8] These emphases and practices provide great benefits to the church: People in the pew become intelligent Bible readers; pastors become more confident proclaimers of God's requirements; people make decisions based on what God says rather than on what humanity says; preachers are forced to speak about as great a variety of topics as the texts they use; the Bible's own authority remains center stage; preachers' and people's loyalty to and knowledge of the precise statements of Scripture grow; Scripture becomes the judge of life and not vice versa.[9]

Yet despite the wonderful benefits of expository preaching, large numbers of contemporary preachers have turned away from this disciplined approach

---

mans, 1988], 125–26]) is further aided by structural guidance that ensures that a sermon remains expository and is not simply a discussion of a topic that is derived from a text but does not reflect the thought as it is developed in the passage. Such a topic may still receive excellent biblical treatment (including commentary from the exposition of other passages). Some subjects a preacher addresses may, in fact, necessitate this topical/textual approach, but a steady practice of mixing texts to make a preacher's point can undermine the authority that comes from preaching the Word according to its own thought development.

5. Robert G. Rayburn, "Expository Preaching—A Method," 4, in his uncompleted work on expository preaching.

6. Ibid., 6; Jerry Vines, *A Practical Guide to Sermon Preparation* (Chicago: Moody, 1985), 7; Haddon Robinson, *Biblical Preaching: The Development and Delivery of Expository Messages,* 2nd ed. (Grand Rapids: Baker, 2001), 21–22; Ilion T. Jones, *Principles and Practice of Preaching* (Nashville: Abingdon, 1956), 109; Andrew Blackwood, *Expository Preaching for Today* (Nashville: Abingdon, 1953), 13; and John A. Broadus, *On the Preparation and Delivery of Sermons,* ed. J. B. Weatherspoon (New York: Harper & Row, 1944), 140–54.

7. Although John Broadus argues for the antiquity of the expository method, his book *On the Preparation and Delivery of Sermons,* first published in 1870, is the seminal volume for the codification and popularization of the expository method as we now know it (cf. Marquart, *Quest for Better Preaching,* 104). The erosion of scriptural commitments that swept the culture after the initial publication of Broadus's work indicates the critical timing of his methodology and why it was so widely adopted by evangelicals.

8. See John Stott's analysis of the anti-authority mood of our culture in *Between Two Worlds,* 50–85.

9. David Waite Yohn, *The Contemporary Preacher and His Task* (Grand Rapids: Eerdmans, 1969), 152–53; and Broadus, *On the Preparation and Delivery of Sermons,* 142.

to the text. Today's pastors may question the continuing validity of expository preaching because they do not understand how to prepare effective expository messages, because they no longer believe the transcendent truths of Scripture can be universally applied, or because they have lost confidence that a generation weaned on sound bites and remote controls can digest serious exposition.[10]

This lack of confidence in so fundamental a form of biblical preaching must be addressed. Our society shows no signs of vacating its anti-authority mood or acquiring a more biblical worldview. Now may be the worst time to abandon a preaching method designed to address the spiritual weaknesses most apparent in our age. Thus, a key to the revival of effective exposition is teaching pastors to hone the structure of their messages so that the truths of Scripture can shine clearly through this long-trusted approach with methods that are sensitive to the currents of our culture but do not capitulate to them.[11]

Outline Purposes

A well-planned sermon begins with a good outline—a logical path for the mind. If you had to instruct someone on how to go from New York to Los Angeles, you would not advise them to "head thataway." You would provide a map identifying landmarks to keep them on course in each stage of their journey. The features of a preacher's outline serve a similar purpose, keeping listeners and speaker oriented throughout a message. The outline of a sermon is thus the mental map that all follow.

The advantages of clear outlines for listeners are obvious: Good outlines clarify the parts and progress of a sermon in listeners' minds. Preachers may forget, however, that outlines are also important for the speaker.[12] In preparation and in the pulpit, good outlines clarify the parts and progress of a sermon for the preacher. Creating an outline for a message helps a pastor crystallize the order and the proportion of ideas. A preacher can thus evaluate at a glance

10. E.g., Michael Rogness, "The Eyes and Ears of the Congregation," *Academy Accents* 8, no. 1 (Spring 1992): 1–2.

11. Although we should be thankful for the new forms of preaching that broaden the horizons and tools of the contemporary preacher (see Bryan Chapell, "Alternative Models: Old Friends in New Clothes," in *A Handbook of Contemporary Preaching*, ed. Michael Duduit [Nashville: Broadman, 1992], 117–31), we should also be thankful for the wisdom of one of the deans of contemporary preaching, James Earl Massey, who writes, "Many voices are being raised advising that the old forms and approaches need to be adapted in the interest of greater variety and wider public appeal. There is much to be said for increased appeal and the need to move beyond stilted stereotypes . . . but when I hear discussions about some sermon form being outmoded I recall something musician Richard Wagner reportedly remarked upon hearing Johannes Brahms play his scintillating *Variations and Fugue on a Theme by Handel*. Although Wagner was not especially fond of Brahms, he was so moved by the composer's genius that he declared, 'That shows what still may be done with the old forms provided someone appears who knows how to use them'" (*Designing the Sermon: Order and Movement in Preaching*, ed. William Thompson [Nashville: Abingdon, 1980], 24).

12. Robinson, *Biblical Preaching*, 132.

whether a message's divisions all relate to a central, unifying theme. At the same time, an outline visually displays the proportions of the various parts of a message while naturally indicating places for supporting ideas, applications, and illustrations. In addition, a pulpit outline, typically refined and reduced from a homiletic outline for use in the pulpit, enables a preacher to keep an eye on the development of a sermon's thought without losing significant eye contact with listeners (see appendix 1 for more on delivery).

No advantage of an outline weighs more heavily, however, than the credibility its organization grants a preacher. Organization not only promotes the communication of a message's content (*logos*) but is also a vital indicator of a pastor's competence and character (*ethos*). "This preacher is so disorganized" is a deadly assessment of any preacher's efforts. Such a characterization means that listeners have concluded that the preacher is either intellectually incapable of ordering thought or cares too little about them to bother. The first conclusion frustrates listeners, the latter angers them, and either removes their reason for listening.

Despite recent debates over the necessity of presenting messages in outline form, there is no question that excellent preaching requires some structure.[13] As preachers mature, they will discover that rhetorical "moves," homiletical "plots," concept-rich "images," thoughtful transitions, implied ideas, and other measures can often substitute for the formal statement of points in their outlines.[14] However, the importance of solid outlines for both student preachers and experienced preachers whose messages have begun to unravel should not be undermined. All well-communicated messages are at least *prepared* via an outline and require outlining skills.[15]

Concerns that preaching from an outline may make a message sound artificial or too segmented are legitimate. Such worries, however, are largely alleviated by using sound transitions, employing regular speaking patterns that reveal the sermon's form without overemphasizing its skeleton, and

13. David Buttrick, *Homiletic: Moves and Structures* (Philadelphia: Fortress, 1987), 23; and Stott, *Between Two Worlds*, 228.

14. Buttrick (*Homiletic*, 28ff.) uses the literary term *move* to argue for using language and images that turn thought (i.e., open, develop, and close a single idea) without stating outline points, which he feels breaks the conscious engagement of listeners, creates artificial separation between preacher and parishioners, and introduces complexity not palatable to contemporary audiences. Later portions of this chapter also offer suggestions for using key word structures and implied ideas as substitutes for the formal statements of outline points. Eugene Lowry, in *The Homiletical Plot: The Sermon as Narrative Art Form* (Atlanta: John Knox, 1980), 25ff., suggests a five-step structure that makes a sermon mimic the dynamics of narrative to involve listeners psychologically and emotionally as well as cognitively in gospel discovery. See also "The Controlling Image: One Key to Sermon Unity," *Academy Accents* 7, no. 3 (Winter 1991): 1–2.

15. Hugh Litchfield, "Outlining the Sermon," in *Handbook of Contemporary Preaching*, 174; James Cox, *Preaching* (San Francisco: Harper & Row, 1985), 137; and George E. Sweazey, *Preaching the Good News* (Englewood Cliffs, N.J.: Prentice-Hall, 1976), 72.

remembering that the goal of good outlining is to make sure listeners can follow a sermon's thought, not reproduce a preacher's outline.[16]

Sometimes a subject contains such complexity that a preacher must help listeners by clearly marking each step of logic in the outline.[17] Other times the outline of a message has an aesthetic value that warrants its display. Usually, however, a preacher who pauses at each road sign on the sermonic journey only wearies those following in the pews. The rather common practice of including outlines in church bulletins can clarify the points of a sermon, but these outlines may also create such "linear consciousness" that most in the pew use them to time the sermon rather than to study it.[18] The same may occur if a preacher gives too much attention to each joint in a sermon's structure. Experience and judgment will guide preachers in making their sermonic landmarks clear and natural enough to orient listeners but not so plodding or patronizing as to frustrate them.[19] Since outlines can greatly affect the quality of a sermon, we need to make sure we understand the principles of constructing them.

General Outline Principles

Sermons typically begin with an introduction that leads to a proposition that indicates what the body of the sermon will discuss. The body includes main points and subpoints that form the skeletal outline of the sermon and structure the sermon's explanation. The explanatory materials, which support the main and subpoint statements, as well as the sermon's illustrations and applications flesh out the skeleton formed by the explanation's points. A conclusion follows the body of the message, summarizing the information in the message and usually containing the sermon's most powerful appeal. Despite modern challenges to this traditional structure, such messages still communicate well if preachers understand the principles to which key features of the outline must adhere.[20]

16. Stott, *Between Two Worlds*, 228–29. See also Sweazey, *Preaching the Good News*, 73.

17. Jay E. Adams, *Preaching with Purpose: A Comprehensive Textbook on Biblical Preaching* (Grand Rapids: Baker, 1982), 55–56; and Broadus, *On the Preparation and Delivery of Sermons*, 113.

18. Attention toward involving listeners in the bulletin outline can overcome some of the linear consciousness. Suggestions include using fill-in-the-blank outlines or focusing the main wording of the outlines on application. See Michael Fabarez, *Preaching That Changes Lives* (Nashville: Thomas Nelson, 2002), 176–81; and Hershael W. York and Bert Decker, *Preaching with Bold Assurance: A Solid and Enduring Approach to Engaging Exposition* (Nashville: Broadman & Holman, 2003), 254.

19. Broadus, *On the Preparation and Delivery of Sermons*, 111–13.

20. It should be noted that many of the modern challenges to traditional sermon structures result from a redefinition of the preaching task from conveying knowledge of biblical truth to the experiencing of spiritual truth. When the Bible loses its authority, sermons are less concerned with communicating its specifics than with leaving religious impressions and making moral challenges. This change of focus necessarily calls for structures more compatible with eliciting human perceptions and less concerned with communicating biblical information. Note that most information-oriented communicators in our culture still use traditional communication structures. This is true whether the field is business,

Unity

Good outlines display unity. Each feature relates to the one thing the sermon is about. This is usually accomplished by making sure that all the main points support or develop the central theme statement or proposition and that all the subpoints support or develop the main point to which they are subordinate. Eliminate everything that does not contribute directly to the focus of the sermon. Avoid all tangents. State each idea in such a way that it directly develops the overall purpose of the sermon or immediately supports a point that does. A good way to check this is by looking over the outline to see if each main point and its anticipated application deal with the stated FCF of the message.

Brevity

State points as concisely as possible. Listeners do not have the opportunity to back up and reread what you just said. Get to the essence of each point and then use subsequent paragraphs of explanation to add proof, nuance, and appropriate qualifications. You do not want to put every thought you have about an idea into the main-point statement that is essentially a summary of the explanation that will follow. Use outline points as pegs on which to hang additional information, remembering that pegs are not useful if they are nine yards long. For example:

> Not this: Because we are offered salvation in the name of Jesus Christ, we must take great care not to live unholy lives lest our testimony damage the honor of Christ, the testimony of the church, and our Christian witness before those in the outside world and those in the family of faith.

> But this: Live worthy of the name by which you are called—Christian.

Try to make each point of your outline pass the 3:00 A.M. test.[21]

Harmony

Main points should echo one another, and the subpoints supporting a single main point should harmonize with one another. Usually this is accomplished through *parallelism.*

---

law, or education (cf. standard business and education seminars and textbooks on making successful speeches or presentations). Many modern approaches to preaching reflect the communication standards of commercial advertisements, political speeches, or entertainment vehicles designed to make impressions rather than develop thought. Preachers must learn the value of many types of communication, but appropriate usage requires that they understand the underpinnings of each.

21. See chap. 2.

PARALLELISM

Parallelism means that nouns, verbs, and modifiers appear in the same order throughout the points, and the wording changes only as much as is necessary to indicate a major turn of thought. William Hogan writes, "It is usually helpful if the main words in each main point are the same form of speech: nouns corresponding with nouns, prepositions with prepositions, verbs with verbs, participles with participles."[22]

Parallelism does more than simply give the impression of unity and form. The repetition of phrasing in a consistent word order is an audio cue that another major idea is being presented. Hundreds of sentences and sentence fragments whistle past listeners' ears during a sermon. Therefore, when congregants hear something that orients their thoughts to earlier expressions, it serves as a landmark they need to keep navigating the message. In the Sermon on the Mount, Jesus used the parallel phrases "You have heard it said . . . , but I say to you . . ." to divide the subjects of his message. The Beatitudes themselves are a beautiful example of parallel wording with key word changes that signal new ideas.

Parallel terms keep a message pointing to its overall theme, cue listeners to significant ideas, and highlight the central concept of each new point by drawing attention to the key words that do change.[23] Parallel wording draws the attention of the ear, and key word changes focus the mind on the new thought by identifying how this point differs from previous points. Consider how you automatically know what each of these parallel main points is about on the basis of the key word changes:

I. Pray, because prayer will reveal your heart.
II. Pray, because prayer will reach God's heart.
III. Pray, because prayer will conquer others' hearts.

What appears redundant in writing gives great power and clarity to speech, for parallelism acts as an audio flag wave to say, "Hey, here's another main idea." Then the key word change indicates what that new idea is.

Skilled use of parallelism helps illuminate the outline of a message without forcing a preacher to enumerate main points woodenly or to break the flow of a message to announce the outline. Sometimes parallel portions of a main point may drift into a transition sentence between points in order to allow key words to become central to listeners' perception. In the preceding example, the second and third points could be introduced with the transition, "This passage indicates that you should pray because prayer will reveal your heart, but why else should you pray?" The answers, "to reach God's heart" and "to

---

22. William L. Hogan, "Sermons Have Structures," *Expositor* 2, no. 1 (April 1988): 3.

23. Charles W. Koller, *Expository Preaching without Notes* (Grand Rapids: Baker, 1961), 52–53; and Farris D. Whitesell, *Power in Expository Preaching* (Old Tappan, N.J.: Revell, 1963), 60.

conquer others' hearts," then form the subsequent main-point statements. Pastors often divide sermons this way. Preachers first indicate in a strong thematic statement (i.e., the proposition) that the message will be about a practice or principle. They then ask transitional questions that reveal the unfolding sermon's divisions in parallel terms. This is a helpful and natural speech technique (known as "interrogating the proposition") that aids the organization of a message for both preacher and listeners.

CORRESPONDENCE

Although parallelism remains the most consistent means of harmonizing the points in a sermon, preachers have a number of other tools that help indicate divisions of thought. Main points and subpoints are almost always better grasped and retained if a preacher makes them correspond to one another in additional ways. Standard techniques include using key words that begin with the same letter (alliteration), sound similar (assonance, rhyme, rhythm), spur interest (created words, word play, contrasts, irony), and/or reflect a logical, a literary, or a pictorial pattern (ready, aim, fire; it was the best of times, it was the worst of times; chocolate sauce, whipped cream, and a cherry on top; bottom of the ninth, two outs, two strikes). These wording techniques may seem frivolous, but even the most sincere preachers strive to use "glow words" that sparkle for attention and gleam in memory. Excellent preaching neither eschews such devices nor employs any one of them too frequently.[24] The psalmist was not too sophisticated to tie truth to a Hebrew acrostic, and a pun was not beneath the dignity of Jesus.

MEMORABLENESS

Expositors covet the words that make truth shine and stick, but it is important to distinguish the communicative value of such words from their long-term memory import. Both external and internal memory are affected by the word choices of a sermon. External memory is what is remembered from a sermon after it is preached. Tests of external memory are usually discouraging to pastors because they are dismayed at how little people remember days or even hours after a sermon.[25] Such discovery may tempt preachers

---

24. Many homiletics texts cite alliteration as a chief offender, not only because its overuse has made it a virtual caricature of preaching but also because preachers may be tempted to warp the meaning of a text to fit their alliterative word schemes. Still, alliteration remains a powerful communication device that serves preachers and listeners well when used with discretion.

25. In order, listeners most commonly remember from a sermon: delivery (but only if it is very bad, very good, or possesses a memorable feature; natural delivery tends to disappear from memory), illustrations (the last, the first, then others), applications most strongly disagreed with, applications most strongly agreed with, the general theme or thrust of the message, and striking ideas within the sermon. Specific wording of main points, subpoints, etc. quickly passes from memory, as do all other features of a sermon's structure and exposition. With such discouraging results, why should we go to all the trouble to craft a sermon? Because a sermon is mostly about a spiritual encounter during its preaching, not about taking a memory test later (see discussion above). And because the most powerful and memorable aspect of

to hammer away at the distinctions of an outline or repeat the main ideas multiple times to increase external memory. Such efforts are more likely to result in pedantic, plodding sermons than in increased memory retention.

More profitable is the recognition that we are not preaching so that people can pass a test given later on the material in a sermon but so that they can understand and respond to the Word of God *during* the sermon. The sermon itself is a "redemptive event," a present tool of the Spirit to transform listeners' minds, hearts, and wills.[26] We craft the wording of a sermon so that while it is being preached listeners can connect ideas and comprehend meaning in order to experience the present conviction and power of the Spirit working by and with the Word. The communication of ideas during a sermon requires the function of internal memory, which allows the ear and the mind to relate ideas according to their proper sequence, proportion, and weight. A preacher uses word choices to further the dynamics of internal memory that enable listeners to distinguish and connect ideas so that the overall truth of a sermon has its proper spiritual impact. A preacher finds ways to harmonize the wording and thoughts of a sermon so that listeners can navigate the progression, development, and flow of the sermon rather than get stuck at its various road signs. Preachers want to provide enough structure to avoid confusion and enough craft to avoid bringing attention to the structure. The goal is to sweep listeners up into the glory and the power of the Spirit's revelation rather than have them worry about whether they have gotten all the points.

This goal makes it clear that as important as verbal tools are for effective communication, nothing warrants bending the truth of Scripture to make it fit a word scheme. When John Calvin bade farewell to the pastors in Geneva, he said, "I have not corrupted one single passage of Scripture, nor twisted it as far as I know, and when I might well have brought in subtle meanings, if I had studied subtlety, I have trampled the whole lot underfoot, and I have always studied to be simple."[27] It is more important to be able to echo these words at the conclusions of our ministries than to make any sermon more interesting at the expense of biblical truth. When shrewd word choices for an outline do not work naturally, state the truth simply and let the Holy Spirit impress it on mind and heart. His truth will do more good than all our cleverness.

Symmetry

Each main point and its supporting features should occupy a roughly identical proportion of a message. If you take twenty-five minutes to explain your first

---

preaching—*ethos*—is damaged when craft or thought is not well in evidence (see Bryan Chapell, *Using Illustrations to Preach with Power,* rev. ed. [Wheaton: Crossway, 2001], 141–42).

26. Greidanus, *Modern Preacher and the Ancient Text,* 5; and Paul Scott Wilson, *The Practice of Preaching* (Nashville: Abingdon, 1995), 20–25.

27. As quoted in Stott, *Between Two Worlds,* 128 (cf. Acts 20:26–27).

main point and then say, "For my second main point . . . ," your listeners are likely to faint, even if you know the second division will take only five minutes.

The ear expects symmetry. If one point is appreciably longer than the others, an understanding of human nature cautions against making it the last point in the sermon. When length must vary, it is typical for the longest main point to come first, with succeeding divisions getting progressively shorter. A few homileticians advise making the second point the longest to keep a congregation from judging the length of the entire message on the precedent of the first main point.[28] Still, all agree that approximate symmetry is the best approach and that elongating the end is surefire disaster. As sermons approach their climax, matters naturally accelerate. Thus, lengthy last points rob messages of powerful conclusions.

Progression

Listeners need to know that their thoughts and understanding are advancing throughout a message. If a point sounds too much like an idea that has already been covered, or if various points do not seem to build to a higher purpose, ire grows and interest withers. No one wants to waste time listening to a sermon leading nowhere. Hence, preachers must maintain a sense of progression by keeping each point distinct and by making each point advance toward a culminating idea.

Distinction

When a point sounds too much like a preceding point, the two are "coexistent." A coexistent error makes listeners feel they are simply spinning their wheels in matters previously covered.[29] Robert G. Rayburn writes, "Subpoints must never be coexistent with the main point. They must be distinct from it and still be a division of it. In the same way, the main points must not be coexistent with the proposition."[30] Points typically become coexistent when preachers become too involved in describing a text rather than in developing a message. As a result, an idea gets restated or redeveloped later in a sermon simply because it is echoed later in a passage. When such redundancy occurs without apparent progression or distinction of thought, listeners feel they have just taken an unnecessary U-turn.

For the same reason, main points must not appear to repeat one another in *concept* or *terminology*. If the first main point of a message is "Pray, because our prayers reveal God's purpose," and the third main point is "Pray, because prayer discloses God's purpose," listeners cannot help but feel that the latter

28. Hogan, "Sermons Have Structures," 3.
29. Broadus, *On the Preparation and Delivery of Sermons*, 114–15.
30. Rayburn, "Sermon Outlining," personal lecture notes, 2.

point is redundant. Even if a distinction between the terms *reveal* and *disclose* exists in the preacher's mind, listeners are unlikely to notice. A preacher will spare listeners much consternation by using words that more obviously differ from each other in concept as well as in terminology.

Example of Outline with Coexistent Errors

Proposition: We must preach Christ at every opportunity.

I. We must preach Christ whenever there is an opportunity.
II. We must preach Christ when it is not convenient.
III. We must preach Christ when it is difficult.

Note: The first main point is coexistent with the proposition, and the second main point is coexistent with the third.

We must clearly distinguish all points. This standard also requires us to examine our subpoints to make sure the developmental ideas under one main point do not sound too much like the ideas already discussed under a previous main point, unless there is intention and purpose in mirroring their development.

Culmination

Points lead toward a climax when there is an apparent sequence to them. Some outlines proceed logically through an argument; others proceed chronologically or biographically; still others paint a picture by organizing the points of an outline around the description of a common experience, a captivating image, or a familiar allegory.[31] Logical, aesthetic, and communication considerations all help determine the order of ideas: Matters typically come first that explain those that follow; positives counterbalance negatives; concretes anchor abstracts; a general principle may lead to particular applications; particular evidences may demonstrate a generic principle; causes render effects; actions imply motives; conclusions call for foundations; internal dynamics balance external forces; appeal follows instruction; impera-

31. Barbara Hunter and Brenda Buckley Hunter list eleven organizational patterns in *Introductory Speech Communication: Overcoming Obstacles, Reaching Goals* (Dubuque: Kendall-Hunt, 1988), 31–32. More possibilities abound (cf. Larsen, *Anatomy of Preaching,* 70). Standard structural alternatives include problem/solution, proof of contention, cause to effect, effect to cause, explanation and application, story with moral, elimination of wrong alternatives (called the chase outline because a preacher chases down wrong leads to find a right answer), answers to a provocative question, and unfolding dimensions of a controlling image, story, or biographical sequence. As an example of these latter forms, one of the best outlines I have heard was prepared by a student who had been a crash investigator for the Air Force. By picturing the life of King Saul as a spiritual crash site, the sermon led listeners through the steps of a disaster investigation to discover point of impact, pilot or mechanical failure, and prevention of recurrence.

tives warrant explanation. Each of these sequences (and many others like them, including their inverses) naturally lead listeners down a recognizable path. Of course, at times a preacher will veil intentions to make an impact, but then the progression is into mystery or toward surprise. This tactic can give a sermon a sense of purpose if the preacher builds suspense that drives home the ultimate concept.

Typically, progression stumbles when points become so compartmentalized that their relationships to the sermon's central purpose disappear. If the impact of the main points is simply "First we see God's wisdom," "In this other point we see God's providence," and "In this last point we gain insight into God's patience," listeners may well wonder what *the* point of the entire discussion is. In this example, these ideas do not appear to lead anywhere. They simply leave listeners with a collection of impressions. If the sermon's overall purpose does not become more and more evident as each point unfolds, a congregation rightly questions why the points were mentioned at all.

Progression also slows when a sermon contains too many divisions. If one main point has five subpoints and the next has seven, no one will remember the subpoints, and the sermon itself will get lost. Elaborate argumentation will tire and confuse rather than stimulate and clarify. Usually it is preferable to limit subdivisions to two or three ideas and then to use the discussion of those ideas to introduce more detailed analysis. A message that is all skeleton and no flesh holds little allure for most.[32]

Specific Outline Features

The general principles of outlining explained above will help you construct organized expository messages. Excellent communicators may purposefully break the rules for a particular purpose, but the principles still guide if only by providing a benchmark by which to evaluate exceptions. These general principles in turn hold implications for the specific features of sermon outlines.

The specifics introduced below reflect a particular method that I have found useful when training students in expository preaching. This method has strengths and weaknesses, as does any other. My desire in presenting these features is not to suggest that preachers should always structure sermons with every specific exactly so but rather that they understand the reasoning behind these structures so that they can construct messages suitable for their own purposes. There is not one right way of shaping expository sermons, and there are always exceptions regarding general principles as well as specific features. I have simply found it more helpful to lay a foundation on which students can build rather than point them to the vast homiletics horizon

32. Rayburn, "The Discussion," personal lecture notes, 1.

with the encouragement to preach as the Spirit moves (see the sermon in appendix 12 that displays many of the elements of this "formal" structure). Glean what best serves your preaching preferences while learning the foundational principles these specifics represent.

The Proposition

DEFINITION AND DEVELOPMENT

Sermons are built on propositions. Classic homiletics describes a proposition as "a statement of the subject as the preacher proposes to develop it."[33] A proposition usually follows an introduction, summarizes its concerns, and indicates what the rest of the sermon will address. As a consequence, a proposition points both backward and forward—reflecting what has preceded and illuminating what will follow. A proposition is the germ of an entire sermon, and as a result, its construction is crucial. In picturesque language that homiletics instructors have virtually made canonical, Henry Jowett once wrote:

> I am of the conviction that no sermon is ready for preaching, nor ready for writing out, until we can express its theme in a short, pregnant sentence as clear as crystal. I find the getting of that sentence the hardest, the most exacting, and the most fruitful labor in my study. To compel oneself to fashion that sentence, to dismiss every word that is vague, ragged, ambiguous, to think oneself through to a form of words which defines the theme with scrupulous exactness—this is surely one of the most vital and essential factors in the making of a sermon: and I do not think any sermon ought to be preached or even written, until that sentence has emerged, clear and lucid as a cloudless moon.[34]

By forming such a proposition, a preacher isolates a message's dominant thought, which will orient all other points in the message, providing both direction and unity. No matter is more vital for effective communication.

Most instructors advise preachers to form their propositions at the end of their sermon research.[35] At this point, study has probably yielded any number of notes, scribbles, and exegetical insights. Thus, the formation of a proposition forces a preacher to determine a central focus. Of course, one's mind does not always think sequentially, and sometimes you will see main points before you have had a chance to determine a proposition that will include them all. Still, preachers ultimately need to form a proposition in order to give listeners

---

33. Broadus, *On the Preparation and Delivery of Sermons,* 54.

34. J. H. Jowett, *The Preacher, His Life and Work* (New York: Doran, 1912), 133. See also Marquart, *Quest for Better Preaching,* 102; Stott, *Between Two Worlds,* 226; Donald E. Demaray, *An Introduction to Homiletics* (Grand Rapids: Baker, 1978), 80; Henry Grady Davis, *Design for Preaching* (Philadelphia: Fortress, 1958), 37; and many others.

35. Davis, *Design for Preaching,* 37; and Stott, *Between Two Worlds,* 228.

direction as a message unfolds.[36] Every proposition should be stated broadly enough so that the main points are divisions of, not additions to, its thought.

Balance

A simple statement such as "the effects of sin touch every life" might serve as an essay theme. A *formal* sermon proposition, however, is more than a theme. It establishes the concern that a message will address and sets the agenda for how it will be handled. Since an expository sermon applies biblical truth, a sermon proposition also reflects a text's truth *and* what it requires. A proposition, then, is not merely a statement of a biblical truth, nor is it only an instruction based on a biblical principle. It is both.

A formal proposition is the wedding of a universal truth based on a text with an application based on the universal truth. A universal truth is a biblical principle for guiding Christian life or thought that is established by the features and the facts of a sermon's dominant text.[37] A biblical principle may be a doctrinal concept or a practice, but in either case it is a principle that can be proven from the text both to be true and to be valid for present listeners. The statement "Jonah eventually went to Ninevah" is true, but it is not a universal truth because it does not provide a biblical principle that can be applied universally. This mere *statement of fact* describes a text, but it does not develop the message of the text.[38] However, the Jonah narrative supports the principle "God's service requires obedience." When this truth is linked to an appropriate application, such as "Because God's service requires obedience, we must seek his will," a proposition emerges.

A truth without an apparent application or an instruction without biblical justification falls short of the requirements of a formal proposition. Thomas Jones writes:

> Two common errors experienced by students of homiletics have to do with the failure to fashion a balance in the [formal] propositional statement between truth and human response. The faulty propositional statement often tells us only: 1) That something is true; or, 2) That something is required.
>
> An example of the statement which tells us only that something is true is given in the following: "Jesus Christ has provided the only hope of salvation through His death on the cross for sinners." This statement is true. The problem with such a statement however is that it leads us nowhere.... It may state a truth, but, as a propositional statement, it needs to do more. It needs to involve the hearer in the consequences of the truth....
>
> The second type of weakness in propositions is the statement which tells us only that something is required ...: "The believer in Christ must be diligent

---

36. Fred B. Craddock, *As One without Authority,* 3rd ed. (Nashville: Abingdon, 1979), 100; and Ronald J. Allen and Thomas J. Herrin, "Moving from the Story to Our Story," in *Preaching the Story,* ed. Edmund A. Steimle, Morris J. Niedenthal, and Charles Rice (Philadelphia: Fortress, 1980), 158–59.

37. Rayburn, "Outlining," 1–2.

38. Ibid., 2.

in the gospel in every way." This statement points us to a definite response to some truth, but it fails to tell us *what* truth.[39]

Propositions meet formal homiletical requirements when they answer both Why? and So what? The "why" question elicits the truth-principle component of a proposition. The "so what" compels a preacher to determine the application component (i.e., the response of thought or behavior that is a consequence of the truth principle as it is developed in this sermon). This applicational goal is ultimately what Scripture—and a sermon—requires on the authority of the truths proven by a text. *Informal* propositions typically provide only half of a formal proposition's components and depend on the main points to supply and develop the other half (see examples).

Informal Proposition Examples

Our God knows our tomorrow.
Jesus came to save sinners.
We must trust God's providence in our pain.

Note: These propositions are all statements of principles that apply to God's people universally.

Most preachers, including me, will take this more informal approach most of the time because the shorter main points make the sermon's delivery crisper and more conversational. Still, it is helpful to train using *formal* components so that beginning preachers grow accustomed and committed to the full obligations of their sermons (i.e., expounding a text so as to communicate both *what is true* and *what to do*).

FORMAL FORMS

There are a number of ways to phrase formal propositions to ensure that they wed principle and application. Two of the most basic are consequential and conditional statements.

A proposition in consequential form states something that should be done as a consequence of a truth. The word *because* is used or implied:

Because Jesus commands his followers to proclaim the gospel, we must present Christ to others.

A proposition in conditional form identifies a condition that warrants a response. The words *since* or *if* are typically used:

39. Thomas F. Jones, "Truth Has Consequences: Or Balancing the Proposition," in *The Preparation and Delivery of Sermons,* ed. Bryan Chapell, Seminary Extension Training curriculum of Covenant Theological Seminary (St. Louis: Multi-media Publications, 1992), 2.

Since all have fallen short of the glory of God, we all should acknowledge our sin.

The phrase with the word *because, since,* or *if* does not have to begin the statement. A proposition works just as well if a preacher says, "We must present Christ to others, because Jesus commands his followers to proclaim the gospel."

These forms work well because they naturally link, in a single statement, a sermon's overall content: a truth principle and an exhortation. This type of proposition allows preachers to apply biblical truth from the very outset of their messages, setting their biblical and pastoral obligations clearly in view in a natural yet compelling fashion. Other grammatical formulas work, but these forms consistently help preachers frame solid propositions.

Conditional or consequential forms also allow a preacher to test whether a proposition contains a universal truth. If the truth principle clause can stand on its own as a general statement of biblical truth, then the proposition has a solid foundation. For instance, "We should pray because of godliness" is a weak proposition because the principle statement ("of godliness") cannot stand alone as a universal truth. However, if this phrase were revised and extended to "godliness requires private devotion," then the preacher would have a solid, universal truth for the proposition.

In some cases, the application and principle clauses may be combined to indicate a universal truth even when the principle clause cannot stand alone. In the statement "We should pray earnestly, because Jesus commanded it," "Jesus commanded it" is not a universal truth. However, the antecedent of the word *it* is the preceding phrase: "We should pray earnestly." Thus, both clauses taken together supply the implied thought of the second phrase: Jesus commanded earnest prayer. This is a universal truth. Similar dynamics occur when propositions begin with "In order to . . ." (e.g., In order to honor God, we must obey his Word.). Here again the universal truth of the proposition emerges when considering the statement as a whole.

Note also that the application clause in each of the above examples is worded as "we should" or "we must." Not too much should be made of these specific forms—the pronoun *you* may work better than *we* in some sermons.[40] Note also that a simple imperative verb sometimes works better than "we must" or "we should" statements.[41] For example, "Because God uses faithful

---

40. I encourage students to ignore the senseless arguments over whether preachers should exhort with the words *we* or *you*. The arguments some preachers make for the exclusive use of one or the other are specious at best. The prophets obviously said, "*You* should . . ." at times (Exod. 20; Matt. 6:9). Yet it was also a prophet who said, "*We* all, like sheep, have gone astray, each of us has turned to his own way" (Isa. 53:6; cf. Rom. 15:4). Obviously, a preacher who never confronts others speaks without the authority Scripture grants, but a pastor who never identifies with listeners preaches with an arrogance even Jesus did not assume.

41. Some homileticians fear too much use of the imperative in sermons. These instructors wisely note that too much preaching simply degenerates into Bible- and head-thumping (see Stott, *Between*

prayer, pray!" includes truth and application as does "Because God uses faithful prayer, you should pray." The important distinction to note among all of these examples is that a formal application clause contains an imperative of some sort. In addition, the imperative is in the active rather than the passive voice. Preachers take passive and "being" verbs (i.e., be, is, was) out of the application clause so that they give definite indications to God's people of what God requires of them. "God's people are prayerful" is true and a helpful description of other people, but the wording merely represents a *statement of fact* that does not necessarily require any immediate response from listeners.

Many preachers like using the word *can* in an application clause as opposed to using *must* or *should*. *Can* takes some of the imperative bite out of the application clause if a sermon needs a gentler tone. There is often wisdom in this word choice, though the word is ambiguous. In colloquial English, we use *can* as an encouragement to action: We can do it! Such usage works well in the exhortation clause of a proposition (e.g., Because God has freed Christians from the power of sin, we can serve him.). However, when *can* simply reflects the dictionary meaning—ability—a proposition may deteriorate into another mere statement of fact rather than providing a principle wedded to an exhortation (e.g., Because God grants forgiveness, he can set the conditions of our pardon.). Such a proposition states what is true but gives no guidance as to our response.

The goal of using *should, must,* or an imperative verb in an exhortation clause is to give pastoral direction to a believer's faith. A message whose content and structure only convey truthful information has lost sight of its transformational purpose without, at least, an implied exhortation to do or believe something in response. Of course, a preacher can exhort later in a sermon on the basis of a proposition that is stated as a simple truth, even if the exhortation is not woven into the wording of the proposition itself. Good preachers do this most of the time with informally worded propositions. Still, the goal of a formally worded proposition is to ensure that the exhortation the Holy Spirit intends is not neglected in the academic confines of much preaching instruction. Making sure that the imperatives properly reflect the intention of a text *and* properly motivate with the grace of the gospel remain challenges addressed later in this book. For the moment, it is important to remember that faithfulness is a blessing of God. Preaching that there is neither expectation nor obligation in the gospel is ungracious to his people.

Perspective

Variations of and exceptions to these standard propositional forms go on *ad infinitum.* A list of such is not important. What is important is gaining a

---

Two Worlds, 54–58; and Larsen, *Anatomy of Preaching,* 68). Yet preaching at its heart remains exhortation based on truth. For this cause, preaching necessarily possesses an imperative character, even when it adopts less strident tones (Stott, *Between Two Worlds,* 156–57; and Adams, *Preaching with Purpose,* 51–52).

sense for what propositions should fundamentally accomplish. A proposition condenses a sermon's content. Since expository sermons answer What does the text mean? and So what? the propositions that encapsulate a message should also show *what is true* and *what to do*. This is accomplished formally by wedding a universal truth to an application. Informal alternatives are too numerous to discuss, but proposition foundations can be reduced to this essential: *A proposition is a universal truth in a hortatory mode*. A proposition should reveal a truth from a text that forms the foundation for a pastor's exhortation for God's people to do (in behavior, attitude, or belief) what his Word requires.

With the perspective that propositions should reveal truth and lay the foundation for application, preachers are able to develop propositions outside the standard forms that still provide listeners with adequate signals of a sermon's direction. A pastor may word a proposition in a nonuniversal form that nonetheless beacons a universal truth. For example, "Jesus witnessed to sinners" meets none of the formal criteria for a proposition. But if a preacher has prepared the introduction to communicate that Jesus' example is normative despite our reticence to follow him, then the proposition implies, "Since our God ministers to unlovely people, we must witness to sinners." The formal proposition lies conceptually beneath the stated proposition.

Sometimes preachers use only one clause of a proposition early in a message and let the other emerge as the sermon develops. Sometimes a question indicates what a sermon seeks to answer, and the actual proposition does not appear until the message's conclusion. A sermon may succeed without a proposition ever being stated if it is clearly implied. Consider how the following sermon introduction uses these principles to establish an unspoken proposition:

> A young woman came to my office some months ago with what she perceived as exciting news. "Pastor," she said, "I've just agreed to get married to the most wonderful man. He's kind and considerate. . . . He doesn't treat me like the other men I've dated who were so coarse and cruel. And what's even better, after we are married I will be able to lead him to the Lord." What would you say to this young woman if you loved her enough to be completely honest with her? What does the Bible say?

Although no formal theme statement appears here, the proposition beacons clearly. The message will answer the question, What standards does the Bible give for Christian marriage? If we were to spell it out, the formal proposition would be "Because God sets standards for Christian marriage, we must marry as he instructs." Here, however, the formal statement will probably never appear in the sermon because the pastor has found another way to beacon a universal truth in a hortatory mode. The proposition appears, but not in traditional garb.

Homiletics instructors get nervous when talking about abbreviated and implied propositions, recognizing that the techniques may cause students to take shortcuts with the discipline and organization of their thoughts. My approach has been to require students to state propositions formally during their early training and then to help them experiment with more creative approaches as preaching experience and exegetical expertise grow. Suffice it to say, a sermon should not fail to have a formal proposition just because a preacher could not come up with one. Preachers build good sermons on solid propositions even when thoughtful communication strategies may cause the formal statements not to appear in the actual messages.

Main Points

Formal main points are also universal truths in hortatory modes. Like propositions, main points may be informally reduced, abbreviated, and implied rather than formally stated. However, preachers benefit from mastering the following foundational principles for main points before experimenting with the infinite variations sound exposition ultimately encourages.

Formal Wording

Each main point is a division of the thought presented in a proposition. As a result, all the main points of a sermon should develop or support its proposition in a similar fashion (i.e., they should answer similar diagnostic questions about the proposition—Who? How? When? Where? Why? and Why else?).[42] Because main points are so closely related to the proposition, it is usually helpful if they reflect the proposition's structure. Thus, just as the main points should parallel one another, they should also parallel the proposition.

In the most formal wording of main points, one clause (principle or application) of a proposition is picked up by the main points and is repeated throughout the outline (see examples below).[43] The main-point clause that is repeated is called the "anchor clause" (see italicized phrases in the examples). If the anchor clause is the truth-principle clause, then the outline is "principle consistent." Each main point then answers, What should be done about this truth? If the anchor clause is the application clause, then the outline is "application consistent," and the main points answer, Why should this be done?[44]

---

42. For instance, if the first two main points urge listeners to use Scripture to discover the standards for public worship, listeners will scratch their heads to discover the connection of a third main point that urges them to prepare to die (cf. Broadus, *On the Preparation and Delivery of Sermons*, 115–17).

43. Robinson shows how to use this structure effectively in expository messages. See *Biblical Preaching*, 129.

44. Note that the italicized anchor clauses indicate whether the outline is principle consistent or application consistent.

Principle-Consistent Outline

Proposition: *Because Jesus commands believers to proclaim him boldly,* we must proclaim Christ at every opportunity.[45]

> I. *Because Jesus commands believers to proclaim him boldly,* we should proclaim Christ in difficult situations.
> II. *Because Jesus commands believers to proclaim him boldly,* we should proclaim Christ to difficult people.
> III. *Because Jesus commands believers to proclaim him boldly,* we should proclaim Christ despite our difficulties.

Application-Consistent Outline

Proposition: Since Jesus alone provides salvation, *we must proclaim Christ to the world.*[46]

> I. Since Jesus alone purchased salvation, *we must proclaim Christ to the world.*
> II. Since Jesus alone possesses salvation, *we must proclaim Christ to the world.*
> III. Since Jesus alone bestows salvation, *we must proclaim Christ to the world.*

The clauses in the main points that do not remain consistent are the "magnet clauses." The magnet clauses naturally draw the explanatory elements of the main points to themselves because they contain the key word changes that focus the attention of listeners. *Thus, subpoints support or develop the magnet clauses because they contain the developmental features of the outline.*

The universal truth found in the anchor clause should be developed either just before or just after the proposition (and/or early in the first main point if necessary), since this premise is the foundation of the message. Usually this means that the anchor clause reflects a concept that requires little proof and is relatively obvious in the text.

Sound communication choices should go hand in glove with the main- and subpoint structures. Make antecedents clear. Do not use pronouns to represent key thoughts in both anchor and magnet phrases (a double-pronoun error).

Not this: Because God loves *us, we* should worship him.

---

45. Note that I have structured the proposition and main points in consequential form. The sentence structures in these examples are varied simply for demonstration purposes. Neither principle-consistent nor application-consistent outlines require conditional or consequential wording exclusively. Preachers use the form that best serves a particular outline's wording and purposes.

46. Note that I have structured the proposition and main points in conditional form.

But this: Because God loves his *children, we* should worship him.

Experienced preachers also try to avoid the use of passive verbs and negative wording in main points.[47] Homileticians refer to this as taking out the *be's* (i.e., passive *being* verbs) and the *not's*. This is done first because application clauses worded with passive verbs do not exhort people to do anything; they simply state what happens to people, usually in the uninvolved third person (e.g., Because God delivers, *believers are secure.*). In addition, when too many main points concentrate on what *not* to do, people must guess what *to* do. Negative words in negative main points form negative messages that result in negative ministries. Keep the gospel the Good News. Make sure people know what the Bible intends as well as what it prohibits.

Advantages and Disadvantages

The advantages of constructing formal main points that reflect the structure of a formal proposition are many:

1. The wording of each main point will keep a preacher true to the dual expository task of exposing and applying biblical truth. There can be no "information only" sermon when the structure itself requires a preacher to prove from the text *what is true* and *what to do.*
2. Consistent parallelism in anchor clauses gives a message unity while clearly signaling the chief divisions of the message.
3. Parallelism vividly highlights the key word changes in the magnet clauses, thus making the subject of each division distinct and the progress of each point clear.

The disadvantages of wording main points in this form should also be apparent. Chief is the length of each main point. Including principle and application in main points makes each point a mouthful. Yet, though formally worded main points are cumbersome, the repetition of the anchor clause acts as a verbal beacon that vital information is at hand. Repeating the anchor clause is redundant for a reader but not for a listener, especially when five to ten minutes of exposition takes place between the statement of each main point. Anchor clauses provide orientation and are used to home in on magnet clauses. (For an example of a sermon constructed with a formal proposition and main points, see appendix 12.)

Shorter Forms

As already indicated, parallelism woven into transitions accommodates more abbreviated and informal wording of main points. With this in mind,

---

47. See similar statements above for the wording of propositions.

preachers can readily convert formally worded main points to more concise statements by following these steps:

Step-by-Step Main Point Reduction Process

1. Note which element (principle clause or application clause) remains consistent in the outline; that is, identify the anchor clause.
2. Develop the concept of the consistent element in the sermon introduction (this element may also appear in the proposition statement).
3. Create an analytical question or implied question(s) based on the anchor clause: (e.g., Who? What? When? Where? Why? How?)
4. Answer the question(s) with the developmental clauses (i.e., magnet clauses), which become the main points. (Note: Often preachers simply state subordinate aspects of a proposition as main points rather than ask and answer questions about it. This is certainly a legitimate approach, but by interrogating the proposition, the logic of a sermon is usually unmistakable for listeners and preacher.)

By using this step-by-step process of forming and then interrogating a proposition, preachers could change the formal outlines presented above into the following *fundamental reductions:*

Fundamental Reduction of Principle-Consistent Outline

Introduction: Develop the idea that Jesus requires bold proclamation.
Proposition: Jesus commands believers to proclaim him boldly.[48]
Analytical Question: What are the consequences?

    I. We should proclaim Christ in difficult situations.
   II. We should proclaim Christ to difficult people.
  III. We should proclaim Christ despite our difficulties.

Fundamental Reduction of Application-Consistent Outline

Introduction: Develop the need to proclaim Christ to everyone.
Proposition: We must proclaim Christ to the world.
Analytical Question: Why?

    I. Jesus alone purchased salvation.
   II. Jesus alone possesses salvation.
  III. Jesus alone bestows salvation.

---

48. Note that in these examples the anchor clause serves as the proposition. Complete propositions may also serve well, even if the main points are reduced.

Although this process is not the only way to reduce main points, it is one way that keeps the principles of expository messages in the forefront. By beginning sermon preparation with main points that present both truth and application, preachers tend to maintain their expository obligations throughout a message. The formal wording sets the agenda, keeping both message and messenger on track. Even if preachers use only the key word changes of the developmental clauses as the eventual main-point statements of their sermons, the reduction process has required them to consider the meaning and requirements of a passage, a healthy process for any preaching occasion.

The primary challenge in using shorter main points is recalling that they should also promote the *goals* of formal expository outlines. Avoid the trap of merely describing a text (i.e., simply outlining the facts of a text in a way that does not disclose the truth principles they support—Noah was old, Noah built an ark, Noah stayed dry).[49] Main points should always remain hortatory in nature. This means they should be stated so as to reveal universal truth principles that a preacher can exhort believers to apply to their lives. Even if reduced main points do not contain an imperative clause, listeners should recognize that the ideas presented in the points provide conceptual leverage for a message's application. It often helps to word informal main points as imperatives or include in them (or the question that introduces them) first- or second-person plural pronouns—"we" or "you."[50] When a preacher says, "What *we* should do" or "What *you* should believe," the sermon automatically moves out of the abstract. Thus, most preachers discover that when they state the main points as truth principles that immediately apply to their listeners rather than as simple descriptions of the facts of a text, their sermons significantly grow in power of expression and engagement of listeners.

Involve listeners by the way you word your points.

Not this: God justifies his people by his grace. (Note that the wording is in the third person—the truth applies to "them," those justified people out there somewhere.)

But this: God justifies *you* by his grace.
Or even better: *We* should rejoice that God justifies *us* by grace.

Even when (and perhaps especially when) preachers use reduced or informal forms, main points should remain as parallel, symmetrical, and progressive as possible. Most preachers do this instinctively as their preaching experience and expertise grow because they discover that these tools are not

---

49. Walter L. Liefeld, *New Testament Exposition: From Text to Sermon* (Grand Rapids: Zondervan, 1984), 20–21.

50. Michael Fabarez, *Preaching That Changes Lives* (Nashville: Thomas Nelson, 2002), 62–64.

artificial impositions on preaching but natural tools of speech that empower effective communication.

Since preachers must state main points within understandable paragraphs of thought, many homiletics instructors advise wording main points in complete sentences.[51] Although there are valid exceptions to this standard, it does aid completeness of thought in preparation and prevents preachers from grasping for words during presentation. Making sure that all main points, even in abbreviated forms, are at least based on complete sentences will keep the thought of a sermon well groomed.[52]

Remember that the reduced forms of main points must promote unity—the very heart of sound sermon preparation. As the magnet clauses grow more distant from the formal statement of the anchor clause, it is easy for a preacher to lose track of the central focus of the sermon. Even reduced main points should "sustain the same kind of relation to the subject."[53] This means that main points in all forms should develop, support, or prove the proposition. For example:

Not this: Jesus is our advocate . . .
 I. We should praise him.
 II. We should pray to him.
 III. His disciples wronged him.

But this: Jesus is our advocate . . .
 I. We should praise him.
 II. We should pray to him.
 III. We should serve him.

In the second outline, each main point answers the diagnostic question, What should we do since Jesus is our advocate? In the first outline, the third main point (even though it is grammatically correct and may reflect a truth in the text) does not answer a similar diagnostic question and thus does not harmonize with the wording or the concepts developed in the other main points. Because diagnostic questions help harmonize a sermon, preachers often ask such questions out loud during a message. Asking a strong diagnostic question after the proposition and then answering the question with the main-point statements make people keenly aware of the purpose of each main point and

51. Paul Borden, "Expository Preaching," and Hugh Litchfield, "Outlining the Sermon," in *Handbook of Contemporary Preaching*, 73, 173, respectively; see also Adams, *Preaching with Purpose*, 49; and Larsen, *Anatomy of Preaching*, 68.

52. Although some main points are only answers to questions or mere sentence fragments, there must be an implied complete sentence behind what the preacher actually says in order for listeners to make sense of the point.

53. Rayburn, "The Discussion," 1.

give the entire message a sense of unity as it progresses. Interrogating the proposition and answering it with the main points is one of the most common and effective ways that pastors can develop sermons week to week.

Perspective

I would never contend that the discussion so far (regarding formally worded or informally reduced main points) exhausts the ways of organizing expository messages. These structures simply provide models that reflect sound homiletical principles and at the same time fulfill expository obligations. I emphasize these models for those wanting foundational guidance for organizing their thoughts because, though I know the Michael Jordans of preaching prefer 360-degree slam dunks, most of us learn by beginning with straight jump shots.[54] By mastering the fundamentals, you fill your future sermons with promise.

Once preachers grasp the principles that undergird outline construction, they can shorten main-point statements to a few key words, highlighting a truth that drives the application. Sometimes formal wording works well; other times a single clause or even a single word works best. I tend to use reduced forms in my weekly preaching. If I find myself struggling to corral my thoughts in sermon preparing, however, I go back to square one and use the discipline of the more formal structures.

Note also that while the example outlines above each contain three main points, there is no need to put three divisions in every expository message. Homileticians enjoy debating why "three points and a poem" has been standard in Western preaching, but most agree that preachers should use the number of points that best serves the purpose of a specific sermon.[55] Three points generally indicate *developmental* thought: problem, plan, and effects; task, tools, and means; beginning, middle, and end; what, why, and how. Two-point messages are usually *balanced* tension: external and internal, spiritual and physical, divine and human, attitude and action. This tension typically holds the real point of the message (which explains why a two-point message with no conceptual counterbalance between the points feels incomplete). Outlines with more than three main points tend to use the divisions as building blocks for a *culminative* or *summative* effect. Preachers listing "five biblical ways to love your spouse" or "seven marks of a godly witness" use the points to build to a summary idea (these types of outlines are variously called catalog, additive, ladder, or diamond-facet forms).

54. For additional information on more novel structures for preaching, see Chapell, "Alternative Models," 117–31.
55. Broadus, *On the Preparation and Delivery of Sermons*, 113; Stott, *Between Two Worlds*, 230; Adams, *Preaching with Purpose*, 56; and Larsen, *Anatomy of Preaching*, 68.

Subpoints

Guidelines

Subpoints are *not* universal truths in hortatory modes. In expository messages, each subpoint is a summary of a biblical proof or feature that supports a precise aspect of a main point (specifically, a magnet clause). This means that subpoints are thought pegs—usually concise sentences or sentence fragments—that introduce the biblical material that supports a main point. Subpoints point to an aspect of a text (remember that *context is part of text*) that substantiates or develops the premise behind a main point. By using the state-place-prove formula of exposition, preachers typically state a subpoint, cite the information in the text that supports the statement,[56] and then explain how that information establishes the truth of the subpoint. When they have completed their outlines, expository preachers should be able to evaluate whether they have exhausted a text by seeing if a subpoint (or a main point) deals to some extent with every verse (or portion) of the text.

There is no standard number of subpoints. Simply because one main point has three subpoints does not mean that the next main point must have the same, and not every main point needs subpoints. When main points appear alone, proceed immediately to state-place-prove. Subpoints, however, should not appear alone. Although subpoints are not required for each main point, when they do occur, there must be more than one. Single subpoints confuse listeners because they sound like an idea competing with rather than complementing a main point. I advise using subpoints whenever the explanation of a main point exceeds a significant paragraph in length. Nothing loses listeners as quickly as mile upon mile of explanation without clear road signs.

Subpoints organize and develop the thought of a main point. They should exhibit parallelism, proportion, and progression; each should relate to the main point in a similar fashion. Like main points, subpoints generally *develop the thought of a message;* they do not simply describe the features of a passage. For example, "Jesus went to Jerusalem" is a weak subpoint. The preacher is likely confusing repetition of the text's facts with a *principle* the subpoint should be stating (i.e., Godliness requires sacrifice). In accompanying exposition (i.e., the paragraph or discursive material around a subpoint), the facts of the text should support or prove the subpoint statement, but they do not form the statement itself. Outlines that describe only the facts or chronology of a text create what Hershael York calls "factoid sermons."[57]

---

56. As has been stated earlier, preachers have a lesser obligation to read specific aspects of narratives familiar to all. Time constraints often make it wise to summarize the contents of long portions of a text that establish a subpoint rather than read lengthy quotations in the body of the message. See the state-place-prove process described in detail in chap. 5.

57. York and Decker, *Preaching with Bold Assurance,* 12.

Example of Subpoints That Merely Describe a Text

Main Point: Because God blesses faithfulness, we should obey him.
1. Israel confronted Jericho.
2. Israel marched around Jericho.
3. The walls of Jericho fell.

Note: These subpoints merely describe the facts and chronology of Joshua 6. They are not worded so as to develop the principle of the stated main point.

Example of Subpoints That Develop the Principle of a Main Point

Main Point: Because God blesses faithfulness, we should obey him.
1. Faithfulness requires facing God's enemies.
2. Faithfulness requires obeying God's Word.
3. Faithfulness results in seeing God's hand.

Note: These subpoints are worded so as to develop/support the main point's principle. The facts of Joshua 6 will be cited to support/prove the subpoints as they are explained. Note that these "principle-ized" subpoints are based on the same facts as the merely descriptive subpoints in the example above.

Experienced preachers do not usually announce subpoints by saying, "My first subpoint is . . ."[58] Hearers understand subpoints by the way they are phrased. When it is necessary to enumerate subpoints, preachers typically say, "First . . ." "Third . . ." or "In addition . . ." not, "Subpoint C is . . ." Public-speaking experts advise numbering subpoints in notes so that you do not have to convert letters to numbers while you are talking.[59] Yet this sound advice should not imply that all subpoints need enumeration. Although an outline is a logical path for the mind, it is usually not necessary for a listener to retain its every detail in order for the message to be effective.

To the ordinary ear, an effective sermon typically sounds like discourse from a thoughtful conversation (remember the Greek *homileo* behind "homiletics" actually means *converse*). A sermon will sound too much like an essay or an encyclopedia if the preacher emphasizes the outline (which can create a stilted or artificial delivery). Listeners, who do not generally evaluate each separate thought of a sermon, want only to follow the preacher's flow of thought. No one leaves church saying, "My, didn't the pastor have a marvelous second subpoint under the third main point?" But if people say, "I can follow him" or "This preacher is easy to understand," then the preacher has well organized and communicated the message. Paul Scott Wilson makes a delightful contribution to modern percep-

58. Sweazey, *Preaching the Good News*, 74.
59. *Be Prepared to Speak*, an instructional video prepared and distributed by Toastmasters International (San Francisco: Cantola-Skeie Productions, 1986).

tions of preaching by comparing the well-wrought sermon to a website that, when well configured, seamlessly guides its viewers to subsequent windows of insight while maintaining its own distinct message.[60]

The goal of organization is to enable God's people to have a clear impression of how the Holy Spirit is confronting them with the truth of God's Word. We organize to guide listeners down a road that we know can lead them to this encounter. Their memory or impression of the road we have laid is insignificant compared to the experience we pray they will have and to its continuing spiritual impact on their lives. Few will remember a sermon's organizational features, but few will forget their encounter with the Spirit if those features have led them to him without distraction or confusion. We should organize to maximize the glory of the Spirit's work, not to emphasize the craft or labor of our work.

Organization usually becomes an issue only when it is absent or belabored. On the best sermon highways, listeners concentrate on their destination and give little thought to the road surface. Only when the sermon's ride gets bumpy do listeners begin to pay attention to the details of the pavement. Keeping parishioner eyes on a sermon's goal rather than on its gravel requires pastors to use the tools of organization and to forego homiletics jargon in sermons (e.g., "My proposition today is . . . ," "My first subpoint for this is . . ."). Subordinate ideas introduced using some of the techniques described below keep subpoints from distracting listeners.

Types

Three types of subpoints occur regularly in expository messages. While these are not the only types of subpoints, the frequency of their use and misuse warrants examination.

Analytical-question responses support or develop a main point by answering an overarching question such as, How do we know this is true? or When should this apply in our lives? Preachers state a main point then ask aloud an analytical question about it that prompts the subpoints. Each subpoint then introduces discussion about the answer it supplies in a standard state-place-prove pattern.

Using Analytical-Question Responses as Subpoints

Main Point	*Because Jesus provides the only hope of salvation,* we must present Christ despite our difficulties.
Analytical Question	In what types of difficulties must we present Christ?

60. Paul Scott Wilson, *The Four Pages of the Sermon: A Guide to Biblical Preaching* (Nashville: Abingdon, 1999), 11–12.

Subpoints   1. In circumstantial difficulties
                            2. In relational difficulties
                            3. In spiritual difficulties

Interrogatives are subpoints initially worded as parallel questions that introduce answers containing a progression of thought. Each separate question (Who? What? When? How? How much? Why? etc.) stimulates an answer that further develops (or supports) the main point.

Interrogative Subpoints

Main Point   *Because Jesus provides the only hope of salvation,* we must
                 present Christ despite our difficulties.
Subpoints   1. What types of difficulties may we face? Christ's enemies
                 2. What helps us face these difficulties? Christ's armies

Interrogative subpoints greatly aid communication because they force a preacher to ask questions listeners would ask if they were analyzing the sermon out loud. As a result, the preacher thinks as parishioners do and produces a much more listener-friendly message.

Preachers who use interrogatives as subpoints should immediately supply an answer to an interrogative in a concise statement that summarizes the truth being established. In other words, they should place and prove a subpoint's answer. Occasionally, an answer to an interrogative can be delayed, but waiting until after the discussion of a subpoint to supply a clear answer can cause listener frustration with the preacher's apparent lack of resolution. In an aural environment, it is difficult to connect an answer to a question that appeared several sentences earlier unless the question is repeated.

The answers to the interrogative subpoints under a single main point are usually parallel in their wording so that their key terms (i.e., changed words) make the distinguishing concepts of the subpoints obvious. These key terms will also "rain" into the illustrations and applications for their development (see the discussion of "expositional rain" in chap. 7).

Bullet statements are the most common form of subpointing that is taught in pastoral training, though the best communicators instinctively and more frequently use variations on the interrogative forms. Bullet statements encapsulate divisions in the explanation of main points in short, crisp statements. These statements may be declarative sentences or sentence fragments that make sense on the basis of transitions and previous discussion.

Bullet Statement Subpoints

Main Point   *Because Jesus provides the only hope of salvation,* we must
                present Christ despite our difficulties.
Subpoints   1. In the midst of busy-ness
                2. In the face of fear
                3. In the storm of anger

Bullet statements underscore the importance of concisely worded subpoints.
If subpoints trail on, they detract from the thought of the main point rather
than develop it. A bullet subpoint works as a verbal hammer stroke that places
a conceptual peg on which listeners can hang additional information.

PERSPECTIVE

Subpoints divide the explanation of a main point into manageable thought
packets. Typically, they also provide the terms that will echo through that
main point's illustrative and applicational features. Since subpoint terminology
is so significant to the structure of a main point, preachers can help listeners by using terms that have been drawn from the biblical text (this applies
to the wording of main points also). Such construction allows listeners to
see in their own Bibles precisely where the preacher deduced the sermon's
thought. Still, using textual terms in subpoints is not so great an advantage
that preachers should use phrases of the text that do not readily express the
truth of the passage as the sermon is developing it. The text will naturally
be quoted as each point develops; thus, we need not worry that an outline
fails to be expository simply because it does not recite the text in the point
statements themselves.

Throughout this chapter, it has been assumed that subpoints *follow* a main
point. It is useful for preachers to train this way, but excellent communication
can occur when subpoints lead to a main-point conclusion rather than prove
a main-point premise. Much homiletical writing in recent years has revealed
the benefits of inductive preaching wherein particular ideas, illustrations, or
instructions lead to more general principles (Jesus' most typical approach), as
opposed to more traditional deductive sermons in which general statements
of principle begin each division of a message (Paul's common approach).[61]
Inductive approaches facilitate applicational responses, while deductive approaches facilitate argumentation. Each may have its place not only in different
sermons but also at different points in a specific sermon.[62]

One note of caution: Listeners need a thought peg to anchor a main
point's development at the outset of each division in a sermon. Almost
any particular will do: a principle statement that will be proven, a specific

61. Ralph L. Lewis, with Gregg Lewis, *Inductive Preaching: Helping People Listen* (Westchester, Ill.:
Crossway, 1983), 61–66. See also Chapell, *Using Illustrations to Preach with Power,* 26–32.
62. Greidanus, *Modern Preacher and the Ancient Text,* 184.

instruction that will be justified, or an illustration whose significance will unfold. In ordinary conversation, we sometimes say what must be done before we say why, or we give an analogy before we make a point. Similarly, in sermons, no canonical order exists for employing explanation, illustration, and application. However, main points should almost never begin with an explanation of grammar, history, or context before the presentation of a reason for the information: a specific main-point statement, an illustration, or a particular application. We do not want to be breezing along in a sermon while our listeners are questioning, "Why is the preacher telling us this?" Explanation needs obvious warrant that a particular will provide before we launch into discussion of "the origin of the pluperfect tense."

The Basic F-O-R-M

Although I have attempted to provide some perspective with which to conclude the discussion of each of these specific features of expository outlines, I recognize that the detailed instructions devoted to each can lead to a paint-by-the-numbers mind-set. This danger is so apparent that most homiletics books state only the general principles for sermon structure that were presented earlier in this chapter. All professors, experienced preachers, and students recognize that attempts to enforce one style of sermonizing is something akin to saying that all artists must paint like da Vinci or that all musicians must compose like Beethoven. The beauty, richness, and craft of noble expression cannot be confined to one form. Still, there are conventions—techniques, if you will allow such a term—that all must learn in order to master their craft. In the hands of experts, these techniques will ultimately become means to meld traditional practice and informed innovation into original masterpieces and even new techniques.

My hope is that students will learn to use the time-honored techniques of preaching that will allow them to prepare sermons with knowledge and confidence. I do not intend that these specific techniques will always rule sermons. In fact, I would be disappointed if this were the case. Rather, it is my prayer that students will become so well informed and experienced in the "tools of their trade" that they will be able to offer rich and powerful messages crafted according to their own insights, choices, and informed innovations as led by the Spirit of God.

Although the discipline needed to learn the tools of the trade may initially seem constraining, my intention is to free preachers from confusion, doubt, and ineffectiveness over never having been introduced to the tools needed for constructing expository sermons. George Sweazey offers compelling insights here:

A sermon that is intelligently planned toward a purpose is not a limitation but a liberation because it enables the preacher to do what he most wants to do. . . . Liberty is not looseness. A kite that is released from its tether gets its looseness, but loses its liberty to be a kite. A "free balloon" is the captive of every passing breeze. Jesus said that we discover real living not by wandering all over the map, but on the definite, narrow way. . . . A preacher does not find freedom by ignoring form and structure; these set him free to be a preacher. In the hours of working on a sermon, there is a kind of buoyancy in developing what is already outlined, but there is a wearisome feeling of heavy going in laboring out a sermon with no clear plan.[63]

In the classroom and in seminars around the country, I find that preachers have more questions about structure than they do about any other aspect of preaching. Candidly, I feel there are more important questions, but the frequency of these concerns indicates that the desire of homiletics instructors to give fair emphasis to the art of sermonizing has left many preachers adrift in a sea of structural possibilities. I have endeavored to be much more specific, recognizing that these standards are a starting point, not an end.

The bottom line for structure simply requires that all expository sermons have F-O-R-M. Every outline should be

*F*aithful to the text
*O*bvious from the text
*R*elated to a Fallen Condition Focus
*M*oving toward a climax

When preachers meet these criteria, sermons of many different shapes represent Scripture and strike the heart with precision and authority.

What about Those New Homiletic Forms?

Much that has been written on preaching innovation during the last twenty-five years has borrowed from the astute observations of speech theorists about how we receive and process communication. There is much to commend and learn from these innovations, but it is also important to understand the presuppositions and consequences of these methods.

Narrative Preaching Forms

People love stories. Narrative theologians and preachers have sought to capture the dynamics of story and convert them to a new homiletical method. Christ's own use of parables and the high concentration of narrative ma-

---

63. Sweazey, *Preaching the Good News,* 71.

terial throughout Scripture attest to the power and appropriateness of using the features of storytelling to communicate eternal truth.[64] We are greatly indebted to the homileticians who have dissected the natural structures and processes of narrative communication so that we can reproduce its features in sermons that are highly attractive in form to today's culture.[65]

Narrative Theory

One of the key observations that has driven narrative theory is that oral communication is not usually heard as "logical points" but rather as a flow of impressions that are built (or turned) through the various "moves" of language.[66] Word and image choices introduce a thought, cause it to be further considered by introducing a complication, and then draw a resolution that typically leads to the next thought (see fig. 6.1).

Figure 6.1

The "Moves" of Communication

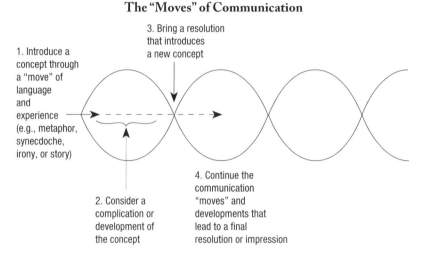

1. Introduce a concept through a "move" of language and experience (e.g., metaphor, synecdoche, irony, or story)

2. Consider a complication or development of the concept

3. Bring a resolution that introduces a new concept

4. Continue the communication "moves" and developments that lead to a final resolution or impression

Listeners interpret these moves not by dispassionately processing a line of logic along its various branches but rather by engaging these moves as a series of experiences that intersect with their previous and present life

---

64. Chapell, *Using Illustrations to Preach with Power,* 40–47.

65. Richard L. Eslinger, *A New Hearing: Living Options in Homiletic Method* (Nashville: Abingdon, 1987), 11–14; idem, *Narrative Imagination: Preaching the Worlds That Shape Us* (Minneapolis: Fortress, 1995), 141–74; Massey, *Designing the Sermon;* Henry H. Mitchell, *Celebration and Experience in Preaching* (Nashville: Abingdon, 1990); and Lucy Rose, "The Parameters of Narrative Preaching," in *Journeys toward Narrative Preaching,* ed. Wayne Bradley Robinson (New York: Pilgrim, 1990), 23–41.

66. Buttrick, *Homiletic,* 23–53. See in relation to the communication thought of Hayden White, *Topics of Discourse: Essays in Cultural Criticism* (Baltimore: Johns Hopkins University Press, 1978), 5, 72–80.

contexts. These experiences then become the new contexts that orient and explain later thought in the message. This analysis of the way most people perceive all oral communication, including sermons, advises preachers not to think of their sermons as debate speeches that wrestle listeners into submission with intricate and indisputable propositions of logic but rather as sequences of impressions that create an experience in which listeners come to understand truth on their own terms.[67]

Emphasis on the importance of personal experience in communicating meaning has naturally led speech theorists and homileticians to study how experiences can be shared in order to maximize communication. If we cannot all go out and walk in a field together to experience the flowers, then how can we know what it means to enjoy them? The answer, of course, is through narrative—re-creating the experience in a story. Based on the assumption that meaning is best communicated when we have shared views of an experience,[68] stories have become for some the primary means of making sure that the truth of a preacher is shared with (i.e., experienced by) listeners. Through a story, listeners are introduced to an experience, vicariously live through the events or impressions described, and take away shared impressions of its implications so that meaning is formed and held in community.

Narrative Methods

Wonderfully insightful and winsome methods of forming sermons based on story structures have resulted, and many books and articles have advocated story as the preeminent and most effective way of communicating meaning. Eugene Lowry's description of the "homiletical plot" remains one of the best-known and most helpful resources for pastors to discern what makes a story work and how to use its features in sermon construction.[69] A story, and a sermon that reflects its development, unfolds the personal meaning of an identified experience with these features: upset the equilibrium (oops!), analyze the discrepancy (ugh!), disclose the clue to resolution (aha!), experience the gospel (whee!), anticipate the consequences (yeah!).[70]

Not only do such structures naturally capture listener interest, but they also may naturally and powerfully reflect the development of the biblical narrative.[71] Virtually every expository preacher has felt the tension of trying

67. Craddock, *As One without Authority*, 57–63.

68. Alfred Schutz, *The Phenomenology of the Social World,* trans. George Walsh and Frederick Lehnert, Northwestern University Studies in Phenomenology and Existential Philosophy (Evanston, Ill.: Northwestern University Press, 1967), 97–138.

69. Lowry, *Homiletical Plot;* and idem, *The Sermon: Dancing the Edge of Mystery* (Nashville: Abingdon, 1997), 56–89.

70. In his later work, *The Sermon,* Lowry reduces the stages to four: conflict, complication, sudden shift, unfolding (81–84).

71. Calvin Miller, *Spirit, Word, and Story: A Philosophy of Preaching* (Dallas: Word, 1989), 139–83.

to squeeze the features of a biblical account into the mold of three points worded in propositional language. The truth of an account may be communicated much better when aspects of the sermon are devoted to giving listeners a realistic impression of what the biblical character was experiencing or what the complications of the event required of God's people. In such cases, narrative forms may reflect more accurately the actual form of the biblical account in relating its truth. Informed understanding of the techniques biblical writers used to construct narratives can help pastors better understand how to construct sermons accordingly.[72]

One form of narrative sermon reflects the parable structure of Jesus. A preacher tells a story, or retells a biblical story in contemporary terms, and then derives a moral or application from the account.

Parable Form
Story
↓
Moral

This approach has much biblical endorsement and great appeal to today's narrative-minded culture. The dangers of this approach include overdramatizing the account, creating truth principles from contemporary details added to aid the telling of the story but that do not have foundation in the text, and outright moralizing that uses the story simply as an allegory rather than as a dimension of God's redemptive plan or instruction.

A second form of narrative preaching involves a preacher using the details and development of a story in the text, a created story, or a series of stories to reveal biblical principles that apply to listeners. In this model, narrative details provide the experiential proofs of the principles that the preacher says Scripture teaches. The details may be redescribed, re-presented, or reflected in a parallel contemporary account so that listeners confirm in their experience of the narrative the truths the Bible communicates. Often the form of the sermon reflects the flow of the narrative. The sermon parallels the structure of the story as the preacher frames each stage (or move) of the story's explanation with questions or statements of principle that reflect the implication, complications, and resolution of the developing narrative situation (plot). Overall, the sermon functions inductively (leading listeners through experience to apparent mutual discovery of biblical truth with the preacher) instead of deductively (having the truth preannounced by the preacher and then proven to the listeners).

72. Robert Alter, *The Art of Biblical Narrative* (New York: Basic Books, 1981); Craig Blomberg, *Interpreting the Parables* (Downers Grove, Ill.: InterVarsity, 1990); Tremper Longman III, *Literary Approaches to Biblical Interpretation,* vol. 3, Foundations of Contemporary Interpretation (Grand Rapids: Zondervan, 1987); Leland Ryken, *Words of Delight: A Literary Introduction to the Bible* (Grand Rapids: Baker, 1987); and Meir Sternberg, *Poetics of Biblical Narrative: Ideological Literature and the Drama of Reading* (Bloomington: Indiana University Press, 1985).

Narrative Form

1. God's people always desire reward for their obedience.
   Plot situation re-presented or described: The disciples wanted privileged positions for their obedience to Jesus.
2. God's people often derive pain from their obedience.
   Plot complication re-presented or described: Jesus promised the disciples persecution for their faithfulness to him, not what they or we expect or desire.
3. God's people grasp the better realities of eternity only through the sometimes bitter realities of obedience.
   Plot resolution re-presented and applied: Jesus' disciples were made able witnesses on earth and more sure advocates of heaven by their obedient suffering.

   Truth Applied: The suffering of obedience loosens our grasp on this world in order to strengthen our grip on the better realities and unshakable joys of heaven.

Deductive sermons approach listeners through the front door by declaring the truth the preacher will prove "up front." Inductive/narrative sermons go through the side door, letting listeners experience the truth of the sermon alongside the preacher through their mutual experience, which is facilitated by narrative. Inductive/narrative sermons also occasionally approach listeners through the back door by keeping ultimate truth veiled until the sermon's final moments or by offering it as an ironic twist toward the end.[73] Narrative sermons can be expository as long as the truths they develop are provable in the text, developed from the text, and cover the scope of the text.

Narrative Cautions

The ability of such techniques to garner listener attention and appreciation cannot be denied, but the presuppositions of the approach require examination before the methods become the mainstay of any evangelical preacher. The philosophical ground from which modern narrative theory sprouts is that propositional truth is not transcendent or transferable.[74] Speech theorists fall back on the importance of shared experience because of their unwillingness to accept any authoritative propositions that are culturally transcendent or universally meaningful for persons from diverse life contexts. Such assumptions are simply not the perspective of the Bible.

73. "Door" analogy provided by homiletics colleague Roy Taylor (personal conversation, January 20, 2004).
74. For a fuller discussion of the philosophical soil from which narrative homiletics spring, see Chapell, *Using Illustrations to Preach with Power*, 177–86.

Scripture presents its truth in propositions as well as in narratives because of its presupposition that we are made in the image of God and are indwelt by his Spirit—the same Spirit that inspired his Word.[75] These truths do not deny cultural and personal hurdles for gospel meaning. Yet these are the very truths advanced by Scripture to show that such barriers can be overcome by the preaching of the Word in all its dimensions. Those made in the image of God already share a context by which to have a natural understanding of his world and his Word, and those indwelt by his Spirit have their minds renewed so that they can understand the spiritual truths of his Word and perceive their world accordingly (1 Cor. 2:9–13; 2 Cor. 2:14–17). Such understanding is not simply formed in community. It is formed in heaven but can be held in community by the body of believers, in whom Christ dwells by the Spirit, who makes him known (Eph. 1:22–23). The "genius of Scripture" is its use of narrative to give propositions culturally transcendent contexts while synergistically using propositions to give meaning to the narratives that are not merely existential but rather eternal.[76]

These spiritual truths do not disregard the power of story, but they do challenge the presumptions that would make its use exclusive or preeminent in preaching. It is possible to mine the riches of narrative without falling into the mineshafts of preaching that have abandoned trust in propositional truth. Much of what modern theorists have written about the techniques and the effects of storytelling may be fruitfully used by expository preachers in innovative sermons or in the illustrative features of traditional expositions (as explained in the next chapter).[77] In addition, as shown in the latter portions of this book, sermons that are Christ-centered inevitably have an implicit narrative structure that is attractive to this culture because our God always comes to the rescue.[78] Sermons that begin with a human interest account that exposes an FCF also have an implicit inductive structure in that they use an introductory experience to identify a human complication that the sermon must then resolve with gospel truth.

Preachers must not avoid all methods that are narrative, but they must avoid the assumption that listeners indwelt by God's Spirit are incapable of hearing the transcendent truths of his Word. Accepting such nonbiblical assumptions will cause preachers to substitute simple, moral allegories for the regular and careful explanation of the biblical truths that are the bread of life for those

75. Ibid., 186–89.

76. Ibid., 186–87.

77. Bruce C. Salmon, *Storytelling in Preaching* (Nashville: Broadman, 1988), 47–51. See also Chapell, *Using Illustrations to Preach with Power,* 28–31, 56–62.

78. Tim Keller makes this important observation in "Post-Everythings," *By Faith* 1, no. 1 (June/July 2003): 29–30. By contrast, the difficulty with so much narrative preaching is that a good story is followed by a simple (human) moral that is incapable of communicating the necessary involvement of the Savior in all that would truly please and serve God.

who believe. Thankfully, awareness of this reality is swinging the homiletics pendulum back to a greater emphasis on the exegesis and explanation of the text in this culture that is increasingly unfamiliar with the Bible.[79]

Mass Communication Models

Preachers who have been trained in an expository tradition are often perplexed by television and radio preaching. Somehow people who struggle to stay awake on a Sunday morning still appreciate listening to someone preach on a car radio.[80] What are the mass media preachers doing that addresses the short attention spans and immediate impact demands of a media-saturated modern culture?

Broadcast sermons may sound similar to traditional messages, but they often include structural variations that keep listener interest and involvement focused. Technology requirements and media pressures have forged aspects of a preaching model that typifies many mass communication sermons. Not every preacher faces these pressures directly, but all of us deal with the expectations indirectly, and there are lessons to learn from those whose ministries must deal with a mass audience. Close examination of a sermon prepared for mass communication indicates that its features are not actually as novel as are their organization and placement. Figure 6.2 shows how a main point develops in a traditional sermon as compared to a sermon modeled on mass communication principles.

Model Distinctions

The distinctions of a mass communication model are apparent in the comparison of its main-point structure with the main-point structure of a traditional expository model.

An expository model (also called an exegetical model) usually begins a main point with a statement of a biblical principle or instruction. Subpoints follow that prove or develop the main-point statement with exposition of Scripture. Each subpoint contains a paragraph or two of information, and therefore, the exposition of a main point is likely to take three to seven minutes. After explaining

79. Fred Craddock, "From Classroom to Pulpit," *Preaching Magazine* 18, no. 6 (May–June, 2003): 19–20. See also the fountain of new works aware of narrative insights but also committed to expository preaching: John Carrick, *The Imperative of Preaching: A Theology of Sacred Rhetoric* (Carlisle, Pa.: Banner of Truth, 2002); Al Mohler Jr. et al., *Feed My Sheep: A Passionate Plea for Preaching,* ed. John Kistler (Morgan, Pa.: Soli Deo Gloria Publications, 2002); Steven J. Lawson, *Famine in the Land: A Passionate Call for Expository Preaching* (Chicago: Moody, 2003); Ramesh Richard, *Preparing Expository Sermons* (Grand Rapids: Baker, 2001); Haddon Robinson and Torrey Robinson, *It's All How You Tell It: Preaching First-Person Expository Messages* (Grand Rapids: Baker, 2003); Jim Shaddix, *The Passion-Driven Sermon* (Nashville: Broadman & Holman, 2003); and York and Decker, *Preaching with Bold Assurance.*

80. For a fuller discussion of these structures, see Chapell, "Alternative Models," 117–31.

Figure 6.2

Traditional and Mass Communication Sermon Comparisons

Traditional Expository Model	**Mass Communication Model**
Statement of the main point	Statement of the main point
1. Subpoint	(Immediate proof, explanation,
2. Subpoint	or definition; 1–2 sentences)
3. Subpoint	
Illustration	Illustration
Application	Application
	Developed
	Particularized
	Qualified and explained
	Further tied to Scripture

and/or proving the truth of the main point, a preacher typically demonstrates that truth with an illustration. The illustration leads into application that, because of the time and energy expended in exposition, all too commonly simply reiterates a sentence or two of abstract principle developed earlier. Information is emphasized, application minimized, and relevance often sacrificed.

The mass communication model (also called an application model) attempts to maintain interest and communicate immediate relevance throughout its development. A main point begins with a statement of a biblical truth or a question of what someone should do in a particular situation. The preacher then offers an immediate proof, explanation, verse recitation, or definition that corroborates the principle being advocated. This corroboration typically occurs in one or two sentences and concludes the "explanation" of the main point. Expecting that listeners will not have the mental patience for lengthy explanations, the preacher quickly progresses to illustration.

An illustration in a communication model sermon is usually life situational with a strong taste of realism that suggests how the truth previously stated can be applied in everyday life. The dynamics that fuel narrative sermons also make such illustrations powerful communication tools within this model. Still, application is really the heartbeat of the mass communication model, dominating both its emphases and its proportions.

The applications that follow the illustration in a mass communication model seek to connect the message of the sermon directly to the lives of listeners. The terms used and the concepts developed thus far prepare listeners for specific instructions. The preacher presents applications with enough detail that listeners know what God requires in particular situations, and the preacher devotes enough time to the application so that important qualifications or limitations can be added. Vague generalities are not used. Whether listeners agree with the applications or not, there is no arguing that they are specific and concrete. Frequently, a preacher will quote additional Scripture verses or offer clarifying commentary during the application. In other words, the explanation details of a traditional expository sermon are woven into the application features of the mass communication model. Application is emphasized, illustrations are riveting, and explanation is simplified and integrated so as not to put off listeners.

Model Strengths and Weaknesses

Each of these models has important strengths. The exegetical focus of the expository model makes it a far better tool for explaining the intricacies of the epistles or other strongly didactic passages. This same advantage enables a preacher to explore the rich implications of small portions of Scripture and give adequate proof for theological principles that require complex development. The broad brush of the communication model enables a preacher to deal with general themes and group ideas without unnecessary complexity. This may actually help a preacher deal with larger portions of Scripture than the exegetical model typically allows and thus give listeners new insights into the way the Bible develops truth. Lengthy biblical narratives are often made plainer when a preacher distills truth rather than covers all the details of an account (which may run for chapters). Still, the real strength of the mass communication model is its devotion to interest and relevance through application. Listeners simply do not walk away from a sermon without knowing what the preacher says God expects. In an age in which profession of faith seems to have so little impact on the conduct of one's life, this advantage is no small contribution.

Each model also has obvious weaknesses. The most consistent criticism of the exegetical model is that its orientation to detail can make it boring. A preacher may belabor the instruction and lose people in unnecessary detail. Time for application can get swallowed up by explanation, and a preacher may feel self-satisfied with the sermon's exegesis even though the people still hunger to know what God's Word means for them today. The mass communication model also has vulnerabilities. The most obvious is that it may not adequately expound a text, and therefore, its application focus can degenerate into messages dominated by personal opinion, legalism, or error. The communication model may also create a listener appetite for milk rather than for meat, with a preacher's distaste for handling difficult subjects (with appropriate complexity) creating and maintaining a congregation of baby Christians.

Model Evaluation

In the 1970s, the overhead projector movement made its entry into the North American preaching world. Thousands of preachers gave projectors honored positions beside their pulpits with the expectation that this new technology would revolutionize the clarity and power of sermons. Within ten years the movement died because of studies regarding the strengths and weaknesses of the technology. Research indicated that such technologies are wonderful means of communicating information but are not effective in promoting persuasion.[81]

The most powerful means of addressing the mind *and* the heart remains the *ethos* of the speaker. To the extent that a technology takes focus away from the voice, character, and person of the preacher, the persuasiveness of the message is reduced.[82] Thus, researchers advised preachers to use projectors to present information but, when it was time for exhortation, to turn them off so that nothing distracted from the person of the preacher. Preachers soon discovered, however, that trying to determine what part of a sermon was not hortatory was usually fruitless, and overheads and transparencies disappeared from stages. This does not mean that overhead projectors, PowerPoint, and visual aids have no purpose for instruction. It does mean that their use must be evaluated according to their strengths and weaknesses.[83]

The same need to evaluate their use without denying appropriate usefulness applies to the various models for presenting sermonic material. Rather than trying to determine which of the models described above is "right" or "correct," preachers should assess what specific purpose a sermon, or even a single main point within a sermon, needs to achieve. Preachers should use the model that best serves the immediate sermonic task. Appropriate models may vary between sermons or even between divisions of a single sermon depending on the message's purpose, proportion, rhythm, focus, subject, and so on.

More important than defending or critiquing the strengths and weaknesses of a particular sermon model is understanding its underlying as-

81. Michael A. Eizenga, "One-Sided versus Two-Sided Messages: An Examination of Communication Theory with Application to the Preaching Context" (Ph.D. diss., Dallas Theological Seminary, 1983), 12–14; Lori Carrell, *The Great American Sermon Survey* (Wheaton: Mainstay Church Resources, 2000), 20–31, 223–27; and Gregory Edward Reynolds, *The Word Is Worth a Thousand Pictures: Preaching in the Electronic Age* (Eugene, Ore.: Wipf & Stock, 2001), 366–67.

82. This research retains significant implications for the use of video clips, audio recordings, and PowerPoint presentations in sermon presentations. See Don Sunukjian, "Weakened by Powerpoint, Strengthened by Connection," PreachingToday.com (March 12, 2003), http://www.preachingtoday.com/index.taf?_function=journal&_op+article&res=200301.22; and Reynolds, *Word Is Worth a Thousand Pictures,* 367–69, 401.

83. David Schuringa, "Hearing the Word in a Visual Age: A Practical Theological Consideration of Preaching within the Contemporary Urge to Visualization" (Ph.D. diss., Theologische Universiteit te Kampen, 1995), 221–32.

sumptions. Again, it may not be necessary to label these assumptions right or wrong. However, it is critical for preachers to determine when and why these assumptions apply in order to be well equipped for the full range of tasks involved in their calling.

Consistent practitioners of the expository model may consciously or unconsciously assume that complexity equals seriousness. Deep down they believe that the way they demonstrate seriousness about the Bible is by detailing its beautiful intricacies. Some ministers think they should speak with complexity even if the people do not want it because such preaching—like vegetables—is good for them. Contrasting with this attitude is the "plain and simple" conviction of mass communication model practitioners. They tire of the "head games" exegetes play. Communication-oriented preachers believe simple sincerity equals seriousness. Deep down they believe preachers cannot speak from the heart if they are on a "mind trip" into the exotica of exegesis. Plain truth plainly spoken is their passion.

Proponents of the expository model often assume that developing higher order truths demonstrates their commitment to orthodoxy. By using biblical proofs to back up statements of universal truth, these preachers believe they have laid the foundations for orthodox commitments in every sphere of life. Such traditional preachers expect properly articulated universal principles to trickle down to correct decision making in every situation. The communication model adherents may scoff at what they consider such stratospheric abstractions. They think high-blown doctrinal precepts really evidence an unwillingness to roll up one's sleeves and deal with the real issues of life. For mass communication preachers, applicability equals orthodoxy. For them, the particulars are what make sermons universal because the particulars connect sermons to the real dimensions of life.[84]

Of course, these assumptions as worded are stereotypical and stated more crassly than any informed preacher would want. Yet the absurdity of each position taken to its extreme underscores the need for every preacher to be sensitive to the task at hand when choosing a sermon model. The newer models are not wrong simply because they are new. The older models are not outdated simply because they are tradition-worn. Preachers are best equipped for a lifetime of leading God's people when they know the variety of tools available to help them construct messages faithful to his Word. Understanding the strengths, weaknesses, presuppositions, and assumptions of each sermon form will provide the Lord's servants with the best options for the occasions he provides.

Questions for Review and Discussion

1. Distinguish among topical, textual, and expository sermons.

84. Cf. Norman Neaves, "Preaching in Pastoral Perspective," in *Preaching the Story*, 108.

2. What are five general principles to observe in constructing homiletical outlines?
3. What two major components compose *formal* propositions and main points?
4. What are anchor clauses and magnet clauses?
5. What are advantages of using glow words in an outline?
6. Identify three main types of subpoints.
7. How does the structure of an expository outline require craft, and how does it reflect art?
8. What are the strengths and weaknesses of narrative and mass communication forms?

Exercises

1. Prepare an example of a formally worded main point in conditional form. Prepare an example of a formally worded main point in consequential form.
2. Create a formally worded homiletical outline of 2 Corinthians 6:14–7:1; 1 Thessalonians 4:13–18; or 2 Timothy 4:1–5.
3. Present the outline you created for exercise 2 above with the main points in a reduced form.
4. Perform a fundamental reduction on the following formal main points framed by Haddon Robinson[85] for Ephesians 1:4–14.
   I. We should praise God because he has elected us in Christ (Eph. 1:4–6).
   II. We should praise God because he has dealt with us according to his riches in grace (Eph. 1:5–12).
   III. We should praise God because he has sealed us with the Holy Spirit until we acquire full possession of our inheritance (Eph. 1:13–14).
5. Create formal main points for these informal main points that Jerry Vines[86] framed for Colossians 2:8–23.
   1. Intellectualism[87] (vv. 8–10)
   2. Ritualism (vv. 11–17)
   3. Mysticism (vv. 18–19)
   4. Legalism (vv. 20–23)

---

85. Robinson, *Biblical Preaching,* 129.
86. Vines, *Practical Guide to Sermon Preparation,* 121.
87. Note that this outline contains an interesting version of what Vines calls "back-door alliteration" (i.e., the end of the key words correspond rather than the opening consonant).

G O A L   O F   C H A P T E R   7

*To explain the why and the how of illustrating
expository sermons*

7

The Pattern of Illustration

Orientation and Definition

To this point we have chiefly examined the explanation component of expository preaching. After introducing the priorities and the parts of an expository sermon, we turned our attention to principles for choosing a text, interpreting what it says, explaining what it means, and organizing the explanation. To prepare for the next stage of sermon construction, we must return to a foundational understanding of what helps grant expository messages communicative power. Merely dispensing biblical information in the form of description, proof, or argument may fulfill academic requirements for preaching, but scriptural priorities demand more.

The most powerful sermons bring truth to life by demonstrating and applying textual truths. Traditional expository messages fulfill these obligations when they include illustration and application along with explanation in every main point. The relationships among these three components of exposition in a main point were represented with a double helix illustration in chapter 4. Although the components of exposition need not always follow this particular order, we will continue to use this depiction of the most common order (see fig. 7.1) as a means of highlighting important instructional principles. We now need to see how a sermon progresses through illustration.[1]

Preachers typically think of illustrations as brief anecdotes that accom-

1. For a more extensive discussion of this subject, see Bryan Chapell, *Using Illustrations to Preach with Power*, rev. ed. (Wheaton: Crossway, 2001), 89–128.

Figure 7.1

**Double Helix
Illustration Perspective**

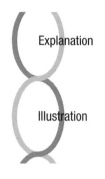

Explanation

Illustration

pany a sermon's propositional statements of truth.[2] More technically, illustrations are stories whose details (whether explicitly told or imaginatively elicited) allow listeners to identify with an experience that further elaborates, develops, and/or discloses the explanation of scriptural principles.[3] Through the details of a story, a listener imaginatively experiences a sermon's truths. An account does not have to be real or current, but a preacher must tell it in such a way that listeners can identify with the experience. A preacher tells the what, when, where, and why of an occurrence to give listeners personal access to the occasion. Each listener is enabled to see, feel, taste, or smell features of the event as though he or she were involved in the unfolding account. Along with sensory details, the preacher also suggests the emotions, thoughts, or reactions that might typify the experience of one living through the situation.[4]

These sensory and emotional descriptions create the "lived-body" details that distinguish true illustrations from figures of speech, allusions, or examples.[5] A quotation from an ancient sage or a statistic from a contemporary newspaper may add interest to a sermon, but neither has the descriptive characteristics of a full illustration.[6] With most quotations, allusions, and examples, a speaker *refers* to an account, whereas with an illustration, a preacher *invites* a listener into the experience. The lived-body details flesh out the illustration in such a way that listeners can vicariously enter the narrative world of the illustration. For example, with an allusion a preacher says, "This reminds me of . . ." With an illustration a preacher says, "I'll take you there. Live through this experience with me so that you will understand fully what this biblical truth means."[7] Whether an illustration is new to a

---

2. Ilion T. Jones, *Principles and Practice of Preaching* (New York: Abingdon, 1956), 141–42.

3. Because he so fears that the term *illustration* will be confused with lesser forms of illustrative material, Jay Adams eschews the use of the word entirely and opts instead for the word *story* as the term that most accurately communicates the essentials of sermonic illustration (*Preaching with Purpose: A Comprehensive Textbook on Biblical Preaching* [Grand Rapids: Baker, 1982], 90–91). J. Daniel Baumann uses the life-situation designation for illustrations that create immediate applications for contemporary life (see *An Introduction to Contemporary Preaching* [Grand Rapids: Baker, 1972], 250).

4. Adams, *Preaching with Purpose,* 86.

5. The "lived-body" terminology is that of Maurice Merleau-Ponty, whose *The Phenomenology of Perception,* trans. Colin Smith, with revisions by Forrest Williams (Atlantic Highlands, N.J.: Humanitas, 1981), xix, 122, 235–40, 274, 383, grants modern insight to the ancient illustrative practice of using the body's perceptions to further understanding.

6. Robert G. Rayburn, "The Discussion," personal lecture notes, 2.

7. See Chapell, *Using Illustrations to Preach with Power,* 20–21, where I construct an illustration hierarchy demonstrating how illustration may be distinguished from allusion, example, analogy, and

listener or can be conjured from memory, a preacher verbally re-creates a slice of life to explain a sermonic idea.

Why Illustrate

He did not want to offend me, but he wanted to be honest. He spoke with great hesitation because he did not want his emotions to get out of control, but it was obvious he felt deeply about what he wanted to say. "Dr. Chapell," he said, "I do not understand why you want us to put illustrations in our messages. I came to seminary to learn how to explain to people what the Bible means. I did not come here to learn how to tell anecdotes. How can we communicate to people the seriousnesss of the truth of God if we have to tell them silly little stories?" I appreciated the honesty of the question; I know other students feel the same way.

I know of no aspect of expository preaching that troubles preaching students and conscientious pastors more than illustration. We do not hesitate to offer explanations that require us to cite commentaries, grammars, and the church fathers, but illustrating a point with a story we concoct makes us question whether we are preachers or entertainers, pastors or babysitters. Students who are required to include illustrations in their messages complain of being forced to manipulate listeners. Pastors who have discovered the necessity of telling a story to keep a congregation listening shamefacedly confess the need of "little tales for little minds."

Such confusing, even conflicting, notions require us to reset our bearings and determine what preachers should include in expository sermons. The journey may begin with less concern, however, when we remember that through the history of preaching virtually every component of exposition has been challenged. The Huguenot reformers questioned whether consistent *explanation* was an improper addition to the pure Word of God and concentrated their services on simple Bible readings. Two generations ago, many seminaries were against *application* on the basis of a *solus spiritus* ethic. They believed that giving specific applications inhibited the work of the Holy Spirit alone in applying his truth individually. Though it has a rich heritage in biblical preaching, *illustration* also receives significant criticism in some traditional circles today because of innovative movements in our culture that seem to have elevated storytelling to a preeminent position in communication.

Few question the pragmatic benefits of using illustrations to keep listeners awake, yet many preachers consider the stories they tell to be a necessary

---

figures of speech based on the degree of lived-body detail in each. J. Daniel Baumann also offers a hierarchy, calling illustrations in simplest form ejaculatory examples, in slightly more complex forms figures of speech and analogy, and in the most artistic forms parable, historical allusion, and anecdotes (see Baumann, *Introduction to Contemporary Preaching,* 173–74).

evil that undermines the seriousness, scholarship, and spiritual integrity of their messages. Such equivocation cannot be tolerated where souls are at stake. We must decide whether illustrations are mere congregational pandering that godly preachers must avoid or have true value. History indicates that preachers have used sermon illustrations for more than two thousand years. Unless sermons degenerate into "just telling stories," people do not complain about illustrations and, in fact, often cite them as the portion of the message they appreciated the most.[8] Have many been so long misled, or are preachers who complain about having to illustrate too easily blinded by their academic interests and unable to see the human factors that are as essential to excellent preaching as propositional proofs?

I was not taught reasons for illustrating other than pragmatice concerns to maintain interest, and I have not always defended the use of illustration in expository messages.[9] But I discovered while pastoring that the mind yearns for and needs the concrete in order to anchor the abstract. This does not mean that illustration should be merely a cognitive crutch or a supplement to sound exposition. Rather, illustrations exegete Scripture in terms of the human condition, creating a whole-person understanding of God's Word. Illustrations are essential to effective exposition not merely because they easily stimulate interest but also because they expand and deepen understanding of a text.[10] Illustrations do not allow mere intellectual knowledge. By grounding biblical truths in situations that people recognize, illustrations unite biblical truth with experience and, in so doing, make the Word more accessible, understandable, and real in ways that propositional statements alone cannot.[11]

Preachers can misuse illustrations as much as they can misuse any aspect of preaching, but potential abuse should not preclude appropriate use. In

8. Byron Val Johnson, "A Media Selection Model for Use with a Homiletical Taxonomy" (Ph.D. diss., Southern Illinois University at Carbondale, 1982), 215; and "Of the Preaching of the Word," in *The Directory for the Public Worship of God,* produced by the Westminster Assembly with the Westminster Confession of Faith.

9. Chapell, *Using Illustrations to Preach with Power,* 11–14.

10. Ibid., 65–81.

11. Walter R. Fisher, "Narration as Human Communication Paradigm: The Case of Public Moral Argument," *Communication Monographs* 51 (1984): 488; and his subsequent article, "The Narrative Paradigm: An Elaboration," *Communication Monographs* 52 (1985): 347–67. Cf. Klaas Runia, "Experience in the Reformed Tradition," *Theological Forum of the Reformed Ecumenical Synod* 15, nos. 2, 3 (April 1987): 7–13. Runia places in proper perspective much of the contemporary secular thought, demonstrating how "experience does not precede the Word but rather follows after it." Encapsulating Calvin's thought, Runia explains, "Experience, however, is not the source of knowledge, in addition to Scripture. It is not an independent road to God, next to the revelation of Scripture." Experience "functions as a hermeneutical key for the understanding of Scripture," which, as Runia and the Reformers make quite clear, is not rooted in or limited by human experience. Objective truth transcends human subjectivity, but full understanding of the Word of God, when opened by the Holy Spirit, is still contextualized for reflection and obedience by the experiential. See also Chapell, *Using Illustrations to Preach with Power,* 49–63.

skilled hands, illustrations are among the most powerful preaching tools that preachers possess. To take full advantage of the power of this dynamic expository instrument, we must learn the functions it best serves and discern its misapplications.

Wrong Reasons to Illustrate

Preachers who illustrate primarily to entertain ultimately destroy the foundation of their messages. An entertainment ethic creates shallow congregations and hollow pulpits. People who attend such a church are implicitly taught that their own desires and sensations are to be the objects of their worship. Such people learn to evaluate the success of a sermon not by the conviction of spirit it brings but by the lightness of heart it offers. This shallow expectation is matched by the hollowness of purpose behind the pulpit: personal acclaim. Such preaching inevitably fails over time. Congregations realize that no one always entertains well. They grow to resent the manipulation of their emotions in a world in need of deep spiritual discernment. Though the dynamic may take years to unfold, ministries that compromise truth for appeal lose their allure.

Ministers who justify their use of illustration on the basis of their congregations' lack of intellectual acumen or spiritual sophistication will also face bitter realities. There are times to use illustrations to simplify or to clarify difficult truths, but preachers should not ordinarily preach in a way that cannot be understood without illustrations. If preachers use illustrations merely to spoon-feed the ignorant in the congregation, then they are either overcomplicating their messages or underestimating the intelligence of the congregation. Either alternative exposes an arrogant, patronizing attitude ill concealed by the pulpit and not long tolerated by most congregations.

Even proponents of illustrations sometimes imply—and may state directly[12]—that the purpose of illustration is to entertain or to spoon-feed. Yet if the primary purpose of illustration is not to keep people from nodding off or to explain what would otherwise be unclear, why does expository preaching require illustrations? To answer we must delve into the ancient history of preaching as well as explore the insights of modern communication researchers.

Right Reasons to Illustrate

THE CRISIS IN PREACHING

Widespread dissatisfaction with preaching has invaded our churches. The disenchantment began to surface almost a generation ago. Young and old alike

---

12. W. E. Sangster, *The Craft of Sermon Illustration* (London: Epworth, 1948), ix; and Chapell, *Using Illustrations to Preach with Power*, 25–26.

complained of preaching that was lost in abstraction and buried in jargon, incapable of forging a clear path for an age in the midst of unprecedented change. Thoughts too lofty to touch the realities of life aroused criticism the like of which American preachers had not endured since battles over slavery eroded public confidence in the pulpit. Preachers scrambled to find answers. Experts studied, surveyed, and assessed. Their conclusions were not always based on biblical priorities, nor were they pleasant to hear, but they defined well the perceptions of the contemporary mind. Clyde Reid surveyed religious professionals and presented their conclusions:

> 1) Preachers tend to use complex, archaic language which the average person does not understand; 2) most sermons today are dull, boring, and uninteresting; 3) most preaching today is irrelevant; 4) preaching today is not courageous preaching; 5) preaching does not communicate; 6) preaching does not lead to change in persons; 7) preaching has been overemphasized.

Reuel Howe spoke to laypeople and catalogued similar complaints:

> 1) sermons often contain too many complex ideas; 2) sermons have too much analysis and too little answer; 3) sermons are too formal and too impersonal; 4) sermons use too much theological jargon; 5) sermons are too propositional, not enough illustrations; 6) too many sermons simply reach a dead end and give no guidance to commitment and action.[13]

These surveys and similar studies triggered an explosion of works advocating novel approaches to preaching.[14] The proverbial baby and its bathwater were often flung out the back door together in a rush to develop new forms. Time will tell whether the "new homiletic" approaches will have enduring value.[15] What is now obvious is that few seem satisfied. The willingness of many to experiment with so important a spiritual task highlights how desperate many consider their situation to be. Both pulpit and pew echo the concern that too many sermons have no direct link to real life. To reconnect sermons with people, preachers must understand their situation.

---

13. Both Reid and Howe are quoted in Johnson, "Media Selection Model," 215. See also Edward F. Marquart, "Criticisms of Preaching," in *Quest for Better Preaching* (Minneapolis: Augsburg, 1985), 19–47. Three decades after the Reid and Howe studies, the situation appears little different. Cf. Lori Carrell, *The Great American Sermon Survey* (Wheaton: Mainstay Church Resources, 2000), 88, 94, 110, 115, 226.

14. Cf. Richard L. Eslinger, *A New Hearing: Living Options in Homiletic Method* (Nashville: Abingdon, 1987); and Chapell, *Using Illustrations to Preach with Power*, 27–32.

15. The "new homiletic" reflects much of modern literary and communication theory, which suggests that meaning is formed in the experience of a listener, and therefore, the obligation of a preacher is to create experiences (typically through stories) in a sermon rather than rely on the statements of propositions to convey biblical truth. See additional discussion in chap. 6.

The Currents of Culture

We are in the "age of visual literacy."[16] The average adult who spends fifty hours a year in a pew will also spend two thousand hours at home watching television. By the end of high school, the average American will have invested more hours in watching television (fifteen thousand hours) than in attending class (twelve thousand hours).[17] Some estimate that most children will spend more time watching television before entering school than listening to their father during their entire lifetime. These same children will have watched 350,000 commercials by the time they graduate from high school.[18] Add to this the influences of movies, video games, grocery packaging, and the Internet, and the conclusion is inescapable: "Ours is par excellence the Age of Illustration, an age when people are habituated to picture thinking."[19]

The average person in the pew does not depend on words alone for information. If the nation goes to war, anticipates election news, or craves information about a tragedy, printed words and expert analysts are not the primary informants. The modern mental palate lusts for visual images more than statistical analysis. Crowds in malls and airports gather around television monitors waiting for the slightest glimpse of news, while newspapers brimming with analyses lie in stacks at neighboring newsstands. All newspapers do not go unread. A few people depend primarily on newspapers or news magazines, and many more use printed sources to get additional details. But even newspaper publishers know that only 4 or 5 percent of their audience reads beyond the first paragraph of the average story and that readership triples or quadruples for a story bearing a picture (the caption being the most read paragraph of the entire account).[20] Audience interest and information consumption increase with sensory involvement even in these media.

Some believe these trends are the result of modern culture's audio-visual addictions. Video and audio media have become the sensory wallpaper of many Americans' daily existence. Electronic sights and sounds accompany every waking moment. Computer software companies and compact disc publishers bank on our need for sensory input by marketing interactive

16. Ralph L. Lewis, with Gregg Lewis, *Inductive Preaching: Helping People Listen* (Westchester, Ill.: Crossway, 1983), 10. See also David Schuringa, "Hearing the Word in a Visual Age: A Practical Theological Consideration of Preaching within the Contemporary Urge to Visualization" (Ph.D. diss., Theologische Universiteit te Kampen, 1995), 176–79.

17. David L. Larsen, *The Anatomy of Preaching: Identifying the Issues in Preaching Today* (Grand Rapids: Baker, 1989), 39.

18. Ibid., 133–34; and David L. Larsen, "Volume of TV Viewing . . . ," *MetroVoice* (April 1993): 4.

19. Ian MacPherson, *The Art of Illustrating Sermons* (Nashville: Abingdon, 1964), 39. See also Schuringa, "Hearing the Word in a Visual Age," 186–94.

20. *Principles of Advertising Design* (St. Louis: Delcom Seminars, 1978), 12, 35; and *How to Write Advertising Copy* (St. Louis: Delcom Seminars, 1978), 22.

learning and game programs everywhere we turn. Whether these trends are a result of recent cultural developments or the exploitation of more basic human thought processes remains to be seen. But there is no question that our culture trains us to reason and react experientially.[21]

Contemporary preachers must acknowledge these cultural challenges even if they are unsure how much to accommodate them. Although we should not too hastily abandon our rich preaching heritage, we must ask how we can best serve present needs.[22] Preaching practices that ignore the importance of experiential discovery indicate insensitivity to a typical parishioner's daily life and learning.

THE FOOTSTEPS OF GIANTS

Contemporary realities make the old preaching admonition to "turn the ear into the eye" more important than ever. Yet many preachers fear that by using multiple images in sermons they surrender to the vices and frailties of this age. A glimpse at the best preaching of all eras will put such fears to rest. With rare exceptions, the most valued preaching throughout history has consistently relied on the inner eye.

Had not the apostles punctuated their words with images of the full armor of God, the race course, living stones, olive trees, or walking in the light, we would strain to remember their instruction. Had not Jonathan Edwards dangled sinful spiders over a pit of flame, no one would know "Sinners in the Hands of an Angry God." If William Jennings Bryan had not decried, "You shall not crucify mankind upon a cross of gold," his political "sermon" would have been forgotten the next day. If Martin Luther King Jr. had not led us through a "dream" and onto a "mountaintop," would the march on Washington have been anything more than a ragged hike across a majestic mall?

Books have extolled the sensory appeals of Charles Spurgeon, the images of Peter Marshall, the characterizations of Clovis Chappell, and the human dramas of Harry Emerson Fosdick. None of these men, of widely varying theological perspectives, preached in a time dominated by visual electronics, yet they dressed their sermons in strong illustrative images—with powerful results. Prior to this "age of visual literacy," these preaching giants tapped something deep and fundamental in the human understanding. We are just beginning to discover what this fundamental something is.

21. Neil Postman, *Amusing Ourselves to Death: Public Discourse in the Age of Show Business* (New York: Viking, 1985), 79–80.

22. James J. Murphy, *Medieval Rhetoric: A Select Bibliography* (Toronto: University of Toronto Press, 1971), 18; see also idem, *Rhetoric in the Middle Ages: A History of Rhetorical Theory from Saint Augustine to the Renaissance* (Berkeley: University of California Press, 1974).

THE PATH TO PERCEPTION

Our generation is witnessing a revolution in thought about the way people understand themselves and their world. Three centuries of relative consensus based on the Cartesian philosophical model of "I think, therefore I am" is being turned upside down. The contemporary model reacts to the purely rationalistic/cognitive model of the past and declares, "I am, therefore I think," or, more specifically, "I can, therefore I am."[23] Abstract thought is no longer seen as the ground of our concept of who we are and our place in the world. Rather, according to some, our interaction with the world gives us our sense of being.[24] Our circumstances, the experiences that affect our physical beings, and situations that stimulate mental activity and emotive responses are the factors, theorists say, that create comprehension.[25] While such theories cannot fully explain spiritual understanding, they do help express how we ordinarily make sense of the world.

The need to promote understanding through experience echoes through the communication disciplines in an array of catch phrases. Advocates say we communicate best when we couch ideas in "human interest accounts,"[26] "life situations,"[27] "life stories,"[28] "experience-centered messages,"[29] "narra-

23. According to Jacques Derrida, as explained in Fisher, "Narrative Paradigm," 351, meaning is a matter of use rather than reference to people and things in the world. The notion is driven home with consideration of Maurice Merleau-Ponty's seminal work on the role of the body in perception that assaults compartmentalized theories of mental versus sensory perception and argues instead that the body itself is a primary structure of consciousness inseparable from mental perception (Merleau-Ponty, *Phenomenology of Perception*, 174, 235, 383).

24. Amadeo Giorgi, "The Body: Focal Point of Twentieth-Century Cultural Contradictions," *South Africa Journal of Psychology* 13, no. 2 (1983): 140; and Esther Lightcap Meek, *Longing to Know: The Philosophy of Knowledge for Ordinary People* (Grand Rapids: Brazos, 2003), 48–50.

25. Merleau-Ponty, in *Phenomenology of Perception*, writes, "We are not, then reducing the significance of the word, or even of the precept, to a collection of 'bodily sensations' but we are saying that the body, insofar as it has 'behavioral patterns,' is that strange object which uses its own parts as a general system of symbols for the world, and through which we can consequently 'be at home in' that world, 'understand' it and find significance in it" (237).

26. The standard journalistic definition of human-interest accounts is that they are stories in which persons recognize sensations or situations they have experienced or could experience. Such accounts picture ordinary or extraordinary persons in ordinary or extraordinary situations that evoke common sensations, emotions, or thoughts with which ordinary people can identify.

27. Lloyd M. Perry and Charles M. Sell provide an excellent discussion of the preachers and authors who use "life-situation" terminology in their book, *Speaking to Life's Problems* (Chicago: Moody, 1983), 15–18.

28. Edmund A. Steimle, Morris J. Niedenthal, and Charles Rice, eds., *Preaching the Story* (Philadelphia: Fortress, 1980), 12. See also Rolf von Eckartsberg, "The Eco-Psychology of Personal Culture Building: An Existential Hermeneutic Approach," in *Duquesne Studies in Phenomenological Psychology,* ed. Amadeo Giorgi, Richard Knowles, and David L. Smith III (Atlantic Highlands, N.J.: Humanitas/Duquesne University Press, 1979), 233.

29. Lewis, *Inductive Preaching*, 41.

tive paradigms,"[30] "firsthand encounters,"[31] "piece-of-life illustrations,"[32] "lived-body experiences,"[33] "identifiable accounts,"[34] and even in "a story that participates in the stories of those who have lived, who live now, and who will live in the future."[35] The variety of terms grants rich expression to the power of personal experience.

We understand most fully what is real to us. Even the formal expositor Jay Adams argued that it is only when a truth touches us experientially or when we sense the impact it could have on us that we can comprehend it fully.[36] Well-known preacher Steve Brown asserts even more boldly, "If you can't illustrate it, it's not true. We forget that doctrine isn't for doctrine's sake and theological propositions are not for theological propositions' sake. Those [illustrations] are ways by which we communicate the reality that we've discovered and that reality's a time-space thing."[37] Illustrations, of course, do not make biblical concepts propositionally true, but they do explain those concepts in the terms of experience that make what the Bible teaches true (i.e., knowable) for our living reality.

The union of knowing and doing—of understanding and experience—has strengthened over time. In the early 1950s, Edgar Dale demonstrated that learning occurs most effectively through direct, purposeful involvement. Teachers trained in the 1960s pondered the implications of a "learning pyramid" that showed that we learn 10 percent of what we hear, 30 percent of what we see, but 60 percent of what we do. In the 1970s, researchers ranked types of experiences that most effectively teach and in doing so discovered that people learn as much from "fully described" experiences as they do from actual experiences.[38]

By the 1980s and 1990s, these discoveries were affecting every segment of culture. Today, distaste for words divorced from experience typifies the contemporary intellect. More and more, schools are turning from lecture- to involved-learning because studies indicate that 70 percent of students of

30. Fisher, "Narration as Human Communication Paradigm," 488. See also Fisher, "Narrative Paradigm," 347–67.

31. Webb B. Garrison, *Creative Imagination in Preaching* (Nashville: Abingdon, 1960), 95–96.

32. Louis Paul Lehman, *Put a Door on It* (Grand Rapids: Kregel, 1975), 27.

33. Merleau-Ponty, *Phenomenology of Perception*, 274, 235–38, 383.

34. In various terms reflected in Kenneth Burke, *A Rhetoric of Motives* (Berkeley: University of California Press, 1969), 55; Craig Brian Larson, *Preaching That Connects: Using the Techniques of Journalists to Add Impact to Your Sermons* (Grand Rapids: Zondervan, 1994), 37–42, 72–79; Craig A. Loscalzo, *Preaching Sermons That Connect: Effective Communication through Identification* (Downers Grove, Ill.: InterVarsity, 1992), 15–24; and Calvin Miller, *Marketplace Preaching: How to Return the Sermon to Where It Belongs* (Grand Rapids: Baker, 1995), 13–31.

35. Fisher, "Narration as Human Communication Paradigm," 6.

36. Adams, *Preaching with Purpose*, 86. See also Marquart, *Quest for Better Preaching*, 74.

37. Interview with Steve Brown, *Preaching* 8, no. 3 (November/December 1992): 4.

38. Johnson, "Media Selection Model," 197.

all ages are not analytic learners. Eight or nine out of every ten junior-high students engage in problem solving without linear reasoning. Six out of ten high-school students learn better through exposure to concrete experiences than through abstract thought.[39] The case-study method, once typical only of law schools, now dominates many forms of professional training. Business professionals expect the weekend seminars they attend to involve them in the examination of numerous case studies, whether they are being taught how to sell tax-free bonds or negotiate a labor contract. Back at the office on Monday, these same professionals will instinctively evaluate the success of the seminar based on how realistic and down-to-earth the sample situations were. The accrediting agencies of our nation's major colleges and universities provide funding for training veteran teachers in all major disciplines to teach using case-study methods. The message is clear: Involve listeners or they will not learn. Preachers must hear this message, not because it is new but because the new research that drives it confirms the wisdom of centuries of preaching with an expositional component.

The Guidance of Scripture

Listeners who experience concepts—even vicariously—actually learn more than those who consider words and ideas in the abstract. What preachers have known instinctively for generations has a solid, scientific foundation: Meaningful thought flourishes when tied to reality.[40] This discovery discloses the hidden value of illustrations. Listeners understand more deeply and more broadly when preachers connect biblical truths to identifiable experiences. Scripture itself guides them to this understanding.

Although the gospel is logical, it is also spiritual, visceral, and impressionistic. The Word itself calls us to worship with our hearts and our souls as well as with our minds (Deut. 6:5; Matt. 22:37). For this reason, illustrations that involve the whole person in the understanding process operate in a manner consistent with the biblical concept of our complex nature. Wayne Oates, professor of behavioral psychology at the University of Louisville School of Medicine, writes:

> The Hebrew-Christian understanding of personality is a holistic one. Jesus states the commandment which is "first of all": "Hear, O Israel, the LORD our God, the LORD is one; and you shall love the LORD your God with all your heart, and with all your soul, and with all your strength." The Greek word, "*holes*," is translated "all" and is repeated four times [in the passage]. My approach to understanding the human personality is to emphasize the oneness and totality rather than the division of personality into separate "faculties." When a person loves with all his or her mind, the whole being is involved,

---

39. Lewis, *Inductive Preaching*, 10.
40. Merleau-Ponty, *Phenomenology of Perception*, 235.

not just one part of the personality. Therefore, when you and I preach to the emotional needs of our audience, we are addressing them as total beings and not just as a "bundle of feelings."[41]

Far from being unethical or unintellectual techniques, illustrations that engage the whole person in the experience of knowing by touching the heart and/or eliciting its responses are powerful, biblical instruments of learning and motivation. Because the Bible teaches that we are more than beings of pure mind, the best preaching never relies on intellectual appeals alone. If holiness were a matter only of mental agility, then computers would be sacred.

This analysis admonishes preachers not to consider illustrations an inane frill of popular preaching but the inherent fabric of effective preaching. Illustrations do more than adorn thought or clarify what is difficult to understand. Because life experiences inform our souls, our psyches, and our thoughts, citations of such experiences function as basic tools of communication. Illustrations persuade, stimulate involvement, touch the heart, stir the will, and result in decisions. *Thus, the primary purpose of illustration is not to clarify but to motivate.* Preachers who fail to understand this will assume that when the point they are making is clear, they do not need an illustration. Preachers who grasp the true power and purposes of illustration know that the most clear points often deserve the best illustrations to make the truth as significant to the hearer as it is in Scripture.

When preachers ignore illustration, which can serve as a real-life intermediary to help interpret and empower their words, then they speak without the most efficient or managed effect. Communication of some sort will still occur, but to understand, listeners will translate words they hear using their own experiences—which may lead them down errant paths. Preacher-chosen experiential accounts are more likely to provide the interpretive contexts and the biblical direction the preacher and Scripture intend. The great preachers of our age know this. Billy Graham, Steve Brown, Charles Stanley, Chuck Colson, R. C. Sproul, John MacArthur, Tim Keller, D. James Kennedy, John R. W. Stott, Chuck Swindoll, and Rick Warren all know how to touch the heart with illustrations that spark biblical responses. Although they know that emotions that operate apart from considered thought are dangerous, these respected preachers also know that rationality without human contexts such as love, gratitude, grief, and even holy rage can be the antithesis of godliness.

The Way of the Master

If the Bible itself does not endorse the use of illustration in expository preaching, then heeding cultural currents, human precedents, learning theo-

---

41. Wayne Oates, "Preaching to Emotional Needs," *Preaching* 1, no. 5 (1985): 6.

rists, or motivational guidance may still seem to be only a capitulation to the wisdom of the age. Though the Bible is not intended to be a homiletics textbook, it indicates valid tools for communication that we should consider valuable for preaching. We do not have to guess whether Scripture validates illustrative communication. The Bible says of Jesus, "He did not say anything to them without using a parable" (Mark 4:34).[42] Relating truth through illustrative narratives, parables, allegories, and images was Jesus' method of communicating. His was not an age of visual literacy (at least in terms of modern technologies and media), yet illustrative materials pervaded his expressions. If in Christ's time illustrations were necessary, how much more, given contemporary influences, must today's preachers weigh the need for illustrative content.

Christ actually followed a long-established pattern. First there was the pre-Christian rabbinic tradition in the form of Haggadah (the way of story, as opposed to Halakah, the way of reasoned reflection on the law).[43] In addition, the Scriptures themselves are replete with symbols, images, and narratives that are the regular instruments of the communication of religious truths. Alister McGrath summarizes this point emphatically: "*Narrative is the main literary type found in Scripture.*"[44] "Remove the narrative content from Scripture and only fragments remain,"[45] says Ralph Lewis. Henry Grady Davis states that this does not mean that propositional truths are not presented but that their proportion is diminutive compared to the experiential descriptions and narratives in the rest of the canon.[46]

The Spirit that inspires Scripture reinforces the conclusion that people tend to seize images more readily than they do propositions, and if they take hold of enough images, they can grasp apt principles.[47] Of course, propositional summary and explanation must still accompany the illustrative material, but the pattern of the Bible is to prepare, clarify, and epitomize truth through illustration, characterization, and example. The tree of life and the tree of the knowledge of good and evil symbolize the Adamic covenant (Gen. 2).[48] God pledged the Noahic covenant with the visual token

42. Note that the passage goes on to indicate that until explanation accompanied the parable, its truth remained unclear. Illustrations alone will not illuminate biblical truth. The genius of Scripture is its linkage of illustration and proposition in which both components of exposition expose and reinforce the truths of the other.

43. Beldon C. Lane, "Rabbinical Stories: A Primer on Theological Method," *Christian Century* 98 (December 1981): 1306.

44. Alister E. McGrath, "The Biography of God," *Christianity Today* (July 22, 1991): 23.

45. Ralph Lewis, "The Triple Brain Test of a Sermon," *Preaching* 1, no. 2 (1985): 10.

46. Henry Grady Davis, *Design for Preaching* (Philadelphia: Fortress, 1958), 157.

47. MacPherson, *Art of Illustrating Sermons*, 40.

48. Note that these symbols are the shorthand of broader narratives. Jay Adams wisely notes that stories and story particles both represent illustrative tools preachers may biblically employ (*Preaching with Purpose*, 90–91).

of the rainbow (Gen. 9). He sealed the Abrahamic covenant with both a traditional contractual ceremony (Gen. 15) and a foreshadowing sign of blood (Gen. 17). The Lord established the Mosaic covenant in signs and symbolic wonders (e.g., the burning bush, the staff turned into a serpent, water turned to blood, and the Red Sea parted), maintained it in symbol and ceremony (e.g., the ark of the covenant, the scapegoat, the Paschal lamb, the temple economy, the phylacteries and feasts), and characterized its truths in symbol-laden narratives (e.g., the provision of manna, the brazen serpent, wandering in the wilderness, and entry into Canaan).

The Old Testament history books are just what their designation indicates—narrative upon narrative that illuminates God's redemptive plan by characterizing his work among his covenant people. There is little propositionally stated systematic theology in the accounts of Joshua, Gideon, Samson, Samuel, Saul, and David. Instead, there is an unfolding pattern of God's dealings with humankind through the events that lead to the establishment of the Davidic covenant and Israel's subsequent history as it initially responds, then rebels, and finally is restored. In all its details and personalities, the Bible illuminates the central truth, "The LORD, the LORD, the compassionate and gracious God, slow to anger, abounding in love and faithfulness, maintaining love to thousands, and forgiving wickedness, rebellion and sin. Yet he does not leave the guilty unpunished" (Exod. 34:6–7). The proposition is infrequently stated in full form, but its truths are clearly explicated, easily understood, long remembered, and readily applied because of the stories that illustrate its essence.

Biblical truths often find their most profound expression in the Hebrew books of poetry. These wisdom books do not ordinarily contain formal narratives (Job is a notable exception) but by their very nature employ metaphor, symbol, and image to bring experiences to mind that touch the heart deeply. Although the prophetic books contain high propositional content, their use of illustrative material remains significant. In Jeremiah 13, God commands the prophet to hide a linen belt and to retrieve it after many days. When Jeremiah retrieves the belt, it is ruined. The Lord says, "In the same way I will ruin the pride of Judah and the great pride of Jerusalem" (v. 9). In Ezekiel 12, the Lord tells the prophet to pack up his belongings in open view of the people of Israel in order to warn them that they will be forced to pack for exile if they do not repent. "Perhaps they will understand, though they are a rebellious house" (v. 3), says the Lord.

Similar episodes appear in the Minor Prophets. God requires Hosea to keep forgiving and receiving his wife, Gomer, though she turns to adultery with others. The Lord says, "Love her as the LORD loves the Israelites, though they turn to other gods" (Hosea 3:1). On a contrasting note, God shows the prophet Amos a basket of ripe fruit because, "The time is ripe for my people Israel; I will spare them no longer" (Amos 8:2). The examples of illustrated truth as well as stated truth are too numerous to mention individually. Suffice it to say that in all the prophetic books, as throughout the Old Testament, the use of illustrative tools remains consistent and is comprehensive. In *The Anatomy of Preaching,* David Larsen summarizes the evidence: "75 percent of the Old Testament is narrative. What an explosive element for contemporary preaching."[49]

The New Testament does not abandon the Old Testament communication principles, as is clearly evident in the Gospels. A. M. Hunter says that the parabolic element in Luke's Gospel amounts to 52 percent of the total.[50] Ian Macpherson estimates that in the whole of Jesus' recorded teachings the illustrative ratio is actually more on the order of 75 percent.[51] The actual words of Jesus comprise 20 percent of the New Testament (the rough equivalent of twelve thirty-minute sermons).[52] This means that a hefty portion of the Gospels is illustrative and that the Lord's own preaching methods and priorities leaned to the illustrative.

Ralph Lewis argues that it took three centuries for the church to abandon Christ's pattern of teaching and institutionalize the homiletical style of "universal abstractions" and "hortatory accent with fewer examples."[53] Even highly doctrine-oriented Paul sprinkled his epistolary messages with allusions to the narrative history of Israel, the arena, the sports field, the military, the marketplace, the temple, the home, and the school.[54] David Calhoun suggests that the chief differences among the four Pauline sermons to unbelievers in the Book of Acts are the allusions Paul chose in relation to the four cultures of those audiences.[55]

The biblical picture of illustration is not complete, of course, without reference to the incarnate Word as embodied truth. In a very real sense, our knowledge and perceptions of God are a product of that most explicit illustration of his nature—Jesus Christ. The glory of God, who cannot be seen, was revealed in the Son, who "made known"[56] the Father (cf. John 1:14, 18). According to A. T. Robertson, the wording translated "made known" traditionally means "to draw out in narrative."[57] In other words, the stories of Christ actually serve to illustrate the heavenly Father. Our comprehension of

49. Larsen, *Anatomy of Preaching,* 90.

50. As cited in MacPherson, *Art of Illustrating Sermons,* 40.

51. Ibid., 40; Larsen put the proportion at 35 percent (154). No doubt varying definitions of "parable" skew the figures, but never so far as to deny the significance of illustrative content in Christ's messages.

52. Lewis, "Triple Brain Test," 11.

53. Ibid.

54. Thomas V. Liske, *Effective Preaching,* 2nd ed. (New York: Macmillan, 1960), 185.

55. David Calhoun, professor of church history at Covenant Theological Seminary (personal conversation, St. Louis, April 24, 1986).

56. First aorist (effective) middle indicative of *exegeomai.*

57. A. T. Robertson, *Word Pictures in the New Testament* (Nashville: Broadman, 1932), 18.

the spiritual involves the interaction of propositions and illustrations. With God's own Word as the endorsement and example, today's preachers have ample warrant to use illustrations for spiritual communication.

How to Illustrate

With the rest of the nation I listened for the reports of the rescuers' progress as they fought rock, equipment failure, and time to rescue eighteen-month-old Jessica McClure from a well shaft in Midland, Texas. Left alone for a few minutes in her aunt's backyard on a bright October day, the little girl had playfully dangled her feet over an innocent-appearing, eight-inch opening in the ground. When she tried to stand up, she fell into the darkness. With one leg up and the other down, Jessica was wedged in the narrow shaft above the water but twenty-two feet below the ground. Rescuers drilled a twenty-nine-foot vertical shaft parallel to the well and then bored a five-foot-long horizontal tunnel through solid rock to reach her. It took far more time than any had anticipated—fifty-eight hours. Medical personnel grew increasingly alarmed and warned that dehydration and shock were becoming greater dangers than the entrapment itself. Finally, rescuers reached Jessica, but they could not pull her out. The way her body was wedged in the shaft foiled their efforts. The health technicians conferred, checked the little girl's vital signs one more time, and then gave these awful orders: "Pull hard! She does not have more time. You may have to break her to save her."

When the rescuers pulled the last time, Jessica came free without additional injury. But when I heard the instructions of the medical technicians to the rescuers, I could not help but relate them to a sermon I was writing. I was explaining how God so desires the salvation of his children that he will even allow them to experience hurt that will convince them of their need of him. As cruel as this providence may seem, it actually expresses a great love because God, who knows that no one's hours on this earth are unlimited, is willing to break us to save us. I believed deeply in what I was saying, but I recognized that the words seemed hollow—dry doctrine that might communicate an uncaring attitude for those who were experiencing such trials or for those with unsaved loved ones who might have to experience the same.

Take a Slice out of Life

The events in Midland came to my rescue. By isolating those events and relating key aspects to the truths I needed to communicate, I was able to tie a biblical principle to an experience that not only reflected real-life truth but also allowed me to demonstrate doctrine in a context of compassion true to God's priorities. Even a snatch of a conversation from an event lasting many days can be the catalyst of a process that is always the first step in the craft of illustrating. Preachers isolate an aspect of an event, conversation, perception, or relationship and associate it with a principle, concept, or proposition they wish to relate. In this way, they provide an experience through which listeners are able to contextualize and interpret their thinking. An illustration thus becomes a snapshot from life. It captures a mood, a moment, or a memory in a narrative frame and displays that slice of life for the mind to see and the heart to know.

The process of isolation and association does not require a particular order. Sometimes preachers see in an experience something that reminds them of an associated concept (a child being rescued from a well's darkness reminded me of how God saves souls from sin's darkness). They may then file that isolated event (in memory or a catalog system) until they preach on a passage whose explanation will benefit by such an association. Other times they first formulate a concept or a proposition and then try to isolate an associated experience that enables them to show others what they mean.

A preacher who wants to use illustrations well must cultivate the ability to isolate and associate experiences. To do this a preacher must learn to see everything as a passing parade of potential illustrations—every event, face, feature, and fantasy holds illustrative promise. A preacher is much like a photojournalist, constantly framing one moment, one event, one sequence after another to find what best communicates the truths of existence. By doing this, what looks common to the ordinary eye becomes significant. Preachers should continually take those snapshots of life's grandeur and simplicity so as to relate both to the consistently awesome nature of God and to the too frequent tedium of their listeners' experience.

Nothing of life goes by us without notice. Preachers who illustrate well do not wait passively for the world to offer them something significant to note. Rather, they steal from the world the treasures others do not notice or do not have the opportunity to display. There is beauty in an oil slick, irony in a detergent ad, pageantry in a barn lot, and grief in an abandoned railroad track if a preacher will but see it. The psalmist saw in the nests of swallows his own heart's longing to be near the Lord (Ps. 84:3), and Jesus recognized faith in a mustard seed (Matt. 17:20). You too can see as much and show as much if you are committed to relating truth through the experiences that enable people to see beyond textbook propositions.

By showing truths in terms of experience with the world, preachers not only enable others to comprehend theological principles but also accustom them to seeing their world in a spiritual frame. These comments highlight the preeminent value of human-interest accounts, that is, life-situation illustrations.[58] D. W. Cleverley Ford writes:

---

58. Baumann, *Introduction to Contemporary Preaching*, 175.

Admittedly, to quote from Dante, Dumas, Dostoievsky, and Dickens is impressive, but ... what a congregation will most readily hear is references by the preacher to objects, events, and people's comments which he has seen and heard himself *in the recent past in the locality*. An illustration drawn from the derelict house in the next street, the aftermath of a recent storm, a local flower show, a current play at the theatre, is the kind that is most serviceable.[59]

This is not to devalue the use of historical examples, fictional allusions, parables, fables, allegories, and other forms of illustration but to suggest that these, too, are used most effectively when they are infused with descriptions of familiar emotions, identifiable dilemmas, known traits, or common situations to which listeners can immediately relate.[60]

If a historical event is used for illustration, it should be presented as a slice of life with enough description of setting, drama, and characters that today's listeners can find themselves in that event. If you must refer to the Spanish Armada, take care to capture the event in identifiable description. Isolate its human features. Let the listeners see the cannons flash, feel the storm, and fear the shoals. No parishioner wants to endure another fourth-grade lecture on the history of England and Spain, hoping it may mean something now, even though it never did before. Meaning occurs when an account is made real (i.e., related) to listeners' experience.

Tell a Story

To present illustrations well, preachers need to learn the storytelling principles of the masters. While no set formula exists for presentation, by its very nature an illustration is a slice of life and has an implied beginning and end, background and development, and a point to make. In short, an illustration is a story.[61] Many of the components of a story may be implied rather than stated or assumed rather than articulated. Jay Adams says that sermon illustrations appear in a variety of forms, from fully fleshed-out narratives to mere kernels of stories, but he insists that these "stories" are what appeal to the senses and involve the audience.[62] Thus, we can agree with Dawson C. Bryan, who wrote decades earlier, "Practically every illustration should be as technically perfect in form as a short story." He was not merely advocating conscientious preparation but indicating the essential form that

59. D. W. Cleverley Ford, *The Ministry of the Word* (Grand Rapids: Eerdmans, 1979), 204.

60. This advice also mitigates against the too common tendency to use old preachers' tales, tired illustrations from steam-locomotive days, and anecdotes clipped from the latest illustration catalog that have not been revised to reflect the immediate situation of persons present. Cf. Lehman, *Put a Door on It*, 27.

61. Adams, *Preaching with Purpose*, 90.

62. Ibid., 90–91.

illustrations should take.[63] Good illustrations take a story form. An illustration usually has an introduction, descriptive details, movement through crisis (i.e., creating suspense that leads to a climax), and a conclusion.[64]

INTRODUCE CREATIVELY

The too frequent form of illustrative introduction is the lame and the unimaginative "Let me illustrate . . ." Bryan provides variations on this theme, including, "Here we have an even more striking illustration of such spiritual understanding . . . ," "Perhaps you will get this distinction best by a single illustration adapted from . . . ," or "Here is a roadside experience taken from the paper which gives vividness to what I mean."[65] Instead of involving listeners, such beginnings seem to put a wall between the illustration and the truth it is supposed to illustrate. Of course, even these bearded techniques occasionally prove to be useful or necessary, but they should be used sparingly if a preacher really intends to involve listeners in a message's thought. The old maxim is still true most of the time: Don't talk about illustrating; just illustrate. "Congregations can recognize illustrations without being told what they are."[66]

Transition statements announcing an illustration may be necessary for readers, but they seem superfluous to listeners when the manner of a preacher should indicate that an illustration is coming. In a very real sense, an illustration is a demonstrative parenthesis coming before or after a passage of formal explanation. As such, illustrations are a change in the flow of things—not so much a break in the action as a shifting of gears. An unobtrusive yet effective way to introduce an illustration is simply to pause. Briefly put in the clutch, as it were, to prepare for the gear shift.[67]

Next, a preacher slices out the context of an illustration. Say when or where the event occurred. Separate the situation of the illustration from the immediate situation of the listeners. Jesus used time separation to introduce the parable of the workers in the vineyard: "The kingdom of heaven is like a landowner who went out *early in the morning* to hire men to work in his vineyard" (Matt. 20:1, emphasis added). We demonstrate this as parents when we intuitively begin children's stories with "Once upon a time . . ."

---

63. Dawson C. Bryan, *The Art of Illustrating Sermons* (Nashville: Cokesbury, 1938), 210.

64. Bryan says that an illustration contains four chief components: a beginning, action, a climax, and a conclusion (ibid., 220). In *Preaching with Purpose*, Adams's list varies somewhat. He says there must be background (briefly sketched), a complication or a problem, suspense, a climax, and a conclusion (93). Both lists anticipate well the conclusions of narrative theorists that a story should describe a situation, upset the equilibrium, bring resolution, and communicate a point (e.g., Eugene L. Lowry, *The Sermon: Dancing the Edge of Mystery* [Nashville: Abingdon, 1997], 56–89).

65. Bryan, *Art of Illustrating Sermons,* 199.

66. Deane A. Kemper, *Effective Preaching* (Philadelphia: Westminster, 1985), 86.

67. Ibid., 86.

The principle never ceases to operate. When a preacher begins with, "It was five minutes to midnight, and she still wasn't home," listeners move to a dimension of experience separate from where they are. Conceptual understanding can also be built with illustration introductions that provide spatial separation, as in the parable of the importunate widow. "*In a certain town* there was a judge" (Luke 18:2, emphasis added).

Separation of time and space can be combined in the description of a situation that introduces a story. The situation may also be defined by the personalities involved (their relationships, accomplishments, or activities); by the event being recounted (its impact, import, or progress); or by the preacher's own reflection on personal, internal responses to an incident, an account, or a relationship. In the introduction to the parable of the sower, Jesus simply says, "A farmer went out to sow his seed" (Matt. 13:3). No specific time or place is mentioned, but the Savior nonetheless defines a particular situation—a life experience with which people can immediately identify.

The goal of a preacher mirrors that of a child operating a box crane in a game arcade. The child tries to use the crane to lift a treasure from a mound of trinkets and place the prize where it can be claimed before time runs out. With an illustration, a preacher attempts to lift listeners from their immediate situations and transport them to an experience that will claim their thought before their interest expires. The introduction of an illustration begins this transporting process by separating listeners from their immediate experience and placing them in the context of another.

Care needs to be taken in these opening moments so as not to lose listeners. In Western culture, *listeners expect an illustration to be about the last thing a preacher said before beginning the illustration.* If you are going to illustrate something you said three minutes ago or even three sentences ago, the matter needs to be summarized and restated before the illustration begins.

Recognize also that a sermon is not a research paper. Unless you are trying to make an impression that requires you to state the source of an illustration, do not burden listeners with unnecessary documentation. Bryan writes, "It is wise to begin at once with the example. The introduction of author, title, and chapter usually has a deadening effect, and, because of such, many an otherwise good illustration is brought forth stillborn."[68] This is more than a matter of artistic preference. By beginning with what an average listener could not read or has not read, a preacher distances listeners from the illustration. Not overburdening listeners with documentation does not mean you can take the credit for ideas not your own. Maintain pastoral integrity by using phrases such as, "The story is told of . . . ," or "I've heard it said

68. Bryan, *Art of Illustrating Sermons*, 199.

that . . ." Such phrases do not damage an illustration but do protect a pastor from accusations or impressions of plagiarism.

Use Vivid and Pertinent Details

To keep listeners engaged until the conclusion of an illustration, preachers must keep all its parts closely tied to experience by using concrete details that enable listeners to relate to it.[69] Webb Garrison explains why concreteness empowers illustrations and furthers understanding: "If I were to talk at length about my having been deeply moved by watching the setting of my son's broken arm, this would constitute a report of my feelings. But when I describe some factors that contributed to my mood, you are brought into the experience and feel with me. To re-create a moving situation is quite different from testifying to having been deeply moved."[70] Make the situation concrete to make the experience accessible and the message it communicates powerful.

The question is, How? How does a preacher make an experience concrete for listeners? Answers R. C. H. Lenski, "Concrete objects, persons, actions, situations, etc., are *fully described*."[71] When Jesus told the parable of the prodigal son, he did not describe the reunion by saying, "The father expressed continued care for his wayward son." Jesus said:

> But while he [the son] was still a long way off, his father saw him and was filled with compassion for him; he ran to his son, threw his arms around him and kissed him.
>
> The son said to him, "Father, I have sinned against heaven and against you. I am no longer worthy to be called your son."
>
> But the father said to his servants, "Quick! Bring the best robe and put it on him. Put a ring on his finger and sandals on his feet. Bring the fattened calf and kill it. Let's have a feast and celebrate. For this son of mine was dead and is alive again; he was lost and is found." So they began to celebrate.
>
> Luke 15:20–24

Jesus fleshed out the details that brought the illustrative experience to life. He described perceptions, actions, dialogue, aphorisms, and scene changes—all to express one idea: The father still loved his son.

Details enable listeners to enter a situation they have not actually experienced.[72] Descriptions of sights, sounds, and sensations that they would take in were they in such a context involve them in that experience. Thus, Lionel

---

69. Davis, *Design for Preaching,* 256.

70. Garrison, *Creative Imagination in Preaching,* 95.

71. R. C. H. Lenski, *The Sermon: Its Homiletical Construction* (Grand Rapids: Baker, 1968), 236, emphasis added.

72. Eugene L. Lowry, *How to Preach a Parable* (Nashville: Abingdon, 1989), 106.

Fletcher once advised, "Don't hurry the telling of your illustrations. Tell them well. Build up the background, picture the whole scene, and make it live before the eyes of the congregation."[73] Garrison adds, "Words that name colors, shapes, sounds, odors, and other tangibles help create backgrounds that evoke moods. Anything that moves you can move your listeners—provided they are brought into firsthand encounter with stimuli that produced the emotion."[74]

Still, even though specifics are important, steer clear of details that are extraneous or extravagant. Preachers may fall in love with the artistry of detail to the extent that they remove an illustration from an identifiable experience. Lehman writes, "A certain amount of description becomes necessary to enable the listener to see the door and cross the threshold with you. This does not mean poetry—just description."[75] Unnecessary ornamentation, inefficient story descriptions, and extraneous detail may so flood listeners' minds with irrelevant thoughts that (although the speaker is admired for erudition) no specific experience can be focused on, lived through, and made meaningful. True eloquence requires a preacher to present vivid details in clear and concise terms. Dispense with the musing of philosophers, the jargon of psychologists, and the rambling of tale tellers in love with narrative embellishments.[76]

Charles Haddon Spurgeon sums up the cautions regarding overdoing illustrative description:

> We are not sent into the world to build a Crystal Palace in which to set out works of art and elegancies of fashion; but as wise master-builders we are to edify the spiritual house for the divine inhabiting [*sic*]. Our building is intended to last, and is meant for everyday use, and hence it must not be all crystal and colour. We miss our way altogether, as gospel ministers, if we aim at flash and finery. . . . Some men seem never to have enough of metaphors: each one of their sentences must be a flower. They compass sea and land to find a fresh piece of coloured glass for their windows, and they break down the walls of their discourses to let in superfluous ornaments. . . . They are grievously in error if they think that thus they manifest their own wisdom, or benefit their hearers. . . . The best light comes in through the clearest glass: too much paint keeps out the sun.
>
> Our Lord's parables were as simple as tales for children, and as naturally beautiful as the lilies which sprang up in the valleys where he taught the people. . . . His parables were like himself and his surroundings; and were never strained, fantastic, pedantic, or artificial. Let us imitate him, for we shall never find a model more complete, or more suitable for the present age.[77]

73. As cited in MacPherson, *Art of Illustrating Sermons,* 214.
74. Garrison, *Creative Imagination in Preaching,* 95–96.
75. Lehman, *Put a Door on It,* 69.
76. Ibid., 203.
77. Charles Haddon Spurgeon, *The Art of Illustration,* Lectures to My Students (London: Marshall Brothers, 1922), 5, 6, 11, 12.

Although Spurgeon's ornamental discussion may in some ways violate the principles he articulates, his point remains valid. Save the ribbons and the flowers for occasions when eternity does not hang in the balance.

Rain Key Terms

Every detail of an account should serve the explanatory point being made.[78] To keep listeners on track, preachers must take care not only to illustrate the last thing said but also to tell the illustration using the key terms with which they first explained the matter. An illustration should not merely reflect the concepts of the explanation; it should echo the terminology of the explanation as well. Ordinarily this means we *rain the key words of the subpoints* (or the key terms of the main point when there are no subpoints) into the sentences we use to tell the illustration.

For example, if an explanation's subpoints indicate that we should pray *fervently* and *consistently*, the illustration should tell a story using those terms. If, instead, the preacher tells of someone who petitions another *devotedly*, listeners may well wonder how the illustration relates to the explanation. In the preacher's mind, "petitions another devotedly" may be synonymous with praying "fervently and consistently," but the listening ear longs for more consistent expression. Such term consistency, or *expositional rain*, keeps an illustration tied to a preacher's explanation. The English teachers who taught us to write essays would advise changing terms to avoid redundancy, but in an oral medium, the repetition of key terms orients the ear to what is important and ties thoughts together. The key terms of the subpoints that were the listeners' signposts through the concepts in the explanation now function in the illustration, enabling it to reinforce the specific truths of the explanation.

Dispensing with these verbal trail guides in the illustration invites confusion and loses listeners. Not only does the lack of expositional rain disconnect the verbal cues linking the explanation and the illustration, but the lack of term consistency actually erodes the credibility of the preacher. In the latter decades of the twentieth century, many speakers were advised to begin public addresses with anecdotes. The humorous stories quickly grabbed attention and were thought to win the goodwill of listeners. However, studies began to indicate that, though interest was quickly raised by such stories, listeners often would grow weary or suspicious of the technique if it seemed purely designed to manipulate their emotions or will. What most aroused suspicions were stories that seemed to have no immediate connection to the subject of the speaker. Expositional rain and discipline in illustrating the last thing

---

78. Bryan, *Art of Illustrating Sermons,* 221. See also Thomas Fuller, as quoted in John R. W. Stott, *Between Two Worlds: The Art of Preaching in the Twentieth Century* (Grand Rapids: Eerdmans, 1988), 240.

said prior to the illustration are important in maintaining the thought of a message and the trust of the preacher. Select the key terms of the subpoints (or main point) that carry the main concepts of the explanation and use them in the telling of an illustration.

CREATE CRISIS

An illustration's descriptive details (of time, place, feelings, sights, etc.) should carry a narrative forward through its crisis. Narrative crisis does not have to be created by the threat of a tragedy. Crisis may be achieved by opening a door to scientific wonder, creating anticipation about how an event will unfold, or creating a new perspective from which to see the commonplace in a special light. At its heart, crisis is the tension of the not yet—not yet knowing the solution, the resolution, the punch line, or even how the punch line will be delivered this time.

Crisis results from having sufficient, relevant facts to create a problem that listeners have an interest in solving and that forces them to journey through a narrative to discover the resolution found in the climax. If preachers do not bring an audience to the edge of wonder, grief, anger, confusion, fear, or discovery, then their words have no point—no hook on which to hang meaning. The internal tensions of illustrations hold a congregation because they spotlight the very types of experiences that bring people to hear the minister.

In the parable of the Pharisee and the publican, the incongruous prayer attitudes of two men who are apparently moral opposites create the tension. The outwardly moral Pharisee prays "about himself" (Luke 18:11). The despised publican, however, "would not even look up to heaven, but beat his breast and said, 'God, have mercy on me, a sinner'" (Luke 18:13). The crisis for Christ's audience is in determining proper prayer and deciding what it reflects about dependence on God's grace rather than on self-righteousness. The complications in the details create a tension between what these opposite men should be saying and what they actually are saying. Without this crisis, the story has no impact. The need to build and release tension to underscore a principle reveals why mere statistics, examples, or allusions do not serve the full purposes or carry the full power of illustrations.

CONCLUDE MEANINGFULLY

Following the advice of the adage "Strike while the iron is hot," preachers should state an illustration's conclusion while "heat" from the crisis is greatest. That is, they should place the climax of an account as close to the illustration's end as possible.[79] An illustration's crisis stimulates interest and pulls listeners into an experience. Having drawn in listeners as much as

79. Bryan, *Art of Illustrating Sermons*, 227–28.

possible, a preacher must make the point being illustrated before interest, attention, and involvement diminish. Thus, illustrative conclusions have two elements: the story's end and the illustration's point.

The introduction isolates the experience, the narrative detail gives it form, the crisis compels involvement, and the conclusion focuses meaning by relating the events in the illustration back to the explanatory point being made. There are a number of ways this can be done, but normally a preacher states the relation in a crisp, verbal hammer stroke that drives the point home.[80] Louis Paul Lehman writes, "The bridge from the illustration itself to the interpretation must not be shaky or ill defined."[81] Such a bridge usually takes the form of a grouping (or interpreting) statement. In this statement (which may take a sentence or two), a preacher quickly reminds listeners of pertinent details in the illustration and ties them to the principle being communicated.

Grouping statements demonstrate similarities between an illustration's details and the sermon's truths. A preacher might conclude an illustration with phrases such as "Even as so-and-so discovered this path, we must . . ." or "In the same manner . . ." or "We too must . . ." or "We learn from this account that just as . . ." An alternative is to cap an illustration with an application phrased in wording parallel to a key phrase or thought that occurred within the illustration. An illustration might end with the statement, "Without his guide, Joe could never have found his way back." The parallel grouping statement might then be, "Without our God, we can never find our way back." Parallel phrases remove the need for prefatory comments that indicate that the preacher is about to relate the illustration's details to the sermon's point because the parallelism automatically implies the relationship.

Donald Grey Barnhouse made many illustrations famous, but none more ably demonstrates how master preachers use interpreting statements than this poignant illustration he told his children when their mother died:

> As he drove his children to his wife's funeral Barnhouse stopped at a traffic crossing. Ahead of them was a huge truck. The sun was at such an angle that it cast the truck's shadow across the snow-covered field beside it. Dr. Barnhouse pointed to the shadow and spoke to his children: "Look at the shadow of that truck on the field, children. If you had to be run over, would you rather be run over by the truck or by its shadow?"
>
> The youngest child responded first, "The shadow. It couldn't hurt anybody."

80. Kemper, *Effective Preaching,* 86; Adams, *Preaching with Purpose,* 93; Sangster, *Craft of Sermon Illustration,* 89; and Bryan, *Art of Illustrating Sermons,* 226.

81. Lehman, *Put a Door on It,* 89.

"That's right," said Barnhouse. "And remember, children, Jesus let the truck of death strike him, so that it could never destroy us. Mother lives with Jesus now—only the shadow of death passed over her."

I have used this illustration at more than one funeral. Not only does it speak movingly of deep biblical truth, but it also does all an illustration must with a great economy of words. Listeners focus their attention on the Barnhouses' situation, see what the children see, and even listen in on the dialogue. Even more crucial than a vicarious experience of the event, however, are the master preacher's final words to his children, which enable them to relate the details of the illustration to Christian death. The interpreting statement is short—two brief sentences. But by reaching into his illustration to grab key terms to weld the illustration and a theological concept together, Barnhouse provides comfort for us as he did for his children. No matter how well they are described, events generally do not interpret themselves. Therefore, such grouping statements at the conclusion of illustrations are crucial. Though a grouping statement can be implied as well as directly stated, its essence must echo in a listener's mind for an illustration to remain faithful to an exposition's purpose.

Concerns Regarding Illustrations

Illustrations that portray realism, integrity, and compassion magnify the persuasive power of a sermon. How we use illustrations and where we find them largely determine their effectiveness.

Illustration Cautions

USE ILLUSTRATIONS PRUDENTLY

Remember that illustrations are a tool for exposition, not a substitute for sound explanation. A preacher who constructs sermons to serve illustration rather than solid biblical exposition inevitably drifts from pulpit to stage, from pastor to showman. Any trained public speaker can select a theme and gather a bundle of stories that will touch an audience emotionally, but this is not preaching. The proper focus of illustrations lies in presenting biblical truth in such a manner that it can be understood deeply and applied readily rather than in promoting popular enjoyment or pastoral acclaim.

Messages that are overloaded with illustrations damage the credibility of a preacher because hearers conclude, "All this one does is tell stories."[82] We achieve balance not through a standard for the number and placement of illustrations but through a commonsense assessment of how and where they

---

82. Marquart, *Quest for Better Preaching*, 153.

will best serve the purposes of a message. According to tradition, each major division (i.e., main point) of a sermon should contain an illustration.[83]

Whether an illustration should follow each main point's subpoints, accompany a single subpoint whose explanation is particularly difficult, or serve as a transition showing the relationship between two points[84] is better left to the discretion of the preacher. The messenger in the situation will have the best feel for what the message as a whole requires. For instance, if a powerful illustration dominates the conclusion of a sermon, it may be wise to distance the final main point's illustration from the conclusion so that it does not impinge on the sermon's climax.[85] Mass communication studies have indicated that it is often best to use an illustration immediately after the first statement of an expositional principle in a main point's development.[86] The technique intrigues while introducing a subject and thus allows the point to be made with a minimum of attention drop or listener argument.[87] This method is especially popular with broadcast preachers.[88]

These alternatives indicate that illustrations may properly appear at the beginning, in the middle, or at the end of a main point, as well as in the transition between main points. Such a conclusion underscores the seductive nature of illustrations. Once a preacher discovers how illustrations elicit audience response and then further realizes that they can surface almost anywhere in a sermon, the temptation is almost irresistable to use illustrations everywhere. Preachers must resist the temptation. If we were to graph the emotional intensity of a sermon, we would see that the peaks tend to rise around illustrations, especially if an application is made with the illustration. But if a sermon is all illustrative climaxes, no portion holds exceptional impact. Preachers who load illustration upon illustration in order to woo an audience find themselves in a classic hedonistic dilemma—people lose interest because of the commonness of the pleasure. Pastors lose credibility when their sermons do not possess adequate explanatory balance.[89] At the same time, preachers who do not construct their sermons to minister to the different personalities, capabilities, and learning styles of their listeners will be perceived as selfish or insensitive. Sermons too full of illustrations choke credibility; sermons too lacking in illustrations strangle goodwill.

83. Bryan, *Art of Illustrating Sermons,* 172; Baumann, *Introduction to Contemporary Preaching,* 180; and Larsen, *Anatomy of Preaching,* 66.

84. Bryan, *Art of Illustrating Sermons,* 173–74.

85. See more discussion of this in chap. 9.

86. Lewis, *Inductive Preaching,* 82.

87. Kemper, *Effective Preaching,* 81.

88. For additional information on the application of this principle to broadcast preaching, see Bryan Chapell, "Alternative Models: Old Friends in New Clothes," in *A Handbook of Contemporary Preaching,* ed. Michael Duduit (Nashville: Broadman, 1992), 118–31.

89. Spurgeon, *Art of Illustration,* 4–5.

The nature of a sermon, the nature of its illustrations, and the nature of the target audience all come to bear on the proper balance of expository components in the sermon. Popular today in some circles is the narrative sermon, which presents a biblical truth in a parable pattern[90]—an extended story (or a narrative structure) leading to a poignant moral or insight. We should not condemn this method since it was often Jesus' manner of teaching. Such sermons can serve important purposes, and the proportion of illustrative content in them is necessarily large. Still, we will recall that Jesus used such an approach in contexts in which he could assume his followers knew (or would become acquainted with) much additional biblical teaching (see Mark 4:10, 34). It is unlikely that Jesus believed a congregation would be fed adequately if this were its only diet.

Determine when and where to use illustrations by assessing what will make a message's application most effective. In some cases, this will mean that illustrations must focus on clarifying the exposition to allow sufficient understanding. In other instances, it is better to use illustrations to create deep feeling about a matter that is so familiar that it no longer stimulates the response it should. Whether the illustration is intended to support an intellectual or attitudinal appeal (or a combination of the two), illustrations work best when a preacher uses them primarily to affect the wills of hearers. Such use ennobles illustrations by taking them from the realm of entertainment and placing them in a servant relationship to a sermon's expository purposes. People are simply more willing to attempt, or even to consider, what they believe to be possible.[91] When they see spiritual truth in scenes, incidents, and circumstances that form the common ground of human experience, acceptance of what a preacher says naturally grows.[92] Illustrations carry compelling evidential weight.

USE ILLUSTRATIONS PASTORALLY

Even if illustrations are not the focus of an expository message, they do focus congregational attention on a preacher's understanding of life and the Bible's relevance to it. Illustrations put pastoral integrity, competence, and compassion in full view. For this reason, preachers must prepare illustrations with a keen awareness of their inherent pastoral implications.[93] Heeding these cautions will help keep illustrations from damaging your ministry:

90. See the discussion in chap. 6; Steimle, Niedenthal, and Rice, *Preaching the Story;* Eugene L. Lowry, *The Homiletical Plot: The Sermon as Narrative Art Form* (Atlanta: John Knox, 1980); Wayne Bradley Robinson, ed., *Journeys toward Narrative Preaching* (New York: Pilgrim, 1990); and Chapell, "Alternative Models," 124–25.

91. John Killinger, *Fundamentals of Preaching* (Philadelphia: Fortress, 1985), 30–31.

92. R. E. O. White, *A Guide to Preachers* (Grand Rapids: Eerdmans, 1973), 171.

93. Chapell, *Using Illustrations to Preach with Power,* 146–64.

Get the facts straight. Adept handling of facts instills listener confidence in a preacher. References to the "Ninety-five Theses of Martin Luther King," "the prison ministry of *George* Colson," "Einstein's discovery of X-rays," and "John Steinbeck's mischievous Huckleberry Finn" do the opposite.

Beware of untrue or incredible illustrations. Resist the temptation to tell an account as though it were true if it is not. Do not say it happened to you if it did not. Even if the account is true, avoid it if it casts doubt on your veracity. You lose much if you lose credibility.

Maintain balance. The illustrations of expository sermons rarely extend beyond a paragraph or two in a written manuscript. Be brief. Avoid stacking too many illustrations together. An illustration clarifying an illustration is a sure sign of danger.

Be real. Appreciate the epic in the immediate. If we too often illustrate with the great saints of yesteryear, we may hopelessly distance faith from the experience of most Christians today. Continually impressing everyone with the prayer life of E. M. Bounds, Charles Simeon, George Mueller, and Moses promotes a false perception of super spirituality. Preachers whose illustrations always fly in the lofty clouds of spiritual idealism ultimately destroy listeners' confidence that faith can be lived in real life.[94]

Do not carelessly expose, disclose, or embarrass. Be careful not to draw illustrations from sources that may inadvertently promote indulgence in or imply approval of entertainments or habits that may compromise your pastoral position (e.g., some congregations may approve of movies for mature audiences, but in other settings parents may wonder why their pastor endorses what they forbid their teens to see). Never disclose counseling confidences in such a way that individuals can be identified. Do not portray family, friends, or parishioners in embarrassing accounts unless you have secured their permission *and* indicate in the sermon that you have done so.

Poke fun at no one but self. Ridicule of ethnic groups, dialects, political parties, gender, age, or any individual automatically calls into question your ability to communicate the grace of God even if people laugh at the joke. The only one you have a right to poke fun at from the pulpit

---

94. Baumann, *Introduction to Contemporary Preaching,* 180. If you question the validity of this advice, ask yourself which of the following grants you more hope for your own usefulness in God's service: the fact that Charles Haddon Spurgeon so struggled with depression that this "prince of preachers" was absent from his pulpit nearly a third of the time in his later life, or the story that he had such mastery of the pulpit that a workman was converted merely by hearing Spurgeon quote John 3:16 while testing the acoustics in an auditorium.

is yourself. (Corollary: The only one you cannot pat on the back in the pulpit is yourself.)

Share the spotlight. Do not let yourself (your kids, your hobby, your dog, your vacation, your illness, your military service, your sports career) be the focus of too many illustrations. Never be the hero of your own illustrations. If any good results, give the credit to God (1 Cor. 1:31).

Demonstrate taste and respect sensibilities. Birthing, blood, bedrooms, and bathrooms do not usually merit graphic description from the pulpit. Where such references are needed, speak matter-of-factly and move along. Profanity or coarse language even of the mildest form can spark more anger from the pew than most preachers ever want to confront. Although people know the terms well, they do not come to church to hear them on their pastor's lips.

Finish what you begin. You cannot leave people hanging, wondering what happened to that little dog, or the boy in the hospital bed, or the neighbor who ran over the garbage can. Even if other aspects of the illustration make your point, unresolved aspects of a story may so dominate listeners' thoughts that they will hear little else you say.

Illustration Sources

Preachers get illustrations from several basic sources: personal experiences (read about, heard from others, or personally lived), news accounts, historical accounts, literary materials, imagination, and the Bible. Seeing illustrations around you, keeping track of them as you read and study, and listening for accounts others tell is a constant challenge that becomes a lifestyle.[95] Preachers can naturally develop the skill of finding illustrations everywhere if they are convinced of the importance of doing so and do not too early fall into the habit of using only the illustrations of others.

Unlike many other homiletics instructors, I am not unalterably opposed to using illustration catalogs *as long as* preachers use the stock accounts as catalysts rather than as crutches. All preachers run into situations in which they know they need an illustration but cannot think of something appropriate (especially in churches where the pastor must prepare messages four or five times a week). Having a reservoir of illustrations that can be revised, updated, and personalized is valuable. However, preachers who only cut and paste others' illustrations will develop messages that are increasingly trite, staid, and impersonal. When you do use another's illustration, be sure to give appropriate credit (see earlier comments in this chapter on simple ways to avoid plagiarism). Then revise the illustration by raining in key terms from your own sermon's explanation. In this way, the illustration

95. Chapell, *Using Illustrations to Preach with Power,* 167–74.

will verbally and conceptually fit you and your message—and will not seem like a foreign import.[96]

DISCOVERY SYSTEMS

Often illustrations will come to mind as preachers prepare a message. If the point to be made is sharply defined, it is more likely to throw mental sparks against a memory or recent experience, and the illustration will immediately flame into light. Most preachers, however, will be seriously handicapped if they rely only on immediate inspiration for sermon illustrations. Most of us find that we must combine illustrations that we have stored with those that spring to mind when we prepare messages.

A number of "systems" have been devised to help preachers save and retrieve the illustrations they discover. Computer programs and subscription services are only recent innovations in a much developed field. No illustration system is more important or more basic than knowing well ahead of time what the subject and/or text of a sermon will be. Having that in hand weeks prior to preaching a message is like having a powerful idea magnet. This does not mean that you should have the entire sermon in hand weeks before it is preached. For most of us, this is simply impossible, and even if it were not, such a practice might rob messages of their spontaneous fire. Still, by knowing in general what a sermon will be about, a preacher can begin to collect, sort, and evaluate illustrations long before they are actually needed.

Often preachers keep a file with a separate folder for each sermon planned for upcoming weeks or months. Then as an illustration comes to mind or an article dealing with the subject is encountered, preachers can simply drop the material into the appropriate folder so that they have a healthy reservoir of ideas on hand when it comes time to prepare the sermon. Not only illustrations will find their way into such a file. Potential outlines, exegetical discoveries, applicational thoughts, and expositional ideas will be drawn to the magnetic "pre-sermon file."[97] A preacher certainly does not have to use all the material collected in such a file. However, even if a pastor ends up using very little of the file for a particular message, over time such a system will undoubtedly put many more—and better—illustrative resources at the preacher's fingertips.

RETRIEVAL SYSTEMS

When you come across an illustration, write it down immediately. Be careful to write it down with sufficient detail so that you can remember what it is about. Most preachers who determine to "write it down more fully later"

---

96. Ibid., 163.
97. See the discussion in chap. 3 of the pre-sermon file.

had best simply resign themselves to forgetting 90 percent of their potential illustrations. Many great communicators have disciplined themselves to carry a pocket notebook so as to record illustrations and other thoughts pertinent to their messages. In recent years, I have mimicked the practice of these experts by keeping a small tablet of Post-it notes in my wallet. This way I always have paper to jot down an illustration. Later, I simply stick the note on a three-by-five-inch card and file it in an appropriate pre-sermon or other illustration file.

My family has long insisted that I be the last to read the daily paper, for when I do, sections tend to get savaged by my scissors. I read magazines with scissors in hand and books with a highlighter within reach. That which I cannot clip, I photocopy, or I jot down enough information so that I can remember and retrieve the illustration when I need it. Then I file the clipping, photocopy, or note with other illustrations. My illustration files may not be pretty, but I am the only one who has to look at them.

What do you do with good illustrations that have no place in your pre-sermon file or that you have used previously? File them.[98] As bothersome as it may be to set them up initially, illustration files will later save large amounts of time and energy. Some preachers may prefer to develop their own topical system for cataloging their illustrations, but you can save yourself much work by purchasing one of the good topical indexes on the market today. Currently, I prefer to attach my wallet notes to three-by-five-inch cards and put them with my collection of clippings in manila folders filed according to a subject index distributed by a major publisher. The file readily accepts all kinds of notes, and I can easily change the topic categories by inserting or deleting tab folders. If I am undecided about which category an illustration best fits, or if I think it fits well in a number of categories, I simply make photocopies and file the illustration in each of the appropriate places.

Computer cataloging systems are also adaptable, and some have high-powered topical search and cross-reference programs (often these can be updated monthly through various subscription services). Typically, computer illustrations may be placed directly into a sermon manuscript using standard word-processing software. The only drawback to computer cataloging is the time needed to input illustrations that are not part of the original or subscription packages. However, it is easier to file duplicate copies of an illustration in multiple topic and text categories using computer processing. Preachers should evaluate their own practices, needs, and budgets to determine which system will best serve them.

---

98. Topic and text files are both extremely beneficial. Excellent discussions of filing procedures are found in Haddon Robinson, *Biblical Preaching: The Development and Delivery of Expository Messages,* 2nd ed. (Grand Rapids: Baker, 2001), 159–61; and Leslie B. Flynn, *Come Alive with Illustrations: How to Find, Use, and File Good Stories for Sermons and Speeches* (Grand Rapids: Baker, 1987), 103–9. For an index of illustration subjects to form headings for your illustrations file, see the Biblical Studies Foundation at www.bible.org/illus/illustoc.htm.

Questions for Review and Discussion

1. What distinguishes an illustration from an allusion or an example?
2. What do listeners automatically assume a preacher is illustrating when an illustration begins?
3. How are the key words of a main point's explanation used in illustration?
4. What is a grouping (or interpreting) statement, and how is it used in illustration?
5. What matters help determine the proportion of illustration in a sermon?
6. What matters help determine the placement of an illustration in a main point? What are appropriate locations for an illustration?
7. What are important cautions to remember when creating illustrations?

Exercises

1. Create an illustration for one of the main points you outlined in the exercises at the conclusion of chapter 6, or create an illustration for the following main point: Because Jesus always intercedes for his people, we must pray consistently and fervently.
2. Choose a topic and create an illustration that uses at least three of the five senses.

G O A L   O F   C H A P T E R   8

To demonstrate how to apply the truths of expository sermons with relevance, realism, and authority

8

The Practice of Application

The Functions of Application

Approximately one-third of American adults say they have had a born-again experience, and the figure has remained consistent for several years. Surveys find little difference, however, when comparing the behavior of these born-again Christians before and after their conversion experiences. In fact, these surveys indicate that in three major categories—use of illegal drugs, driving while intoxicated, and marital infidelity—behavior actually deteriorates after a commitment to Christ. The incidence of drug use and illicit sex roughly doubles after conversion, and the incidence of drunk driving triples. Recent surveys also indicate that the incidence of divorce is actually higher among those identifying themselves as evangelical Christians than among the general population. A Zogby poll reported that Internet pornography sites were visited by 18 percent of surveyed born-again Christians, a figure just two percentage points lower than the national average.[1]

Reasons for these troubling statistics vary widely, but they make clear the fact that faith can remain abstract idealism for too many. John Calvin's observation still rings true: "If we leave it to men's choice to follow [what] is taught them, they will never move one foot. Therefore the doctrine of

---

1. For these and other survey reports, see Michael Fabarez, *Preaching That Changes Lives* (Nashville: Thomas Nelson, 2002), xiii, 203; and Gallup and Roper Organization survey results in National and International Religion Report (October 1990), 8.

itself can profit nothing at all."[2] Preachers make a fundamental mistake when they assume that by providing parishioners with biblical information the people will automatically make the connection between scriptural truth and their everyday lives.[3]

Application fulfills the obligations of exposition. Application is the present, personal consequence of scriptural truth. Without application, a preacher has no reason to preach, because truth without actual or potential application fulfills no redemptive purpose. This means that at its heart preaching is not merely the proclamation of truth but truth applied.[4] The Westminster divines understood this when they formulated the answer to the catechism question, "What do the Scriptures principally teach?" The answer, "What man is to believe concerning God and what duty God requires of man,"[5] clearly specifies the dual task of the preacher who would unfold the meaning of a biblical passage. The exposition of Scripture remains incomplete until a preacher explains the duty God requires of us.[6]

The duty that God requires in a passage is the "so what" of expository preaching that causes application. David Veerman summarizes:

> Simply stated, application is answering two questions: So what? and Now what? The first question asks, "Why is this passage important to me?" The second asks, "What should I do about it today?"
>
> Application focuses the truth of God's Word on specific, life-related situations. It helps people understand what to do or how to use what they have learned. Application directs and enables people to act on what they have been persuaded is true and meaningful.[7]

As helpful as these familiar distinctions are, a word of caution needs to be added before summarizing the obligations of application. Too much emphasis on duty, action, and What do you want me to do? can leave the impression that application always requires a pastor to dictate behavior in a sermon.

Application may be attitudinal as well as behavioral. In fact, the frequent mark of immaturity among preachers is too much (or too early) an emphasis on behavior. Mature preachers do not ignore behavior, but they carefully build an attitudinal foundation for whatever actions they say God requires. This is more than a rhetorical tactic. Its source is the biblical insight that out of the

---

2. From Calvin's sermon on 2 Timothy 4:1–2, as translated in *Sermons on the Epistles to Timothy and Titus* (Edinburgh: Banner of Truth Trust, 1983), 945–57.

3. David Veerman, "Sermons: Apply Within," *Leadership* (Spring 1990): 121.

4. Jay E. Adams, *Truth Applied: Application in Preaching* (Grand Rapids: Zondervan, 1990), 39.

5. Westminster Shorter Catechism, q. 3.

6. The impact of this truth on Puritan preaching is detailed in Fabarez, *Preaching That Changes Lives*, 57–59.

7. Veerman, "Sermons," 122.

heart come the issues of life (Prov. 4:23). Sermons that merely instruct—don't drink, don't smoke, don't lust, don't procrastinate—will lead to little spiritual maturity, even if parishioners do all they are told. Many applications exhort action (e.g., share the gospel with a neighbor, turn from a sinful practice, give to a worthy cause), but just as many should identify an attitude needing change (e.g., prejudice, pride, or selfishness) or reinforce a faith commitment (e.g., grasping the freedom of forgiveness, taking comfort in the truths of the resurrection, or renewing hope on the basis of God's sovereignty). Transformation of conduct *and* heart are both legitimate aims of application.

Application justifies exposition. If there is no apparent reason for listeners to absorb exegetical insights, historical facts, and biographical details, then a preacher cannot expect what seems inapplicable to be appreciated. No doctor will have much success saying to patients, "Take these pills," without explaining why. Application explains why listeners should take a sermon's expositional pills. Through application a preacher implicitly encourages parishioners to listen to a message's explanations because they establish the basis, reasonableness, and necessity of particular responses. Thus, John Broadus, the father of modern expository preaching, declares, "Application is the main thing to be done."[8] An informed preacher uses every aspect of a sermon as leverage to move the message's application based on sound exposition (see fig. 8.1).

Figure 8.1

The Sermon as Application Leverage

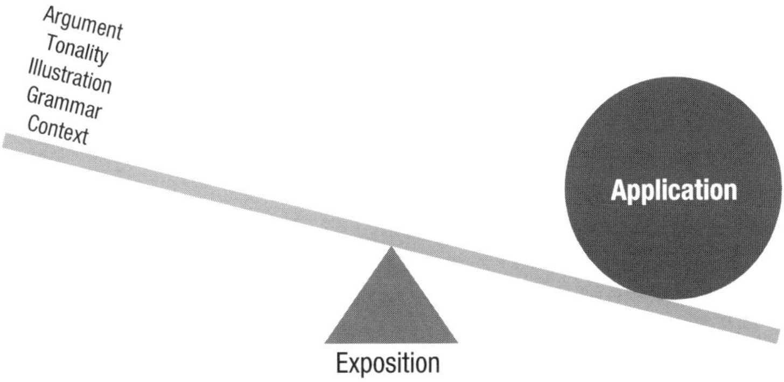

Application also focuses exposition. Exegesis and explanation are bottomless pits of commentary possibilities if a preacher has no clear purpose

---

8. John A. Broadus, *On the Preparation and Delivery of Sermons,* ed. J. B. Weatherspoon (New York: Harper & Row, 1944), 210. See also earlier comments in chap. 4 of this book.

in mind. Many books containing entirely legitimate information could be written on almost any biblical passage.[9] But preachers have only a few minutes each week to expound what a passage means. How do they choose what to say? Application answers by forcing them to determine what information most strongly supports particular responses a passage requires of listeners in light of the Fallen Condition Focus (FCF) of the message. The application points to the FCF, saying, "This is what you must do about that problem, need, or fault on the basis of what this passage means." Preachers select explanatory arguments and facts from the infinite possibilities on the basis of how readily they will support the application. Application gives exposition a target on which to focus (see fig. 8.2).

Figure 8.2

Application as Expositional Target

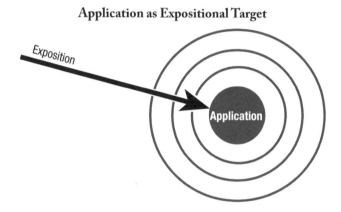

If the application loses sight of the FCF, the message will degenerate into a handful of legalisms tacked onto randomly selected observations. Without building the exposition to support the application directed at the FCF, preachers will simply choose to comment on what is most prominent in their own thought. In other words, by not identifying an FCF that a text addresses, preachers speak more about what is on their mind than what is in the text, even though they believe they are doing the opposite.

Accurate exposition requires preachers to complete their sermon research by identifying an appropriate application that will focus the exposition according to a text's priorities. Therefore, although preachers should not definitively determine application until completing their study of a passage (i.e., not deciding what a text requires before determining what it means), they should have the thrust of application clearly in mind before beginning sermon construction. If they start writing a message before determining

9. See chap. 2.

what a sermon needs to accomplish, then the components of the message are not appropriately geared toward the sermon's goal. Application—at least its general direction—must precede final decisions about structure, exegetical emphases, wording, and even the tone of a message, or else a preacher will be designing a highway without knowing its destination.

For my preaching students, I have devised what I call "the left-field rule." The rule comes into effect when, after writing the explanation and illustration of a main point, a preacher internally questions, "I wonder how I should apply this?" The question itself indicates that a preacher is out in left field (that is, lost or oblivious to chief obligations). If a preacher did not know what application an exposition was driving at, how did he choose the route? What determined the wording of the ideas, the choice of facts, the grammar to highlight, and the illustrations told if the preacher had no idea what response the text required? Without application, a preacher simply swings blindly, hoping that the ball of application will hit the bat of exposition. Home runs are more frequently hit when the batter sees the ball before swinging.

Although the precise details of application may take shape only as the rest of the sermon takes form, decisions about the general thrust of the application of each stage of the message should precede the development of that portion of the message. Homiletics instructors vary as to how they express this, referring variously to the "aim," "big idea," "telic purpose," or "transformation" to which all aspects of a message drive. The richness of expression underscores the importance of one consistent principle: Do not fire off information without having a target. Preachers should exegete a text *and* their congregation to decide the response they intend before they craft the words of the sermon.[10]

If this advice seems to devalue the importance of explanation in expository preaching, recognize that the chief purpose of application is not simply to give people something to do. Application gives ultimate meaning to exposition. Even if the explanation of a sermon defined every Greek and Hebrew word for prayer; quoted at length from Calvin, Luther, and E. M. Bounds on prayer's meaning; cited fifty passages that refer to prayer; and described the prayer practices of David, Jeremiah, Daniel, Paul, and Jesus, would listeners truly understand what prayer is? No. Until we engage in prayer, we do not really understand it. Until we apply a truth, understanding of it remains incomplete. This means that until a preacher provides application, exposition remains incomplete.[11]

No preacher really interprets what a text means at the human level by merely identifying its historical and grammatical roots. "God caused the

10. Adams, *Truth Applied*, 41. A preacher should have at least the general instructional specificity in mind before constructing a message.

11. Sidney Greidanus, *Sola Scriptura: Problems and Principles in Preaching Historical Texts* (Toronto: Wedge, 1970), 157; and John F. Bettler, "Application," in *The Preacher and Preaching*, ed. Samuel T. Logan (Phillipsburg, N.J.: Presbyterian & Reformed, 1986), 332.

Word spoken in those days to be put in writing with a view to us and our salvation. . . . A respect for the true nature of the Bible opens the way for applied explanation in preaching"[12] (cf. Rom. 4:23–25; 1 Cor. 10:6–13). Preachers must translate what a text means. This is more than an exegetical task. They must make the meaning of a text concrete for contemporary people in their situations. If preachers do not place the proclamation of gospel truth in the present world, it will have no continuing meaning for listeners.[13] By this I do not mean that a biblical truth has no intrinsic or eternal meaning apart from application but rather that Scripture has no individual meaning for those unaware of what difference the message of the Bible can make in their lives. Sidney Greidanus writes, "To put the issue succinctly: since the message was first addressed to the ancient church, it requires explication; since that message now needs to be addressed to a contemporary church, it requires application."[14]

Traditional homiletical distinctions between explanation and application still have merit. Preachers do need to provide explanations of a text that demonstrate the validity of application, and listeners should ignore applications that have no clear biblical warrant. Preachers simply must not let application become a tacked-on task. Application is an aspect of exposition that grants present significance to a text's enduring meaning.[15] How people are able to respond to God's truth as well as what they know about it make meaningful their understanding of God's Word (see Rom. 12:1–2).[16]

The Components of Application

Expository messages require preachers to ensure that the applications they make answer four key questions: *What* does God now require of me? *Where* does he require it of me? *Why* must I do what he requires? *How* can I do what God requires?

What (Instructional Specificity)

Preachers answer the question, What does God now require of me? by providing instructions that reflect the biblical principles found in the bibli-

12. C. Trimp, "The Relevance of Preaching," *Westminster Theological Journal* 36 (1973): 27.

13. John Frame, *Doctrine of the Knowledge of God* (Phillipsburg, N.J.: Presbyterian & Reformed, 1987), 81–85; and Daniel M. Doriani, *Putting the Truth to Work: The Theory and Practice of Biblical Application* (Phillipsburg, N.J.: Presbyterian & Reformed, 2001), 20–27.

14. Sidney Greidanus, *The Modern Preacher and the Ancient Text: Interpreting and Preaching Biblical Literature* (Grand Rapids: Eerdmans, 1988), 183.

15. D. Martyn Lloyd-Jones, *Darkness and Light: An Exposition of Ephesians 4:17–5:17* (Grand Rapids: Baker, 1982), 200–201. See also introductory discussions of the relationship of exposition and application in chaps. 2 and 4 of this book.

16. Frame, *Doctrine of the Knowledge of God,* 93–98.

cal text. This *instructional specificity* translates the text from ancient history to present guide. For the guidance to reflect accurately the Bible's intent, a preacher must discern the biblical principles reflected in the text that were directed to the people of that time and apply them to the people of this time. These universal principles are then applied by giving instructions consistent with and derived from the text that direct believers in present actions, attitudes, and/or beliefs.[17]

The need to base instructions on principles found in a text further justifies the prudence of phrasing main points as universal truths that a sermon's explanation will support. Since a preacher must acknowledge the discontinuity between ancient people and the present congregation, mere description of a text will not support application. The application must be built on principles that the details of the text support.[18] The "what should I now do?" dimension of application fails if the preacher does not explicate the text in terms of principle development.

Opinion, arbitrariness, or ignorance appear to dictate applications that are simply slapped onto the conclusion of a sermon that rehearses a text's details. The fact that Paul went to Jerusalem to deliver gifts no more supports an exhortation to tithe than the fact that Jesus wore sandals obligates us to use open footwear.[19] Preachers must demonstrate that the facts of a text support application instructions because the instructions naturally follow from biblical principles that the explanation establishes.[20] The goal of a text's explanation should be to establish the validity of the principles on which the application must be based.

A simple and effective way of ensuring the cohesion of explanatory principles and sermonic applications is to use the key *concepts* and *terminology* of a main point's explanation to frame the application (see fig. 8.3 and the discussion of expositional rain in chap. 7). For example, preachers could use subpoints indicating that devoted prayer is "consistent" and "fervent" to frame and phrase the instruction that people should pray "consistently" and "fervently." By phrasing the application's instruction with the key terms of the explanation, preachers help listeners not only understand why they were listening to the explanation but also connect the instruction of the preacher with the authority of Scripture.[21] When preachers apply a text with the same terms that they have explained a text, listeners conclude, "We must do this because it is what the Bible says." Again, although an

17. Greidanus, *Modern Preacher and the Ancient Text,* 167; and Veerman, "Sermons," 122–23.

18. Greidanus, *Modern Preacher and the Ancient Text,* 172–74.

19. Douglas Stuart, *Old Testament Exegesis* (Philadelphia: Westminster, 1980), 73.

20. Krister Stendahl, "Preaching from the Pauline Epistles," in *Biblical Preaching: An Expositor's Treasury,* ed. James W. Cox (Philadelphia: Westminster, 1983), 307–8.

21. Note how this procedure again underscores the necessity of having application in mind before settling on the phrasing and the form of an explanation.

English teacher would encourage you to use different terms in a written essay, in an oral presentation, the repetition of key terms is one of your most powerful communication tools. *Apply what you explain and the way you explain.*

Where (Situational Specificity)

Instructional specificity uses biblical principles to establish what contemporary people should do, but if preachers never specify *where* in real life these principles apply, the instructions remain irrelevant abstractions. The mere exhortation "We should love our neighbors more" hardly adds new challenge or insight to anyone's walk of faith, even if the instruction accurately reflects a biblical principle. Who did not know this general teaching before sitting down in the pew? The instruction moves from generic principle to poignant application when a preacher identifies the contemporary situations that listeners should address with the biblical principle evident in the text (e.g., loving the neighbor who supports a different political party, raises hateful children, laughs at your faith, or backs into your car and drives away without leaving a note).[22]

The aptness, relevance, and realism of *situational specificity* is frequently a distinguishing mark of mature and powerful preaching.[23] The applications of beginning preachers often seem to fall into one of two categories: simple generalization (go and do likewise) or instructional multiplication (e.g., buy this book, pray in these phrases, associate with these people, give to this cause, think this way, act this way, believe this way). The generality error evidences a lack of thought; the multiplication error demonstrates unfocused thought. The latter occurs when preachers think they will exhibit depth of insight by greatly multiplying the instructions a passage implies. Instead, such a shotgun approach makes a preacher seem to be scattered and reaching for any possible idea rather than discerning a text's particular purpose.[24] When preachers find themselves dispensing lists of instructions that even they had not considered prior to preaching the sermon, then they are probably burdening God's people rather than ministering to them. *The best preaching takes truth to struggle.* Preachers should consider the biblical truth that their explanation has disclosed and then pastorally consider how people in the congregation will be aided in their life struggles by the right application of this truth. In this way, sermons heal rather than burden God's people, and by applying the Word of God to the former purpose, preachers themselves discover the joys of pastoring as they preach.

---

22. Stuart, *Old Testament Exegesis*, 47.

23. David L. Larsen, *The Anatomy of Preaching: Identifying the Issues in Preaching Today* (Grand Rapids: Baker, 1989), 96; and Herbert H. Farmer, *The Servant of the Word* (New York: Scribner's, 1942), 84–97.

24. Adams, *Truth Applied*, 41.

Seasoned preachers identify a biblical principle that a text supports and then approach application by going in through the "who" door. They ask, "Who among my listeners needs to hear this?" In the sermon, they do not identify the persons but pastorally apply biblical truth to situations listeners are facing. Tact and pastoral sensitivity should determine the level of specificity appropriate, but ignoring the situations people face daily is not a pastoral option.[25] By exegeting the people as well as the text, a preacher will discern applications that sink deep into individual experience rather than skip across the surface of life's possibilities. Directing all applications toward different facets of a precise, poignant FCF will keep the entire sermon's application focused and will provide the preacher with the time for deep exploration of the heart and life implications of the text.

By mentally identifying the struggles of persons to whom a biblical principle applies, a preacher naturally connects the situations parishioners face and the guidance a text offers.[26] To be fair, pastors who have the most experience in life often have the greatest skill in developing powerful applications. Still, even beginning preachers can hone the craft of application by taking seriously the need to present scriptural principles in the context of situational specifics by studying the life of a congregation as well as the details of a text.[27] Think through the types of people—young parents, harassed clerks, lonely teens, new believers, tired saints—whose situations require scriptural guidance, comfort, and challenge. Preachers cannot speak to all groups every week, but since people confront no temptation but such as is common to all, speaking to specifics will have some relevance for each person (1 Cor. 10:13). The extent to which preachers keep specifics in touch with the more common concerns in a congregation, the more their applications will speak to all.[28] The following categories of common concern may help you begin to consider specifics in your congregation that need application of the principles in a text:

1. Building proper relationships (with God, family, friends, coworkers, church people, etc.)
2. Reconciling conflicts (in marriage, family, work, church, etc.)
3. Handling difficult situations (stress, debt, unemployment, grief, fatigue, etc.)

25. D. Martyn Lloyd-Jones, *Preaching and Preachers* (Grand Rapids: Zondervan, 1972), 137–38.

26. Jerry Vines, *A Practical Guide to Sermon Preparation* (Chicago: Moody, 1985), 98; and Edmund A. Steimle, Morris J. Niedenthal, and Charles Rice, eds., *Preaching the Story* (Philadelphia: Fortress, 1980), 108.

27. Veerman, "Sermons," 124.

28. See Bryan Chapell, "Alternative Models: Old Friends in New Clothes," in *A Handbook of Contemporary Preaching*, ed. Michael Duduit (Nashville: Broadman, 1992), 118–31.

4. Overcoming weakness and sin (dishonesty, anger, addiction, lust, doubt, lack of discipline, etc.)
5. Lack or improper use of resources (time, treasures, talents, etc.)
6. Meeting challenges and using opportunities (education, work in or out of church, witnessing, missions, etc.)
7. Taking responsibility (home, church, work, finances, future, etc.)
8. Honoring God (worship, confession, prayer, devotions, not compartmentalizing life, etc.)
9. Concern for social/world problems (poverty, racism, abortion, education, injustice, war, etc.)

The goal of exposition is always to reveal and prove from a text the principles for life and obedience (usually stated as a sermon's points) that can be applied to spiritual struggle. A text may also mandate specific practices (e.g., shun profanity, pray, repay debts), but such specific imperatives are less common. More often a pastor will have the obligation and the privilege to indicate contemporary situations listeners face in which they can apply the principles that a text establishes. These applicational aims require a preacher to (1) prove that the sermon's principles come from the text, (2) demonstrate that the textual situation parallels the contemporary situation, and (3) word the principles so that they are readily applicable today.

The best applications move beyond abstract instructions that are as easily dodged as they are acknowledged.[29] This application ethic derives from the preaching rule that "the cure for dullness in the pulpit is not brilliance but reality," and its derivative, "generalization in the pulpit gives sin security in the pew." Applications that are true to the goals of expository preaching explain how believers today have to live in specific situations to remain faithful to Scripture. This is no easy task. In fact, the strain of developing balanced, relevant, and fair situational specificity underscores why application is the most difficult task of expository preaching.[30] The biblical text contains information for instructional specificity, but the experience, courage, care, and spirituality of a preacher provide the material for situational specificity (i.e., instructional specificity is supplied to you; situational specificity is supplied by you). Without situational specificity, sermons will typically run out of steam after the preacher repeats the standard encouragements to practice the means of grace more: pray more, read the Bible more, go to church more. But when messages are designed to apply biblical truth to the

29. Larsen, *Anatomy of Preaching,* 97.
30. The historic *Directory for the Publick Worship of God* says of the preacher, "He is not to rest in general doctrine ... but to bring it home to special use, by application to his hearers ... albeit a work of great difficulty to himself requiring much prudence, zeal, and meditation" (from the section "Of the Preaching of the Word" approved by the Westminster Assembly in 1645).

struggles of life, then applications will be as varied and as relevant as the situations God's people face every day.

Why (Motivation)

Applications must provide proper *motivation* as well as relevant instruction. We need only consider the example of the Pharisees to recall that it is more than possible to do all the right things for all the wrong reasons and to be no holier than those whose behavior is far less moral. A friend of mine is fond of saying, "There is a longing for heaven and a fearing of hell that is straight from Satan because it is nothing but sanctified selfishness." Preachers must make sure their listeners know *why* they should heed applications.

Because much of part 3 of this book deals with proper motivation in preaching, I will not belabor the point here except to highlight this basic precept: Make sure that you motivate believers primarily by grace, not by guilt or greed. If God has freed his people from the guilt and power of sin, then preachers have no right to put believers back under the weight Jesus bore.[31] For many preachers, this is a particularly difficult imperative because in their own experience they have been so motivated by unrelenting guilt or by subtle appeal to greed that they have no real concept of what else could motivate people to serve God. In fact, they fear that without the burden of guilt ("God will get you if you don't") or the leverage of greed ("God will give you more if you do"), they will have no means to motivate obedience.

The alternative to motivating by guilt is its antidote: grace. The alternative to motivating by greed is its antithesis: grace. Believers need to serve God preeminently out of loving thankfulness for the redemption he freely and fully provides. All Scripture labors to put this mercy motivation before us (Luke 24:27; 1 Cor. 2:2). Informed expository preaching discloses the grace all passages contain and their applications require.[32] This grace exposure is necessary not merely because God's mercy is the foundation of our faith but because it is the most nourishing source of our service (Rom. 12:1). If we serve God primarily because we believe he will love us less if we do not, punish us more if we do less, or withhold blessing until we are sufficiently holy, then we are not obeying God for his glory but are pursuing our own self-interests. In such cases, the chief goal of our obedience is personal promotion or personal protection rather than the glory of God.[33]

31. Cf. Bryan Chapell, *In the Grip of Grace* (Grand Rapids: Baker, 1992), 15–40.

32. Kenneth J. Howell, "How to Preach Christ from the Old Testament," *Presbyterian Journal* 16 (January 1985): 9.

33. Jay E. Adams, *Preaching with Purpose: A Comprehensive Textbook on Biblical Preaching* (Grand Rapids: Baker, 1982), 152.

God does promise blessings for obedience, and it is proper to encourage faithfulness with the blessings he bestows. However, it is important to understand that these blessings are more certain in regard to our relationship with him (assurance of his love, peace of conscience, joy in the Holy Spirit) than in regard to the satisfaction of earthly desires (absence of pain, poverty, or persecution). The consequence of making personal gain our primary motivation for obedience is that our seemingly moral activities will become a transgression of the first commandment to have no other gods before God. The motivations that spring from full apprehension of God's grace do not change the rules but do change the reasons for our obedience. Grace encourages and enables us to serve God out of love for him and desire for his glory. Grace makes true obedience possible because a thankful response to unearned merit is motivated more by love for God than by love for self.

Guilt drives sinners to the cross, but grace must lead us from there or we cannot serve God. Christ-centered preaching keeps redemption by grace alone as central to the message of sermons as it is to the scope of Scripture. This is necessary because there is no more powerful motivation for holiness than loving God in response to the revelation of his redeeming character and eternal promises.[34] When love motivates, then the Lord, his purposes, and his glory are our aim. Without this motivation, no application challenges believers to serve any object greater than self. Whether the explanation component of a main point or the material immediately associated with the application supplies the grace motivation depends on a preacher's expositional choices. The application of an expository sermon, however, is not complete until the pastor has disclosed the grace in the text that rightly motivates obedience.[35] Listeners who fully apprehend the grace of God toward them will also discover their greatest strength for obedience, which is a greater love for God that produces a desire to please him—a desire that also provides their greatest satisfaction when it is fulfilled.

How (Enablement)

Along with motivation, an expository preacher must also supply the means, or *enablement*, of listeners' faithfulness. To placate constituents but avoid action, elected officials have been known to pass bills that require sweeping changes but lack enablement clauses. As a result, plans that sound great never get implemented. Preachers must be careful not to fall into the same pattern by telling people what they must do and at the same time neglecting to tell them how.

34. Ibid., 147; and Greidanus, *Sola Scriptura*, 41, 135.
35. Remember that context is part of text. For additional discussion on finding and disclosing the grace inherent in every text, see chaps. 10 and 11.

How can one who hates now love? How can an addict leave the drug? How can the negligent mature? How can one with no past discipline consistently express devotion? How can a lifelong pursuit of self be transformed into a passion for selfless care? Simply saying it should be so doesn't make it so. Complete application requires a preacher to spell out the practical steps and the spiritual resources that make the aims of a sermon attainable. Fuller treatment of this subject occurs in part 3 of this book, but a few preliminary comments will set a helpful course for application.

Why must a sermon include information on how to obey as well as what to do, where, and why? An obvious but frequent example of failing to provide listeners with the instruction necessary for action occurs when preachers conclude a sermon with a call to salvation, although the sermon did not indicate what an unbeliever must do to repent of sin and commit to the Savior. Such preaching assumes that listeners will know what to do despite the fact that those most needing to respond are the ones least likely to understand what God requires. If we tell God's people what, where, and why to do something, they still will struggle to obey if they do not know how.

An additional theologically significant reason to include enabling concepts is that the human reflex is to seek God in one's own strength. By such means, what seems to be holy practice is really just human striving. Too many applications are simply human-centered exhortations to do better in the power of the flesh. Thus, preachers must take care not to fall inadvertently into a self-help gospel in regard to application. When preachers tell their congregations to love their neighbors as themselves but do not point to the Spirit, who alone makes this love possible, then people may assume that this love is something they can stimulate in themselves. Preachers may assume that people will not try to do as the Bible instructs without seeking God's enabling power, but this is a naive expectation. If preachers can neglect to mention divine dependence, why should they be surprised when people forget to seek divine enablement?[36]

The power to do what God requires resides in God. Responsible preaching does not tell people their responsibilities without also informing them of how to plug into this power. Jay Kesler, former president of Taylor University, says that a sermon without enabling instruction is like shouting to a drowning person, "Swim! Swim!" The advice is correct but not helpful. It simply tells someone to do what in their situation they have no means to accomplish.[37]

Information regarding enablement may occur within the explanation that supports the application or in the application itself. In an expository sermon,

---

36. Sadly, there is little discussion in most homiletics texts on application's enablement. Even the experts give rare thought to how people can do what God requires. It is so much easier to say what to do than to enable the doing.

37. Veerman, "Sermons," 121.

however, the steps that will help listeners apply the truths of the sermon must have textual foundation. The how of application includes practical steps that will aid obedience (flee places of evil, seek mature counsel, count to ten) and the use of the means of grace (prayer, study, and fellowship), but it implies much more because these activities too may be perceived as the human efforts that bribe God for blessing rather than free provisions from God that enable us to walk in his wisdom and presence. Preachers must exegete Scripture with an eye not only for what act(s) of devotion and avenue(s) of discipline it advocates but also for what means of dependence it supports that enable the application.[38] It does no good for an application's principles to have biblical precedent if a preacher suggests (or allows) purely human means to fulfill biblical commands. Our power to obey is entirely through our union with Christ (John 15:5). This fact again emphasizes the importance of determining the aspects of divine dependence that a text's content discloses before finalizing the statements and the structure of the application.

The need to answer what, where, why, and how explains why preachers should dedicate a significant portion of expository messages to application.[39] A sentence at the end of twenty minutes of survey will not do. Application that ignores any one of these four critical questions is not merely incomplete; it is unbiblical because it fails to equip God's people for their service to him.

The Structure of Application

Understanding the components of application prepares us to consider how they fit into the structure of a standard expository message. Qualification offered in previous chapters needs to be reiterated here. There are many good ways to organize expository messages. The structure detailed in this section exhibits certain instructional principles without intending to suggest that there are no other proper expository forms. At the same time, this structure can serve as a standard without making its specifics normative.

38. These three D's (devotion, discipline, and dependence) summarize the aspects of biblical application traditionally associated with Christian enablement. All are valuable, but the last is indispensable for Christ-centered preaching because without dependence the other two D's can actually prompt unbiblical behavior disguised as means of soliciting God's aid. Prayer, for instance, rightly expressed is a confession of our weakness that seeks God's sovereign intervention (i.e., devotion and discipline with dependence); however, prayer can be used as a human attempt to leverage God (i.e., devotion and discipline without total dependence). In the latter case, the application's "how" ultimately seems to reside in the degree, frequency, or fervency of a human effort. Means of enablement that reflect biblical priorities are not behaviors alone but rather acts of devotion and discipline resting on divine mercy alone that direct, stimulate, and allow the human heart to rest, rely, and rejoice in God's work alone.

39. The what and where questions of application should be answered in virtually every main point, but the why and how questions may need to be answered with concepts developed through/by the sermon's entirety.

If a main point unfolds according to the standard expository format described earlier, the exposition begins with a statement of a main point addressing the FCF. Explanation—usually in subpoints—then supports, clarifies, or proves the main point. If an illustration follows the subpoints, then the subpoints first need to be summarized, since the ear expects an illustration to reflect the last thing said. This summary thus serves as the de facto introduction to the illustration. Because such a summary encapsulates the explanation of the main point, it will likely sound very similar to the main-point statement that the subpoints all support. The illustration of that statement unfolds in a narrative that echoes key terms of the explanation. These key terms rain into the illustration to keep its concepts and terminology consistent with the explanation. The illustration then concludes with a grouping (or interpreting) statement that reaches into the narrative and pulls the key thoughts into another summary statement. Since this statement summarizes a story that itself unfolds from a summary statement of the explanation, it is likely that the illustration's summary statement will also echo the main point.[40] But more than merely concluding the illustration, this grouping statement is also an introduction to the application (see fig. 8.3).

Figure 8.3

Main-Point Application Development

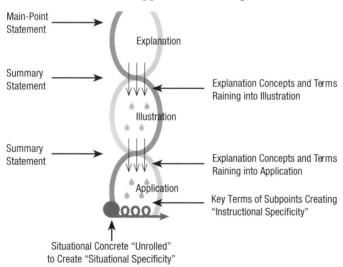

40. For more discussion of this process as it relates to illustration, see chap. 7. At this point it should also be evident that the two major strands of this expositional double helix are composed of the concepts and terms that ultimately develop and unify all the components of the main point.

The illustration's summary statement acts as the introduction to the application and serves as or sets up a general statement of principle that begins the application.[41] Almost all preachers use these overarching statements of biblical principle to begin their application. They conclude their explanations with a generic statement such as, "You, too, should examine your heart to see if you love your neighbor as you ought" or "Pray with the fervor that indicates you are serious about the salvation of the lost." Far too many preachers also conclude their applications at this point. Having proven a biblical principle, these preachers believe that they have fulfilled their expository obligations and that people will automatically translate the principles into their lives. For reasons already mentioned, this is too often a false hope.

The overarching statement of principle is merely the beginning of sound application. A magnification of the graphic in figure 8.3 will help explain what should characterize well-developed application (see fig. 8.4).

Figure 8.4

Application Magnified

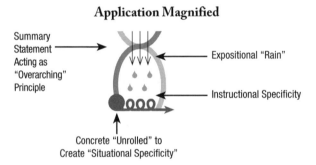

The overarching principle statement needs real-life delineation. Therefore, preachers give specific instructions that reflect what people can (or should) do, believe, or affirm in order to apply the general principle to their lives. Preachers should word these instructions with the key concepts and terms of the explanation that have rained through the illustration and now

41. Note that this structure assumes that each main point contains application according to the standards of a traditional expository method. I recognize, however, that preachers may choose to build to an application concentrated at the conclusion of the message as is characteristic of a "Puritan" sermon. We simply must question whether an approach that requires listeners to pay attention for twenty minutes (or more) before a preacher makes the message relevant will communicate well in our times. A modifying approach has the preacher offering general conclusions throughout the message that are made more particular in the conclusion or (in contrast) offering particular applications throughout the message that the conclusion gathers into a more generic and powerful thrust. Each approach has value. However, sound communication principles require preachers to avoid offering entirely new applications in sermon conclusions (see further discussion in chap. 9).

flow through the application (see sample sermon in appendix 12 with key words boldfaced in illustration and application to show "expositional rain"). This expositional rain keeps the instructions in contact with the earlier explanation, calling to the listeners' minds and ears the biblical authority that backs them. By providing this instructional specificity, a preacher fulfills the obligation of answering the what question. Why and how questions are also often answered at this stage if they have not already been addressed in the explanation.

To answer the where question, a preacher should identify concrete situations to which the general principle and the specific instruction(s) apply. Listeners need the sermon to draw the instructions down into a real-life situation (see fig. 8.4). Typically, the description of this concrete (that is, real-life) situation involves detailing circumstances and a specific explanation of how the instructions would function (or what they would require) in such a situation. In essence, a preacher makes the biblical instruction live the realities of the listeners. No single example, however, is likely to identify a situation that all listeners confront (one of the prime reasons why preachers in another generation were advised to let the Holy Spirit do all the application of a message). If a preacher simply stops here, the sermon may have arrived at a destination many find irrelevant. As a result, a preacher needs to unroll the initial concrete example into further situational possibilities by briefly mentioning other situations or struggles common in the congregation to which the biblical truth of the text applies.

Rarely will a preacher have the time to discuss these additional possibilities in the same detail as the initial concrete situation. The goal of the initial example is to expose listeners to a situation in which a biblical principle applies (i.e., becomes meaningful) and to stop them from thinking that the principle applies *only* to that situation. The initial situation makes the principle real; the unrolled specifics make it relevant to all. The identification of the additional situations breaks down the fence of any impression that the biblical truth could be confined to the first situation mentioned. The unrolled specifics do not (and cannot) encompass all the relevant situations listeners face. The unrolling process simply demonstrates that the principle cannot be limited to the first example so that listeners are more open to consideration of how the Holy Spirit will apply the principle to similar situations in their lives. For instance, a preacher might describe the obligations of loving a next-door neighbor who has caused hurt in one's life and then remind listeners that these instructions also apply to neighbors at work, school, and even church. The initial example allows the preacher to shine the light of Scripture into a dark corner of life. The details in that corner allow the preacher to focus the beam realistically before directing it and the listeners' attention to other areas of their lives (see fig. 8.5).

Figure 8.5

Focusing Application with Situational Specificity

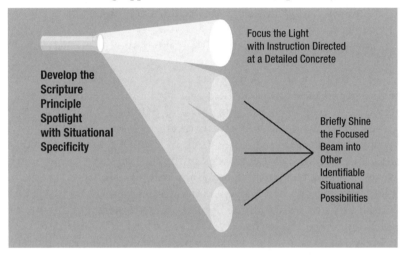

The greater the relevance and the realism of the initial situation for the majority of listeners, the more likely the application will apply to an entire congregation. Often the additional situational specifics that a pastor unrolls after the initial concrete example will include listeners who may not have been able to identify with the first example. Still, preachers should not be overly concerned that neither the concrete example nor its specifics precisely match what everyone in the congregation is facing. By presenting real-life specifics, preachers identify a dilemma, a stress, a temptation, or a concern that resonates with something that is common to the human condition. For instance, in the loneliness we all have felt, we can identify with the loneliness of an elderly widow whose family does not visit—even if we have not faced precisely this same set of circumstances. Even though a company may not have collapsed beneath us, we all have had enough failures to identify with the businessman whose greatest efforts have come to naught (cf. 1 Cor. 10:13).

By providing situational specificity, preachers are far more likely to include and involve all listeners than they are by speaking only in terms broad enough to cover all possibilities. Norman Neaves writes of the embracing power of the specific:

I'm tired of sermons that do not live where people live, that don't connect with the real stories and struggles by which their lives are shaped, that never touch the earth or breathe the air that the congregation breathes. Maybe there are those who enjoy developing the universal sermon, the one that can be preached everywhere and anywhere, that has a quality of being timeless. But as far as I am concerned, everywhere and anywhere really means nowhere; and those who strive to be timeless, are usually, simply not very timely. . . . The particular is higher than the universal.[42]

This perspective not only echoes the situational specificity of Scripture, which states general principles in small proportion relative to personal accounts, but also reminds us how integrated expository components may become in mature preaching.

An illustration may serve to indicate an application as well as to demonstrate an explanation. Often, experienced preachers focus on illustrating an application to give relevance and realism to the principles of a message. An illustration of a main point serves as a double-edged sword when it both sharpens the truth of an explanation and cuts away abstraction from an application. Most of the time, however, the application is not a full illustration but does contain enough description to bring a definite circumstance, emotion, failing, feeling, challenge, or need to listeners' minds.

By combining a general principle of application with instructional specifics that apply in other identifiable situations, a preacher provides truly usable biblical exposition.[43] Listeners gain an understanding of the principles they must heed when a sermon is removed from the realms of generality and irrelevance. Listeners comprehend and understand what underlies the advocated actions as well as the real-life consequences, thus producing mature, committed believers.

The Difficulty of Application

Identifying the Breaking Point

The specificity that makes application powerful also exposes why it is the most difficult aspect of expository preaching. The thought that is required to be specific strains mental and spiritual resources. Although accurate explanation can hardly be called easy, at least the unmined raw material lies within the pages of Scripture. Preachers derive application from far less obvious

42. Norman Neaves, "Preaching in Pastoral Perspective," in *Preaching the Story,* 108. One need not agree with all the philosophical roots of Neaves's thinking to appreciate the pastoral wisdom in his words.

43. Adams comments, "When I say that preaching is truth applied, I mean that the truths of a passage are not merely expounded; they are so expounded (applied) as to effect change in the listener. . . . Creeds should lead to deeds. . . . You ought to be proclaiming God's Word in order to accomplish the purpose for which He sent it" (*Truth Applied,* 42–44).

terrain. Sound explanation requires good scholarship. Solid application requires deep spirituality. A pastor who is keenly aware of the soul's struggles and who is intimately acquainted with scriptural remedies has what it takes to produce sound applications. Such a pastor knows not to harangue over obvious misbehaviors, not to remind others tritely to employ "the means of grace" (i.e., pray more, read the Bible more, go to church more), and not to rely on a habit-hewn appeal to come to Christ.

Application requires creativity and courage: creativity to imagine the battles of daily life fought with the truths of God, and courage to talk about this reality on a personal level. Apart from all the homiletical jargon about form, structure, and content, preachers know instinctively what makes application the most difficult part of preaching: the rejection they invite by being specific. J. Daniel Baumann writes:

> What is it that causes some sermons to be ineffective? One of the results of Ziegler's studies was that the sermons which contained applications to the daily lives of the congregation were the sermons that were unanimously rejected by the congregation. The frequency of rejection and the intensity of the rejection exactly paralleled the amount of daily application contained in the sermon. I would suggest that individuals are becoming more and more reluctant to accept that kind of application, religious or otherwise, to their daily lives. That kind of prescription implies that one person is in a position to tell others just what they should do with their daily lives.[44]

When listeners conclude that a pastor has "stopped preachin' and gone to meddlin,'" the sermon fails. Insightful application seems almost to invite this accusation.

Throughout the explanation and illustration of a main point, listeners can happily nod in agreement or nod off in security. But application requires commitment and action, not assent and neutrality. Sound application ventures out of hypothetical abstraction and elbows its way into business practices, family life, social relationships, societal attitudes, personal habits, and spiritual priorities. Application disrupts lives and as a result is the point at which listeners are most likely to tune out a sermon. Whether we like it or not, the breaking point of most sermons is application (see fig. 8.6).

A denial of the breaking point will accomplish nothing. Blaming others for this human frailty only leads to frustration. Believing that mature congregations are guilty of no such fault only exposes naïveté. Should preachers avoid application to keep rejection at a minimum? No! The Bible will not allow such neglect of God's instructions. Our calling obligates us to reveal

44. J. Daniel Baumann, *An Introduction to Contemporary Preaching* (Grand Rapids: Baker, 1972), 250.

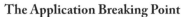

Figure 8.6

The Application Breaking Point

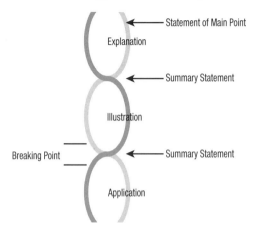

humanity's duty to God in clearest terms. God does not charge preachers to dismiss the breaking point but to overcome it.

Overcoming the Breaking Point

Forewarned is forearmed. When preachers know that specific application will likely spark a negative response to a message (but so also will meaningless, abstract applications), they have the opportunity to prepare a sermon so as to maximize its impact. We should not perceive such preparations as openings to soft-pedal God's requirements but as means to gain them an optimum hearing. Sermons must sometimes offend to remain faithful to the gospel (Rom. 9:33), but preachers must make sure that the offense is in the truth itself, not in the failure to present it wisely and well (1 Cor. 10:32–33). We should grieve for pastors who seem to believe that the mark of their orthodoxy is their offensiveness and who forget that the origin of the offense should be God's message, not their manner (2 Cor. 6:3, 6–7). Believers in whom the Spirit has worked have the capacity to receive the most convicting truths with joy when they represent the compassion of God rather than a power play of a preacher (1 Thess. 1:6). The following are tools that preachers can use to overcome application's breaking point without abandoning the priorities of Scripture.

Conclusive arguments. The primary tool of preaching that convicts and transforms is undeniable truth. Preachers should apply that which they have logically demonstrated God's Word requires. Unfortunately, a conclusive argument does not always persuade. The truth of the maxim "A man convinced against his will, is of his own opinion still" often exhibits itself in churches. If preachers are unwilling to confess the truth of this line, they have only to examine their own hearts. Why do preachers, who have so much knowledge of God's requirements, still sin? The answer is that conclusive arguments (as indispensable as they are to biblical preaching) do not always result in obedience. Even preachers do not always do what they know to do, and for this reason, they need additional tools to help them craft effective application.

Disarming illustrations. Deane Kemper writes, "One of the most important uses of stories and quotations is to short-circuit emotional reaction. When you are advancing ideas that may receive a less-than-receptive hearing or even be met with resistance, an illustration can provide an indirect lead-in that is more likely to gain a fair hearing than a more frontal, didactic approach."[45] The nature of the narrative can demonstrate the goodwill of the preacher. A story also has the ability to guide hearers along a narrative trail that leads to scriptural conclusions, which is better than immediately confronting listeners with arguments that raise their defenses.[46] Kemper also indicates that select quotations from respected experts may open listeners' minds to ideas they might not consider on a preacher's authority alone.

Commonsense proposals. Applications should be relevant, realistic, and achievable. Applications lacking in common sense destroy the credibility of a preacher and impede the acceptance of scriptural truth. Three types of applications are typically lacking in credibility and are thus lacking in persuasive power:

Pie-in-the-sky principles. "Smile more every hour," "Love all your neighbors with all your heart," "Work so that no one will ever go hungry," and "Resolve never to fear again" exemplify applications that live only in pastoral idealism and spiritual hyperbole. The instructions as stated are *unrealistic* because their goals are unattainable. As a result, they have no connection to real life and should not have been uttered. These applications will convince listeners either that they cannot do what Scripture requires or that their preacher lives in a make-believe world.

High hurdles. These applications are based on behaviors beyond the capacities of all but a few listeners. "You should learn Greek and Hebrew so that you can confirm the truth of my words" or "Everyone here should go to the Holy Land so that you can see the type of geographical challenges Jesus faced." No one would deny that such goals would be nice to accomplish, but they are *unachievable* for most people in the pew whose lives are full of other, appropriate obligations.

45. Deane A. Kemper, *Effective Preaching* (Philadelphia: Westminster, 1985), 87.
46. Craig Blomberg, *Interpreting the Parables* (Downers Grove, Ill.: InterVarsity, 1990), 54; and Bryan Chapell, *Using Illustrations to Preach with Power,* rev. ed. (Wheaton: Crossway, 2001), 144–46.

Narrow focus. Applications that a preacher knows almost no one will do even if they are able are not worth the breath and the time. For example, too many preachers endorse and encourage the purchase of books from the pulpit. But unless the book obviously makes a dramatic impact on a large number of people, how many in the congregation will actually take the time to drive to the local bookstore, make the order, and plop down their money? One, two, any? How many will even remember the name of the book by Sunday dinner? Preachers are considered *irrelevant* who too often offer applications that too few can apply.

Of course, the likelihood of implementation should not alone determine whether a preacher applies biblical truths. People may reject biblical instruction simply because of the hardness of their hearts (Isa. 6:9–10; Zech. 7:12). Courage, not common sense, is the issue in this case. God does not excuse ministers from proclaiming his truth simply because people do not want to hear it, but neither does he want preachers to remove his Word from the reach of his people. Even proper applications can be presented at inopportune times or when people are not ready (or able) to hear. Those at the Jerusalem council who gave instructions to the church at large wrote, "It seemed good to the Holy Spirit and to us not to burden you with anything beyond the following" (Acts 15:28). And even Jesus said to his apostles, "I have much more to say to you, more than you can now bear" (John 16:12). Pastoral prudence as well as biblical prescription must govern application because patience and faithfulness are both scriptural mandates (Gal. 5:22).

Task sensitivity. The minister who angrily explodes, "How can the people in this community know how friendly we are if you won't invite your neighbors?" probably makes an impact opposite to that intended. The tone must match the task. A preacher whose application compels love must speak in love. A preacher who says, "If we really understood the resurrection, we would not struggle with grief," should realize that the words will more likely condemn than comfort. Some applications require stern expression (Titus 1:10–13); others need gentleness (2 Tim. 2:24–26). Jesus drove moneychangers out of the temple with a whip, and yet Scripture says that he would not break a "bruised reed" (Isa. 42:3). The authority that the Word of God grants its proclaimers does not mean they must always speak in rebuke. Their authority also grants them the right to encourage (Titus 2:15).

Mature guidance. If only a preacher decides what parishioners should do, they will not grow. Nothing creates and perpetuates spiritual babies more than pastors who will not allow people to come to their own conclusions and take responsibility for their own actions. On occasion, preachers must point to situational specifics and at the same time provide sufficient information and guidance for adults (and sometimes children) to make their own decisions. Even those with apostolic authority practiced this sort of participatory application in order to foster spiritual maturity (e.g., Acts 15; 2 Cor. 1:23–24; 2:9; 2 Tim. 2:24–26; Philem. 8–9, 14, 21). We need both "direct and indirect application"[47] in sermons. Prudence and discretion may indicate that it is better to help listeners build up their own faith resources by giving them the information needed to make correct decisions than by confronting them with the decisions they must make.

Mandate clarity. Preachers who cannot differentiate between a scriptural mandate and a good suggestion drain biblical power from their ministries. You must make sure that Scripture—not you—demands what your application requires. Preachers may suggest many things that help listeners fulfill God's demands, but they err greatly when they imply (or believe) that their suggestions are the Bible's requirements. A twenty-minute devotional every day is a good suggestion, as are reading the Bible as a family at meals, engaging in a small-group Bible study, and enrolling in a Scripture memory course. The Bible, however, requires none of these specific practices. When preachers take a good suggestion and make it a biblical mandate, they not only arrogate their own thoughts to the canon of Scripture but also inevitably preach a pharisaism implying that people can earn grace by meeting these particular standards. Practical suggestions for meeting a biblical requirement are often needed in application, but these suggestions are proffered, not commanded.

Respect for complexity. One of my favorite radio commentators says, "For every complex problem there is a simple answer 'that is wrong!'" A preacher's willingness to admit that a sermon deals only with a narrow aspect of a large concern or that more extensive answers must await later occasions may do far more to bolster application than flip responses, quick solutions, and cliché condemnations. Young preachers often feel that they will damage their credibility if they confess, "I don't know" or "I will have to study more before I have a good answer." Yet such responses may best display the wisdom of the preacher. Thoughtful congregations know no one has all the answers to every concern. Preachers destroy their credibility when they pretend otherwise. They usually offer the worst applications when they preach outside their expertise (e.g., advising congregations on what a union contract should say, specifying how to advocate for a particular legislative bill, dictating legal or medical procedures). Where clear biblical principles apply, preachers have warrant to address all of these issues. Unfortunately, preachers too often confuse the desire to say something with the right to say anything.

Respect for the complexity of life's concerns does not mean that all applications have to be complex. Preachers should not be afraid of simple applications spoken with sincerity and thoughtfulness that make them

47. Larsen, *Anatomy of Preaching,* 100.

powerful.[48] Applications should be true but not trite, apparent but not painfully obvious, and sufficiently plain yet poignant enough to get beneath the skin. No one wants to languish in a pew for thirty minutes listening to the proof for an application they knew before they sat down. Providing new (or fresh) motives, reasons, benefits, consequences, or means for commonly accepted duties remains every pastor's challenge.

At the same time, preachers must be cautious not to make simplistic applications about controversial subjects without offering sufficient exposition to enable uninformed or non-agreeing listeners to handle the instruction. Keeping an FCF in view from the introduction through the conclusion will help keep application from dangerous steps off the path of exposition.[49] A sermon dealing with the need for fidelity in marriage is probably not the best place for a line such as, "And, similarly, faithfulness to God requires that we not participate in the lottery, abort the unborn because of their gender, or ignore the homeless." Applications are not always legitimate simply because somewhere a sermon will support what you say. If a particular sermon does not adequately support an application, think twice before offering it. Preachers should not raise more snakes of controversy in a sermon than the exposition provides biblical sticks to kill.

Spiritual integrity. Application also requires personal trustworthiness. Why should people listen to a preacher tell them what they do not want to do, have not done, or will need to change? If the answer is not "Because they know the preacher loves them and the Lord too much to withhold the truth they need," then the application will fall on deaf ears. Even when it hurts, people listen to application from a preacher whom they perceive possesses spiritual integrity. Such trust does not rise from academic exegesis or homiletical structure but results as a pastor's life reflects sensitivity to and dependence on the indwelling Spirit.

So many pastoral matters require prudence, judgment, and discernment. How do we know when to tackle an issue head-on and when to exercise patience? How do we know when to say precisely what to do and when to let others make their own decisions? When does gentleness become compromise, and when does forcefulness degenerate into arrogance? How do we know when to say, "I don't know"? No textbook can answer these questions. Preachers remain dependent on the Word and the Spirit. Only preachers whose minds and motives are conformed to God's will by the Spirit's daily work will reflect the wisdom and the maturity of judgment that grants power over application's breaking point.

Preachers' lives will confirm the heart behind their applications of the Word (1 Thess. 2:8–12). Ultimately, sermons have power because the wisdom

---

48. Veerman, "Sermons," 121.
49. Larsen, *Anatomy of Preaching,* 99; and Adams, *Truth Applied,* 41, 69.

and compassion evident in preachers' actions demonstrate the presence of the Spirit in their words. Applications are not a license for preachers to take potshots from behind the pulpit (e.g., "We need leaders in this church who will lead by example in giving") or to preach their personal interests (e.g., respect my position, attend my prayer meeting, join my church). Preachers who employ such applications may believe that their brass indicates courage, but thoughtful people eventually recognize preachers who substitute personal polish for spiritual fire and heed them little. Ultimately, the Spirit alone can apply the truths of his Word, and therefore, sermonic application succeeds only when preachers preach for his purposes and in dependence on his work.

The Attitudes of Application

Application focuses the impact of an entire sermon on the transformation(s) God requires in his people as a consequence of his Word. This is not the time to mince words or abandon care. From the pulpit, say exactly what you mean exactly as you would say it to a loved one. The spiritual welfare of others requires that you not obscure your meaning in abstract idealism that disturbs no one and has no potential to get you in trouble. If the young people need to stop seeing violent or pornographic movies, tell them so. If the church will not heal until gossip stops, say so. If political differences are dividing believers, address the problem. Speak with tact. Speak with love. But do not fail to say what the situation requires and what the Bible demands.

In application, preachers pour out their hearts. Without application, preachers have difficulty preaching with fervor. After all, who can say with heartfelt conviction, "Paul went from Iconium to Lystra"? The need of the people of God to sense the impact of his Word draws feeling from preachers' own hearts. Exposition not powered by application usually falls flat and robs a message of serious consideration. This is because there is something fundamentally irrational about paying attention to persons who say they have something important to proclaim but who speak without the passion that signals its importance.

Passion comes naturally to sermons when preachers speak as though they are addressing a real concern with a friend. If a friend were to come to our door one evening and confess that his teenage son is destroying his family, we would invite the friend to sit at our kitchen table, and we would talk plainly. The hurt in our friend's eyes would dissuade us from pompous idealisms, the need to offer real help would make us turn to the Bible for practical aid, and our friendship would keep us speaking with love even if we had to say hard things. The best preaching offers no less. Application presented as though we are speaking to a friend across a kitchen table has more spiritual potential than a dozen sermons designed for delivery from Mount Sinai. When Jesus spoke, the Bible records, the common people delighted to hear him because he spoke so plainly about their concerns. Preaching that represents him should still speak as he did.

Our voices will fade, however, if we do not maintain a final attitude in making application: forgiveness. A mark of naive or inexperienced preaching is the expectation that, because the preacher says the right thing, the people will do the right thing, right away. Some sins are corrected in a conversation, and some require faithful preaching over a generation—or more. Faithful preachers must be able to tell people what the Bible requires and still love them when they act as though the words were never spoken. Frustration, anger, and despair are the sure companions of a preacher who cannot forgive the regular failure of God's people to apply his Word. Such attitudes inevitably diminish the joy and zeal of the preacher. Application that remains strong and steady week after week arises from a mind fixed on God and from a heart that beats for broken people in a fallen world.

Questions for Review and Discussion

1. What is the main thing to be done in an expository sermon?
2. What are four basic questions that complete application must answer?
3. What distinguishes instructional specificity from situational specificity? Why are both important?
4. What is expositional rain?
5. What is a sermon's breaking point, and how is it overcome?
6. Why and how should a preacher differentiate between a scriptural mandate and a good idea?

Exercises

1. Create two paragraphs of application for one of the main points you outlined in the exercises at the conclusion of chapter 6, or create two paragraphs of application for the following main point: Because Jesus always intercedes for his church, we must pray consistently and fervently.
2. Explain how the following verses bear on the attitude with which a preacher should express application:
   1 Thessalonians 2:7–12
   2 Timothy 2:24–26
   2 Timothy 4:2
   Titus 1:10–13
   Titus 2:15

G O A L   O F   C H A P T E R   9

*To present principles for constructing effective
introductions, conclusions, and transitions*

9

Introductions, Conclusions, and Transitions

Necessary Pieces

A good friend once began a wonderful sermon with this artful dodge: "Two of the foods I most admire are products of childhood memories. I remember the delight I took in my aunt Bessie's sour pickles. Using a secret recipe and cucumbers from her own garden, Aunt Bessie made pickles so crisp they would snap like a firecracker when you crunched down on that first sour bite that puckered your lips before drenching your tongue in a sweet dill that made you ache for more. Those pickles always added some spark to the fall picnic in my home church, but they were only a prelude to the real treat. Between the morning and afternoon preaching, the women gathered around great kettles placed over open fires lit behind People's Bible Church in rural Red Bank, Mississippi. There in those magic caldrons beneath the smoke that danced between the steeple and nearby woods, a brew of cinnamon, sugar, sweet dough, and tart apples from local orchards somehow coalesced into fried apple pies so delicious that a large mouthful could almost make you swallow your tongue. All my adult life I have been in search of sour pickles like my aunt Bessie's and fried apple pies like those cooked at People's Bible Church in Red Bank, Mississippi. But as with the search for an introduction to this sermon, I have yet to find anything that meets the requirements."

So began this supposedly introductionless sermon. Yet whether the preacher intended it or not, his denial of having an introduction was his message's introduction. Introductions, conclusions, and transitions cannot be avoided. Regardless of our intentions or abilities, our sermons will have introductions, conclusions, and transitions. The first words you say introduce your message, the last words you say conclude it, and the material that ties these two events together inevitably contains transitions. The real question is whether these necessary pieces will serve or burden the message. Knowing the purposes and structures that characterize the best of these components will help answer that question.

Purposes of Introductions

To Arouse Interest in the Message

The assumption that one's listeners automatically share one's own interest in the sermon is a mark of an inexperienced preacher.[1] Such a preacher reasons that because God's people *should be* interested in God's Word, they *will be* interested in a discussion of it. Only in a perfect world would such an expectation have merit.

The tiresomeness of so many sermons; the weekly assaults on the realities of faith from family, friend, and foe; the weariness prompted by work stress; the overdone Saturday-night fun; the competing influences of the entertainment media; the seeming irrelevance of prophets and apostles dead for at least two millennia; and the mere redundancy of a lifetime of Sunday morning rituals combine to make congregational interest in any message a minor miracle that no minister should ever take for granted. Explains William Hogan:

> You must remember that you come to the pulpit having spent hours in the study poring over the passage on which you are to preach. You have been thinking over your subject for days, or weeks, perhaps even for years. But your people have probably not thought about it at all. Indeed, they may not even know what it is going to be before you stand up to speak. (Pray that they will know after you have finished.) The chasm separating their thoughts from biblical ideas may be vast. In the introduction you must enter their world and persuade them to go with you into the world of biblical truth, and specifically the truth that is the burden of the sermon.[2]

---

1. Haddon Robinson says introductions should "command attention," which— though not the classic terminology—could hardly be stated better (see *Biblical Preaching: The Development and Delivery of Expository Messages*, 2nd ed. [Grand Rapids: Baker, 2001], 166).

2. William L. Hogan, "It Is My Pleasure to Introduce . . . ," *Expositor* 1, no. 3 (August 1987): 1.

Sermon introductions are never superfluous. A preacher who, after commanding, "Open your Bibles to . . . ," immediately launches into a discussion of the history and grammar of the text has not exegeted the nature and the circumstances of those who must listen and thereby forfeits a hearing.

Today's communication researchers say that audiences generally decide within the first thirty seconds of a presentation whether they are interested in what a speaker will say.[3] This modern reality underscores the importance of gaining attention in the opening moments of a sermon, but the insight is not new. The Roman orator Quintilian said that "a flawed introduction is like a scarred face"—you want to turn from it.[4] An introduction is so crucial to the likelihood of listeners hearing the rest of a sermon that preachers have long adopted the maxim "Well begun is half done."[5] Only the conclusion rivals the introduction for determining whether listeners will digest the sermonic food offered them. No matter how good the meat inside, if these surrounding "slices of bread" are moldy, we should not expect anyone to take a bite.

An introduction should present listeners with an arresting thought that draws them away from apathy or competing interests and makes them say, "Hey! I need to hear this." An introduction may pique curiosity, concern, mirth, or wonder, but no matter what avenue a preacher takes, the task remains the same: Get their attention! If the opening sentence does not stimulate interest when it stands alone, reject it. Make the opening words count. After you step forward to begin the sermon, pause, square your shoulders to the congregation, look directly at your listeners, gather your breath, and then speak with evident confidence in your first words.[6] You may not have a second chance to make that first impression that garners attention for matters of eternal consequence.

The key to arousing interest is to involve listeners.

Involve their imaginations.
Involve their sense of wonder.

3. Only a generation ago, the time allowance for this judgment was sixty seconds (cf. D. W. Cleverley Ford, *The Ministry of the Word* [Grand Rapids: Eerdmans, 1979], 215). The media influences of our culture continue to compress our attention spans.

4. Quintilian 4.1.61.

5. To which John A. Broadus adds the quip, "Ill begun is apt to be wholly ruined" (*On the Preparation and Delivery of Sermons,* ed. J. B. Weatherspoon [New York: Harper & Row, 1944], 103).

6. Michael J. Hostetler adds these important comments about opening sentences: "First, let the opening sentence *be* an opening sentence. Let silence separate it from all that precedes it, whether music, Scripture reading, or pulpit small talk ('Thank you, Mrs. Murphy, for that truly wonderful solo.'). It takes discipline not to muddle or to mumble into the sermon. Good preachers are not afraid of the silence, especially that moment of quiet immediately before the sermon's opening sentence that sets the sermon apart from the preceding item in the liturgy" (*Introducing the Sermon: The Art of Compelling Beginnings,* The Craft of Preaching Series [Grand Rapids: Zondervan, 1986], 30). See also Robinson, *Biblical Preaching,* 166.

Involve their appreciation of the past.

Involve their fear of the future.

Involve their outrage.

Involve their compassion.

In some way, make them need to go with you into the body of the message. What makes an introduction most interesting are features that indicate that the message will have an impact on listeners' lives.

To Introduce the Subject of the Message

An introduction must indicate what a message will be about. An introduction that arouses interest but does not focus attention on the subject actually gives listeners a false lead. Confusion and resentment can result. The all-too-common practice among after-dinner speakers, business seminar instructors, and not a few preachers of beginning messages with humorous anecdotes may elicit laughter but may also create distrust of the speaker. When it is obvious that the joke has nothing to do with the subject, listeners know they have been manipulated, and they typically adjust their expectations toward more enjoyment while bracing against any persuasion from one so calculating.[7]

A preacher may begin with a thought-provoking question, a story, a quotation, an anecdote, or a host of other attention-getting alternatives. Still, the introduction succeeds only when at its end the central thought in listeners' minds is the subject of the sermon. Jay Adams writes, "The purpose of an introduction is to lead the congregation into the matter to be discussed. If it fails to do that, it fails."[8] An introduction may illustrate, demonstrate, state, imply, indicate by contrast, or in some other way signal what a preacher will address. By the conclusion of the introduction, however, every listener should know that the message is about "Christian leadership," "the path to marital happiness," "the means of sanctification," "the marks of a sound church," or "an answer to loneliness," because the introduction has aroused interest in that specific subject.

To Make the Subject Personal

An introduction is a preacher's handshake of good intent. With the opening words, a preacher welcomes listeners into the sermon while assuring

7. Cf. Ralph Lewis, *Speech for Persuasive Preaching* (Wilmore, Ky.: Asbury Theological Seminary, 1968), 95; Donald E. Demaray, *An Introduction to Homiletics* (Grand Rapids: Baker, 1978), 68; Hogan, "It Is My Pleasure," 2; and Robinson, *Biblical Preaching*, 166.

8. Jay E. Adams, *Preaching with Purpose: A Comprehensive Textbook on Biblical Preaching* (Grand Rapids: Baker, 1982), 59.

them that what they are about to hear is important and good for them. As was discussed in chapter 1, nothing is more important for the credibility of a speaker and the reception of a message than listeners' perception of the preacher's concern for them. "Your job is to so describe the problems that people face and the solutions that Scripture gives that listening to God's Word becomes important—nothing less than an event."[9] No hearer has reason to progress beyond a sermon's introduction if it does not point to an obvious personal consequence.

In an introduction, a preacher indicates why listeners should listen to the message by identifying the Fallen Condition Focus (FCF) of the sermon.[10] The failure to do so is one of the most common and deadly omissions in evangelical preaching.[11] Preachers are almost universally adept at using introductions to indicate what sermons will be about, but they are too frequently unskilled at explaining why hearers need to listen. Preachers introduce subjects without reasons. Listeners must know the reason it is important for them (in their lives today) to listen to a sermon on justification, perseverance, or God's sovereignty. Simply providing the biblical material that logically explains or theologically categorizes such concepts does not constitute a sermon designed to minister to God's people. Until preachers identify a fallen condition that makes it clear why a message is important and will be helpful for listeners' walk with God, they give the average person no more incentive to listen than to attend a lecture on quantum physics. Haddon Robinson explains:

> Early in the sermon, therefore, your listeners should realize that you are talk-ing to them about themselves. You should raise a question, probe a problem, identify a need, open up a vital issue to which the passage speaks. Contrary to the traditional approach to homiletics, which holds the application until the conclusion, application starts in the introduction. Should preachers of even limited ability bring to the surface people's questions, problems, hurts, and desires to deal with them from the Scriptures, they will bring the grace of God to bear on the agonizing worries and tensions of daily life.[12]

The more specific, poignant, and personal a preacher makes the presenta-tion of the FCF, the more powerful will be the introduction (see fig. 9.1). There should be no question what the FCF of a message is by the end of the introduction. Normally, a preacher states the precise FCF toward the end of the introduction in a concise sentence that acts as the obvious launching pad

---

9. Jay E. Adams, *Truth Applied: Application in Preaching* (Grand Rapids: Zondervan, 1990), 72.

10. See the discussion of the Fallen Condition Focus in chap. 2.

11. Cf. Robinson, *Biblical Preaching*, 106–7.

12. Ibid., 171; see also Sidney Greidanus, *The Modern Preacher and the Ancient Text: Interpreting and Preaching Biblical Literature* (Grand Rapids: Eerdmans, 1988), 184.

for the rest of the sermon. It is not enough to present the FCF in general terms—as though there is a problem out there somewhere that someone should be concerned about sometime. A preacher must frame the FCF in such a way as to make it immediately and personally apply to listeners.[13]

Figure 9.1

The Introduction Chain

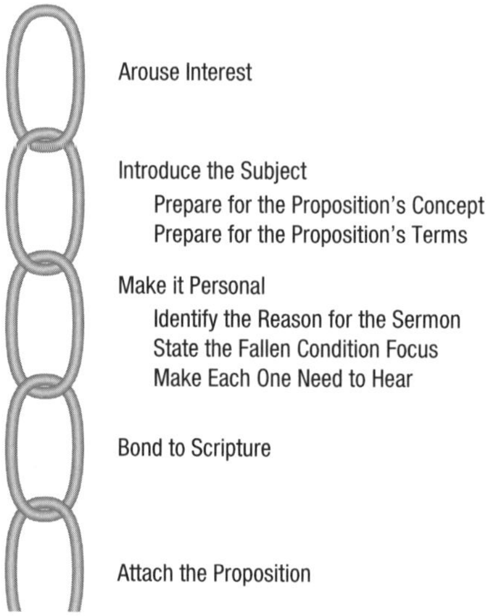

Arouse Interest

Introduce the Subject
    Prepare for the Proposition's Concept
    Prepare for the Proposition's Terms

Make it Personal
    Identify the Reason for the Sermon
    State the Fallen Condition Focus
    Make Each One Need to Hear

Bond to Scripture

Attach the Proposition

Specific statements such as these can capture the FCF that drives the development of a sermon: "When you cannot see God's purposes, God's promises can make you angry"; "It seems impossible to raise godly teens in a culture in which all values are relative"; or "When we know we are guilty, the gift of grace does not feel like it costs us enough." An FCF states the negative—the problem in the human condition—that the truths of a text will redemptively address by God's grace for our good and his glory. By directing a text's truth to human struggle in the introduction, a preacher begins to develop application at the sermon's outset. In addition, a preacher discerns the focus of the message to which all remaining applications should relate in order to develop the deep implications of the text's significance rather than to develop lists of imperatives that simply skip across the surface of the text. In this way, the truths of a text drive ever more poignantly and powerfully into the concerns of the heart, and the minister is able to pastor as well as to preach in every subsequent aspect of the sermon.

Even if a preacher only implies the FCF, it should still be so clear that

13. Adams, *Preaching with Purpose,* 64; and Hogan, "It Is My Pleasure," 3.

people feel compelled to listen. Almost every minister knows that there are three kinds of preachers: those to whom you cannot listen, those to whom you can listen, and those to whom you must listen. No factor more assures that we will be among those whose sermons are most compelling than our willingness to form introductions that convince people they must hear what follows. Lest this goal appear to be mere pandering to the desires of the day, consider this ringing exhortation of Ian Pitt-Watson: "Every sermon is stretched like a bowstring between the text of the Bible on the one hand and the problems of contemporary human life on the other. If the string is insecurely tethered to either end, the bow is useless."[14] Identifying the FCF in the introduction not only gives people a stake in the message but also convinces them that their preacher is in touch with their world, wants to help, is open to their needs, and truly desires to make the Word of God an authentic instrument of God's healing and glory in a broken world.[15]

When the FCF is framed in the introduction, the whole message penetrates daily experience with an application thrust that begins with a preacher's first words.[16] This emphasis not only makes listeners expect and desire answers but also gives preachers a weekly zeal for their messages. When we see that our sermons have real answers to real problems and that people really want to listen, our calling reignites with each message. We have cause to preach! No preaching rationale provides greater purpose or joy. No preaching approach more directly gives listeners cause to glorify God.

To Prepare for the Proposition

Homiletics texts unanimously agree that an introduction prepares listeners for the body of a sermon.[17] Since this is an introductory text, however, more specific directions may prove helpful. In a formally constructed sermon, an introduction prepares for the body of a message by leading to the proposition. Because the proposition is the theme of the overall message, an introduction that leads into the proposition automatically orients listeners to the body of the message. This orientation will go astray, however, if a preacher does not recognize that the proposition is not a theme tacked onto an introduction. The proposition is actually a summary of the introduction as well as a thematic statement of the sermon's subject.

14. John Stott cites this and similar statements attributed to D. Martyn Lloyd-Jones, Phillips Brooks, C. H. Spurgeon, Jonathan Edwards, Chrysostom, and others while making the same point in *Between Two Worlds: The Art of Preaching in the Twentieth Century* (Grand Rapids: Eerdmans, 1988), 146–50.

15. Demaray, *Introduction to Homiletics,* 68.

16. Cf. David L. Larsen, *The Anatomy of Preaching: Identifying the Issues in Preaching Today* (Grand Rapids: Baker, 1989), 99; Greidanus, *Modern Preacher and the Ancient Text,* 182; and Adams, *Truth Applied,* 41, 73.

17. Robinson, *Biblical Preaching,* 171–72; Demaray, *Introduction to Homiletics,* 69; and Jerry Vines, *A Practical Guide to Sermon Preparation* (Chicago: Moody, 1985), 138.

If listeners feel unprepared for ideas stated in the proposition, then the introduction has not properly led into the proposition. This occurs if the *concepts* stated in the proposition did not originate in the introduction or if the *terminology* used in the proposition does not originate in the introduction. For example, if the introduction is a story about a child lost without a guide, then listeners will scratch their heads in consternation at a proposition urging them to "tithe because God is gracious." The concepts are not related.

Listeners also become disoriented if a preacher uses inconsistent terminology. When an introduction repeatedly refers to "a child who is lost," but the proposition speaks of "sinners who do not know the Lord," the change of terms can confuse listeners, even if the preacher has the same concept in mind. If a proposition does not echo significant terms of the introduction, then listeners feel like one given a map to a city whose main streets have been renamed. *The introduction, therefore, should prepare for the proposition in concept and terminology.* All key terms of the proposition should beacon in the introduction before they appear in the proposition. For formally worded propositions, this means that the key words of both the application and the principle clause should appear in the introduction.

Recognition that an introduction prepares listeners for the proposition warns preachers against separating the introduction from the body of the sermon with a Scripture reading.[18] Although occasionally there are good, creative reasons for such a sequence, it often damages the thought flow and cohesion that propositions are designed to facilitate.[19] Preachers who regularly introduce a sermon before reading the Scripture text may be confusing a *sermon* introduction with a *Scripture* introduction (see this chapter's section on Scripture introductions). Reference to the Scripture passage certainly has a place in traditional sermon introductions—not through a reading of the text but by an indication of how the text will address the FCF. After stating the FCF, a preacher usually ties the sermon to Scripture by indicating how (or at least that) the text addresses the subject.[20] This bonding to Scripture usually occurs through a brief sentence or two immediately preceding the proposition and establishes (1) hope for an FCF solution and (2) authority for the proposition's assertions.[21]

18. Broadus, *On the Preparation and Delivery of Sermons,* 102.

19. When time constraints are tight or there is a high likelihood that listeners will tune out the Scripture reading, there are good reasons to begin a sermon without a prior Scripture reading. In such cases, preachers use the introduction to prepare listeners for the reading of the text. Such a practice usually requires the introduction to set up a problem or situation that the preacher promises the Scripture passage will address. Then it is read to show its immediate relevance/application to the concern the introduction raised.

20. Hostetler, *Introducing the Sermon,* 50.

21. Note that traditionally one of the primary purposes of introductions was to establish the authority of the speaker (see Demaray, *Introduction to Homiletics,* 69–70; and Broadus, *On the Preparation and Delivery of Sermons,* 102).

The introduction chain (fig. 9.1) pictures the overall character and ordinary sequence of components in effective introductions. Observe how the links in this chain take form in an analysis of an introduction adapted from an account by John Alexander[22] in *The Other Side* (table 9.1).

Table 9.1

A Sermon Introduction Analyzed

Arouse Attention	The stench was unbearable. It was a poor section of town even by Haiti's standards, and as missionary
Introduce Subject Dealing with overwhelming worldly misery.	leader John Alexander walked through the market, he did not want to *open* his *eyes* to the *misery* around him. Awful food being sold in a shantytown without sewers; the crowd so dense he could hardly move; and kids with red hair. He knew that Caribbean children do not usually have red hair unless they are starving. The whole situation sickened him and led him close to despair.
Note: Key (italicized) terms of the proposition echoing throughout the introduction.	He had *seen* it all before in other towns, in other countries, on other trips. But this time he wrote, "I couldn't stand it. I went home and took a nap. Sometimes I'd like to take a nap for the rest of my life. Not that I'm suicidal. But I'd sure like to shut the truth out somehow." The *vision* of reality before Alexander's *open eyes* was too much for a weary heart that day.
	I do not like the missionary's words any more than the one who wrote them, but I understand their
Statement of FCF: Wanting to close one's eyes to misery. **Making It Personal:** Identifying the listeners' own feelings and concerns with the FCF.	cause. We all know *the temptation of not wanting to open our eyes to the misery of the world because we fear the sight will overwhelm us.* You know this feeling too. Whether it is because of *misery* in your own life, in the lives of those you love, or in the lives of those you pity, you know the near-overwhelming desire just to shut *your eyes* to the *despair* and take a nap. What we have no *might* to stop we have no energy to face.

22. Hostetler directly quotes the article in *Introducing the Sermon*, 60.

**Bonding
to Scripture**

Proposition

But neither resignation nor *despair* is a biblical response to human suffering. The *almighty God,* who does not shield his *vision* from our hurt, offers *faithful* people more purpose and our world more hope than snoring oblivion. Here in the fourth chapter of Amos, the prophet phones in this wake-up call: *Open your eyes* to this world's *misery,* because the *almighty God* uses *faithful vision* to overcome *despair.*

Types of Introductions

Human-interest account. The John Alexander account is an example of an introduction based on a human-interest account—a brief story of someone's experience with which hearers are made to identify.[23] The story may be real or fictional, and it may involve ordinary or extraordinary persons in ordinary or extraordinary situations, but it always creates personal interest or concern. Because of their natural ability to involve listeners' thoughts and emotions, *human-interest accounts are ordinarily the most dependable and effective way to introduce sermons.*[24] Whether the account is serious or humorous, derives from history or the neighborhood, comes from something read or personally experienced, the unrivaled ability of such stories to capture attention and to direct people toward biblical concerns makes them foundational forms of sermon introductions.

Simple assertion. When listeners are already primed to consider the subject of a sermon, a simple assertion of intent may serve as an introduction. This is particularly true if the subject is so troublesome, pressing, tragic, or controversial that a human-interest account might seem to trivialize the matter. "Today, I want to talk to you about how gossip is hurting our church and what we should do about it" is an arresting opening that will perk interest. Note, however, that some of the most difficult issues in Scripture have been introduced with human-interest accounts (e.g., 2 Sam. 12:1–4; Matt. 21:28–32; Luke 15:1–2).

Startling statement. This brief form of introduction is designed to jolt a congregation to attention. Jay Adams offers this wonderful example:

23. See definition of human-interest account in footnote 26 of chap. 7. Although Lloyd Perry lists thirty-six different types of "instruments or materials" for use in sermon introductions (*Biblical Sermon Guide* [Grand Rapids: Baker, 1970], 36–37), Michael Hostetler says they can all be boiled down to two categories: "what you have experienced or read" (*Introducing the Sermon,* 29). I attempt to list only some of the most basic forms of introduction here.

24. For further discussion of how and why human-interest accounts communicate so effectively, see chap. 7.

There is a murderer sitting in this congregation today. . . . Yes, I mean it. Just yesterday he murdered someone. He didn't think that anyone saw him, but he was wrong. I have a written statement from an eyewitness that I am going to read. Here is what it says, "Everybody who hates his brother is a murderer." [1 John 3:15][25]

These lines have also been used effectively:

"What this world needs is fewer churches and more bodies of Christ."
"Your arms are too short to box with God."
"I hate him for what he did to me, and I hate me because I can't forgive him."

Two strong cautions must accompany startling statements. First, you cannot begin with a startling statement every week—only infrequent use of this tool makes it effective. Second, do not forget that an introduction requires more than an opening line. Even a startling statement must flow into a personalized FCF and a clear proposition. This second caution also applies to the additional types of introductions listed below.

Provocative question. Asking a question that provokes thought or initiates an unvoiced discussion with listeners is often a strong way to begin a sermon. "Why does grass grow in my driveway and not in my lawn?" "What does God require when you no longer love the one you married?" Haddon Robinson offers this crisp series of questions sure to perk up ears: "Can a woman who works be a good mother? What do you say? What does the Bible say?"[26] Whether complex or simple, a provocative question can provide an engaging start to a sermon.

Catalog. Grouping or listing items, ideas, or persons in such a way that they reveal the central concept of a sermon is a standard form of introduction. When the children in *The Sound of Music* sing, "Raindrops on roses and whiskers on kittens, bright copper kettles and warm woolen mittens," they engage in a catalog song making the point that simple pleasures make life tolerable. A list of disasters at the beginning of a sermon may well make the point that the uncertainties of existence make life without faith intolerable. Lewis Smedes offers this poignant combination of a catalog introduction and a human-interest account while describing the participants in a church service whose everyday lives require a supernatural hope:

25. Adams, *Preaching with Purpose*, 61–62.
26. Robinson, *Biblical Preaching*, 170.

A man and woman, sitting board-straight, smiling on cue at every piece of funny piety, are hating each other for letting romance in their marriage collapse in a tiring treadmill of tasteless, but always tidy, tedium.

A widow, whispering her Amens to every promise of divine providence, is frightened to death because the unkillable beast of inflation is devouring her savings.

A father, the congregational model of parental firmness, is fuming in the suspicion of his own fatherly failure because he cannot stomach, much less understand, the furious antics of his slightly crazy son.

An attractive young woman in the front pew is absolutely paralyzed, sure she has breast cancer. . . .

A submissive wife of one of the elders is terrified because she is being pushed to face up to her closet alcoholism.

Ordinary people, all of them, and there are a lot more where they come from. What they all have in common is a sense that everything is all wrong where it matters to them most. What they desperately need is a miracle of faith to know that life at the center is all right.[27]

Other options. Interesting quotations, striking statistics, biblical accounts with contemporary descriptions, correspondence excerpts, parables, familiar or pithy poetry, object lessons, and a host of other creative options may also serve well as sermon introductions. Nothing works all the time; some types of introductions work well only when used infrequently; almost all work best if a preacher varies the introductory approach from week to week.

Chief offenders. Two of the most commonly used but ineffective types of sermon introductions are historical and literary (or logical) recapitulation. With these introductions, preachers perform the vital expository task of establishing the context, background, and limits of a text. These concepts are important but misplaced if they occur in an introduction. Many people sit in pews assuming that the ancient writings of Scripture have nothing to do with contemporary life, and in the first two minutes of the sermon, the preacher does nothing but convince them they are right. William Hogan writes:

> What is the first unspoken, even unconscious, question in the average listener's mind? Probably it's this: *is it worth the effort to listen to what the preacher is going to say?* Listening, after all, is hard work. . . . But will those first two or three sentences make them want to keep listening? Imagine a sermon that begins as follows (and I have heard plenty that were almost as dull): "In this difficult passage the sacred writer refers to a long-forgotten custom of the Moabites." Difficult? Sacred writer? Long-forgotten? Moabites? Can you blame a listener who concludes that it is easier and more worthwhile to think about the starting lineup for today's game for the next half hour?[28]

27. Lewis B. Smedes, "Preaching to Ordinary People," *Leadership* 4, no. 4 (Fall 1983): 116.
28. Hogan, "It Is My Pleasure," 1; cf. Vines, *Practical Guide to Sermon Preparation*, 139.

Information about a text is absolutely crucial to its faithful exposition, but few (and perhaps none) will hear that information if a preacher makes little effort to ensure that listeners can hear and that the introduction has not turned off listeners' receptivity. Jay Adams offers this stark advice:

> Do not begin with the text; begin with the congregation as Peter and Paul did. Turn to the passage of Scripture only when you have adequately oriented your congregation to what they will find there *and only when you have sufficiently stirred up in them a concern to know about it.*[29]

If you must begin by recapping forty years of Israel's history that precipitate a prophecy, the argument of Paul that precedes a problem text, or the events in David's life that punctuate a lament, at least paint the summary well. Contemporize your comments with enough narrative details, current language, and modern parallels that people can identify with the biblical situation. Give the recap a human-interest-account feel that invites listener interest and causes personal concern.

Cautions for Introductions

Distinguish the "Scripture" Introduction

Much confusion exists over what sermon introductions should accomplish because pastors have not been taught the ancient wisdom of preparing a Scripture introduction. Confusion begins at the moment that a preacher invites listeners to turn to the biblical passage the sermon will expound.[30] After the preacher has said, "Please turn with me in your Bibles to Romans 6:15–23," what comes next? Does the preacher simply stand in an awkward silence while parishioners thumb through their Bibles to find the text? Does the preacher immediately commence reading with the hope that people will catch up when they find the passage? The best answer is neither.

After announcing the text, two obligations immediately fall on the preacher. The first of these obligations (although it may not come first in actual sequence) is to *contextualize* the text so that listeners will understand the reading. This may involve offering brief background comments (a sentence or two at most), providing definitions for unfamiliar words, or otherwise quickly orienting listeners to the passage. Second, the preacher must *create a longing* for the Word (see table 9.2). For many listeners, the Bible is simply a fog too dense

---

29. Adams, *Truth Applied,* 71, emphasis added. Cf. Stott, *Between Two Worlds,* 245; and Edward F. Marquart, *Quest for Better Preaching* (Minneapolis: Augsburg, 1985), 107.

30. The following comments assume the practice of reading Scripture immediately before the sermon. However, even if someone reads the text for the sermon earlier in the service, similar principles still apply for those who truly want parishioners to follow in their Bibles.

for navigation. Others look at the Bible as a mountain of trite and tired truths they have scaled too often and from which they expect no new vistas. Those eager to read, those scared to read, and those calloused to reading all sit before the minister, who must draw each within the confines of the Word.

Table 9.2

Example of a Scripture Introduction

Creation of Longing	Christians are rarely uncertain about Christ's commands to forgive—and they are often haunted by their own inability to forgive. If you know what it is to hate your own bitterness . . . if you want to know how to let the poison drain from your own soul, . . . then this passage is for you.
Brief Contextualization	You need not be ashamed that you need to listen because here in Matthew 18 Jesus tells his own disciples how to deal with their unforgiving hearts. If you are as human as they are, read with me what we all need to know.

Homileticians identify the phase of the sermon prior to the Scripture reading as the ante-theme.[31] In these moments, a preacher hints at the issues a sermon will address to stimulate a congregation's interest in the passage as well as in the message. The ante-theme quickly makes people sense enough promise and/or interest in the text to venture forward with the preacher. If the Scripture introduction labors beyond four or five sentences, it is usually too long. With the Scripture introduction, the preacher primarily prepares for the reading of the Word, not for the complexities of the entire sermon.

The argument over whether the traditional prayer for illumination should precede or follow the Scripture reading is less pivotal than whether listeners follow the reading. If preachers use such a prayer, they should place it where it best serves the thought, flow, and purpose of the message. Many variations have good warrant (see fig. 9.2).

One additional obligation of the Scripture introduction is easily met—but easily forgotten: Reannounce the text. Preachers should anticipate what their listeners are doing when they finally get to the page in the Bible of the previously announced passage. They lean over to their neighbor and ask, "What verses did the preacher say?" The experienced preacher knows human nature well enough to anticipate and answer the question with a second (and even third) announcement of the specific chapter and verse reference.

---

31. Thomas Chabham of Salisbury (fl. 1230), in his *Summa de arte praedicandi*, offered pioneering guidance in the use of the pro- or ante-theme.

Figure 9.2

A Common Pattern for Effective Sermon Beginning

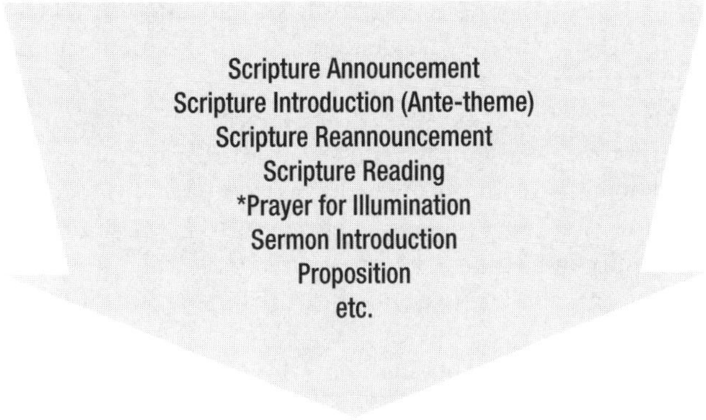

Scripture Announcement
Scripture Introduction (Ante-theme)
Scripture Reannouncement
Scripture Reading
*Prayer for Illumination
Sermon Introduction
Proposition
etc.

*Also functions well prior to Scripture introduction or the Scripture reading.

Scripture introductions can also relieve preachers of certain textual obligations. A preacher can use the ante-theme to *summarize* portions of a lengthy narrative so that the Scripture reading does not last too long. Providing a general synopsis along with specific readings of briefer portions of a text allows listeners to focus on verses pivotal to a sermon's development. A preacher may also *slice out* more specific purposes for a sermon in the Scripture introduction, indicating that the message will be about only particular verses or particular subjects from the reading. In this way, an expositor can put the larger context of a passage before a congregation without seeming to neglect or skip matters that are not the focus of the sermon. The preacher simply predefines the narrower territory that the message will cover.

Hone the "Sermon" Introduction

Be brief. Sermon introductions that roam more than two or three standard-length paragraphs (two to three minutes) usually drift into danger. "He took so long setting the table that I lost my appetite for the meal" is an accusation variously applied to some historic preachers[32] and best avoided by contemporary ones. "If you can't strike oil in three minutes, you should quit boring."[33]

Be focused. An introduction is often called the porch of a sermon, and preachers are frequently cautioned that listeners "do not want a porch on a porch."[34] Focus the introduction. Try not to make one story lead

32. Cf. Broadus, *On the Preparation and Delivery of Sermons,* 107; and Robinson, *Biblical Preaching,* 165.
33. Vines, *Practical Guide to Sermon Preparation,* 139.
34. Broadus, *On the Preparation and Delivery of Sermons,* 105, 107; and Vines, *Practical Guide to Sermon Preparation,* 139.

into another. Excise extraneous details and tangential comments. There should be no opportunity for listeners to wander from the focus of the message. This caution also advises against the tendency to quote Scripture passages other than the text the sermon should expound. An introduction should act like a directional beacon leading all airborne thoughts to a single landing strip.

Be real. This is the age of conversational speech. Although highly impassioned or argumentative comments have a definite place in preaching, they usually do not serve introductions well. A preacher who starts off in high gear while listeners are just getting their thoughts on the track is likely to race alone. Theologian Robert Dabney once gave this practical advice to preachers who might be tempted to slight the situation of their hearers:

> Just as you must lead their thoughts from where they are to where you want them, so you must lead their affections to higher levels. Be careful not to give vent to the full fervor of your emotion at the outset. One master teacher of homiletics has warned, "When he [the preacher] is all fire and they [the congregation] as yet are ice, a sudden contact between his mind and theirs will produce rather a shock and a revulsion than sympathetic harmony." His emotion is to their quietude extravagance. He must raise them first a part of the way toward his own level.[35]

Lay the kindling before starting a fire.

Be specific. Broad generalizations and obvious abstractions are immediate turnoffs. Who wants to listen to a sermon that begins with the so-called insight that "goals are important in life"? Academic training habituates preachers to state the generic first and then to work toward the particular. However, the best introductions start with specifics.[36] Instead of offering the obvious (e.g., "Some people believe God is arbitrary."), state the personal consequence ("My friend says that because he sinned God gave his son cancer."). Instead of opening a message with textbook principles (e.g., "God saves us by faith alone."), speak of the human concern ("When will you be good enough for God?").

Be professional. Because so much of a preacher's credibility, a congregation's interest, and a sermon's progress ride on the opening words, they must be well prepared.[37] A preacher is most vulnerable to grasping for words and to nervous error in these opening, heart-racing moments, but simply reading a manuscript to avoid mistakes will not provide the credibility or the impact good sermons demand. Dynamic delivery and consistent eye contact are requisites for effective introductions and credible speakers.

---

35. Robert L. Dabney, *Lectures on Sacred Rhetoric* (Carlisle, Pa.: Banner of Truth, 1979), 141.
36. Broadus, *On the Preparation and Delivery of Sermons,* 106.
37. Robinson, *Biblical Preaching,* 174–75.

Preachers should write out the opening paragraphs so they are sure what to say, and then they should commit the opening sentence(s) to memory so that they have immediate credibility with listeners. Although homileticians vary over the best time to write an introduction, most preachers begin to construct an introduction after they have roughed out a sermon's outline, and then they continue to hone its elements as their preparation progresses.[38] Preachers should not try to memorize the entire introduction word for word. Beyond the opening sentence(s), they should memorize concepts, not words, so that their delivery has a natural, conversational flow. Knowing precisely what they intend to communicate and the proposition to which the flow of the introduction leads will keep the introduction naturally powerful, even if they do not recite it. Nothing so manages nerves and empowers delivery as a clear destination.

Even if your message makes you feel inadequate for its proclamation or you are unprepared for the task, introduce the message without spoken or implied apologies. The outset of a sermon is no time to prejudice a congregation against you, your message, or the potential of the Holy Spirit to work in spite of human weakness.[39] Look directly at your listeners, square your shoulders, take a breath as you pause and pray for the Spirit to work beyond you as well as through you, and then begin—with confidence in his working and his Word.

Purposes of Conclusions

Were one to graph the conceptual and emotional intensity of a well-constructed sermon, the results would usually look like figure 9.3. A message that starts with a gripping introduction should end with an even more powerful conclusion.[40] Because listeners are more likely to remember a conclusion than any other portion of a message,[41] and because all a sermon's components should have prepared for this culmination, a conclusion is the climax of a message.

38. Broadus, *On the Preparation and Delivery of Sermons*, 107; Hogan, "It Is My Pleasure," 2; Adams, *Preaching with Purpose*, 64; and Demaray, *Introduction to Homiletics*, 76–77.

39. Broadus, *On the Preparation and Delivery of Sermons*, 104; Hogan, "It Is My Pleasure," 2; and Demaray, *Introduction to Homiletics*, 105.

40. Broadus, *On the Preparation and Delivery of Sermons*, 123.

41. With the exception of their perception of the speaker, which is what they most remember, what people are most likely to remember of a sermon can be seen in this "Sermon Component Retention Hierarchy":

    Some striking aspect of delivery
    Concluding material
    Introductory material
    Illustrations (particularly of the conclusion and/or introduction)
    Specific applications (particularly if listener strongly disagrees or agrees)
    Basic idea of the message

Figure 9.3

Sermon Intensity Graph

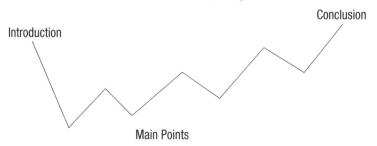

Note overall upward progression of the entire message.

The last sixty seconds are typically the most dynamic moments in excellent sermons. With these final words, a preacher marshals the thought and emotion of an entire message into an exhortation that makes all that has preceded clear and compelling. A conclusion is a sermon's destination. Ending contents are alive—packed with tension, drama, energy, and emotion. This never means bombast and does not necessitate grandiloquence, since deep feeling and powerful thought are often expressed in the most quiet, sincere terms. Masterful conclusions sometimes thunder, and other times they crackle with an electricity barely audible to the ears, but the best endings always soundly register in the heart.

Good conclusions require careful craftsmanship. G. Campbell Morgan said, "Every conclusion must conclude, include, and preclude."[42] To conclude, a conclusion must truly end a message. To do this well, it must include what was previously said and preclude the possibility that the implications and the consequences of the message will escape listeners. To accomplish these purposes, conclusions contain these components:

Recapitulation (i.e., concise summary). A preacher should briefly place before listeners the key thoughts of the preceding exposition.[43] Most of the time a preacher can simply summarize the main ideas of a sermon by restating the key terms of the main points (not entire main-point statements) or by threading these (or other) key terms through a final illustration. A preacher

---

An interesting thought in the message

A main-point statement

An expositional concept

For a discussion of the implications of this hierarchy (that when properly analyzed argues for the importance of each component), see Bryan Chapell, *Using Illustrations to Preach with Power*, rev. ed. (Wheaton: Crossway, 2001), 141–42.

42. G. Campbell Morgan, *Preaching* (Grand Rapids: Baker, 1974), 87.

43. Robinson, *Biblical Preaching*, 176; and Demaray, *Introduction to Homiletics*, 95.

only reminds listeners what has preceded and does not preach the sermon again. If the summary portion of a conclusion lasts more than two or three sentences, it is probably too long. One sentence of concise recap within the larger conclusion will usually suffice. Concluding summaries should sound like hammer strokes, not sonatas.

Exhortation (i.e., final application). Although we have already examined the inappropriateness of delaying all the applications of a sermon until the conclusion, this does not mean that conclusions are devoid of application. In a conclusion, a preacher summons previous thought and present emotions and then exhorts the congregation to act in accord with the thrust of the message.[44] Usually, and for maximum impact, preachers incorporate this exhortation into the conclusion's last sentence or two.

> It is in the conclusion that the appeal to "believe," or "go" or "do" something or other is made. . . . The purpose of the conclusion, then, is not merely to bring the sermon to an end. It does that. But the principal function that it serves is to capsulize and capitalize on the sermon *telos* [i.e., purpose]. The listener goes away with the conclusion, which always calls for some change on his part, in mind. It must be powerful.[45]

In a conclusion, a preacher exhorts people to act on the principles or concepts the sermon has already made clear.[46] Thus, the primary purpose of a conclusion is motivation. Ordinarily, *there should be no new exposition or application in a conclusion* but rather a determined effort to mobilize the wills of the listeners to conform to previously specified imperatives. This means that the concluding exhortation is often broader than (or the culmination of) the applications in the main points. The final challenge urges listeners to consider all that has preceded and inspires them to do what has already been made clear. Now is not the time to reargue the case or prove new specifics. Bring horizons into view, melt hearts, and prod the will.[47] Sage preachers once taught, "If there is no summons, there is no sermon."[48] The advice remains sage: The minister who does not seek this pinnacle effect likely possesses little contemporary impact.

Elevation (i.e., climax). Thought and emotion should arrive at their greatest height and most personal statement in the conclusion. Such elements indicate that a message has led to consideration of matters that are significant, vital, and moving. If the content of a message and the manner of the messenger do not indicate such import at the end, the sermon will probably

---

44. Stott, *Between Two Worlds*, 246–53.

45. Adams, *Preaching with Purpose*, 69.

46. Cf. Broadus, *On the Preparation and Delivery of Sermons*, 125; Demaray, *Introduction to Homiletics*, 95; Larsen, *Anatomy of Preaching*, 124–25; and Robinson, *Biblical Preaching*, 167.

47. Stott, *Between Two Worlds*, 247–48.

48. Broadus, *On the Preparation and Delivery of Sermons*, 210.

fail. John Broadus writes, "Weakness in manner, thought, or words draws the nails instead of driving them deeper. Deep passion, thoughts that burn, strong words are the instruments required, whether the conclusion be a direct drive on the will or an appeal to the heart."[49] If you are not moved, do not expect anyone else to be. To exhaust oneself prior to the conclusion so that the sermon ends weakly may seem noble, but it will strike listeners as indicative of little forethought or, worse, little courage.

Termination (i.e., a definite end). Like the first sentence of a sermon, the last should also make a significant impression.[50] The final sentence structure should demonstrate craftsmanship and fully prepared thought—bearing the entire sermon in nugget form. The wording of this terminus should also be striking enough to echo in the mind of listeners throughout the week. These expectations require a preacher to plan for a definite, purposed, pointed end. W. E. Sangster admonishes:

> Having come to the end, stop. Do not cruise about looking for a spot to land, like some weary swimmer coming in from the sea and splashing about until he can find a shelving beach up which to walk. Come right in, and land at once. If the last phrase can have some quality of crisp memorableness, all the better, but do not grope even for that. Let your sermon have the quality that Charles Wesley coveted for his whole life: let the work and the course end together.[51]

Sangster's advice reminds us that even if conclusions do not meet other homiletical ideals, they are still good if they end crisply.

Types of Conclusions

Although as many resources can be used for conclusions as for introductions,[52] two types of sermon endings predominate: *grand style* and *human-interest account*. In a grand-style conclusion, a preacher heightens the manner of expression and the choice of words to indicate that a message has come to its climax. Summary, final exhortation, and end are stated in elevated language with an intensified delivery that communicates the import of the thought. This style allows a preacher to state a message's point directly while depending on vocabulary choices and delivery skills to express the intensity that effective conclusions require. Student preachers may find this direct approach appealing, but they frequently lack the confidence and the

---

49. Ibid., 126.

50. Demaray, *Introduction to Homiletics,* 101; and Broadus, *On the Preparation and Delivery of Sermons,* 107, 126.

51. W. E. Sangster, *The Craft of Sermon Construction* (Grand Rapids: Baker, 1972), 150.

52. See "other options" above in the discussion of types of introductions. Cf. Larsen, *Anatomy of Preaching,* 123–27.

freedom of powerful expression to make it succeed. Experience will cultivate the instincts and the skills to use grand style effectively, but the sense of climax needed for effective conclusions is consistently available at an early stage of training through human-interest accounts.[53]

For all the reasons stated earlier in this chapter and in chapter 7, human-interest accounts involve listeners as few other sermon components can. If the account chosen for a conclusion is both personally gripping and apt for a sermon's subject, then a preacher has the opportunity to rally both the hearts and the minds of listeners and to motivate their wills. Manipulation of emotions with a story that does not drive home the principles that have been developed in a message ranks among the worst abuses of preaching. But nearly as great an offense is committed by failing to engage the heart, stimulate the will, excite the mind, and elevate the soul concerning eternal truths at this most crucial stage.[54] Preachers who ethically use a human-interest account to elicit honest emotions, stir genuine feelings, and provoke appropriate convictions are following biblical injunctions to urge, persuade, and encourage.[55] Conclusions should neither contrive emotions nor avoid them.

Cautions (Hints) for Conclusions

Poems and quotations. The stereotypical three-points-and-a-poem sermon holds little promise for persuasive power in this age of low literary appreciation. The modern mental palate has little appreciation for difficult words, remote references, and high-blown speech.[56] Not only does a preacher give the final word to someone else when concluding with a poem (or hymn) quotation,[57] but the citation of flowery expression also turns off many contemporary hearers. Unless the poem says precisely what you intend, says it better than you could, and touches a deeper chord than you can reach, frame your own final words. But if you do use an appropriate quotation, use as brief a portion as possible, signal the significance of the lines before you cite them, and vocally emphasize the key ideas. Remember also that it is almost criminal at a sermon's most convicting moment to break eye contact, bury your head in a manuscript, and flatly read obscure words. Conclusions need to be largely committed to memory and movingly spoken from the heart.

High notes. Try to end on a high note. Even the most darkly convicting messages need to end with a ray of hope. If Scripture requires you to take

53. Demaray, *Introduction to Homiletics*, 97.

54. Ibid., 103.

55. Adams, *Preaching with Purpose*, 69.

56. Ibid., 66–67.

57. Larsen, *Anatomy of Preaching*, 127; and David Buttrick, *Homiletic: Moves and Structures* (Philadelphia: Fortress, 1987), 105.

people to the mat, do so. But do not abandon them there. A preacher who leaves a congregation depressed, despairing, and pessimistic about their sin or situation has failed to preach.[58] Remember that the gospel is the Good News. Conclusions should challenge and lift the heart. Clovis Chappell rightly asserted, "No man has a right so to preach as to send his hearers away on flat tires. Every discouraging sermon is a wicked sermon.... A discouraged man is not an asset but a liability."[59]

Anticlimax. Sustain a climax by avoiding common causes of anticlimax. When a preacher seems to have raised the emotions, hammered home the point of a message, and called hearers to action and then launches anew into more oratory, listeners despair or grow angry. William Jennings Bryan's own mother once scolded him, "You missed several good opportunities to sit down."[60] Conclusions work best if there is only one per message.

One way of avoiding an apparent dual ending is to move the illustration of the final main point early into that point's exposition (especially if the conclusion is a human-interest account). In this way, the dynamics of the final point's illustration will not impinge on the thoughts and emotions of the conclusion. Phillips Brooks consistently used the third main point of his messages as the conclusion in order to keep the power of his culminating point from competing with (or diminishing) the power of the conclusion.

Extending a sermon for more than a few sentences beyond its climax creates an anticlimax that will rob the entire message of power. By contrast, ending a message prior to a climax will make it seem to have ended abruptly or simply to have been ill prepared.[61] Although a sudden stop can have a beneficial arresting effect, simply running out of words does not justify its use.[62]

A sermon also dodges anticlimactic tendencies if the summary of the message is placed before the conclusion's climax rather than after it.[63] If the summary comes after the climax, make the recap extremely brief. Lengthy summaries or new explanations of matters not previously addressed will usually disrupt the culminating power of a sermon. An understanding of the way people listen and are motivated strongly cautions against introducing new exposition in a conclusion. Forcing new arguments into a conclusion or preaching a point in the prayer following the conclusion because you forgot it during the message are also surefire ways of blunting a sermon's ending.[64]

Rhetorical questions. Preachers often end sermons by using questions as launching pads for listener reflection. Unfortunately, questions at the end of

58. Larsen, *Anatomy of Preaching,* 129.
59. As quoted in Demaray, *Introduction to Homiletics,* 100.
60. As quoted in Vines, *Practical Guide to Sermon Preparation,* 145.
61. Demaray, *Introduction to Homiletics,* 99.
62. Robinson, *Biblical Preaching,* 176, 181.
63. Broadus, *On the Preparation and Delivery of Sermons,* 127.
64. Demaray, *Introduction to Homiletics,* 99; and Robinson, *Biblical Preaching,* 169–70.

sermons also have a tendency to make the sermon's message dissolve into space. When preachers conclude with a rhetorical question, they intend for listeners to consider more deeply the matters discussed in the sermon. Instead, generic questions frequently tend to drain off the power a conclusion should have (e.g., "And what do you think?"). If you use such questions, be very specific about what you want listeners to consider.[65] Too often rhetorical questions simply demonstrate that a preacher did not think of a more fitting conclusion.

Wraparounds. A highly professional way of concluding is to hearken back to material mentioned in a sermon's introduction (or other earlier portions of the message).[66] Complete a story, echo an earlier thought, refer to character or story specifics in a previous illustration, resolve a tension, repeat a striking phrase, refer to the opening problem, or in some other way end where you began. This wrapping up of the sermon[67] gives the message a sense of being packaged and thus communicates craft, thoughtfulness, and conscientious preparation.

Professional preparation. Professionalism radiates from conclusions that are relatively brief (not more than two or three significant paragraphs), focused, and end poignantly. Conclusions do not always need impassioned speech, but they do need telling words.[68] The last sentence of a conclusion needs special preparation. A powerful phrase—perhaps one that echoes an earlier point in the message, a verse of Scripture movingly quoted, or a simple, clear sentence—marks quality preaching.[69] Each requires careful preparation.

Homiletics experts differ as to when preachers should prepare conclusions.[70] Idealists argue that the conclusion to a sermon should be the first component written so that the sermon has a clear and definite destination while it is being prepared. Realists want the conclusion prepared after the sermon has taken shape so that it definitely reflects the specifics of the developed message. Such realists often argue that a late-formed conclusion does not prematurely affect the direction the Spirit may take a sermon's thought. Realism of another sort, however, requires the recognition that a preacher often has little thought or energy left for conclusions formed late in the sermonic process. Regular practitioners understand that there can be no ironclad rules

65. I recognize that formal rhetoric would not categorize these as rhetorical but rather as maieutic questions (i.e., questions whose answers have already been supplied). True rhetorical questions have no answers. Jay Adams suggests modifying rhetorical questions with "cluster-question" endings (multiple questions grouped together to refine a point) that leave no question about what the conclusion specifically requires (see Adams, *Preaching with Purpose,* 68).

66. Larsen, *Anatomy of Preaching,* 127.

67. "Circular closure" is a common artistic device in literature, rhetoric, and music.

68. Broadus, *On the Preparation and Delivery of Sermons,* 128.

69. Brian L. Harbour, "Concluding the Sermon," in *A Handbook of Contemporary Preaching,* ed. Michael Duduit (Nashville: Broadman, 1992), 221–22.

70. Cf. Broadus, *On the Preparation and Delivery of Sermons,* 123; and Stott, *Between Two Worlds,* 243.

regarding when conclusions are formed. A conclusion sometimes jumps onto the field of preparation and declares its presence before any other sermonic team members arrive, and other times it has to be dragged from bed and pummeled into service long after the other members have assumed their positions. Probably the most balanced approach lies in generating a basic plan for a conclusion during a sermon's embryonic stages but modifying the conclusion to conform to the message's specifics as it develops.

Whatever the timing of their preparation, however, all master preachers agree that conclusions take time. We cannot emphasize too strongly the need for preparation since too many preachers delay constructing a conclusion until they are worn out from preparing the meat of the sermon. As a result, these preachers are tempted to extemporize (rationalized as letting the Holy Spirit inspire) that portion of the sermon that holds the potential for greatest impact. David Larsen recommends that his students spend two-thirds of their time on the last one-third of a message.[71] You may not agree with this time allotment, but you should at least acknowledge that it makes no sense to spend the least amount of preparation on that aspect of a sermon that holds the greatest spiritual potential.

Finally. It is best not to announce the conclusion.[72] Let your manner and thought indicate the culmination. If you say, "Finally . . ." or "In conclusion, . . ." you have tacitly told everyone to stop looking at you and to glance at their watches. Of course, if a sermon has lulled listeners into oblivion, such an announcement can serve as a final, desperate effort to raise the eyelids of those who have abandoned hope for an end. If you do say, "Finally, . . ." mean it. Nothing so frustrates listeners as an announced conclusion that never arrives. R. E. O. White chides:

> An apostle may say "Finally, brethren . . ." and go on for two more chapters: but not you. A troubled English vicar asked a farm-labourer why he came to church only when the assistant preached. "Well sir," said the labourer, "young Mr. Smith, he says 'in conclusion' and he do conclude. But you say 'lastly' and you *do* last."[73]

Purposes of Transitions

An introduction charges into a message. Explanations, illustrations, and applications congregate in the body. Conclusions cap the whole. Each component performs separate, vital functions, but if the pieces remain too

---

71. Larsen, *Anatomy of Preaching,* 121.

72. Vines, *Practical Guide to Sermon Preparation,* 144; Demaray, *Introduction to Homiletics,* 100; and Robinson, *Biblical Preaching,* 181.

73. R. E. O. White, *A Guide to Preachers* (Grand Rapids: Eerdmans, 1973), 111; cf. Robinson, *Biblical Preaching,* 171.

segregated, the sermon will feel like patchwork and the prominence of the seams will obscure the overall design. Something must sew the components together. This is the job of transitions.

Although they contain little raw information, transitions greatly contribute to the thought of a message—aiding its flow, progress, and beauty. Skilled transitions are often the distinguishing mark between mundane messages and excellent sermons.[74] With transitions, a preacher demonstrates the relationship of the introduction to the body of a sermon, the parts of the body to one another, and the conclusion to all that has preceded it.[75] These relationships are most frequently logical connections, but transitions are also psychological, emotional, and aesthetic links. Good transitions harmonize the conceptual and emotional rhythms that run through a sermon.

Transitions not only tie the components of a sermon together but also signal progress and direction to listeners. But the job of transitions is not merely to point forward. They must also relate present matters to previous discussion. Since listeners cannot see the outline of a sermon, transitions cue them as to which thoughts are major, which are minor, and how they relate. For instance, the summary of the explanation is typically also the introduction to the illustration, and the summary of the illustration usually serves as the introduction to the application—and both of these summaries strongly echo the original main-point statement (see fig. 9.4).

Figure 9.4

Double Helix Transition Perspective

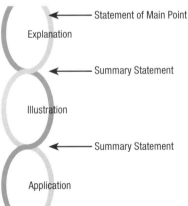

Sometimes preachers insert transitions into a sermon simply to distinguish ideas. When a preacher states a subpoint in the sentence immediately

74. Broadus, *On the Preparation and Delivery of Sermons,* 120.
75. Robinson, *Biblical Preaching,* 135.

after a main-point statement (or states the first main point on the heels of the proposition), listeners often cannot discern which was the major idea. They may wonder if the second statement is really a new thought or if it is merely a refined (or corrected) version of the first statement. Although preachers can do a great deal with voice and gesture to limit confusion, simply separating a major idea from subordinate ideas with a sentence or two of transition often helps avoid problems.

My wife once said of a pastor, "Everything he said was true; he just didn't seem to have a clue how to pull it all together." Such a characterization will not apply to preachers who remember that they must use transitions to review where they have gone, preview where they are going, secure an immediate matter to a larger theme, and/or remove questions about how varying ideas relate to one another. Consistent ties to a sermon's major theme (especially the FCF) at significant junctures throughout the message strongly indicate a preacher's awareness of congregation and communication needs.

Types of Transitions

Knitting statements. The phrase *Not only . . . but also . . .* is the foundational form of transition. The words reach back into previous comments, point toward upcoming discussion, and pull the two together.

The essence of this transition is manifested in many forms. The statements "If this is true, then these are the implications . . ." "Our understanding is not complete until we also consider . . ." and many similar variations capture the significance of the not-only-but-also concept. Parallel wording that picks up key terms summarizing earlier thought and then repeats them in a slightly different form to signal upcoming thought accomplishes similar purposes.[76]

Not-only-but-also variations come in many lengths. Even the simple word *next* reminds listeners that something has preceded and something more will follow. Other connector words (e.g., however, therefore, consequently, yet, etc.) can also provide this service.[77] A short series of sentences can stimulate similar dynamics. Consider how this brief paragraph glues what is ahead to what is behind:

> We have seen how this text demonstrates God's love. But knowing that God means well is not enough warrant to offer him our trust. Good intentions do not make everything work out all right. That is why the apostle Paul continues his argument with proof of God's sovereignty. God does not just

76. See examples of parallel wording in the grouping statement discussion of chap. 7 (e.g., "Just as we cannot turn to God without faith, we will not turn to another without trust.").

77. George E. Sweazey, *Preaching the Good News* (Englewood Cliffs, N.J.: Prentice-Hall, 1976), 78.

desire what is good for us; he accomplishes it. Because God is sovereign, we can trust his love.

Statements such as these that knit together strands of previous and following thought accomplish transitions' most fundamental purpose.[78]

Dialogical questions. A preacher can also signal progress by asking questions that stimulate further discussion. A preacher who can hear the questions playing on listeners' minds and then asks those questions *out loud* employs a powerful rhetorical tool. The dialogue a preacher initiates on listeners' behalf not only convinces them that the preacher respects their thought and is sensitive to their concerns but also invites listeners to continue progressing through the message to satisfy their concerns.[79]

Examples of questions that involve listeners while orienting them to a sermon's progress are: If this approach won't work, what will? What plan does God offer for this? What must come next? Make listeners dive into an explanation with you by asking, "What in the world does this verse mean?" or "How do we know what this verse means?" You can introduce an illustration with, "How can we see this more clearly in our own experience?" Listeners will never tire of the question "How can we apply this truth in our lives?"

Loading a sermon with questions that move listeners into and through the sermon stimulates interest in the message as long as the answers are clear. Following the proposition with a strong overarching question that the main points answer is an effective way to begin a message.[80] But the dialogue should not cease after interrogating the proposition or in the sermon's early moments. Even the most apathetic listener wants to know answers to questions such as these: What else do you do when all else fails? Did God forget that he was a sinner . . . then why would God choose him? How can you face loneliness in the eyes of one you love? Using such questions to frame and set up subpoints[81] can take advantage of this dynamic and energize an entire message.

Numbering and listing. There is little artistry in simply numbering ideas, but a preacher who lists ideas as first, second, and third readily orients listeners to specific stages of a sermon's thought. Preachers who make such encyclopedic references to their ideas need to remember, however, that hearers are not reading the sermon's outline. Listing subpoints as A, B, and

---

78. Recall also that the nodes between the expositional components act as transitions if a preacher properly uses the summary of one component as the de facto introduction to the next component (see discussion in chaps. 7 and 8).

79. Larsen asserts that Jesus' recorded teachings include one hundred questions (*Anatomy of Preaching*, 154).

80. A good diagnostic question that establishes the subject of a sermon can also substitute for the proposition. See further discussion of the uses of analytical questions to set up main points in chap. 6.

81. See the discussion of subpointing in chap. 6.

C shows insensitivity to how we speak to one another in regular conversation. Saying "first" and "second" for each main point *and* for each subpoint causes great confusion for hearers who will struggle to categorize the third, fourth, and fifth mention of "first" through the course of the sermon. Also be careful not to say, "In the third place, . . ." if you have not previously announced what came first and second.[82]

As a final caution, remember that simply numbering one's way through a sermon is a fairly dry and pedantic way to proceed. Unless the ideas require exceptional clarity, other forms of transition are usually more stimulating.

Picture painting. When a controlling image[83] forms the basis of a sermon's outline, a preacher can often make transitions by referring to other aspects of that image. A simple reference to "the flip side of the coin is . . ." draws an image that alerts listeners that the preacher is about to contrast thoughts. Of course, sermons can be built on much more complex images that indicate progression of thought (e.g., "Since God is the architect of our salvation, he does not merely plan his love for us. He designs our love for him. Next, we need to see what characterizes that design."). A separate illustration can also act as a transition between main points, with images or relationships within the story indicating how ideas in the sermon connect.

Billboards and branches. An important but often neglected area of transition arises between the introduction and the body of a message. Here skilled preachers often preview how they will handle issues raised in the introduction by use of a billboard. Billboards are crystallized statements of the main points (typically using only key words) in the order they will appear (e.g., "To have an assurance of your relationship with God, you must believe that the love of Jesus is greater than *sin, circumstances,* and *Satan.*").

Sermon billboards usually occur just before or just after a proposition (and are occasionally incorporated into the proposition) to indicate the direction and organization of a message. Billboards quickly orient listeners to a sermon's plan and bind a preacher to a certain path. Failure to follow the path signaled will confuse and frustrate listeners. Reiterating key features of the billboard through the course of the message keeps listeners on track and can be an efficient way of summarizing the entire message in the conclusion.

Mini billboards may appear throughout a message as preachers preview subpoints or signal the development of other subordinate ideas. One automatic way of doing this is to use conjunctions in main-point statements. A preacher who says, "Since God commands love without partiality, we must love the lovely and the unlovely," has already implied, "First I will talk about love for the lovely. Then I will discuss love for the unlovely." Conjunctions in main-point statements indicate branches in a preacher's thought. If a preacher

---

82. Cf. Sweazey, *Preaching the Good News,* 78.
83. See chap. 6 for a discussion of types of outlines.

does not intend to follow such branches in a sermon's development, he should eliminate conjunctions from main-point statements (and propositions).

Billboards and branches help preachers meet the first and last obligations of the following traditional rhetorical instruction:

1. Say what you will say.
2. Say it.
3. Say what you said.

Despite the antiquity of this maxim, homileticians in the past and in the present have questioned the wisdom of announcing a sermon's divisions ahead of time.[84] Legitimate concerns about making a message too boxy, linear, time-conscious, and anticlimactic need to be weighed when deciding to use billboards. Certainly, if a preacher intends to build suspense or arrange an ironic twist, preannouncing points serves no good purpose. However, where the train of thought is complex, the discourse lengthy, or interest difficult to stimulate or maintain, then some form of billboarding may well serve the sermon. Clarity will also be promoted by a bird's-eye perspective on the relationship among the main points.

Ultimate Measures

This chapter cannot exhaust all the possible functions and forms that introductions, conclusions, and transitions assume. Appropriate exceptions abound, and many variations are needed. Specific purposes will supersede all rules for a preacher who taps the wisdom of the refrain "Never do anything always."

Remember also that no amount of homiletical skill will substitute for the Spirit's work. The ultimate measure of a sermon's success is not whether it had a great introduction, a powerful conclusion, or smooth transitions but whether it communicated transforming truths. Sermons succeed when the Holy Spirit works beyond human craft to perform his purposes. Only the most arrogant servant, however, will impose on the Master's goodness by anticipating blessing for shoddy work. We serve best when we not only depend on the Holy Spirit to empower our words but also craft them so as to honor him.

Questions for Review and Discussion

1. What are four major purposes of sermon introductions?
2. What are five major types of sermon introductions? What are two common but *ineffective* types of introductions?

84. Cf. Broadus, *On the Preparation and Delivery of Sermons,* 118; Buttrick, *Homiletic,* 85; and Sweazey, *Preaching the Good News,* 73–74, 78.

3. What is the difference between a sermon introduction and a Scripture introduction?
4. In what two ways should a sermon introduction prepare for a proposition?
5. What are four major purposes of sermon conclusions?
6. What are two major types of sermon conclusions?
7. What is the most basic form of transition?

Exercises

1. Create a sermon introduction for the message you previously outlined from 2 Timothy 4:1–5; 2 Corinthians 6:14–7:1; or 1 Thessalonians 4:13–18; or create a sermon introduction for an alternative message. (Attach the proposition to make sure it flows from the introduction.)
2. Identify the following components in the introduction you created for exercise 1: interest arousal, introduction of the subject, statement of the FCF, making it personal, bonding to Scripture, and terminological preparation for the proposition (see the example following fig. 9.1).
3. Create a conclusion for the message you previously outlined from 2 Timothy 4:1–5; 2 Corinthians 6:14–7:1; or 1 Thessalonians 4:13–18. Or create a conclusion for an alternative message. Identify the concise summary, climax, final exhortation, and definite end in your conclusion.

PART 3

A Theology of Christ-Centered Messages

CONTENTS OF CHAPTER 10

Reviewing the Fallen Condition Focus
   Grounding the Fallen Condition Focus
   Incorporating the Fallen Condition Focus
Deciphering the Redemptive Signals
   Sub-Christian Messages in Preaching
   A Biblical Theology for Preaching
   A Biblical Focus for Preaching
Expounding the Redemptive Message
   Topical and Textual Approaches
   Expository Approaches
      Text Disclosure
      Type Disclosure
      Context Disclosure
Recognizing Nonredemptive Messages
   The Deadly Be's
      "Be Like" Messages
      "Be Good" Messages
      "Be Disciplined" Messages
   The Bottom Line

GOAL OF CHAPTER 10

To present the overarching theological concern
for constructing sermons as indicated in
previous chapters

10

A Redemptive Approach to Preaching

Reviewing the Fallen Condition Focus

Why does the development of expository sermons depend on the clear identification of a Fallen Condition Focus?[1] To this point, the most obvious answer relates to homiletical structure. A clear FCF provides a sermon with a distinct aim so that a preacher can organize an entire message to address a unified purpose. An FCF not only targets the information in a sermon but also directs a preacher to relevant application supported by the particular text. Beyond these standard homiletical goals, however, there are theological reasons for preparing sermons directed toward a passage's FCF.

Grounding the Fallen Condition Focus

The theological basis for designing messages with an FCF derives from a principle evident in 2 Timothy 3:16–17, a touchstone verse for all biblical preaching. As already observed (see chap. 2), the fact that "all Scripture is God-breathed . . . so that the man of God may be thoroughly equipped for every good work" (2 Tim. 3:16–17) necessarily implies that even the most gifted and good persons remain spiritually incomplete apart from God's revelation (cf. Col. 2:9–10). God uses his Word to make us what we could not be on our own. In this sense, God's Word acts as an instrument of his redeeming work. Scripture continually aims to restore aspects of our

---

1. See the discussion and definition of the Fallen Condition Focus in chap. 2.

brokenness to spiritual wholeness so that we might reflect and rejoice in God's glory. Our condition as fallen creatures in a fallen world requires this redemptive work not merely for the initial work of salvation but also for our continuing sanctification and hope (Rom. 15:4). Jesus said, "Apart from me you can do nothing" (John 15:5). Thus, all Scripture—and by corollary, all expository preaching that unfolds its meaning—focuses on an aspect of our fallen condition that requires and displays God's provision. *Preaching that remains true to this God-glorifying purpose specifies an FCF indicated by a text and addresses this aspect of our fallenness with the grace revealed by the text.*

As already discussed, a preacher determines an FCF for an expository message by asking the following three questions: (1) What does the text say? (2) What concern(s) did the text address in its context? (3) What do listeners share in common with those to (or about) whom the text was written? Expository preachers are ready to prepare a sermon only after they have identified a fallen condition shared by those in the biblical context and those in the contemporary context. This premise is derived from the understanding that God intended the Bible to serve both an original purpose and a present use.[2] These are not separate purposes. The original intent reveals proper present use by highlighting a common aspect of the human condition that is addressed by the scriptural truths of the text.

Scripture itself teaches that determining what is biblically meaningful for us hinges on identifying an original FCF that is applicable for present purposes. Using an Old Testament passage in this way, the apostle Paul wrote to the Corinthians of the New Testament:

> It is written in the Law of Moses: "Do not muzzle an ox while it is treading out the grain." Is it about oxen that God is concerned? Surely *he says this for us*, doesn't he? Yes, *this was written for us*, because when the plowman plows and the thresher threshes, they ought to do so in the hope of sharing in the harvest. If we have sown spiritual seed among you, is it too much if we reap a material harvest from you?
>
> 1 Corinthians 9:9–11, emphasis added

Moses wrote for his own situation, but Paul recognized that proper understanding of original concerns (i.e., insensitive greed should not drive God's people to deprive even oxen of a share in the product of their labor) had implications for God's people in a much later time. Paul even wrote that Moses "says this for us" and "this was written for us." Through the Old Testament passage, Paul taught that New Testament believers should

---

2. Sidney Greidanus, *The Modern Preacher and the Ancient Text: Interpreting and Preaching Biblical Literature* (Grand Rapids: Eerdmans, 1988), 166.

not be so concerned about their own gain that they do not provide for the ministers who labor to feed the churches with God's Word.

Over and over again the apostle used the Old Testament in this freshly applied way. In the next chapter of the same letter to the Corinthians, he alluded to the devastations that came on ancient Israel when it yielded to temptation in order to command certain behaviors of New Testament believers who were similarly tempted:

> Now these things occurred as examples to keep us from setting our hearts on evil things as they did. Do not be idolaters, as some of them were.... We should not commit sexual immorality, as some of them did.... We should not test the Lord, as some of them did.... And do not grumble, as some of them did.... These things happened to them as examples and were written down as warnings for us.
>
> 1 Corinthians 10:6–11

In the apostle's mind—and in the Spirit's plan—the initial intent of the record made in a previous millennium provided definite guidance for present practices.

But original purposes did not merely provide behavioral instruction. They were also signposts to faith.[3] For those people who might be tempted to believe that their salvation depended on their works, Paul also wrote, "The words 'it was credited to him' [i.e., Abraham] were written not for him alone, but also for us, to whom God will credit righteousness—for us who believe in him who raised Jesus our Lord from the dead" (Rom. 4:23–24). Paul recognized that identifying the concern that a passage originally addressed was the key to applying its truths to present needs of faith as well as behavior.

Every passage was written to bring glory to God by addressing some aspect(s) of our fallen condition (affecting faith and/or practice with divine provision). By correction, warning, diagnosis, and/or healing of this fallenness, a text reveals God's means for enabling his people to glorify him and to know his grace both in the passage's original context *and* in the present situation. This realization of the underlying spiritual design of all Scripture underscores priorities discussed in earlier chapters of this book:

1. Until we have determined its FCF, we do not really know what a text is about even if we know many true facts about it.
2. We should never preach on a passage until we have determined an FCF the Holy Spirit intended the passage to address.

3. Westminster Confession of Faith, VII.5, VIII.6, XIX.3.

Expository preachers must ask, "What is an FCF behind the inspiration of this text?" before they can accurately expound its meaning. They must determine the target the Holy Spirit intended to strike in order to aim their exposition of the text accurately. Thus, identifying a current need that listeners share with those in the biblical situation that required the inspired writing is prerequisite for every expository sermon.

Incorporating the Fallen Condition Focus

The approaches to expository preaching proposed in this book have already prepared you to incorporate an FCF into your exposition. We have developed each element of a sermon to support the principles of an FCF. The unifying theme of a sermon—the one thing that a message is about—is how the truths of a passage address an FCF. The introduction of a message identifies this FCF by revealing the reason the truths of the passage were inspired in the biblical context and the reason they are needed in the present situation. The introduction also prepares for the proposition, which formally states how the preacher will present the truths of the passage in light of this FCF (see examples in chap. 9 and in the example sermon in appendix 12).

The structure of the proposition, whether it is stated formally or appears in an abbreviated form, further supports development based on an FCF. By making sure that the proposition indicates how the truths of the passage will be applied, the preacher ensures an understanding that something must be done as a consequence of the text's instruction. This understanding makes listener transformation—rather than the static acquisition of information—the goal of the message. Such a goal indicates that human brokenness has to be addressed in active terms. Our sin-corrupted world is not merely an abstract principle—not a theological phantasm for philosophical consideration. Fallenness is rather the daily reality that corrodes our souls unless we receive the balm and the correction of Scripture.

The body of the sermon indicates how the scriptural balm should be applied to our lives and what regimens God requires for our spiritual health. Main points formulated to reflect and support the principles of the proposition provide the information that acts as biblical leverage for the preacher's exhortations. Explanation and illustration unfold and demonstrate meanings that supply the reasoning and the reality that make the sermon's applications authoritative, accessible, and possible. The conclusion drives the matter home, marshaling the forces of heart and mind for a final exhortation that calls listeners to respond to their fallen condition with the biblical guidance that the sermon has disclosed.

Deciphering the Redemptive Signals

Thus far we have emphasized the negative—focusing the development of a sermon on the mutual problem or burden that both original and present targets of the text share. There is, however, a necessary and welcome reverse. Why does all Scripture reveal an aspect of our fallen condition? The clear answer is: to supply the warrant for (and to define) the character of the redemptive elements in Scripture that we can, in turn, apply to our fallenness. The Bible's ultimate aim is beautifully positive. Scripture addresses features of our incompleteness only because such a focus concurrently signals the work of God that makes us whole. The goal of expository preaching is to decipher these redemptive signals so that listeners understand a text's full meaning in the context of its God-glorifying, gospel intent.

Sub-Christian Messages in Preaching

Unless we identify the redemptive purposes of a text, it is possible to say all the right words and yet send all the wrong signals. I witness this miscommunication almost daily as the top-rated radio station in our city broadcasts a "meditation" during the early morning. In each meditation, the preacher addresses a topic with a Bible verse or two. The subjects run the gamut from procrastination to care for children to honesty on the job. The station turns up the reverberation during the inspirational minute so that it sounds as though the words come directly from Mount Sinai. Not to pay attention seems like a sin. As the speaker reminds us to practice punctuality, good parenting, and business propriety, I imagine thousands of listening Christians are nodding their heads and saying in unison, "That's right . . . that's how we should live."

I have played tapes of these meditations to seminary classes and asked if anyone can discern error. Rarely does anyone spot a problem. The speaker quotes from the Bible accurately, he advocates moral causes, and he encourages loving behaviors. Thus, students are usually astonished when I point out that the radio preacher is not a Christian. He actually represents a large cult located in our region.

How can this be? How can so many Christians (even those well informed) readily grant assent to one whose commitments are radically anti-Christian? Some answer that their lack of protest results from the radio preacher's care to avoid saying anything controversial. They contend that he hides his heresy beneath a veil of right-sounding orthodoxy. Such defenses miss the point, even as his proponents have missed the problem. The radio speaker has not hidden his heresy; he exposes it every time he speaks by what is missing from his message. The more significant problem is that evangelical preachers inadvertently and frequently present such similar messages that

Christians fail to hear the difference between a message that purports to be biblical and one that actually is.

A message that merely advocates morality and compassion remains sub-Christian even if the preacher can prove that the Bible demands such behaviors. By ignoring the sinfulness of humankind, which makes even our best works tainted before God (Isa. 64:6; Luke 17:10), and by neglecting the grace of God, which makes obedience possible and acceptable (1 Cor. 15:10; Eph. 2:8–9), such messages necessarily subvert the Christian message. Christian preachers often do not recognize this counter-gospel impact of their preaching because they are simply recounting a behavior clearly specified in the portion of the text in front of them. But a message that even inadvertently teaches others that their works merit God's acceptance inevitably leads people away from the gospel. By themselves, moral maxims and advocacy of ethical conduct fall short of the requirements of biblical preaching.[4] Jay Adams explains with impassioned eloquence:

> If you preach a sermon that would be acceptable to the member of a Jewish synagogue or to a Unitarian congregation, there is something radically wrong with it. Preaching, when truly Christian, is distinctive. And what makes it distinctive is the all-pervading presence of a saving and sanctifying Christ. Jesus Christ must be at the heart of every sermon you preach. That is just as true of edificational preaching as it is of evangelistic preaching.
>
> . . . Edificational preaching must always be evangelical; that is what makes it moral rather than moralistic, and what causes it to be unacceptable in a synagogue, mosque, or to a Unitarian congregation. By evangelical, I mean that the import of Christ's death and resurrection—His substitutionary, penal death and bodily resurrection—on the subject under consideration is made clear in the sermon. You must not exhort your congregation to do whatever the Bible requires of them as though they could fulfill those requirements on their own, but only as a consequence of the saving power of the cross and the indwelling, sanctifying power and presence of Christ in the person of the Holy Spirit. All edificational preaching, to be Christian, must fully take into consideration God's grace in salvation and in sanctification.[5]

A textually accurate discussion of biblical commands does not guarantee Christian orthodoxy. Exhortations for moral behavior apart from the work of the Savior degenerate into mere Pharisaism, even if preachers advocate the actions with selected biblical evidence and good intent. Spirituality based on personal conduct cannot escape its human-centered orbit though it aspires to lift one to the divine.

---

4. Michael Fabarez, *Preaching That Changes Lives* (Nashville: Thomas Nelson, 2002), 112–14.

5. Jay E. Adams, *Preaching with Purpose: A Comprehensive Textbook on Biblical Preaching* (Grand Rapids: Baker, 1982), 147.

A Biblical Theology for Preaching

But how do expository preachers infuse the redemptive essentials (i.e., Christ-centeredness) into every sermon without superimposing ideas foreign to many texts? Many Old Testament passages make no explicit reference to Christ's "substitutionary, penal death and bodily resurrection." New Testament texts abound that commend moral behaviors with no mention of the cross, the resurrection, the Holy Spirit, or God's enabling grace. Can we really be expositors and bring out of a text what it does not *seem* to mention? The answer lies in an axiom mentioned earlier: Context is part of text.

No text exists in isolation from other texts or from the overarching biblical message. Just as historico-grammatical exegesis requires a preacher to consider a text's terms in context, correct theological interpretation requires an expositor to discern how a text's ideas function in the wider biblical message. Some meanings we discern by taking out our exegetical magnifying glass and studying a text's particulars in close detail. Other meanings we discern by examining a text with a theological fish-eye lens to see how the immediate text relates to texts, messages, events, and developments around it. Accurate expositors use both a magnifying glass and a fish-eye lens, knowing that a magnifying glass can unravel mysteries in a raindrop but can fail to expose a storm gathering on the horizon.

The branch of Bible study devoted to examining Scripture in the light of the overarching themes that unite all its particulars is called biblical theology. The insights of biblical theology are as critical for preachers who want to expound a text as are the contributions of all other features of exegesis. The intent of all the dimensions of exegetical study, including biblical theology, should be to enable preachers to convey the meaning of a specific passage in a way that is consistent with the gospel message of all Scripture.

In the introduction to his seminal volume on biblical theology, Geerhardus Vos outlined the keys that will keep preaching on track. He began with the simple observation that "revelation is a noun of action relating to divine activity."[6] All scriptural revelation discloses God. In its proper context, every verse in the Bible in some sense points to his nature and work. Yet because God is God, no single verse, no single passage, no single book contains all we need to know about him. In fact, had God totally revealed himself to our earliest faith ancestors, they would not have had the theological background or the biblical preparation necessary to take in all that God has since disclosed to humankind about himself. For this reason, God's revelation through biblical history is *progressive*. This does not mean that early revelation differs from or in any sense contradicts

---

6. Geerhardus Vos, *Biblical Theology* (Grand Rapids: Eerdmans, 1975), 5.

what God ultimately reveals. Says Vos, "The progressive process is *organic:* revelation may be in seed form which yields later full growth accounting for diversity but not true difference because the earlier aspects of the truth are indispensable for understanding the true meanings of the later forms and vice versa."[7] God uses each verse, each recorded event, and each passing epoch of biblical history to build a single, comprehensive understanding of who he is. Even though an aspect of God's revelation may not be in full bloom in some portion of Scripture, that does not mean that the truth is absent in seed form.

Our understanding of who God is remains inextricably bound to what he has done. Writes Vos, "Revelation is inseparably linked to the activity of redemption. . . . Revelation is the interpretation of redemption."[8] This means that for us to expound biblical revelation from any passage, we must relate its explanation to the redeeming work of God present there. The redemptive dimension of a particular Scripture passage may not seem to dominate the text's landscape because the redemptive features of a passage sometimes appear only in seed form. Still, exposing the revelation properly requires understanding a passage's redemptive content and context.

We must relate even seed-form aspects of a text to the mature message they signal or for which they prepare us in order to interpret fully and rightly what the passage means. You do not explain what an acorn is, even if you say many true things about it (e.g., it is brown, has a cap, is found on the ground, is gathered by squirrels), if you do not in some way relate it to an oak tree. In a similar sense, preachers cannot properly explain a seed (or portion) of biblical revelation, even if they say many true things about it, unless they relate it to the redeeming work of God that all Scripture ultimately purposes to disclose.[9] In this sense, the entire Bible is Christ-centered because his redemptive work in all of its incarnational, atoning, rising, interceding, and reigning dimensions is the capstone of all of God's revelation of his dealings with his people. Thus, no aspect of revelation can be thoroughly understood or explained in isolation from some aspect of Christ's redeeming work.

7. Ibid., 7.

8. Ibid., 5, 6.

9. It cannot be denied that the Scripture writers (or at least the divine Author) intended for particular passages to be viewed from multiple perspectives to provide various opportunities to emphasize moral obligation, doctrinal articulation, historical sequence, character development, or worship instruction. Still, expositors must not forget the one who is the yes and the amen of all God's promises, the alpha and the omega of all God's purposes, the beginning and the end of all holy endeavor, the first and the last means of performing all scriptural duty (2 Cor. 1:20; Rev. 22:13). Preachers should be well aware of the various perspectival purposes and layers individual texts may contain. But the absence of grace from whatever instruction a preacher ultimately offers will automatically identify a focus grown too narrow for Christian purposes (cf. John 5:39, 46).

A Biblical Focus for Preaching

All Scripture is redemptive revelation that is inspired to address humanity's fallen condition (or incompleteness) with divine provision. Preachers who recognize this pervasive scriptural dynamic have discovered the means for uncovering the positive focus in all Christ-centered preaching. The discovery occurs when they see that a text's FCF defines God's mercy at the same time that it reveals human need.

When I was a child, my mother spent an afternoon making a special chocolate pudding for our family of eight. When she brought the fabulous dessert to the dinner table, however, the impact was marred by the deep imprint of a child's finger in the middle of the bowl. Someone had sneaked an early taste. My mother asked, "Who?" No one fessed up, but that did not stop my mother's investigation. She simply began matching the index finger of the six children to the hole in the top of the pudding until she found the digit that fit (it wasn't mine). The impression not only revealed the pudding's incompleteness but also identified the one who could fill the hole. God's imprinting of our incompleteness on a passage of Scripture does not merely demonstrate an aspect of our fallenness; it also reveals the nature and the character of the One who can make us whole.

Although every biblical passage addresses an FCF, no text tells us what we can do to complete ourselves or to make ourselves acceptable to God (by our actions), for then we would not be truly fallen. No passage tells us how to make ourselves holy (as though we could achieve divine status by our own efforts). The Bible is *not* a self-help book. Scripture presents one, consistent, organic message. It tells us how we must seek Christ, who alone is our Savior and source of strength, to be and do what God requires. To preach what people should be and do and yet not mention him who enables their accomplishment warps the biblical message. God's redemptive work is integral to every biblical passage's proper exposition. Thomas Jones writes:

> True Christian preaching must center on the cross of Jesus Christ. The cross is the central doctrine of the holy scriptures. All other revealed truths either find their fulfillment in the cross or are necessarily founded upon it. Therefore, no doctrine of Scripture may faithfully be set before men unless it is displayed in its relationship to the cross. The one who is called to preach, therefore, must preach Christ because there is no other message from God.[10]

These words are not hyperbole but rather reflect the ethic of the apostle Paul, who wrote to the Corinthians, "As I proclaimed to you the testimony about

---

10. Thomas F. Jones, "Preaching the Cross of Christ" (essay presented at the homiletics lectures, Covenant Theological Seminary, 1976–77), 1.

God . . . I resolved to know nothing while I was with you except Jesus Christ and him crucified" (1 Cor. 2:1–2). Paul echoed this ethic many times:

> Jews demand miraculous signs and Greeks look for wisdom, but we preach Christ crucified: a stumbling block to Jews and foolishness to Gentiles, but to those whom God has called, both Jews and Greeks, Christ the power of God and the wisdom of God.
>
> 1 Corinthians 1:22–24

> The god of this age has blinded the minds of unbelievers, so that they cannot see the light of the gospel of the glory of Christ, who is the image of God. For we do not preach ourselves, but Jesus Christ as Lord, and ourselves as your servants for Jesus' sake.
>
> 2 Corinthians 4:4–5

> May I never boast except in the cross of our Lord Jesus Christ, through which the world has been crucified to me, and I to the world.
>
> Galatians 6:14

Paul's commitment to make his ministry reflect "nothing but Jesus Christ and him crucified" may strike us as not only infeasible but also not genuine. After all, we could reason that Paul addressed church worship standards, biblical discipline, stewardship, family relationships, governmental responsibilities, and the history of Israel. He even quoted Greek poets. Doesn't this prove that the apostle did more than talk about Jesus and the crucifixion? Apparently not to Paul. In Paul's mind, every subject, every address, and every epistle had a focus. Everything he did centered on making the cross *and* its implications evident. In this sense, the "cross" reference functions as synecdoche, representing the entire matrix of God's redemptive work past, present, and future, including the resurrection, advocacy, and reign his victory through the cross provides.[11]

Sidney Greidanus explains the redemptive scope of the cross in Christ-centered preaching:

> Even the seemingly limited focus found in 1 Corinthians 2:2 of Paul knowing "nothing among you except Jesus Christ, and him crucified" may contain a much broader perspective. John Knox helpfully explains, "At first sight this last phrase ['and him crucified'] seems to leave out the Resurrection entirely. But it seems to do so only because we suppose Paul's thought was moving, as ours customarily does, in a forward direction. . . . But when Paul wrote the

---

11. Cf. John Calvin, *Institutes of the Christian Religion*, 2.16.13; *Commentary on Acts*, 4:33; and *Commentary on 1 Corinthians*, 1:2.

phrase, he was thinking first of all of the risen, exalted Christ and his thought moved backward to the cross. . . . Thus, far from omitting reference to the Resurrection, Paul's phrase takes its start from it; the word Christ means primarily the one now known as the living and present Lord."[12]

In this sense, though the apostle addressed many topics and drew from many sources, the panorama of subjects was displayed only to reveal the Redeemer's work on the cross in richer detail. Christ-centered preaching (whether it is referred to as preaching the cross, the message of grace, the gospel, God's redemption, or a host of similar terms) reflects Paul's intention to preach nothing "except Jesus Christ and him crucified." Just as Paul's preaching involved more than the message of the incarnation and atonement—and yet kept all subjects in proper relation to God's redemption through Christ—so also *Christ-centered preaching rightly understood does not seek to discover where Christ is mentioned in every text but to disclose where every text stands in relation to Christ.* The grace of God culminating in the person and work of Jesus unfolds in many dimensions throughout the pages of Scripture. The goal of the preacher is not to find novel ways of identifying Christ in every text (or naming Jesus in every sermon) but to show how each text manifests God's grace in order to prepare and enable his people to embrace the hope provided by Christ.

This apostolic ethic of maintaining a Christocentric perspective when preaching reflects the principles of exposition that the Savior himself revealed. Jesus propositionally stated the redemptive focus of all Scripture when he walked with the two disciples on the road to Emmaus. There, "beginning with Moses and all the Prophets, he explained to them what was said in all the Scriptures concerning himself" (Luke 24:27; cf. John 5:39, 46). Jesus said that all Scripture is about him. This does not mean that every phrase, punctuation mark, or verse directly reveals Christ but rather that all passages in their context disclose his nature and/or necessity. Such an understanding compels us to recognize that failure to relate a passage's explanation to an aspect of Christ's person or work is to neglect saying the very thing that Jesus said the passage is about. Jesus said the passage is about him. If this is so, then we cannot faithfully expound any text without demonstrating its relation to him.

What Jesus verbally said on the road to Emmaus he visually displayed on the mount of transfiguration. When the archetypal representatives of the Old Testament law and prophets, Moses and Elijah, appeared with Jesus near the culmination of his earthly ministry (Matt. 17), they testified that all preceding Scripture directs the believer's gaze to this One. Thus, the testimony of Scripture encircles Jesus.[13] The law and the prophets that precede

---

12. Sidney Greidanus, *Preaching Christ from the Old Testament* (Grand Rapids: Eerdmans, 1999), 6.
13. John Calvin, *Institutes of the Christian Religion,* 2.6.3.

and the apostolic ministry that follows the work of the cross make Jesus their center. Prophets, apostles, and the Savior testify that all Scripture ultimately focuses on the Redeemer. How then can we rightly expound them and not speak of him? Expository preaching is Christ-centered preaching.

Expounding the Redemptive Message

Assenting to the redemptive focus of all Scripture is often far easier than disclosing it. How one gets redemptive truth out of a text and into a sermon can stretch both exegetical and preaching skills. Commitment to the insights of biblical theology requires a homiletical methodology that grants preachers and listeners access to the redemptive truths each passage contains. The next chapter deals with this methodology in greater detail, but it is appropriate at this juncture to identify some errant paths and to point in the directions that lead to faithful exposition of a text.

Topical and Textual Approaches

A topical sermon may allow a preacher to add redemptive truth to a message because the preacher is not bound to disclose the precise meaning of a specific text in such a message.[14] The much repeated line of Charles Spurgeon that "no matter where he began in Scripture, he always took a shortcut to the cross" exemplifies a method that bypasses the direct statements in a text. This is not to say that a topical sermon necessarily leads to unbiblical conclusions or to inappropriate redemptive connections. Such an approach simply progresses without clear biblical authority.

The same authority vacuum exists for textual sermons that include redemptive truth through analogy, illustration, or addition. An analogy or illustration may well bring to mind an aspect of the redeeming work of God, which gives entry to a redemptive focus. Unfortunately, the redemptive focus results from a preacher's words rather than from the Word. Devising a redemptive focus by adding material not exegeted from a text invites homiletical moves and conceptual developments without clear biblical warrant. Several years ago I heard a well-known preacher deliver a sermon on the subject of procrastination. In each phase of the message, he told us why the Bible requires us to "make the best use of the Lord's time." The message then ended with an altar call. No mention of the redeeming work of Christ, no development of the necessity of the atonement, no scriptural instruction on the need of salvation preceded the call to come forward. In the call itself, the preacher explained the essence of the gospel, but this explanation had

---

14. See the technical definition of topical and textual messages in chap. 6.

no origin in or connection to the text before us. The redemptive truths were simply added to the message—not developed out of the text.

Expository Approaches

Expository preaching will not allow a preacher to add material to a text in order to derive a redemptive focus. An expositor develops the message of a sermon out of the material in a particular text. How, then, can expositors always uncover a redemptive focus that remains fair to the text?

TEXT DISCLOSURE

A text may make a *direct reference* to Christ or to an aspect of his messianic work. Specific mention of Jesus or his saving activity may occur in a Gospel account, a messianic psalm, an epistle's development, or a prophetic utterance. In such cases, the task of the expositor is plain: Explain the reference in terms of the redemptive activity it reveals. A preacher who does not see redemptive work in an account of Christ's exorcism of a demon, a scene from the crucifixion, or a prophecy of the Savior's dominion over the world cannot properly expound the text. When features of God's plan to defeat Satan and restore spiritual wholeness reside on the plain face of a text, a preacher places the passage in proper redemptive context simply by presenting its contents accurately. But, though many biblical passages specifically mention Christ's person and work, many more do not. What other alternatives may preachers pursue to stay Christ-centered in their preaching?

TYPE DISCLOSURE

God's redemptive work in Christ may also be evident in Old Testament *types*. Typology as it relates to Christ's person and work is the study of the correspondences between persons, events, and institutions that first appear in the Old Testament and preview, prepare, or more fully express New Testament salvation truths.[15] Debates have swirled through the centuries over what constitutes a legitimate type and what merely reflects an interpreter's overactive imagination. Current research into literary methods and structures promises to aid our understanding of biblical typology, but where New Testament writers specifically cite or unmistakably echo how an Old Testament person or feature prefigures the person and work of Christ—as with Adam, David, Melchizedek, the Passover, and the temple—a preacher may safely use typological exposition.[16]

15. David L. Larsen, *The Anatomy of Preaching: Identifying the Issues in Preaching Today* (Grand Rapids: Baker, 1989), 166; and Dan McCartney and Charles Clayton, *Let the Reader Understand: A Guide to Interpreting and Applying the Bible* (Wheaton: Victor, 1994), 153–60.

16. Gordon P. Hugenberger, "Introductory Notes on Typology," in *The Right Doctrine from the Wrong Texts? Essays on the Use of the Old Testament in the New*, ed. G. K. Beale (Grand Rapids: Baker,

Types allow a preacher to approach appropriate Old Testament passages with a biblically certified pre-understanding of their redemptive connotations. These connotations may not be apparent if the texts are examined without the New Testament information. On the basis of this inspired input, explanations of such passages remain incomplete if a preacher does not take into consideration what the Bible itself reveals about a text's ultimate purposes. Of course, this does not mean that every time an Old Testament passage contains a type, a preacher must identify it as such. Where typology exists, however, it may prove to be a profitable avenue for redemptive exposition, particularly when other alternatives seem remote.

Context Disclosure

Texts that specifically mention Jesus or reveal him typologically are few relative to the thousands of passages that contain no direct reference to Christ.[17] How can a preacher remain Christ-centered and expository when dealing with these apparently Christ-silent texts? When neither text nor type discloses the Savior's work, a preacher must rely on *context* to develop the redemptive focus of a message.

By identifying where a passage fits in the overall revelation of God's redemptive plan, a preacher relates the text to Christ by performing the standard and necessary exegetical task of establishing its context. Preachers concerned about Christ-centeredness recognize that their exegetical method has necessary implications for their theological conclusions if they are to deal consistently with Scripture.[18] In its context, every passage possesses one or more of four redemptive foci. The text may be:

- predictive of the work of Christ
- preparatory for the work of Christ
- reflective of the work of Christ and/or
- resultant of the work of Christ

These categories do not exhaust the possibilities of how texts may reveal the redemptive work of God, but they do provide dependable means of exploration and explanation.

1994), 337–41; Edmund Clowney, *Preaching and Biblical Theology* (Grand Rapids: Eerdmans, 1961), 100–112; and idem, *The Unfolding Mystery: Discovering Christ in the Old Testament* (Phillipsburg, N.J.: Presbyterian & Reformed, 1988), 14–16.

17. Of course, the number will vary greatly depending on how one defines a type. Cf. the implication of Gerard Van Groningen's discussion of the wide and narrow notions of the messianic concept in *Messianic Revelation in the Old Testament* (Grand Rapids: Baker, 1990), 19–23.

18. Walter C. Kaiser Jr., *Toward an Exegetical Theology: Biblical Exegesis for Preaching and Teaching* (Grand Rapids: Baker, 1981), 139–40.

Predictive. Some passages *predict* God's redemptive work in Christ by making specific mention of his coming person or work. Messianic psalms and passages from prophetic and apocalyptic literature provide many examples. A sermon from Isaiah 40 that offers comfort to God's people without mention of Christ's coming plainly misses the future source of comfort the passage identifies in its context.

Other texts reveal what Christ will do or be without making specific reference to him. Examples include those passages relating to the Old Testament sacraments, the exodus, the purification codes, and so on. The predictive nature of these passages may be apparent only in New Testament light, and the expositor assumes an unnecessary and inappropriate blindness when attempting to handle such texts without this illumination. We are New Testament believers and have both the right and the responsibility to view God's earlier revelations from the full perspective that his Word grants us. Interpreting Old Testament passages without considering how their features anticipate Christ's coming actually diminishes reverence for the organic nature of Scripture.[19]

Preparatory. The inspired intention of some texts that make no specific mention of Jesus is to *prepare* the people of God to understand aspects of the person and/or work of Christ. When Paul writes to the Galatians that the purpose of the Mosaic law was to lead the people of God to Christ, we not only learn why God provided the commands (3:24) but also understand why a sermon that only exhorts believers not to steal is incomplete. As was every tenet of the law, the eighth commandment was more than a moral standard. It was also a theological lens picturing the frailty of the soul.[20]

Old Testament believers were to understand their need of faith in the Redeemer based on their inability to keep any divine imperative perfectly (Gal. 2:15–21). Exposition on the law that fails to make this point advances an implicit legalism and misses the explanation that the Bible itself offers for God's commands.[21] People today must understand that neither a sophisticated understanding of a commandment nor the most vigorous attempts to heed it will merit grace. Comprehensive explanation of what God requires falls short of adequate exposition if it fails to say why God set the standard.

God prepared for Christ's work by planting the perception of need in the hearts of Old Testament saints. He also prepared them (and us) by helping them to understand how the need would be satisfied. Paul wrote of Abraham, "Now it was not written for his sake alone, that it [i.e., righteousness] was

---

19. Geerhardus Vos, *Biblical Theology* (Grand Rapids: Eerdmans, 1975), 7–8.

20. Vern Poythress, *The Shadow of Christ in the Law of Moses* (Phillipsburg, N.J.: Presbyterian & Reformed, 1991), 104–6.

21. Calvin, *Institutes of the Christian Religion*, 2.7.1–3, 9.

imputed to him; but for us also, to whom it shall be imputed, if we believe on him that raised up Jesus our Lord from the dead; who was delivered for our offences, and was raised again for our justification" (Rom. 4:23–25 KJV). The apostle's statement alerts us to the fact that imbedded in the narratives and proclamations of the Old Testament is the theology of grace. For the sake of the original as well as the present readers, God prepared a testament establishing what Christ would have to do and how his work would apply to us. Exposition fair to this grand purpose of all Scripture excavates Old Testament texts to expose implicit spiritual, experiential, or theological preparations that enable us to embrace redemptive truths, even where there is no explicit statement of them.

Reflective. The path to implicit aspects of the gospel of grace that are imbedded in every biblical passage does not require tortuous expeditions of logic or theological safaris to remote mountains of higher learning. When a text neither plainly predicts nor prepares for the Redeemer's work, an expositor should simply explain how the text *reflects* key facets of the redemptive message. This is by far the most common tool for constructing Christ-centered messages when there is no direct reference to Jesus' person or work. A preacher who asks the following basic questions takes no inappropriate liberties with a text: *What does this text reveal of God's nature that provides redemption? What does this text reflect of human nature that requires redemption?*

Without doing damage to the integrity, authority, and exegesis of a passage, these questions actually place every biblical text within a redemptive context. These questions act as natural lenses that form the spectacles that enable us to view every text redemptively. This does not mean that the lenses make the person or name of Jesus magically arise from the bushes of every biblical account. Rather, they enable us to see reflected aspects of divine character and human fallenness that provide or require the grace of God ultimately manifested in the person and work of Christ.

When we consistently ask these two interpretive questions, grace will be as naturally evident in an Old Testament command as in a New Testament promise, because both will reflect inherent dimensions of our fallen condition and of God's eternal character that contextualize his redemptive work. Preachers should not pretend that every text specifically mentions Jesus if one has the right decoder ring. Rather, they should demonstrate how every text reflects aspects or needs of his grace that are made plain in the fullness of time. In this way, preachers demonstrate the unity of Scripture, God's unchanging but progressive plan of redemption, and the ways that all Scripture coordinates to reveal the grace of the Savior and the futility of any other hope.[22]

---

22. Vos, *Biblical Theology*, 5–6.

By asking what a text reflects of God's nature that prompts the work of Christ, an expositor can examine any narrative, genealogy, commandment, proverb, proposition, or parable to see what it reveals of God's justice, holiness, goodness, lovingkindness, faithfulness, provision, or deliverance. These attributes of God's redemptive character emanate from texts that make no mention of Christ but make sense of Paul's assessment that "everything that was written in the past was written to teach us, so that through endurance and the encouragement of the Scriptures we might have hope" (Rom. 15:4). Because everything that was written is the self-revelation of the God whose mercy endures forever (Ps. 136) and in whom there is no shadow of turning (James 1:17), all Scripture possesses an aspect of redemptive hope.

All Scripture reveals God in either his words or his doings. The redemptive truths made evident by these means may appear in seed form or in mature form, but Scripture, by its revelatory nature, bares these divine features for those with eyes to see. This grace may appear in a direct New Testament statement of Christ's work through the cross and resurrection. It may also appear in Old Testament clothes woven from the fabric of the persons and events that the Holy Spirit uses to reflect the redemptive character of God, which is ultimately revealed and fulfilled in Jesus.

This theocentric nature of all Scripture should not lead us to slight the redemptive lessons that God may be presenting through the human characters in the Bible.[23] The Creator may reveal himself in contradistinction to his creatures. We should not be surprised at the poverty of moral perfection and the absence of consistent heroics in the partriarchs, apostles, and persons who dominate the biblical accounts, because their weaknesses reveal the deep human need in even the most spiritually privileged saints. There are certainly commendable aspects of character in many biblical figures, but Scripture seems to take great care to demonstrate how deeply flawed the entire human race is so that all will acknowledge dependence on the Savior for justification, sanctification, and all spiritual blessing.[24]

Preachers who ignore the human flaws in biblical characters out of deference to the reputation of past saints or out of a desire to hold a moral example before present believers unconsciously distract attention from the only hope of true faithfulness.[25] By demonstrating throughout Scripture his love and his use of those who are shamefully human, God reveals himself to be a Savior of sinners (1 Tim. 1:15) and the Deliverer of those who cannot help themselves (Ps. 40:17).[26]

---

23. Sidney Greidanus, "Redemptive History and Preaching," *Pro Rege* 19, no. 2 (December 1990): 14.

24. Calvin, *Institutes of the Christian Religion,* 2.6.1.

25. Clowney, *Preaching and Biblical Theology,* 80.

26. Kenneth J. Howell, "How to Preach Christ from the Old Testament," *Presbyterian Journal* 16 (January 1985): 8.

Unquestionably, God uses persons in Scripture as both positive and negative models of the behaviors and commitments he requires (cf. 1 Cor. 10:5–6), but he never implies that human actions alone can procure or secure a relationship with him.[27] Had God wished to communicate to us that our acceptance hinges on our goodness, he would have chosen another sort of person than those he most typically uses in the Bible to reveal the basis for our faith. But then he would have revealed himself to be a different kind of God. Expository preaching faithful to the intent of Scripture neither shies away from the flaws in biblical saints nor flaunts their strengths apart from the divine aid that makes the redeeming God the ultimate hero of every text.[28]

Aspects of his redemptive character, which God presents in Scripture through his own activity or through human contradistinctions, may be specifically stated in a text or may be implied by the place of the passage in the history of redemption. Yet whether a preacher gleans these conclusions from the historical sweep of Scripture, its doctrinal statements, or God's relational interaction with his people, the redemptive themes must be harvested lest preaching sow mere moral commentary and reap Pharisaism as its inevitable fruit.[29]

Resultant. Scripture includes many instructions that are often mistakenly preached as conditions for divine love and acceptance. Such preaching errs not by detailing what God requires but by implying, if not directly stating, that a relationship with God is a consequence of obedience.[30] The true gospel proclaims that obedience itself is a blessing that *results* from God's love for us. The love we have for him that is engendered by deep apprehension and appreciation of his unconditional mercy (made available through

27. Greidanus, "Redemptive History and Preaching," 14.

28. Sidney Greidanus, *Sola Scriptura: Problems and Principles in Preaching Historical Texts* (Toronto: Wedge, 1970), 145; see similar comments by the same author in *Modern Preacher and the Ancient Text*, 305–6.

29. Howell, "How to Preach Christ from the Old Testament," 8–9.

30. To be sure, some passages *seem* to present a conditional character to God's love for his children. However, in such cases the interpreter almost always will gain a more biblically consistent and spiritually healthy perspective on the passage either by (1) properly identifying the subjects of the apparently conditional love as unregenerate persons whose acceptance depends entirely on their works rather than on the finished work of Christ (Matt. 12:31; John 15:1–8); (2) understanding Scripture simply to be stating what is (or will be) the situation of those *characterized* by such behavior rather than by establishing a cause-and-effect relationship between a particular action and God's love—statement of fact versus statement of cause (Matt. 7:1–2; 18:35; Heb. 10:26); (3) understanding that the biblical writer may be speaking of the instrumentality by which blessings come rather than the merit by which they are earned (more on this in the next chapter's section on the means of change); (4) discerning that the writer is exhibiting means by which God shows his approval of the obedience he inspires in his children rather than the means by which we are made or maintained as his children (Heb. 11:6; James 5:16); or (5) determining the doctrinal idea a biblical writer wants to communicate through a hypothetical situation understood by the writer to be impossible (a common though debated approach to Heb. 6:4–6).

Christ alone) stimulates our desire and efforts in obedience. Still, even this desire and ability to do what he requires is of his Spirit and is never cause for boasting before our God or for behaving as though he were in our debt (Rom. 3:27; 8:5–13; 1 John 2:16). Many passages that describe the privileges or blessings of obedience cannot be rightly interpreted without an explanation that makes them an ultimate result of what Christ has done rather than a direct result of what we do.

Divine love made conditional upon human obedience is mere legalism, even if the actions commended have biblical precedent. The only obedience approved by God is that which he himself enables and sanctifies through the union with Christ he provides.[31] For example, my prayers in themselves cannot earn, deserve, or require God's blessing. God will be no one's debtor (Job 41:11). God is pleased by sincere prayers and promises to bless according to his purpose what is offered in obedience to him. However, though my prayers may be the instrument by which God blesses, the merit of my prayers is never the basis of his care. With their mix of human motives and their reflection of my own frail wisdom and resolve, my prayers could never by their own worth determine or demand a holy God's blessing.[32] I pray not to gain or barter my righteousness but as a result of the access to the Father that Jesus provides for me (and allows me to use) by his death, resurrection, and continuing intercession. Thus, the writer of Hebrews enjoins, "Therefore, since we have a great high priest who has gone through the heavens, Jesus the Son of God, let us . . . then approach the throne of grace with confidence, so that we may receive mercy and find grace to help us in our time of need" (4:14, 16). God mercifully receives and honors prayer humbly offered in love to him, not because our prayers are inordinately good but because he is surpassingly gracious.

The promised blessings of prayer (as well as the opportunity for fellowship with God) encourage my obedience in offering prayer, but the acceptance of the offering is a result of Christ's ministry and not the sufficiency of my sincerity or diligence. To segregate a Scripture promise regarding the blessings of prayer from mention of Jesus is to consign Christian prayer to the same hopeless and self-righteous folly of spinning prayer wheels and reciting incantations.

To preach matters of faith or practice without rooting their foundation or fruit in what God would do, has done, or will do through the ministry of Christ creates a human-centered (anthropocentric) faith without Christian distinctions. Truly Christian preaching must proclaim, "There is now no condemnation for those who are in Christ Jesus, *because* through Christ Jesus the law of the Spirit of life set me free from the law of sin and death"

31. Westminster Confession of Faith, XVI.2–6.
32. Calvin, *Institutes of the Christian Religion,* 3.15.3.

(Rom. 8:1–2, emphasis added). Christ's work unites us to him and releases us from the guilt and the power of our fallen condition. Now what we do in faith as those whose pasts he sanctifies, whose resolves he strengthens, and whose futures he secures must be seen as a result of what he has done and is doing in and through us (1 Cor. 15:16–17, 58; Phil. 1:12–13; 1 Pet. 4:10–11). Every aspect, action, and hope of the Christian life finds its motive, strength, and source in Christ, or it is not of Christ. The truths of Scripture that do not anticipate or culminate in Christ's ministry must at least be preached as a consequence of his work, or we rip them from the context that identifies them with the Christian message.[33]

By recognizing that all Scripture predicts, prepares for, reflects, or results from the ministry of Christ, preachers unfold the road map that keeps them traveling to the heart of the Bible no matter where they journey in its pages. Such a road map makes this seemingly quaint advice of Spurgeon to a young preacher ring with great spiritual wisdom:

> Don't you know, young man, that from every town and every village and every hamlet in England, wherever it may be, there is a road to London? . . . So from every text in Scripture there is a road towards the great metropolis, Christ. And my dear brother, your business is, when you get to a text, to say, now what is the road to Christ? . . . I have never found a text that had not got a road to Christ in it, and if ever I do find one . . . I will go over hedge and ditch but I would get at my Master, for the sermon cannot do any good unless there is a savour of Christ in it.[34]

By identifying the redemptive content, character, or context of a passage, one can heed Spurgeon's instruction so as to discern not merely the savor of Christ in every text but also his pervading presence made evident by his grace.

Recognizing Nonredemptive Messages

Messages that are not Christ-centered (i.e., not redemptively focused) inevitably become human-centered, even though the drift most frequently occurs unintentionally among evangelical preachers. These preachers do not deliberately exclude Christ's ministry from their own, but by consistently preaching messages on the order of "Five Steps to a Better Marriage," "How to Make God Answer Your Prayer," and "Achieving Holiness through the Power of Resolve," they present godliness entirely as a product of human endeavor. Although such preaching is intended for good, its exclusive focus

---

33. Jones, "Preaching the Cross of Christ," 1; and Adams, *Preaching with Purpose,* 152.

34. Charles Haddon Spurgeon, "Christ Precious to Believers," in *The New Park Street Pulpit,* vol. 5 (London: Passmore & Alabaster, 1860), 140.

on actuating or accessing divine blessing through human works carries the message, "It is the doing of these things that will get you right with God and/or your neighbor." No message is more damaging to true faith. By making human efforts alone the measure and the cause of godliness, evangelicals fall victim to the twin assaults of theological legalism and liberalism—which despite their perceived opposition are actually identical in making one's relationship with God dependent on human goodness.

Preachers may protest, "But I assume my people understand they must base their efforts on faith and repentance." Why should we assume listeners will understand what we rarely say, what the structure of our communication contradicts, and what their own nature denies? Can we not as preachers confess that even we feel holier when our devotions last longer, when we parent well, when we pastor wisely, or when tears fall during our repentance? While there is certainly nothing wrong with any of these actions, we deny the basis of our own faith when we begin to believe or act as though our actions, by their own merit, win God's favor. Were this true, then instruction to "take hold of those bootstraps and pick yourself up so that God will love you more" would not be wrong. But *sola bootstrapsa* messages are wrong, and faithful preachers must not only avoid this error but also war against it.

The Deadly Be's

Messages that strike at the heart of faith rather than support it often have an identifying theme. They exhort believers to strive to "be" something in order to be loved by God. Whether this equation is stated or implied, inadvertent or intentional, overt or subtle, the result is the same: an undermining of biblical faith. Such damage is usually inflicted by preachers striving to be biblical and unaware of the harm they are causing because they see their ideas supported in the narrow slice of Scripture they are expounding. They can point to the five steps for a better marriage in the text. They can support the standards of holiness they advocate with flawless exegesis. What they do not see is the erosion of hope they cause weekly by preaching messages biblical in origin but not biblically complete. We can recognize such incomplete messages by the "be" category into which they frequently fall.

"Be Like" Messages

"Be like" messages focus the attention of listeners on the accomplishments of a particular biblical character. After identifying the exemplary characteristics of the character, the preacher exhorts listeners to *be like* that person in some commendable aspect of his or her personality or practice. In what is often called biographical preaching, pastors urge congregants to be like Moses, Gideon, David, Daniel, or Peter in the face of a trial, temptation, or challenge.[35] Such exemplars, of course, can be used beneficially for instructing God's people in proper conduct and character. Biblical writers clearly intend for certain biblical characters to represent specific characteristics of godliness. A difficulty with much biographical preaching, however, is that it typically fails to honor the care that the Bible also takes to tarnish almost every patriarch or saint within its pages. Without blushing, the Bible honestly presents the human frailties of its most significant characters so that we will not expect to find, within fallen humanity, any whose model behavior merits divine acceptance. For instance, while many sermons exhort listeners to emulate David's courage, wisdom, and love for God, such messages hardly present a full (or honest) picture of the shepherd king's life without mention of his adultery, murder, and faithlessness. Were we to ask David whom believers should emulate, can we imagine that his answer would be, "Me"? If even the biblical characters themselves would not exhort us to model our lives after theirs, then we cannot remain faithful to Scripture and simply command a congregation to be like them. Neither do we help others by encouraging them to be like Jesus if we do not simultaneously remind them that his standards are always beyond them, apart from his enabling grace.

Preachers may quickly protest that in encouraging listeners to be like a biblical character, they are really only encouraging them to imitate the commendable aspects of the person the Bible itself praises. To be faithful to Scripture, we must not shy away from passages that encourage us to use people in the Bible as examples (e.g., 1 Cor. 11:1; Heb. 11:39). Still, before we preach on such passages, we must be sure to identify the source of the character quality that Scripture commends. Since the source of any holy trait is God's grace, we must echo the biblical caution, "Where then is boasting?" In addition, we must make it plain to listeners that grace cannot be self-stimulated or self-sustained. Since empowering grace is entirely of God, its fruit offers no personal merit in terms of justifying us before God (cf. Rom. 3:27; 1 Cor. 3:5–23). Simply telling people to imitate godliness in another person without reminding them that true holiness must come from dependence on God will force them either to despair of spiritual transformation or to deny its need.

The commendable aspects of biblical characters function in Scripture like aspects of God's law: They are necessary to know, proper to follow, and are the instruments of God's blessing in our lives. But these same righteous standards become spiritually deadly when they are perceived or honored as the basis of God's acceptance. Preachers should teach God's people to esteem and emulate the righteous actions of godly people in the Bible, but preachers must also make it plain that such godliness can come only as a response to God's unconditional love and as a result of his enabling Spirit

35. Greidanus, *Modern Preacher and the Ancient Text*, 161–81.

(Phil. 1:19–21). Sermons that preach imitation of saints in isolation from the Savior profit nothing (see John 15:5; Eph. 3:16–19). Without the provision of his grace, we cannot be people he desires.

"Be Good" Messages

Similar to focusing on biographies apart from enabling grace is an emphasis on behaviors alone that also results in nonredemptive messages. Again, preachers of such messages are usually unaware of the harm of devoting an entire sermon to telling people to be good or holy. God expects holiness. He commands it. He devotes innumerable passages in Scripture to telling us what to do and what not to do. So what could possibly be wrong with exhorting people to be good? Again, the problem often lies not in what preachers say but in what they fail to say.

When the focus of a sermon becomes a moralistic "Don't smoke or chew or go with those who do" (or even a more sophisticated "Renew your heart by doing what God commands"), listeners will most likely assume that they can secure or renew their relationship with God through proper behaviors. Even when the behaviors advocated are reasonable, biblical, and correct, a sermon that does not move from expounding standards of obedience to explaining the source, motives, and results of obedience places persons' hopes in their own actions. In such a situation, each succeeding Sunday sermon carries the implicit message, "Since you weren't good enough for God last week, hunker down and try harder this week."

Preaching of this sort sounds biblical because the Bible can be quoted at length to support the exhortations. As it runs its course, however, such preaching destroys all Christian distinctives. Preachers caught in a purely moralistic mode of instruction end up speaking in tautologies: "Be good because it's good to be good, and it's bad to be bad. Christians are good. So be good!"

Ringing clearly through such preaching is the implied promise, "Obey God because he will love you if you do and will get you if you don't." A following week's sermon may be an evangelistic appeal to come to the cross for grace freely offered, but what grace means in this context probably has little to do with biblical teaching. Evangelical preaching that implies we are saved by grace but kept by our obedience not only undermines the work of God in sanctification but ultimately casts doubt on the nature of God (i.e., he loves us only when we are good enough) and thus makes salvation itself suspect when we honestly assess our imperfections.

The natural tendency of all believers is to base our estimation of our justification on our personal progress in sanctification.[36] We estimate whether we are okay with God on the basis of *how we did today*. Were we good enough?

---

36. Richard Lovelace, *Dynamics of Spiritual Life* (Downers Grove, Ill.: InterVarsity, 1979), 101.

Did we fail to honor our ideals? Did we hurt anyone or break any commandments? Yet the truth of the gospel is that sanctification is based on *what Jesus did eternally*. Because Jesus died and rose again on our behalf, we are cleansed of our sin and reconciled to God. "There is now no condemnation for those who are in Christ Jesus" (Rom. 8:1), and we progressively live for God in the confidence that we are in union with his life and power solely on the basis of what he has fully and finally accomplished on the cross (Gal. 2:20). Our *experience* of his blessings, pleasure, and nearness still relies on our obedience, but the *reality* of our relationship is not and never was based on our goodness.[37] God has fully and completely applied to us the merits of Christ's righteousness, even though we are striving to live in conformity with his law in loving response to his redeeming work (Rom. 5:15–21; 1 Cor. 6:11; Eph. 5:25–27).[38]

If God were to make his love conditional on our goodness, then we might obey him, but we would not like him very much. The consequence would be that both love for God and true obedience would be destroyed, since only those who love him really do what he commands (John 14:15). Preaching applications should readily and vigorously exhort obedience to God's commands, but such exhortations should be based primarily on responding in love to God's grace, not on trying to gain or maintain it (Rom. 12:1).

"Be Disciplined" Messages

Close kin to "be good" messages are sermons that exhort believers to improve their relationship with God through more diligent use of the means of grace. Such messages do not merely advocate moral behavior but typically encourage believers to practice more regularly, sincerely, or methodically those disciplines that allegedly will lift them to higher planes of divine approval (or, if left undone, will reap divine displeasure). Such preachers intone, "Pray more, read the Bible more, go to church more, and have better quiet times with God." If pressed to explain these exhortations theologically, few would actually say that they believe the practice of these Christian disciplines earns believers extra points with God. Few, however, will argue with the parishioner who says, "I had a terrible day today. This always seems to happen when I get up too late for my quiet time."

37. See Bryan Chapell, *Holiness by Grace: Delighting in the Joy That Is Our Strength* (Wheaton: Crossway, 2001), 126–32.

38. While our common usage limits the term *sanctification* to progress in the Christian life, the biblical understanding of sanctification is more a pervasive concept that includes God's initial work of salvation (definitive sanctification), *whereby we are declared righteous despite our sin;* continuing work of salvation (progressive sanctification), *whereby we become more righteous as we grow in Christlikeness;* and final work of salvation (entire sanctification), *whereby we are made perfect in glory for eternity,* all of which are fully accomplished in the cross and resurrection, even though they are realized at different stages of the Christian life.

The reason so few preachers will object to such a statement is that many of us live as though our disciplines make us acceptable to God or earn us credit with him. Because our identity is so tied to observances of our religious practices, we feel unworthy if we have neglected daily prayer or shortchanged our Bible memorization. Something in us also believes that the day would probably have gone better if we had only been more diligent. There are, of course, real consequences of faithlessness. Shortchanging sermon preparation tends to result in poor sermons, and regular neglect of prayer tends to result in a perceived distancing of God's hand. The warping of faith and preaching occurs, however, with the belief that disciplines ward off God's ire or buy his favor. In such a case, the problem is not the biblical discipline we practice but the type of God we perceive. He becomes the ogre in the sky who requires the daily satisfaction of our toil to dispense his favor or restrain his displeasure.

Few preachers intentionally paint this picture of a God so readily vexed, but when they present the Christian disciplines in isolation from the grace that motivates, sanctifies, and secures, such a portrait necessarily emerges. If devotion to disciplines procures our position or privileges with God, then grace becomes something we manufacture by our works, making grace meaningless. And since no degree of human diligence can compensate the Lord for all we truly owe him, an insistence on more exercise of disciplines to satisfy God only makes those most honest about their merits less sure of their standing. Brownie points count for little in an economy in which absolute holiness remains the only acceptable currency.

The true efficacy of spiritual disciplines is not their power to bribe God but their usefulness in opening hearts to the perception and exercise of his power. Spiritual disciplines enable those made righteous by Christ's work to breathe more deeply the resources that God freely and lovingly provides for the wisdom, joy, and strength of Christian living. Through disciplines, we inhale more deeply the air God provides for the Christian race, but such disciplines do not produce or maintain the oxygen of God's love. Preachers should encourage more prayer, stewardship, study, and fellowship not to manufacture blessing but so that believers can experience more fully the benefits of union with Christ that God freely offers. With this perspective, disciplines become regular refreshment for those who hunger and thirst for ever deeper fellowship with the God they love (Ps. 19:10). The same disciplines, however, will become distasteful duty or bitter pride for those who think that their devotion keeps them on the good side of a God whose measure of love is determined by the grade of their performance.

The Bottom Line

"Be" messages that contain only moral instruction imply that we are able to change our fallen condition in our own strength. Such sermons communicate (although usually unintentionally) that we make the path to grace and that our works earn and/or secure our acceptance with God. However well intended, these sermons present a faith indistinguishable from that of morally conscientious Muslims, Unitarians, Buddhists, or Hindus. The distinctive of the Christian faith is that God provides the way to himself because we cannot make our way to him. This is just as true for progressive sanctification as it is for original justification. A sermon no different from a childhood imperative to be a "Do Bee" rather than a "Don't Bee" places more responsibility on a child of God than the gospel will allow.

The fundamental biblical truth that differentiates the gospel from a morality lesson is the declaration that our works always remain tainted by our humanity. Of themselves our actions can never earn God's blessing or secure his favor (Isa. 64:6; Luke 17:10). Although there are blessed consequences to heeding divine commands designed for our good, mere conformity to biblical commands offers no heavenly merit.[39] If we had to earn grace prior to or after we came to Christ, it would not be grace that we gained.

There are many "be" messages in Scripture, but they always reside in a redemptive context. Since we cannot be anything that God would approve of apart from his sanctifying mercy and power, grace must permeate any exhortation for biblical behavior. *"Be" messages are not wrong in themselves; they are wrong messages by themselves.* People cannot do or be what God requires without the past, present, and future work of Christ. "From him and through him and to him are all things" (Rom. 11:36). Simply railing at error and hammering at piety may convince people of their inadequacy or move them toward self-sufficiency, but these messages also keep true godliness remote. Thus, instruction in biblical behavior barren of redemptive truth only wounds. Though it is offered as an antidote to sin, such preaching either promotes Pharisaism or prompts despair. Christ-centered preachers accept neither alternative. They understand that if they wound, they are obligated to heal. People pierced to the heart by awareness of the magnitude of their biblical obligations and personal limitations find salve for their souls when preachers proclaim the fulfillment of God's holy standards in Christ and by his Spirit.

Christ-centered preachers do not hesitate to present the moral imperatives the Lord demands, but neither do they deny him the position of honor in all that his Word says or in all that his creatures do.[40] Challenges to holiness must be accompanied by a Christ focus or they will promote only human-centered, doomed-to-fail religion. When we exhort congregations to stand for God against the assaults of Satan, we must never forget the balance of the Pauline imperative: "Finally, my brethren, be strong in the Lord, and in

39. Adams, *Preaching with Purpose,* 146.
40. Regarding a balanced approach, see James A. De Jong, "Principled Paraenesis: Reading and Preaching the Ethical Material of New Testament Letters," *Pro Rege* 10, no. 4 (June 1982): 26–34.

the power of his might" (Eph. 6:10 KJV). Amid his most strident "be" message, the apostle remained Christ-focused. Today's preacher has no lesser obligation. We should not preach God's requirements in isolation from God's grace because the holiness God requires he also must provide. If we neglect the means of grace, then we deny the possibility of obedience.

Faithful expository preaching unfolds every text in the context of its redemptive import. The success of this endeavor can be assessed by a bottom-line question every preacher should ask at the end of each sermon: When my listeners walk out the doors of this sanctuary to perform God's will, with whom do they walk? If they march to battle the world, the flesh, and the devil with only me, myself, and I, then each parades to despair. However, if the sermon has led all persons to God's grace, then they may walk into the world with their Savior—and with fresh hope. Whether people depart alone or in the Savior's hand marks the difference between futility and faith, legalism and true obedience, do-goodism and real godliness.

Questions for Review and Discussion

1. How does clear identification of an FCF prepare a preacher to construct a redemptive message?
2. How can a message advocate biblical behavior and still remain sub-Christian?
3. How does biblical theology act as a fish-eye lens?
4. What are four possible redemptive foci that characterize biblical texts?
5. The most common method of identifying a redemptive message in a text that makes no specific mention of Christ requires a preacher to ask the question, What does this text reflect of God's nature that _____ redemption and/or human nature that _____ redemption?
6. What are the "deadly be's"? Explain why they are not wrong *in* themselves but become dangerous *by* themselves?

Exercises

1. Explain how you could present redemptive messages on three of the following passages:
    Judges 7
    Proverbs 5
    Ezra 2
    Colossians 3:18–4:1
    James 2:14–26
2. Discuss how the redemptive thrust of all Scripture should affect the way you instruct listeners about matters of Christian obedience.

GOAL OF CHAPTER 11

To explain how to construct expository sermons that reflect the redemptive content of every biblical text

11

Developing Redemptive Sermons

Methods of Redemptive Exposition

Once preachers recognize the danger of preaching messages that imply that a person is able to achieve self-justification or self-sanctification, they have a natural compulsion to preach Christ-centered messages. Such messages will not simply tell people to hunker down and try harder this week. Rather, these grace-oriented messages will lead people to understand that Christ's work rather than their own supplies the only basis for God's acceptance and that Christ's strength rather than their own provides the only hope of Christian obedience. Such messages are difficult to develop for two reasons: They go against the flow of so much that we are accustomed to hearing in the evangelical church, and they seem to stretch the bounds of precise expository preaching. Understanding how to overcome these difficulties is the next step in developing Christ-centered sermons.

Capture the Redemptive Flow

"The Menace of the Sunday School" is the title of a rather notorious portion of a book that sadly captures the essence of much evangelical teaching. In an effort to promote moral behavior and deter sin, the stereotypical Sunday school teacher implores children to be good little boys and girls so that Jesus will love them and take care of them. The stereotype is unkind and unfair, but it comes painfully close to characterizing much contemporary preaching that portrays God as a perpetual Santa Claus who is making a list and checking it twice to punish the naughty and reward the nice. I recognize that even as I write these words there are readers who wonder what is wrong with that characterization. The problem lies in the fact that such teaching becomes a menace to faith because it makes the ministry of Christ irrelevant by seeming to make God's love dependent on our works.

Proper concerns to gain holiness and/or compel purity engender much improper teaching by making human activity the basis of our standing with God. Almost every generation has to rediscover grace because humanity has no natural capacity to receive (or perceive of) the notion that we can do nothing to gain God's acceptance. "We cannot by our best works merit pardon for sin ...nor satisfy for the debt of our former sins."[1] After we have done everything we have been told to do, we are still unworthy servants (Luke 17:10). Because our works are mixed with so much weakness and imperfection of motive, they remain defiled before a holy God.[2] Our best works are as "filthy rags" to him (Isa. 64:6). They become acceptable to him only to the degree that their defilement is covered by Christ and to the extent that they proceed from his Spirit.[3]

While there are blessed consequences to moral behavior and God honors the homage we offer him in the name of his Son, our actions *in themselves* offer us no opportunity for boasting and no leverage against heaven. Since our ability to do good works is from God, our goodness alone neither merits his blessing nor secures his acceptance (Ezek. 36:26–27; John 15:4–6; Phil. 2:13).[4] Apart from the provision of God's pardoning and sanctifying grace, our best works are actually deserving of God's reproof rather than meriting his reward.

As apparent as these truths may seem in theological discussion, we too easily divorce them from our homiletical methods. We may regularly encourage people to improve their relationships, polish their ethics, and discipline their habits without mentioning the enabling power of the Spirit or the grace that keeps their best efforts from offending God. One reason for this failure is the fact that Babel is never far from any of us. In our common humanity, we consistently ignore Scripture and continue to practice obedience as a way of bribing God to dispense his favor. In doing so, we not only ignore the limitations of our humanity but also tar God's character. We turn him into the ogre in the sky who shows his favor only when he is paid with enough

---

1. Westminster Confession of Faith, 16.5.

2. Ibid. This classic statement of Christian orthodoxy reads: "*We cannot by our best works merit pardon for sin,* or eternal life at the hand of God, by reason of the great disproportion that is between them and the glory to come; and the infinite distance that is between us and God, whom, *by them we can neither profit,* nor satisfy for the debt of our former sins, but *when we have done all we can, we have done but our duty, and are unprofitable servants;* and because, *as they are good, they proceed from His Spirit; and as they are wrought by us, they are defiled,* and mixed with so much weakness and imperfection, that they cannot endure the severity of God's judgment" (emphasis added).

3. Westminster Confession of Faith, 16.3–6.

4. Ibid., 16.3.

"filthy rags." This is part of the reason why, when the message of grace goes underground in the history of the church, the worst abuses of faith occur. Without a proper perspective on the provision of God, humanity's efforts toward righteousness inevitably lead to intolerance, futility, and despair.

These historical patterns can repeat themselves in the lives of believers in a local church if the pastor tends to preach mere moral precepts from the Bible. But even preachers who see the fault in such preaching may wonder what else they can do if they are committed to expository preaching from the whole of Scripture. How can one preach a redemptive message from a passage of the Bible in which there is no mention of Jesus, the cross, the resurrection, the atonement, or other central redemptive themes? In other words, our natural tendency to try to gain God's acceptance by achievement is not all that tempts ministers to preach messages that contain no reference to Christ's work. Expository commitments to remain faithful to the truths of a text motivate many pastors to neglect preaching grace. Such preachers rightly question, "How can we make a message Christ-centered when the passage contains no Christ reference?" This legitimate exegetical concern deserves a biblical response.

Lay the Redemptive Foundations

IDENTIFY THE FALLEN CONDITION

A good place to begin the construction of a Christ-centered sermon is with a clear statement of the Fallen Condition Focus of a text.[5] This is not done simply to surface a need that will make listeners want to hear the message. Clear identification of a fallen condition automatically locks a preacher into a redemptive approach to the exposition of a biblical passage. Because each text was inspired to complete hearers in some way, when preachers specify a text's purpose, they are pressed to redemptive perspectives. From this perspective, listeners take on the appearance of Swiss cheese—they have holes in their spiritual being that God alone can fill. What determines whether a message is truly redemptive (and true to the scope of Scripture) is what the preacher specifies will fill the holes—mere human effort or divine provision.

The simple step of making sure that they identify the spiritual hole (i.e., fallen condition) that a text addresses keeps preachers from offering solutions that are merely human responses. Fallen creatures cannot remedy true fallenness by an act of their will. Legalistic, moralistic, self-help messages become self-evident and self-defeating when a preacher begins with a strong awareness of the fallen state that is the burden of a text and the condition of listeners.

Real exegetical problems arise, however, when a preacher recognizes that human effort will not alleviate a fallen condition but a text seems to offer no

---

5. See discussions of the Fallen Condition Focus in chaps. 2 and 10.

Christocentric solution. Many passages seem to offer only positive or negative character examples (e.g., the faith of Moses, the courage of Joshua, or, conversely, the deceitfulness of Saul, the rashness of Peter), moral instruction (e.g., do not lie, do not steal), or spiritual-discipline exhortation (e.g., pray more, show more concern for others, be more faithful). How does an expository preacher proclaim redemptive truths when a text seems to present none?

Specify the Christ Focus

Two answers to this question need to be rejected at the outset. First, we must reject the answer that denies the validity of biblical instructions, disciplines, or examples provided in passages with no obvious redemptive theme. Second, we need to dispense with attempts to make Jesus magically, figuratively, or allegorically appear in every biblical account by insisting that a text somehow refers to the incarnate Christ even when there is no evidence in the text (e.g., seeing aspects of Christ's triumphal entry in the account of Balaam's donkey because both "prophets" rode the same kind of animal). Both of these wrong answers arise from an errant view of Scripture that does not properly perceive the organic nature of the entire biblical record.[6] Proper exposition does not discover its Christ focus by disposing of a passage or by imposing Jesus on a text but by discerning the place and the role of a text in the entire revelation of God's redemptive plan, which is ultimately fulfilled in Christ (2 Cor. 1:20; Rev. 22:13).

Following the creation passages at the outset of Genesis, all of Scripture is a record of God's dealings with a corrupted world and its creatures. But the record does not merely recite historical facts. It reveals an ongoing drama whereby God systematically, personally, and progressively discloses the necessity and the detail of his plan to use his Son to redeem and restore fallen humanity and creation itself.[7] Sidney Greidanus states the implications that this organic view of Scripture holds for proper exposition of a text:

> The unity of redemptive history implies the *Christocentric* nature of every historical text. Redemptive history is the history of Christ. He stands at its center, but no less at its beginning and end. . . . Scripture discloses the theme, the scopus of its historiography right at the beginning. "Gen. 3:15," Van't Veer says, "places all subsequent events in the light of the tremendous battle between Christ coming into the world and Satan the ruler of this world, and it places all events in the light of the complete victory which the Seed of the woman shall attain. In view of this, it is imperative that not one single person be isolated from this history and set apart from this great battle. The place

---

6. Sidney Greidanus, *Sola Scriptura: Problems and Principles in Preaching Historical Texts* (Toronto: Wedge, 1970), 135; and Geerhardus Vos, "The Idea of Biblical Theology" (inaugural address upon assuming the new chair of biblical theology at Princeton Seminary, n.d. [1895 probable]), 16.

7. Geerhardus Vos, *Biblical Theology* (Grand Rapids: Eerdmans, 1975), 5–7.

of both opponents and 'co-workers' can only be determined Christologically. Only in so far as they received their place and task in the development of *this* history do they appear in the historiography of Scripture. From this point of view the facts are selected and recorded."[8]

A passage retains its Christocentric focus and a sermon becomes Christ-centered not because a preacher finds a slick way of wedging a reference to Jesus' person or work into the message but because the sermon identifies a function that the text legitimately serves in the great drama of the Son's crusade against the serpent. Rahab does not represent the work of Christ because her cloth is blood red but because God demonstrates through her that he delivers the despicable (her) and the destitute (the Israelites) through means neither naturally possesses or deserves. In such ways, grace appears in Old Testament clothes and New Testament expression without direct mention of Jesus but with an unmistakable tracing of God's redemptive nature and work ultimately achieved through his Son.

This mature view of Christ-centered preaching warns preachers not to believe they have properly expounded a text simply because they have identified something in it that reminds them of an event in Jesus' life and ministry. When a preacher uses a geographical reference to a well in the Old Testament to introduce a discussion of Jesus' conversation with the woman at the well, no real explanation of the original passage's place and meaning in redemptive history has occurred. The preacher has only engaged in a bit of word play. The same is true when a preacher leapfrogs to the New Testament from a feature of Moses' law or an event in Israel's kingship simply because a detail in the account seems similar to something Christ did (see fig. 11.1).

Figure 11.1

Imaginative Leapfrogging to Christ

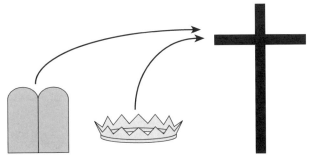

The preacher says, "This passage *reminds* me of . . ."

8. Greidanus, *Sola Scriptura,* 135.

When preachers interpret Rahab's red cloth, the nail in Jael's hand, the saddle on Rachel's camel, and the spices in Solomon's house (to name only a few possibilities) as directly reflecting an aspect of Christ's earthly ministry, their conclusions may sound biblical. However, if Scripture does not confirm the interpretation, such preachers actually relate only what their minds suggest rather than what a text means. A minister's imagination is a poor place to discern what a biblical passage means. After all, some preachers may say that Rahab's red cloth stands for the blood of Christ, while others may conclude that the scarlet represents sin. These nearly opposite interpretations may relate to biblical truths found elsewhere in Scripture, but neither interpretation relates a definite meaning of the immediate text.

Similar interpretive errors occur when pastors believe they must find Christ hiding behind every bush on the plain of Old Testament history. Feeling the obligation to discern Jesus in such passages, these preachers search out the implications of tiny "messianic lights" in pre-crucifixion texts in order to make some reference to the atonement.[9] The water in a lake becomes the water that flowed from Christ's pierced side, the rocks in the desert translate into the solid hope we have in his solitary death, trees metamorphize into crosses, oil transubstantiates into blood, and mountains conform to the contours of Calvary.

The problem with these nonexpository explanations is that they suggest that Christ is adequately represented only when a preacher declares that a textual detail is a direct reference to Jesus' incarnation or atoning work—regardless of a text's statements or purpose. Since Scripture as a whole is God's revelation of his redeeming activity in Jesus Christ,[10] a preacher needs only to demonstrate where and how a particular text functions in the overall redemptive plan in order to show its Christocentric focus. As indicated in the previous chapter, that function may be predictive, preparatory, reflective, or resultant of Christ's work. Other redemptive purposes may also be discerned that do not require figurative references to Jesus.

The Word of Christ and the Word about Christ operate in every Scripture passage as God unfolds the mystery of his grand design.[11] Writes Greidanus:

> This conception of Christ as the eternal Logos actively at work throughout history removes the props from the traditional insistence that every sermon must somehow point to Christ Incarnate in order to be Christocentric. It bursts the confining mold which has caused so many aberrations throughout the history of preaching; it creates more room for the text itself to speak. The preacher is no longer required "to land with an acrobatic leap at Golgotha" in

9. Ibid., 143.
10. Vos, "Idea of Biblical Theology," 11, 14.
11. See Edmund Clowney, *The Unfolding Mystery: Discovering Christ in the Old Testament* (Phillipsburg, N.J.: Presbyterian & Reformed, 1988), 9–16.

order to *make* the text and the sermon Christocentric, for Christ is already present at that point of redemptive history which the text relates.[12]

Expository preaching need not mention Golgotha, Bethlehem, or the Mount of Olives to remain Christ-centered. As long as a preacher uses a text's statements or context to expose the theological truths or historical facts that demonstrate the relation of the passage to the overall war between the Seed of the woman and Satan, Christ assumes his rightful place as the focus of the message. This also means, however, that mere reflection on an aspect of Jesus' nature or an event from his life is *not* an adequate explanation of a passage's meaning as it relates to him. The aroma of the atonement and/or the perfume of gracious provision must permeate a message for it to be truly pleasing to God and edifying for his people. Preaching that is true to the Christocentric nature of all Scripture discloses a text's relationship to Christ's messianic character and redemptive purposes.[13]

Discern the Redemptive Purpose

As unlikely as it seems, this perspective concerning the overall purpose of Scripture means that even if a preacher does not specifically mention an aspect of Christ's earthly ministry in a sermon, it can still be Christ-centered. As long as a preacher explains the ways in which God uses a text to reveal his plan, purposes, and/or reasons for redemption, the sermon leads listeners away from human-centered religiosity. Exposition is Christ-centered when it discloses God's essential nature as our Provider, Deliverer, and Sustainer whether or not Jesus is mentioned by name. By concentrating on what God is accomplishing with the record of every event, the account of every character, and the principles in every instruction, a preacher keeps a message from degenerating into mere human hero worship. God remains the hero of every text. This does not mean that biblical characters have no exemplary qualities for us to emulate (e.g., Rom. 15:4; Phil. 3:17). We must understand, though, that when these positive qualities appear, grace is the cause (Rom. 11:36).

> The slighting of biblical characters cannot be justified. . . . The first thing to notice about biblical characters is that they are incorporated into the biblical text not for their own sake but to show what God is doing through, in and for them—to show how God advances his kingdom through the efforts of human beings and sometimes in spite of them.[14]

When preachers place a text within the context of what God is revealing about his nature that provides redemption or about human nature that requires redemption, self-reliance vanishes.

12. Greidanus, *Sola Scriptura*, 145.
13. Sidney Greidanus, *Preaching Christ from the Old Testament* (Grand Rapids: Eerdmans, 1999), 54.
14. Sidney Greidanus, "Redemptive History and Preaching," *Pro Rege* 19, no. 2 (December 1990): 14.

Theocentric preaching inevitably becomes Christocentric not because a sermon simply cites the name of Jesus or draws to mind an event from his life but because the sermon demonstrates the reality of the human predicament that requires divine solution *and* identifies that solution.[15] Theocentric preaching is Christ-centered preaching because to proclaim God as he has revealed himself is to make known the providing nature and character that are eternally manifested in Christ (Heb. 13:8). A focus on God's redemptive activity sets the stage for Christ's work, alerts the human heart to its necessity, and/or exposes the divine character as Deliverer. When we see God at work, Christ's ministry inevitably comes into view (John 1:1–3; 14:7–10; Col. 1:15–20; Heb. 1:1–3).[16] A sermon remains expository and Christ-centered not because it leapfrogs to Golgotha but because it locates the intent of a passage within the scope of God's redemptive work (see fig. 11.2). Thus, the sermon's purpose remains faithful to the text's original aim of enabling the people of God to understand his redemptive activity—predicting it, preparing to understand its nature, reflecting its need, and/or detailing the results of Christ's work in our lives.[17]

Figure 11.2

Christ-Centered Exposition

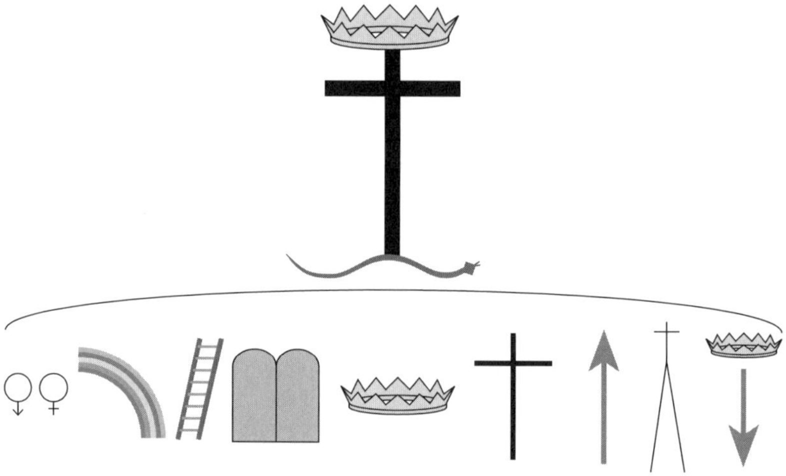

A preacher explains the role of any epoch, event, person, and passage within the divine crusade of redemption (i.e., the sovereign victory of the Seed of the woman over Satan).

---

15. Ibid., 12–13; see also Greidanus, *Sola Scriptura*, 143–44; and Michael Fabarez, *Preaching That Changes Lives* (Nashville: Thomas Nelson, 2002), 114–16.

16. John Calvin, *Institutes of the Christian Religion*, 2.6.4.

17. See further discussion of these four uses of biblical texts in chap. 10.

With this perspective of God's redemptive plan (and Scripture's organic presentation of it), each person, precept, and event in the biblical record assumes its proper role in faithful exposition.[18] Preachers will not present biblical patriarchs whose conduct was often far from exemplary as perfect models for listeners to emulate. The ancient saints will be presented as God intended—hopelessly fallen creatures whose faith and favor are entirely the product of God's mercy and deliverance.[19]

Sermons on the law will not merely detail moral precepts but will show the contemporary people of God what the standards were intended to teach: the necessity of divine dependence as well as holy conduct (Gal. 3:24).[20] Preachers will not inadvertently teach that God's acceptance depends on our righteousness when they consistently demonstrate that the law itself pointed to the need of a greater provision of righteousness than human accomplishment.

Messages on the times of the judges and kings will remove the veils we so often put over these giants of faith to shield their reputations from their too frequent flaws. Preachers will then more freely herald all dimensions of the biblical leaders' characters because they understand that their weaknesses underscore a righteousness that comes from God.[21]

Even New Testament instruction on marriage, stewardship, church relationships, and worship practices will cease to function as an aberrant reinstitution of Old Testament law qualifying God's people for his approval. All biblical standards (whether presented in the form of written precept or human example) will function as God intends—guiding God's people into the paths that reflect his glory, promote their good, and satisfy their souls as the natural outflow of loving thankfulness for what he has done on their behalf and what he alone can further do.

Dead Ends and Bridges

The preceding examples demonstrate how different portions and features of the Bible function in revealing God's overall plan of redemption. As the

18. Jonathan Edwards, in his remarkable "Letter to the Trustees of the College of New Jersey," proposes such an approach to all of Scripture "considering the affair of Christian Theology, as the whole of it, in each part, stands in reference to the great work of redemption by Jesus Christ" as the "summum and ultimum of all divine operations and decrees." See Clarence H. Faust and Thomas H. Johnson, eds., *Jonathan Edwards* (New York: American Book, 1935), 411–12.

19. Edmund Clowney, *Preaching and Biblical Theology* (Grand Rapids: Eerdmans, 1961), 80. See also idem, "Preaching Christ from All the Scriptures," in *The Preacher and Preaching*, ed. Samuel T. Logan (Phillipsburg, N.J.: Presbyterian & Reformed, 1986), 163–91.

20. Calvin, *Institutes of the Christian Religion,* 2.7; 10.3–5.

21. For excellent discussion of how God's redemptive truths are presented in the various epochs and genre of Scripture, see Graeme Goldsworthy, *Gospel and Kingdom: A Christian Interpretation of the Old Testament* (Carlisle, U.K.: Paternoster, 1994); and idem, *Preaching the Whole Bible as Christian Scripture* (Grand Rapids: Eerdmans, 2000).

history of God's redemption unfolds, it is apparent that God is teaching his people various aspects of salvation that they must understand to put full faith in Christ. So that the covenant people would have no hope in their own righteousness, God provided the law, which—despite its blessings—dramatically revealed human frailty and finiteness. So that people would not believe that simply doing what was right in their own eyes would bring fulfillment, God allowed the covenant people to experience the painful period of judges. To know the folly of depending on human authorities (even of splendid gifts and great power) for security and peace, God allowed the disappointments of the period of the kings. These historical features and epochs, and the particular events and people involved, demonstrate that human paths to salvation are *dead ends*.

Our failures before the law indicate that we need someone else to fulfill it perfectly on our behalf. The pain and anarchy that result from trying to exercise autonomous judgment over our lives reveals the need for a more perfect Judge. The limitations and failures of the best of human kings clearly show the necessity of a greater King. By taking us to the end of hope in each of these (and other) human paths through his revelation of redemptive history, God directs us to a better path that leads to Christ. Preaching that is faithful to the purposes of redemptive revelation details the nature of the dead ends (rather than allegorically making details refer to an event in Jesus' life) to direct hearts to the one who is the way, the truth, and the life.

Some passages of Scripture also fulfill their redemptive purposes by providing *bridges* in the place of (or along with) the dead ends. With the law were the Old Testament sacraments and temple features that foreshadowed (or typified) the aspects of grace made available and complete in Christ. With the frustrations and disappointments of the judges and kings of Israel were the prophetic ministries that yet provided hope in a coming Redeemer. An expositor rightly interprets many Old and New Testament passages by explaining how their figures or features lead us forward in our understanding of what Christ did or ultimately will do.

Macro and Micro Messages

The process of interpreting the redemptive truth evident throughout biblical history is known as the redemptive-historical method. This is a vital and foundational tool that expositors need to accurately and gracefully interpret texts in their full context. However, the macro dimensions of a method that requires us to take into account the broad sweep of events across millennia can have unfortunate preaching repercussions. Some preachers may think they have to preach from Genesis to Revelation in every message and thereby construct sermons that are too academic, complex, and long for regular worship. Other preachers so fear that they may not discern precisely the right function of a passage in the scope of biblical history that they dispense with trying to discern a text's redemptive purpose.

Both repercussions can be minimized and much fruitful preaching facilitated by learning to discern the micro as well as the macro messages of grace the redemptive-historical method reveals. It is not always necessary to push the exposition of a text to the most distant horizons of Scripture to discern the grace present. In fact, while these horizons provide the general (and necessary) frame of reference for Christ-centered preaching, an individual sermon can reflect the redemptive truths evident in the immediate context of the passage. These truths may be made evident from *doctrinal statement* in the text or from the *relational interaction* between God and the persons in the text—or between persons in the text who are intended to represent God's redemptive character.

The *doctrinal statement* that "Abram believed the LORD, and he credited it to him as righteousness" certainly has broad theological implications for the history of redemption. But this clear Old Testament explanation of the nature of saving faith also has significant implications within the immediate context of Genesis 15 that can be profitably expounded. Preachers can show the nature of God's provision of his grace through faith by expounding what this statement means within the bounds of the passage. Dimensions of grace can be exposed and explained within the passage. Nothing prohibits a preacher from expounding the wider context of the biblical record, but nothing requires it either. The redemptive themes that make the message Christ-centered (i.e., focusing on what God provides for our need beyond our ability) are evident within the immediate passage if the preacher chooses to go there.

Similarly, the fact that God maintained his promise to David despite the king's grievous sins has vast historical import. But rather than always going to the distant horizons of Scripture, preachers may choose to excavate the grace of the text from the *relational interaction* God had with David in the immediate context of the narrative. God forgave David. This grace on a micro level may prove equally (or more) meaningful as demonstrating on a macro level how the preservation of David's lineage resulted in the birth of the Messiah. Both levels of explanation are appropriate, and the macro and micro aspects of redemptive-historical interpretations do not have to be mutually exclusive. Often they reinforce one another. Still, it usually comforts preachers to realize that redemptive truth can most often be found right in the immediate context of the passage being preached. Through the way that God relates to his people (or those representing him relate to others), the nature of God's character and work reflect the grace we need to know to turn from confidence in ourselves and to faith in his provision. As a consequence, preaching continually motivates others with the mercy of God even when preachers preach from passages that make no explicit mention of his provision of Jesus.[22]

Measures of Redemptive Exposition

A Procedure for Redemptive Exposition

Knowing that the Lord is always revealing his grace in the biblical record through the broad and narrow expanses of Scripture, a preacher needs tools to extract accurately and faithfully the redemptive truths of particular passages. The three-step expository procedure described below is one such tool.[23] It not only serves as a means of tracing how the redemptive truths that course through biblical texts should appear in sermons but also provides a measure of assurance that a preacher will disclose a text's ultimate purposes.

A Procedure for Christ-Centered Exposition

I. Identify the redemptive principles evident in the text.
   A. Reveal aspects of the divine nature, which provides redemption.
   B. Reveal aspects of human nature, which requires redemption.
II. Determine what application these redemptive principles were to have in the lives of the original hearers/readers of the text.
III. Apply the redemptive principles to contemporary lives in the light of common human characteristics or conditions contemporary believers share with the original hearers/readers.

This procedure obviously echoes the process by which a preacher determines the FCF of a message, with two substantive differences. First, this procedure is not merely directed toward determining why listeners need to hear a message. Rather, it makes the aim of a message the determination of what God expects listeners to do, believe, or accept as a result of his dealing with this need. The second difference is a product of the first. As a result of this redemptive focus, the aim or emphasis of a message shifts from a human orientation to what God has done, is doing, or will do.[24]

22. I use "mercy" here synecdochically, as Paul does in Romans 12:1, to refer to the great matrix of redemptive truths (past, present, and future) that are God's means of rescuing us from our sin and self-reliance. In this usage, even strong imperatives and warnings of consequences for transgression are "mercy" because they demonstrate how God desires to turn us from our sin to his safekeeping.

23. Cf. Kenneth J. Howell, "How to Preach Christ from the Old Testament," *Presbyterian Journal* 16 (January 1985): 10. Note that this procedure moves beyond what is commonly called the redemptive-historical method to a redemptive-doctrinal approach that expounds in light of redemptive truth as well as redemptive context.

24. Jay E. Adams, *Preaching with Purpose: A Comprehensive Textbook on Biblical Preaching* (Grand Rapids: Baker, 1982), 152. Cf. John Piper, *The Supremacy of God in Preaching* (Grand Rapids: Baker, 1990), 17–46.

Although an FCF reveals why people need to listen and why God chooses to act, the redemptive exposition keeps the solution divine and precludes human presumption. Such exposition returns preaching to its foundational function of transformation. Men and women are still called to devotion, but preachers issue the summons on the basis of God's actions and by his power. Preachers never inadvertently teach others to seek answers without his truth, perform his bidding without his strength, or reap his blessing without the acceptance he alone provides. Faithful preaching is the practice of pointing others to a provision beyond themselves so that they are able to do what God requires *and* what the regenerate heart desires. The doxological focus of redemptive exposition keeps this process intact.

Models of Redemptive Exposition

What does redemptive exposition look like? How do these principles actually shape the structure of an expository message? Standard cues rather than a standard form tend to designate a Christ-centered sermon. At times, a preacher may begin a message by underscoring the redemptive truths that underlie the instruction in a passage (see the redemptive foundation model below). On other occasions a preacher may build a redemptive case as the instructions unfold (see the redemptive development model below) or provide all the instructions and then in the sermon's waning moments point out the redemptive truths that will enable or properly motivate faithful service (see the redemptive "twist" model below). Preachers should be cautious of this last alternative because it may simply be a human-centered message with a Christ-mentioned ending, but an ironic twist in a message can make a powerful theocentric thrust—if the preacher does not practice this method too often.

Nonredemptive Model

I. Cleanse yourself from all unrighteousness.
II. Follow God in renewed righteousness.
III. Lead others to proper righteousness.

Note: This is a classic "be holy" sermon whose structure and wording make the adequate performance of the believer the sole instrument of redemption.

Redemptive Foundation Model

I. God provides our righteousness.
II. Claim the righteousness God provides.
III. Express the righteousness God provides.

Note: This message lays God's provision as the foundation for the righteousness that he both requires and multiplies. The message calls believers to obedience only after establishing that the source of their righteousness is God.

Redemptive Development Model

I. Confess that God requires the righteousness you lack.
II. Recognize that God provides the righteousness you lack.
III. Ask that God provide the righteousness you lack.

Note: God is the hero of the text. He makes requirements for the good of his people, provides for the fulfillment of what he requires, and enables its accomplishment.

Redemptive "Twist" Model

I. Cleanse yourself from all unrighteousness.
II. Lead others from all unrighteousness.
III. Depend on God to fulfill all righteousness.

Note: This model makes clear the obligations and blessings of obedience but then clarifies that following such instruction is hopeless apart from the saving, sanctifying, and enabling work of God.

Redemptive preaching does not require a preacher to make a Christ connection at one "correct place" in a message. If preachers expound every passage with an arbitrary standard of where or how much Christ needs mentioning, they will inevitably fall into the error of making imaginative rather than expository references to Christ or of tacking on a mention of Calvary. An expository sermon based on redemptive truths is not "Three Points Plus the Cross." Approaching messages this way will only cause messianic leapfrogging, parallel word play (parallelomania), and similar event- or personal-example comparisons (fig. 11.3).

Figure 11.3

"Three Points Plus" Problems

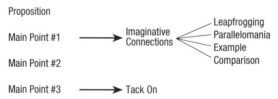

The Christ-centered aspects of a message do not arise
from the natural exposition of a text when arbitrary
standards determine when to mention the cross.

A truly expository Christ-centered sermon is not as concerned with the proper location of the cross in a message as with the necessity that each listener walk away from the sermon with a keen awareness of the personal import of God's redeeming work (see fig. 11.4). When listeners depart, do they focus on themselves or on their Redeemer? Do they look to their own works as their source of hope or to God's work on their behalf? Has the message as a whole directed people to a fuller understanding of grace as the only hope for their justification and the chief motivation for their obedience? Answers to these questions rather than an imposed homiletical structure will determine whether a message has expounded the counsel of God in the light of his historical, theological, and personal purposes. A preacher may develop a redemptive theme in the first main point, the second main point, the conclusion, the introduction, or a combination of these. The ultimate Christ-centeredness of a sermon will be determined by the development of the text and the purpose of the message rather than by an artificial standard for the placement of the grace features. Artificiality will be replaced by a genuine exposition of what a text means within the scope of the biblical record and according to God's interaction with people in the specific biblical situation.

Figure 11.4

Grace-Directed Preaching

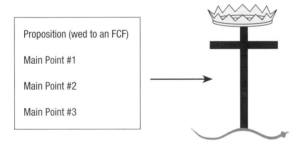

The message as a whole leads listeners to understand the place of the text and/or the role of its features in God's redemptive plan.

Messages of Redemptive Exposition

As preaching efforts mature into explaining how a text functions as well as what it says—expounding its aim as well as its words—we naturally desire confirmation that our messages reflect Scripture's intent. Surely a method of exposition that reveals God's redemptive work in all of Scripture will have characteristics that distinguish it in terms of the grace it discloses. Such preaching will necessarily war against legalism or license that elevates works or cheapens grace. In other words, Christ-centered preaching is not merely an interpretive method; it is an exegetical obligation with necessary implications for the saving and sanctifying messages we preach.

The distinguishing marks of exposition true to the redemptive character of all Scripture emerge when preachers identify the types of messages that typify Christ-centered sermons. Because Christ-centered preachers consistently proclaim the grace evident in all Scripture, their messages highlight the central themes of the glory of God revealed in Christ's love, sacrifice, and victory as they relate to all the issues of faith and life. These themes, the messages they spawn, and the subjects they address typically fall into four categories.

Grace despite our sin. The theme of God's faithfulness despite human faithlessness often arises when pastors must deal with passages that detail the waywardness or frailties of the covenant people. Messages that typically result focus on our adoption as children of God and the assurance this relationship brings despite our rebellion and weakness.[25] Topics preachers consider in these messages include the privilege believers have of resting in God's love (the Sabbath principles of Scripture) and our confidence in God's love (the glory of our divine sonship through union with Christ).

Grace canceling the guilt of sin. Messages on justification and forgiveness flow from the theme of cleansing grace. Topics of such messages quickly move to the need for confession, repentance, and confidence in the sufficiency of Christ's sacrifice.

Grace defeating the power of sin. Messages of sanctification and spiritual enablement reverberate from the Bible's proclamation of the spiritual efficacy of the resurrected and ever present Christ. With such messages of overcoming grace, preachers equip the saints to do battle with the world, the flesh, and the devil by concentrating on the victory available in the power of the Spirit and the truth of his Word.

Grace compelling holiness. When believers see that the whole of Scripture—the entire sweep of biblical revelation—is a stage for the portrayal of grace, their hearts respond in awe, joy, and humility. Such responses ground messages of worship and obedience in their proper motivations and make the application of all biblical truth the fruit of love as it is expressed in thanksgiving, praise, gratitude, and worship. Christ-centered preaching does not abolish the normative standards of Christian conduct but rather locates their source in the compelling power of grace. *In Christ-centered preaching, the rules of Christian obedience do not change; the reasons do.* Believers are exhorted to serve God in response to his sure mercy rather than in payment for his conditional favor.

Marks of Redemptive Exposition

How preachers motivate others to be holy (the chief concern of the last theme of the previous section) is often the telltale sign of Christ-centered

---

25. Robert A. Peterson, *Adopted by God: From Wayward Sinners to Cherished Children* (Phillipsburg, N.J.: Presbyterian & Reformed, 2001), 131–44.

preaching. Legitimate concern for the necessity of obedience has historically caused much criticism of grace-centered preaching because it is difficult to remove obedience as a qualification for divine love without seeming to remove biblical standards of conduct as imperative for Christians.[26] Consistently preaching the necessity *and* the proper motivation for holiness is one of the most difficult tasks that preachers face in every generation.[27] Successful (i.e., biblical) Christ-centered preaching bears the marks of grace-motivated obedience—insisting on the contemporary application of biblical mandates while grounding the source of Christian behavior in appreciation of God's glory and provision.

Understanding the Effects of Grace

HISTORIC UNDERSTANDING

Historians tell us that one of the amazing features of the life of John Bunyan was his refusal to let prison deter him from his pursuit of ministry. The author of *Pilgrim's Progress* wrote many of his most influential words while incarcerated. In fact, prison helped strengthen and galvanize much of his thought. Bunyan's theology took more concrete form when, though facing great deprivations, he debated with fellow religious prisoners whether the assurance of God's love promoted holiness or license. Fellow prisoners challenged Bunyan saying, "You must not keep assuring people of God's grace because they will do whatever they want." Bunyan responded, "That is not true for God's people. If you keep assuring God's people of his grace, then they will do whatever he wants." Through his own experience, Bunyan recognized that love was a far more powerful motivator than fear of harm or threat of rejection.[28] He maintained his convictions and his testimony despite persecution, not so much because he dreaded the retribution of his God but because he possessed such an overwhelming love for his Savior. Had intimidation alone motivated him, Bunyan would have quickly yielded to the more immediate threats of his persecutors with the intention of appeasing God later. Love for the Savior kept the suffering pilgrim faithful.

26. Consider also the similarity of current "lordship salvation" debates with the Marrow Controversy in Reformation history. Cf. Greidanus, *Sola Scriptura,* 131–33.

27. Cf. Rom. 6:1; Gal. 3:21–22; 5:13–26.

28. The word *fear* here is not used in the full, biblical sense of reverential awe but according to the more common usage of a response to intimidation or threat of personal harm. Note that the fear the Bible commends involves giving proper regard to God and can exclude neither joy nor trembling before him (Pss. 16:1; 112:1; 130:4; Jer. 5:22). However one defines this proper fear, it is important to recognize that it cannot mean a terror that alienates or minimizes God's love because Christ also possesses this fear (Isa. 11:2–3). Cf. Jerry Bridges, *The Joy of Fearing God* (Colorado Springs: Waterbrook, 1997), 97–113.

Bunyan's realization reflects the understanding that characterizes the applications of Christ-centered preaching. Since every instruction of Scripture functions within the frame of God's provision and explanation of his redemptive work, grace must be the means to urge others to implement what is expounded. Grace does not merely aid righteous conduct; it also aids in the apprehension of the never-diminishing and nondeterred love of God that makes human righteousness possible. If obedience were merely a defensive posture that listeners assume to avert divine wrath or to curry divine favor, then human holiness would be but a euphemism for selfishness. When self-protection and self-promotion become the *primary* motivations of Christian obedience or preaching, then we have inadvertently made self-satisfaction the Lord of our faith.[29]

The promises of divine blessing and the seeking of reward are not foreign to biblical motivation, but they are never first.[30] The pursuit of holiness is futile until we come to the realization that our best works merit us nothing by their own goodness. As mentioned earlier, they are only filthy rags and unprofitable service until sanctified by the blood of Christ. The reason that we knowingly offer our best works to God, despite our knowledge of their inadequacy, is out of love for him, not to persuade him to love us.

The historic Heidelberg Catechism asks one of the most honest questions in all theological discourse about the nature of obedience: "Since we are redeemed from our sin and its consequences by grace through Christ without any merit of our own, why must we do good works?" The paraphrase is simply, "If salvation is because of grace, why be good?" The answer is: "So that with our whole life we may show ourselves grateful to God for his goodness and that he may be glorified through us."[31] We offer service to God not to gain his affection but in loving thankfulness for his affection. The rewards that he grants—and that we may properly desire—in response to our obedience do not annul our chief desire to please him in response to his mercy. Such blessings would actually be empty of true satisfaction for Christians if the main purpose of their pursuit were pleasure. The Spirit makes our greatest pleasure what delights the Lord we love, and we cannot find deep joy in what fails to put his honor and glory first (Pss. 1:2; 37:4;

---

29. Here I do not mean to devalue the goodness and power of the satisfaction God intends us to experience through our union and communion with him but rather to highlight the emptiness and danger of making our life's priority the satisfaction of our natural affections (cf. Rom. 15:1–3).

30. The priority of motivations in the Christian life is God first, others second, and self last. This does not mean that love of self has no place in the Christian life. By virtue of Christ's work, I am precious to God and have a right to a proper self-love. Self-loathing that parades as piety is actually destructive to Christian living and demeans the completed work of Christ. We properly loathe our sin and the weakness that allowed it, but this hatred of sin, in part, should be due to the damage it does to one made as precious to God as I by Jesus, in addition to the greater offense of grieving the God who gave his Son for me.

31. Heidelberg Catechism, q. 86.

43:4; 119:35). Loving service offered in Christ to God in response to his mercies not only pleases him but also satisfies the deepest longings and dearest aspirations of a believer's heart (Matt. 25:21–23; Heb. 13:21).

This proper expression of gratitude is not a warped sense of trying to repay God the eternal debt of our sin with more filthy rags from our finite hands but the sincere desire to demonstrate our love, thanksgiving, and appreciation for grace freely offered and received by faith alone (1 Cor. 6:19–20; Col. 3:15; Heb. 12:28).[32] J. I. Packer captures the necessity and power of this biblical motivation:

> The secular world never understands Christian motivation. Faced with the question of what makes Christians tick, unbelievers maintain that Christianity is practiced only out of self-serving purposes. They see Christians as fearing the consequences of not being Christians (religion as fire insurance), or feeling the need of help and support to achieve their goals (religion as crutch), or wishing to sustain a social identity (religion as a badge of respectability). No doubt all these motivations can be found among the membership of churches: it would be futile to dispute that. But . . . a self-seeking motivation brought into the church is not thereby made Christian, nor will holiness ever be the right name for religious routines thus motivated. From the plan of salvation I learn that the true driving force in authentic Christian living is, and ever must be, not the hope of gain but the heart of gratitude.[33]

Self-promotion, self-protection, servile dread, and slavish fear evaporate as motives when we recognize that the revelation of God's affection and redemption enables us to "glorify God and enjoy him forever."[34]

If both logic and Scripture make it apparent that motivations of selfish fear and gain are a menace to holiness,[35] why does the debate persist over whether a divine threat of retaliation or a promise of grace better stimulates holiness? The simple answer is that preachers feel the need for a corrective. We wonder how we can compel others, or even ourselves, to pursue righteousness if we lose the leverage of threatening with retribution or rejection.

---

32. John Piper offers a helpful warning against some expressions of "gratitude" that create a "debtor's ethic" to repay God for his *past* redeeming grace. We can never repay the debt of Christ's sacrifice with our filthy rags and should instead look in faith to God's past, present, and future provision as our hope and for our strength. Gratitude, in the historic usage of the churches of the Reformation (and in my usage here), refers to this faith response. Biblical gratitude (i.e., loving thankfulness) stems from the faith that we are eternally loved, bought, and secured by divine efforts we can neither earn nor compensate. This faith creates compelling expressions of love in response to all aspects of God's grace (past, present, and future) and underscores the necessity and power of preaching that consistently stirs renewed love and joy for Christ's redeeming work. Cf. John Piper, *Future Grace* (Sisters: Ore.: Multnomah, 1995), 41–49.

33. J. I. Packer, *Rediscovering Holiness* (Ann Arbor, Mich.: Servant Press, 1992), 75.

34. Westminster Shorter Catechism, q. 1; Westminster Larger Catechism, qq. 32, 97, 168, 174, 178; Heidelberg Catechism, qq. 1, 2, 32, 86; cf. Westminster Confession of Faith, 16.2; 19.6, 7; 20.1; 22.6.

35. Cf. Rom. 8:15; 2 Cor. 5:14; 1 John 4:18.

We recognize that each of these approaches is powerfully persuasive, and in the secrecy of our hearts question, What reason will God's people have to obey if we keep assuring them of his love?

Personal Understanding

Ultimately, the issue all preachers must confront is what they believe to be the relationship between people's conduct and God's acceptance. Are we holy for God's acceptance, or are we holy because of God's acceptance? I did not understand the importance of that question until after several years of pastoring. Despite my good intentions, an honest assessment of my congregation revealed many who seemed far from the Lord. Their spiritual emptiness was all the more discouraging to me because the church was almost two centuries old. Many of the families had attended for generations. Some knew their Bibles far better than I, and due to the history of the church, everyone knew very well how Christians should act. Most conscientiously observed a community code of conduct—they were faithful to their spouses, dressed modestly, had respectable occupations, and did not drink to excess or swear in polite company. Outward conformity to accepted Christian conduct was definitely expected and consistently exhibited.

Attitudes, however, were not so exemplary. I could not understand how people who were so knowledgeable about God could be so bitter, so guilt-ridden, so often depressed, so cold to one another, and so intolerant of the faults of newer Christians. Their words and external behaviors professed loyalty to Christ, but love, joy, peace, patience, and long-suffering were in scant supply. I used to get so angry at those people for their lack of heart response to the Word they said they loved. Then I began to realize that the problem was not so much them as it was my preaching—and the preaching of others like me.

I was using shame and fear to motivate people to obey God. What I had to confess was that though my messages often secured changed behavior, my ministry seemed to produce little spiritual maturity. For instance, I told couples whose marriages were coming apart that they were in trouble because they were not honoring the Word of God in their relationships with each other. I also told them that if they changed their behaviors, God would bless them, but that as long as they continued in their disobedience, they could not expect his love. As a result, I saw changed behavior but few signs of real spiritual growth. Instead, a year or two later, these same people were suffering from depression, pursuing addictive behaviors, or growing spiritually disinterested.

Finally, the Lord opened my eyes to my error. I recognized that I was telling people that the way to get rid of their guilt before God and to acquire his love was by behaving differently. But what did this imply? If people expect a change in behavior to rid them of their guilt, whom are they trusting to take their guilt away? Themselves!

I was forcing people to question, "What action of mine will make me right with God?" No wonder their faith did not mature. I had taught them to trust in what they could do to fix their own situations with God. It was also no mystery why depression, anything that would numb the spirit, and spiritual disinterest were so common among those I had counseled. By encouraging people to look to themselves rather than to the cross for freedom from guilt and assurance of love, I was depriving them of hope. Without my conscious intent—and contrary to the theology in my head—I was driving the wedge of human works between my hearers and God. The people who listened to me, though they may have changed an aspect of their lives to get my approval and secure God's affection, were actually farther away from understanding God than when I had originally begun to minister to them.

Works righteousness had jumped into my ministry without my even knowing it. I was implying (if not directly stating) that we become acceptable to God by being good enough. No wonder the people were so hard and bitter and cold. I was teaching them that if they just offered God more filthy rags, he would care more for them.

What a cruel God I had painted for them. What a merciful God I had denied them by teaching them that God's love was dependent on their goodness. I was the one who had made them intolerant of less mature believers or even unbelievers who visited the church. Because they listened to me, the people who were so well- and long-churched gauged their holiness by their works. This meant that there was no better way to confirm their own righteousness than by finding greater faults in others inside or outside the church. No one was more culpable than I for the bad attitudes and spiritual hardness among God's people that made me so mad at them.

Formulaic Understanding

If behavior change erases guilt or overcomes its effects by satisfying the holy requirements of God, then the Pharisees were right (i.e., God loves and favors those who are more righteous than others). We can represent such an understanding of faith with this simple formula:

$$\text{Guilt} \neq> \text{canceled by feeling guilty} + \text{behavior changes} = \text{God's acceptance}$$

Evangelical preachers have no desire for the formula above to represent their messages, but this is the message hearers receive when they are not assured that Christ is the sole cause of divine care and that love for him must be the prime impetus of human righteousness. Only when believers act with the conscious awareness that God accepts them and their works solely as a result of the work of his Son does their righteousness have the potential to glorify God. If our works or feelings were the basis for God's faithfulness, then obedience could only be a means of buying blessings from a stingy divinity and the goal of our righteousness would be some form of selfishness—self-protection or self-promotion. But since grace alone accounts for God's faithfulness, believers can respond to God with full confidence of his abiding and unconditional love. Loving service results as our hearts fill with the desire to glorify the One whose goodness, mercy, and love never cease. Instead of trying to barter our blessings by fulfilling distasteful duties, we discover that the priorities of God become our greatest pleasure. True repentance results as our hearts increasingly reject the priorities of the world, acknowledge and sorrow for the evil and emptiness of our sin, and delight in glorifying our Savior with the gifts his Spirit bestows.

When grace is perceived as the means of God's acceptance, it becomes the motivation for our obedience. Then the dynamics of obedient living could be characterized this way:

$$\text{Guilt} \neq> \text{canceled by grace} = \text{God's acceptance} \rightarrow$$
$$\text{yielding repentance} + \text{loving service}$$

Guilt for sin drives us to the cross, but love for God that is the fruit of his grace should propel us from it.[36] Conformity to God's will thus becomes a form of praise rather than an attempted bribe. Self-seeking performance and groveling petitions for favors dissolve into the reality of the divine embrace that inspires confidence in God's love, instills a desire to return to his ways, and empowers the sacrificial pursuit of his purposes with joy. Without the perceived need to use servile duty to compensate God for our guilt, repentance can become an expression of deep love for God. Obedience naturally follows as loving service to our faithful God becomes our delight. Understanding this proper source of our faithfulness challenges preachers to recognize the danger of sermons that do not contextualize their instructions with redemptive truth. When explanation of God's full provision and unfailing love does not accompany exhortations for corrected behavior and right conduct, then spiritual damage must occur.

Employing the Means of Grace

Commanding people to do what is right without explaining why or how inevitably hurts them because they are left to consider their works and abilities as the cause of God's acceptance or affection. As a result, much well-intended instruction dispensed with the motive of helping people hurts them. If all they hear are the "shoulds" (i.e., what you should do), believers will either face despair or feign self-righteousness. Healing of the soul begins with

---

36. Ultimately, the Spirit leads us to understand that our guilt, too, is graciously revealed to us so that our Savior might relieve us of its misery and consequences.

the message that God graciously accepts our works offered to him in the love and thanksgiving that result from apprehension of the mercy of God in Christ. Our acceptance and our ongoing sanctification are never a result of anything but grace.[37] Christians cannot gain or earn any more of God's love because grace has already granted and secured all the love there is to have. We may experience more of God's blessings and sense more of his fellowship as a result of our obedience, but we do not risk God's rejection because we have not progressed sufficiently in holiness.

Our works do not cause God's love, and our weaknesses do not jeopardize it. This does not mean that sin has no effects in the lives of believers. We may experience divine discipline as a result of our sin or simply have to face the natural and painful consequences of ignoring standards that God gives for our good. Nevertheless, each of these forms of fatherly discipline, even when harsh, expresses love for a child and concern for his or her welfare (Heb. 12:5–11). Just as a child is emotionally healthier when there is not a question about his or her parent's unconditional love, so God's children are spiritually healthier when they are taught that there is no question about their heavenly Father's unconditional love.

We are saved by grace alone.

We are sanctified by grace alone.

We are secured by grace alone.

Preaching that is faithful to these biblical truths never prods believers toward holiness with the threat of divine retribution, for to do so would make our works rather than his grace the foundation of our relationship with God. The guilt of our past, present, and future sin was placed upon Christ in his sacrifice on the cross (2 Cor. 5:21; Heb. 10:10–12; 1 Pet. 3:18). We may properly feel remorse for the sin we commit, but this *subjective guilt* that we feel and that grieves the Holy Spirit does not annul the finished work of Christ, which removes all *objective guilt* from our account. Subjective guilt is the feeling graciously impressed on our hearts by the conviction of the Holy Spirit so that we will turn from sin and not experience its temporal consequences (John 16:8–16; Eph. 4:30).[38] But the justice of God that is the basis of the objective guilt and the eternal condemnation of our sin has

---

37. Charles Hodge, *Systematic Theology*, vol. 3 (New York: Scribner, Armstrong, 1875), 231–32; Louis Berkhof, *Systematic Theology*, rev. ed. (Grand Rapids: Eerdmans, 1953), 532, 535; cf. Anthony Hoekema, *Christian Spirituality: Five Views on Sanctification*, ed. Donald Alexander (Downers Grove, Ill.: InterVarsity, 1988).

38. There are also forms of subjective guilt that are improper and are tools of Satan to assault weak, uninformed, or oversensitive consciences in order to erode believers' peace, confidence, and strength (cf. Rom. 8:15; Rev. 12:10).

been fully satisfied by Christ's atonement (Rom. 8:1). The completeness and the endurance of this atoning work do not deny preachers the right and the responsibility to challenge the impenitent with the necessary changes that will avert discipline and evidence true faith. Among God's people, however, we simply do not use the denial of love as leverage for holiness. The former cannot produce the latter.

THE MOTIVES OF CHANGE

Nowhere are the effects of Christ-centered exposition more apparent than when preachers apply biblical truths to everyday life.[39] Motives for obedience that allow grace responses to take priority over self-protection or self-promotion include the following.

A response to the love shown us by Christ. Concentration on the love God lavished on us makes righteousness a gift we offer God in loving devotion for his full provision for our sin (Rom. 12:1; Heb. 13:15). Without this appreciative response, obedience cannot maintain its doxological intent or grant proper vent to the guilt we feel as a consequence of our sin.

When love motivates Christian obedience, the subjective guilt we feel for spiritual failure rightly stems from remorse over forsaking the One who loves us enough to sacrifice his own Son on our behalf. This "good guilt" is not the shame of divine rejection or the self-oriented payment of an emoted penance. It is a reaffirmation of our value and standing before God that produces repentance for wrong, renewed zeal for his purposes, and a deeper sense of the measure of his grace. Philip Yancey writes:

> True saints do not get discouraged over their faults, for they recognize that a person who feels no guilt can never find healing. Paradoxically, neither can a person who wallows in guilt. The sense of guilt only serves its designed purpose if it presses us toward the God who promises forgiveness and restoration.
>
> I once thought Christians went through life burdened by guilt, in contrast to carefree unbelievers. I now realize that Christians are the only persons who do not have to go through life feeling guilty. Guilt is only a symptom; we listen to it because it drives us to the cure.[40]

These affirmations do not endorse a sappy unwillingness to preach with convicting authority but rather reverberate from the solid conviction that love—not fear or hate or self—is life's most powerful compulsion. Faithful preaching surfaces guilt to break and drive believers to true repentance. Yet for that repentance to be genuine and fruitful, it must yearn for and be convinced of the power and magnitude of God's kindness (Rom. 2:4).

---

39. Recall that application in expository preaching must answer four questions: what, where, why, and how (see chap. 8).

40. Philip Yancey, "Guilt Good and Bad," *Christianity Today* (November 18, 2002): 112.

That is why the apostle Paul, who identified love as his greatest motivation in ministry (2 Cor. 5:14), urges us to offer ourselves as living sacrifices "in view of God's mercy" (Rom. 12:1).

Grace defined according to the world—as a license to sin or belittle God's law—ignores the Bible's perspective that grace compels the heart renewed by the Spirit to want and to do what God wants. Grace alone motivates us to deny ourselves and enables us to live for God (Titus 2:11–12). This is because at the most fundamental level of our being we consistently can do only what we most love to do. Thus, it is the aim of God to renew the affections of believers so that their hearts will most desire him and his ways. The desires of new creatures in Christ Jesus can be rightly nourished only by the truths of grace. When preachers nourish these affections with love for God, new affections drive out the desires of the world and thereby strengthen the will to serve God rightly and well.[41] In addition, when rich apprehension of Christ's love makes the fulfillment of God's will our greatest delight, then his glory becomes our greatest pleasure and compulsion.

These truths of holiness by grace teach us that, as counterintuitive as it may seem, nothing more powerfully compels holy living than *consistent adulation of the mercy of God in Christ.* Mercy acts as a lens for preceiving the fullness of the glory of God that prompts greater love for him—and hence, greater zeal for his purposes.[42] Sermons of this sort not only empower God's people for his purposes but also make preaching itself the sustaining joy and glory God intends it to be for the proclaimer of his Word. The joy of the Lord is strength for both the dispenser and the recipient of God's truth (Neh. 8:10). With Christ-centered preaching that demonstrates the hope God provides in all Scripture, we maintain the joy that strengthens all expository preaching.

Because many view their obedience as the dues that maintain their membership in the kingdom, preaching grace as the motive of Christian conduct and service has risks. Many preachers think that the goal of good preaching is to bludgeon people with their guilt, just as many parishioners believe it is their duty to take it. Both parties are habituated to feel relief only after one has felt bad enough long enough to gain grace. For such people, guilty feelings and laborious obedience are penance they do not wish to be denied. Even the shallowest apprehension of the true holiness of God and the real heinousness of sin will soon convince them of the futility of such gestures and will either callous or break them. True holiness flows not merely from

41. Thomas Chalmers, "The Expulsive Power of a New Affection," in *Sermons and Discourses,* vol. 2 (New York: Carter, 1846), 271.

42. For book-length treatments of this subject, see Bryan Chapell, *Holiness by Grace: Delighting in the Joy That Is Our Strength* (Wheaton: Crossway, 2001); Walter Marshall, *The Gospel Mystery of Sanctification* (Grand Rapids: Reformation Heritage, 1999); and Rose Marie Miller, *From Fear to Freedom: Living as Sons and Daughters of God* (Wheaton: Harold Shaw, 1994).

a heartrending awareness of the malignancy of sin but also from a deep apprehension of the ability of grace alone to cure it.[43]

A love for others loved by God. When an appreciation for God's love despite our sin motivates our obedience to him, then the need to establish our righteous standing by comparisons with others dies. Love for God overflows into the desire to please him by caring for others he loves. Pride and judgmentalism vanish. Christians associate with and aid the needy precisely because grace assures them that they can "afford" to do so. Only Christ-centered preaching produces such fruitful confidence.

Personal resonance with the desires of God lifts the concern of Christians from solely individual interests. The aims of God to redeem his creation, reflect his glory throughout the earth, express his love to all peoples, and extend his rule to every corner of creation become the heartbeat of those whose desire is to fulfill the will of the sovereign Lord they love. This means that much of the individualistic and self-absorbed religion that can be an unintended consequence of overemphasizing a "personal" relationship with Jesus can be undermined by Christ-centered preaching. Proper emphasis on what the Lord has done for us and desires to be done for others raises the eyes of believers beyond the walls of self to consider (and truly love) the underprivileged, unprotected, and unrepentant for Christ's sake.

A proper love for self in Christ. The Bible consistently and in many ways motivates believers through their desire to experience the blessings of obedience or to avoid the consequences of sin revealed by a loving God. Preachers should not interpret the blessings of obedience Scripture promises or the consequences of sin Scripture reveals to be indications that God's love is conditional or that love for him is still not our highest motivation. God bends to our weakness and shepherds our joy by offering a variety of incentives for obedience so that when our love for him wavers we may be motivated by both love for our good and fear of sin's consequences. Neither of these concerns for self is automatically wrong since a proper love for self as one precious to God and indwelt by the Spirit is biblical. Still, love for God is necessarily the highest and strongest of motivations for a life of enduring

---

43. Cf. Richard Lovelace, *Dynamics of Spiritual Life* (Downers Grove, Ill.: InterVarsity, 1979): "Only a fraction of the present body of professing Christians are solidly appropriating the justifying work of Christ in their lives. Many have so light an apprehension of God's holiness and of the extent and guilt for their sin that consciously they see little need for justification, although below the surface of their lives they are deeply guilt-ridden and insecure. Many others have a theoretical commitment to this doctrine, but in their day to day existence they rely on their sanctification for justification drawing their assurance of acceptance with God from their sincerity, their past experience of conversion, their recent religious performance or the relative infrequency of their conscious, willful disobedience. Few know enough to start each day with a thoroughgoing stand on Luther's platform: you are accepted, looking outward in faith and claiming the wholly alien righteousness of Christ as the only ground for acceptance, relaxing in the quality of trust which will produce increasing sanctification as faith is active in love and gratitude" (101).

fellowship and faithfulness, making Christ's ministry of mercy our main message and motivation.

This instruction does not mean that grace should deter us from mention of sin's biblical consequences. Instead, we should present biblical identification of sin's consequences as the gracious revelation of a loving Father who wishes for us neither to experience the consequences of our rebellion nor to face the discipline he must dispense in order to turn us from even more serious harm. If God did not love, he would not warn. Preaching corrective discipline in the context of divine love should keep us from characterizing the wrath of God toward his people as punitive damage and should enable listeners to understand the occasional need for God's severe mercy.

An illustration tells of a mother who took an ailing son to the doctor. The doctor determined that the boy needed a shot. The mother quickly tried to calm the boy's fear of pain by saying, "Don't worry, Johnny, it won't hurt." The doctor could not go along with the empty promise. Instead, he said to the boy, "Son, I may hurt you, but I will not harm you." God speaks to us similarly in his Word. It is not wrong to preach that sin has consequences or that God's discipline hurts (Heb. 12:11). It would actually be ungracious to pretend or to preach otherwise and thus not provide the warning that Scripture so lovingly offers. What is unloving and ungracious is to preach that God disciplines out of vengeance, divine retribution, or the desire to harm us because we have crossed him. The full penalty that our sins deserved God put on his Son so that we would not have to suffer for the guilt of our sin. Now his discipline (even if it hurts) is not intended to harm us but to help us by turning us from the sin whose consequences would cause even greater pain (1 Cor. 10:11; Heb. 12:7–10).

The Means of Change

Applications of biblical truth are not complete until a preacher explains how to plug in to the power that God provides.[44] Since Christ-centered preaching teaches people that they cannot be the instrument of their own spiritual healing, preachers must also explain how to obey God. Just as the "shoulds" of Christian conduct can lead one astray if not practiced for the right reasons, right motivation (why) without the right means (how) of obedience profits little.[45]

By Means

Many passages speak of various disciplines of grace that equip believers to see or do what God requires. It is important to stress that these are means

---

44. Ian Pitt-Watson, *A Primer for Preachers* (Grand Rapids: Baker, 1986), 18–19.
45. C. John Miller, *Outgrowing the Ingrown Church* (Grand Rapids: Zondervan, 1986), 90.

of grace, not means *to* grace.[46] As indicated earlier, such practices are not the way that we manufacture or merit God's grace. Despite the impression of many Christians that their disciplines are bargaining chips to impress God or obligate his favors, the human performance of disciplines cannot be a path to God's love or the purchase of his rewards.

Prayers, Scripture reading, and church attendance do affect our experience of God's blessings and are means (i.e., instruments) whereby God nourishes our love for him and ushers his grace into our lives.[47] Thus, the practice of these disciplines is both important and blessed. Still, the performance of these disciplines could never be correct enough, long enough, or consistent enough to obligate the God who requires perfect obedience and unsullied holiness. Preachers should preach the practice of the disciplines of grace to enable believers more fully to claim in faith and experience the goodness God has made freely available by his mercy, not on account of our discipline.[48]

Preachers may object that many texts indicating what people should do make no reference to the disciplines of grace or any other means of doing what God commands. For example, the Ten Commandments seem only to list God's imperatives. In such passages, the basic rubrics of Christ-centered exposition rescue God's people from hopeless legalism or attempted holiness by purely human means. By virtue of their inclusion in the redemptive record, all texts participate in proclaiming the message of God's adequacy and human inadequacy.[49] Thus, even if a passage makes no direct reference to the typical *means of grace* by which believers seek God's enablement (e.g., prayer for his work, trusting in his providence, meditating on his Word, partaking of his sacraments, acting on his truths, seeking the advice and accountability of fellow believers), aspects of the text or its context point us away from self solutions and toward seeking God's provision.

---

46. See discussion of how (enablement) in chap. 8.

47. John Murray, *The Collected Writings of John Murray*, vol. 4, ed. Iain H. Murray (Carlisle, Pa.: Banner of Truth, 1982), 233. John Murray, *Collected Writings of John Murray*, vol. 4 (Carlisle, Pa.: Banner of Truth Trust, 1976) offers helpful discussion of how the unconditional nature of salvation intersects with the conditional nature of experiencing the blessings of obedience: "Frances Turretin resolves the question by his characteristic method of distinguishing the different respects in which the term condition may be understood. If condition is understood as meritorious cause, then the Covenant of Grace is not conditioned: it is wholly gratuitous and depends solely upon God's good pleasure. But if understood as instrumental cause, receptive of the promises of the covenant, then it cannot be denied that the Covenant of Grace is conditioned" (233). Helpful comment also comes in the phrasing suggested by Old Testament scholar Jack Collins: "Our share in the grace of God is unconditional with respect to merit, and conditional with respect to instrumentality" (private memo, September 20, 1996). See also Thomas Manton, *A Treatise of the Life of Faith* (Ross-shire, U.K.: Christian Focus, 1997), 65. See also C. S. Lewis, *Mere Christianity* (New York: Macmillan, 1952), 59–61.

48. Jerry Bridges, *The Discipline of Grace: God's Role and Our Role in the Pursuit of Holiness* (Colorado Springs: NavPress, 1994), 13–19, 78–79.

49. Pitt-Watson, *Primer for Preachers*, 22.

By Faith

Scripture's more universal pattern of exposing human inadequacy and divine provision indicates that God does not simply expect exceptional diligence in his disciplines to enable us to partake of the power of his grace (2 Cor. 12:9). As redemptive sermons lead people to understand the lack of their own ability to be or to do what God requires, preachers naturally lead listeners to a confession of their need for God. This most basic and humble of Christian postures is the essential path to divine power.[50] In our humility, we do not trust in the power of our performance but rely on the truth of what God has promised. His word says that we can understand what he requires (1 Cor. 2:12), that we are loved apart from our works (Rom. 5:10), and that we are now equipped for—and enabled to do—divine service (Phil. 4:13).

Faith that we are new creatures in Christ Jesus provides us with the confidence that we can do what God requires, and thus we employ the power his Spirit has already instilled within us (2 Cor. 5:17; Gal. 6:15). Without faith it is impossible to please God (Heb. 11:6). But with the faith that the Spirit within us is greater than the powers of this world (1 John 4:4), we are enabled to act according to the will that he has renewed within us (Rom. 8:4; Col. 3:10). In our pre-Christian experience, we were not able not to sin (*non posse non peccare*), but as children of God made alive by his Spirit and united to Christ, we have within us the same power that raised Jesus from the dead and we are able to overcome the sin the Holy Spirit reveals to our hearts (cf. Rom. 8:7–9; 1 Cor. 2:14).[51] Faith that this spiritual transformation is true—and, as a consequence, tomorrow does not have to hold a repeat of yesterday's failures—is power for believers. We act faithfully because we have faith we can through our union with Christ. Satan does not want us to believe in such power. He wants us to believe that we are powerless against sin and that the battle against his wiles is hopeless. Thus, faith that Satan is defeated and that we are secure in the love of God by the work of Christ alone is power that God provides for Christian living.[52]

The practices/disciplines of the Christian life that confirm and build this faith are means by which God empowers and blesses our lives, but the faith rather than the practices that aid it is the actual conduit of the power and the blessing of God's grace. This is not meant to imply that greater efforts to muster more faith are now the basis of God's love and blessing. Faith is itself a gift of God, and Christ-centered preaching reinforces the basis of the gift and its fruit (Eph. 2:8–10). Faith in Christ's work means that obedience is the result of a relationship with him that his grace alone secures.

50. John Colquhoun, *Repentance* (Carlisle, Pa.: Banner of Truth, 1965), 17.
51. John Murray, *Principles of Conduct* (Grand Rapids: Eerdmans, 1957), 216–21.
52. Chapell, *Holiness by Grace,* 141–56.

In classic theological terms, this means that every *imperative* of Scripture rests on the *indicative* of our relationship with God, and the order is not reversible (Acts 16:14–16; Col. 3:1–5; 1 John 5:1–5).[53]

We do what God requires (the imperatives) because we are his people (the indicative relationship his grace alone establishes). We do not become his people by obeying his imperatives. We see ourselves as beloved, beautiful, and precious to him through faith in his redeeming love for us. Thus, preaching that assures God's people that their relationship with him is secure by virtue of God's provision nourishes the faith that becomes the motivation and enablement of true holiness. God's people serve God out of love for him and with confidence of his provision. If preaching purposefully or unintentionally implies that a relationship with God rests on works, then it reverses the biblical order of grace and works, thereby undermining the faith foundations that provide the power of obedience.

Why we serve God is also *how* we serve him. Overwhelming love based on an understanding of the sufficiency, efficacy, and majesty of his grace makes us willing and able to obey God. Because the joy of the Lord is our strength, when our wills are conformed to God's, we discover that our strength and the Spirit's power are aligned. The way that our wills become conformed to God's is through love for him. Thus, consistent adulation of the mercy of God in Christ is a preacher's primary instrument to stimulate a passion for God and his ways. The motive and means of change converge.[54]

Preaching that stimulates ever greater love for God drives the affections of the world from the heart so that it beats ever stronger for God's purposes. This is how Scripture has always motivated and empowered obedience. Even Moses preceded the Ten Commandments with a recounting of God's deliverance, not only so that the Israelites would not believe that their salvation had been by their hands but also so that their hearts would turn toward God.[55] Provision of divine redemption in the face of spiritual need is the consistent message of Scripture and the chief means by which human hearts flood with love for God that is power to obey his commands. Awareness of the power of proclaiming the goodness of God not only helps govern the priorities of preaching but also brings the joy to preaching that will make it a sustaining privilege for a lifetime of ministry.

No precise formula should instruct preachers how to maintain a Christ-centered perspective regarding the application of biblical truth.[56] However,

---

53. H. Ridderbos, *Paul: An Outline of His Theology* (Grand Rapids: Eerdmans, 1975), 253.

54. See the discussion in this chapter on the motives of change, and see previous discussion in chap. 8 on "The Practice of Application."

55. Howell, "How to Preach Christ from the Old Testament," 9.

56. Daniel M. Doriani, *Putting the Truth to Work: The Theory and Practice of Biblical Application* (Phillipsburg, N.J.: Presbyterian & Reformed, 2001), 264–67, 294–304.

when people walk away from a message understanding that grace both motivates and enables them to serve God, futile human striving and vain self-vaunting vanish. As a consequence, preachers should make God's redemptive work the content, the motive, and the power behind all biblical exposition. The goal of such Christ-centered preaching is not to equip preachers to develop or debate some novel interpretive science. The goal is to encourage preachers to see and proclaim the relationship God establishes with his people and reveals in all Scripture so that they may glorify and enjoy him forever. Only when people look beyond themselves for spiritual health do they find their sole hope and source of power to do what God requires. Preaching the message of God's deliverance that beacons in all Scripture turns God's people away from self and to God as the provider of their present healing and eternal hope. This is the bottom line of Christ-centered preaching: When a sermon is done, do people look to themselves or to God for their security? Only when they know to look to God alone has a sermon been truly beneficial and biblical.

In a well-known image, Francis Schaeffer taught that we must approach God with hands empty of our own works in order to claim his salvation. Similarly, Schaeffer taught that we must bow *twice* for progress in sanctification.[57] We must bow before the redeeming work of God accomplished by his divine power alone, *and* we must bow to the moral obligations in his Word. Schaeffer said, however, that if we bow to the moral obligations before we bow before the divine accomplishment, then our actions are both "irrelevant and wrong."[58] Christ-centered preaching puts these acts of obedience in order. In such proclamation of God's Word, homage to the truths of divine redemption precedes and empowers service. Thus, the hands of believers remain empty of self both before and after conversion, and God's people are equipped to experience the fullness, goodness, and power of his grace.

Questions for Review and Discussion

1. How does Genesis 3:15 relate to the Christocentricity of all Scripture?
2. What is the difference between allegorical leapfrogging to the New Testament Christ and true redemptive exposition?
3. In what ways may theocentric preaching ensure a Christ-centered message even if there is no specific mention of Jesus?

---

57. Francis Schaeffer, "True Spirituality," in *The Complete Works of Francis Schaeffer*, vol. 3 (Wheaton: Crossway, 1982), 200; and idem, *The God Who Is There* (Downers Grove, Ill.: InterVarsity, 1968), 134.
58. Ibid.

4. What is the proper place for the Christ-centered focus in an expository sermon?
5. What themes typify Christ-centered preaching?
6. How does Christocentric preaching affect sermonic application?

Exercises

1. Explain why love for God must be the primary motive behind Christian obedience if our deeds are to be truly holy. What are other legitimate biblical motives?
2. Explain how the key to Christian power resides in humility.
3. Explain how Christ-centered preaching maintains the doxological focus of all Scripture and all life.

Appendix 1

A Philosophy of Delivery and Dress

A Philosophy of Delivery

The elocution movement that taught speakers there was one correct way to gesture, stand, or sound died nearly a century ago. Natural delivery now rules the day. The preachers most respected are those most able to sound like themselves when they are deeply interested in a subject. Bombast and oratorical flourishes remind one of pulpit caricatures; they do not stimulate pastoral respect. At the same time, staid, unenthusiastic solemnity communicates irrelevant tedium rather than sincere seriousness. Congregations ask no more and expect no less of a preacher than *truth expressed in a manner consistent with the personality of the preacher and reflective of the import of the message.* Today, pulpit excellence requires that you speak as you would naturally talk were you fully convinced that God had charged you to deliver a life-changing, eternity-impacting message.

Delivery Hurdles

The great challenge for today's preachers is to maintain this natural expression of urgency that both pulpit mimicry and public timidity deny. Two hurdles contribute to the challenge. The first is the mistaken notion that our preaching will reach its zenith when we sound like our grandfathers or like pulpit idols. If God had wished for George Whitefield or Billy Graham to be in your pulpit, he would have placed him there. You should learn all you can about delivery from previous generations and contemporary greats, remembering that from a universe of possibilities God chose you, with your personality, insights, manner, and gifts, to preach in this place at this time. Do not undermine his wisdom by adopting a delivery not your own.

The second great hurdle to naturalness is intimidation. We do not speak in a manner true to ourselves when we are too concerned about the people watching our every move and listening to each syllable we utter. When speaking at our kitchen tables, we move our hands when expressing something that excites us. When we do not concentrate on how we are saying particular words, our voices move up and down to emphasize different thoughts, our voice intensity varies to reflect different degrees of seriousness, and our volume naturally rises to reach everyone while overpowering no one. Were we secretly to videotape a meal in your home, you would discover that you too express these natural delivery skills. Thus, you already have excellent delivery ability.

But something happens when we move from kitchen tables to church pulpits. All those eyes staring at us somehow straitjacket our gestures and paralyze our expressions. We seem to lose the ability to speak naturally when standing in front of others. The real challenge of pulpit excellence, therefore, is not to add something to our delivery that is atypical of us but to reclaim the naturalness that is most true to us.

Heightened Conversation

When you speak to others in the way most natural to you, your voice and gestures are conversational. If what you have to say is important and you want a number of people to pay attention, you intensify your expressions. This heightening (not changing) of your normal speech is the most natural and effective way to communicate important matters. In such heightened conversation resides the key to truly powerful preaching.[1] Preachers who use this mode of expression recognize the oddity of speaking without enthusiasm about eternal matters and of adopting a peculiar manner to expound so vital a message. A speaking style that is most true to you contains the most effective delivery tools.

Even the most skilled preachers experience some intimidation when they face a congregation (if you have no concerns about preaching, you have not fully comprehended the magnitude of the task). In fact, most preachers learn to appreciate the butterflies that energize their preparations and presentations. So how can we speak naturally when we feel (and even value) the pressure

---

1. The heightened-conversation concept is common in contemporary homiletics but is not new. John Wesley advised the same (Woodrow Michael Kroll, *Prescription for Preaching* [Grand Rapids: Baker, 1980], 85), as did Charles Spurgeon (John Stott, *Between Two Worlds: The Art of Preaching in the Twentieth Century* [Grand Rapids: Eerdmans, 1982], 273).

of the occasion? Understanding what characterizes natural delivery helps. The delivery guidelines described in the next section keep preachers plugged into the power of natural expression. Although instructors sometimes teach these skills as rules others must heed, students of preaching will benefit when reminded that these standards simply reflect the natural expression of persons who feel confident and free to be themselves.

An important caution should precede these standards: When delivery techniques (skilled or unskilled) dominate a sermon's impressions, listeners tend to reject the message.[2] Listeners remember the delivery of poor speakers; they remember the content of good speakers. We communicate messages best when our delivery is transparent. Neither showy oratory nor a staid presentation accomplishes this goal because both draw attention to themselves.

Excellent delivery disappears from the awareness of listeners. Thus, the goal of a preacher is to get out of the way of the message, to deliver the sermon so aptly that its thought alone dominates listeners' thoughts. We achieve this goal by practicing[3] sound delivery skills until they become so natural to us that we use them as unconsciously as we would in conversation. When our manner of expression naturally reflects the content of our words, we are able to concentrate on getting the message *into* others rather than *out of* ourselves. At that point, our delivery becomes a tool for presenting the message rather than a stage for displaying our skills.

Components of Delivery

Voice and gesture are the primary tools of delivery. Each can be subdivided into various features that are best employed when their use is appropriate, varied, and purposeful. The nature of the occasion, the congregation, the message, and the speaker contribute to determining appropriate delivery. Each delivery tool also has a greater impact if a preacher varies the way it is used. The purpose a preacher has for each delivery feature determines which standards of delivery are best employed—or are better broken. The study of these features may seem foreign to the preaching task (we can too easily emphasize technique over the anointing of the Spirit), but faithfulness in

2. Ralph Lewis offers this list of delivery techniques that create listener distrust of speakers: obvious skills, artifice, or cleverness; labored didacticism; forthright sermonizing; loud haranguing—especially too much volume too early; constant hard driving; persistent aggressiveness; ornateness; too evident use of technical skills; high-flown language; and glib tongues (see *Speech for Persuasive Preaching* [self-published, 1968], 95).

3. Let no one make you ashamed of practicing. Great communicators are made, not born. While it is possible to overpractice to the point that a message becomes mechanical, the far more likely result of conscientious preparation is excellence. The best speakers practice. Only poor speakers, and those who were once good, feel no need to hone their gifts. Practice in the early stages of ministry is especially crucial.

communicating God's truth requires us to pay attention to how we present his Word. Haddon Robinson explains:

> Research and experience agree that if nonverbal messages contradict the verbal, listeners will more likely believe the silent language. It seems more difficult to lie with the whole body than with the lips alone. . . . A pastor's words may insist, "This is important," but if our voice sounds flat and expressionless and our body stands limp, the congregation will not believe us. If a preacher shakes a fist at hearers while saying in scolding tones, "What this church needs is more love and deep concern for each other!" the people in the pew will wonder whether the preacher knows what the Bible is talking about. Since a vast amount of preaching involves attitudes that either reinforce or contradict what our words proclaim, a preacher dare not ignore delivery.[4]

When our manner conforms to our sermon's content, it becomes obvious that our message has had an impact on us. Thus, delivery acts as a window to our sincerity, which ultimately carries the power of our words.

Voice

The many aspects of professional vocal delivery can dizzy us with their intricacies, rules, and exceptions. Basically, one point is key: Fill the room, but speak to individuals. Learning how volume, variety, and intensity of speech affect your speech will help you accomplish this goal.

Volume. The most natural way of determining the proper volume for a message is to speak so that those most distant from you can easily hear. As you begin your sermon, look at those in the back row and address them. Your voice will automatically rise to reach them, and those in the front rows will unconsciously adjust to (and forgive) the increase in volume that they all know is needed. Understand that reaching everyone does not require blasting anyone. Save the explosions for the moments they are needed. Recognize, however, that beginning preachers unaccustomed to speaking with power consistently drop their volume at the end of sentences to express seriousness and fervor. Most of us have to be reminded to keep the volume up when we are learning to preach.

If you use a microphone, do not depend on electronics to carry your voice. Pulpit microphones work best (carrying the full dynamics of your voice) if you project over them rather than speak into them. Microphones in large auditoriums spare you from having to shout, but they do not allow you to drop your voice to a normal speaking register without serious damage to your delivery. Move your shoulders and body in a wedge-shaped pattern (but keep facing across the pulpit) when using a pulpit microphone so that your voice

---

4. Haddon Robinson, *Biblical Preaching: The Development and Delivery of Expository Messages,* 2nd ed. (Grand Rapids: Baker, 2001), 194.

consistently pours over the microphone while you address different segments of the congregation (fig. A1.1).

Figure A1.1

Microphone Use

Keep shoulders and face toward the microphone as your body turns to address different segments of the congregation.

Variety. Volume, tone, and pace should vary to emphasize the many thoughts and feelings present in a sermon. Many types of monotone impair effective delivery, but three predominate: low and slow; high and fast; and rhythmic. Each results from different responses to pressure. Some speakers respond to intimidation by becoming very deliberate. These persons speak in low tones at a slow pace. Others overreact to the pressure by filling every space with sound. They speak without pause, at a high pitch, and frequently at great speed. Such animated and energetic speaking hardly seems like a monotone, but the rapid-fire delivery gives equal emphasis to every word. Everything sounds the same, and the constant barrage will ultimately make listeners glaze over. Rhythmic speakers find a comfortable pattern of speech (e.g., starting a sentence at a low frequency and ending high, or vice versa) and return to that haven over and over again. The pattern itself contains a variety of expression, but the constant repetition of the pattern has a homogenizing effect.

The best way to break all forms of monotones is to say things as though you mean them. If you say someone grieves, do not say the word as though their sorrow has no consequence for you. Say the word *grieves* as though you are grieved. Whether you are expressing joy, humor, seriousness, or contemplation, use the tone, pace, and volume that indicates what your words mean. Learn to use silence to emphasize your thought. The best speakers not only vary their expression from thundering to whispering[5] and their pace from crawling to

5. A whisper in the pulpit is not actually said so softly that no one can hear you. Keep volume up while sounding as though you are whispering by pouring breath over your voice.

racing but also let their most telling statements echo in pauses that emphasize thought. In public speaking, one of the ways that we underline a concept is by putting a silent pause before or after the statement of the thought. Repetitive, vocalized pauses (e.g., "uh," "okay," "you know") fill the spaces that skilled preachers prefer to leave silent for powerful effects.

Intensity. We speak with intensity when love for our listeners, commitment to the Word of God, and conviction of the importance of our words dominate our manner. Even though intensity is difficult to quantify, others readily perceive it. The fervor of one who preaches with Richard Baxter's compulsion to speak "as a dying man to dying men" cannot be masked or feigned for long (cf. Rom 9:1–2; 1 Cor. 9:16). Remember, however, that if you say everything with maximum intensity, then nothing will make an exceptional impression. Whether we speak of the horrors of hell, the wonders of grace, or the necessity of repentance, our voices should convey the import of our words.

We help maintain intensity of expression through both spiritual and physical preparation. Praying for the peace of the Holy Spirit can calm nerves and grant confidence, allowing us to preach with power. Often you can expend some of the adrenaline affecting nervousness by walking around, taking a few deep breaths, talking to others, or animatedly reading your text aloud. Remember, a degree of nervousness serves you by fine-tuning your physical and mental faculties. You usually will preach best when well rested, physically fit, and not too recently well fed (milk products, carbonated drinks, heavy foods, and being quite full can negatively affect vocal delivery). Be aware that some medications create dry mouth and may slow thought. Practical suggestions for maintaining fervor aside, however, remember that nothing substitutes for the unction the Spirit alone grants to the heart set afire by his work and set free for his purposes.

Gesture

Our bodies combine with our voices in the communication process. Our eyes, faces, hands, and movements participate in what we say or may carry a message all their own that we never intended to communicate. Some communication studies have actually concluded that we communicate more by what we gesture than by what we vocalize. The precise weight our gestures carry will always be debated, but no one denies that they heavily influence what others perceive. The following guidelines help keep our gestures saying what we intend.

Eye contact. The primary instrument of gesture is the eyes. A speaker who will not look people in the eyes is deemed aloof, afraid, and/or incompetent. One who looks at the ceiling while explaining how Jesus held little children appears distracted. One who looks at the floor while exhorting others to repent seems intimidated. One who looks over heads (or even at foreheads) instead of in the eyes of listeners seems untrustworthy. Preachers too tied to notes, especially when seeking to exhort, project a lack of preparation or a preoccupation with their own thoughts.

You must look at people. The eyes can spit fire, pour out compassion, and preach Christ in you. When you deny people your eyes, you really deny them yourself. No one else talks to them without looking at them—unless to insult them. Everyone expects you to glance at your notes from time to time and even to read an occasional quotation, an anecdote, or a carefully worded thought, but preachers greatly err when they think that by reading every word precisely as written they have better communicated. Far better to stumble over a phrase, smile confidently, and correct it than to speak perfectly while displaying the top of your head as you read the bulk of the sermon.

Include everyone. Scan the entire congregation while pausing briefly on particular sets of eyes as you make special emphases. Take encouragement from those who look at you with appreciation. Take note of those who seem troubled or confused so that you can clarify or adjust your message in appropriate ways. Gifted preachers need eye contact in order to monitor this feedback, which in turn allows them to improve and more precisely refine their messages even as they preach.

Facial animation. If you can smile in the pulpit, you can convey every other needed expression. Too often students of preaching try to control the thumping in their chests by showing no expression. This feels all right because the message is serious, but the result is a dead-pan look that implies, "I have no feeling about what I am saying." If our faces do not move, our voices get tied down. We have trouble expressing a variety of tones or emotions when our faces do not reflect what we want to communicate. Try this experiment. See if you can make your voice sound joyful, while not smiling, when you say, "The love of God frees us from our sin." It is practically impossible not to smile and sound joyful or to sound sincere and not furrow your brow. For your words to express what you want, you have to free your face from the deep freeze.

When you have managed to animate your expressions, make sure that others can see them. Keep your face toward the congregation. Push your notes high on the pulpit (or lift your Bible high) and stand a half step back from it so that even when you look at your notes you are facing forward and not down. In this way, not only will your voice project outward when you read but the congregation will also be able to read your face.

Hand gestures. Perhaps no aspect of pulpit speech seems as unnatural as keeping your hands in natural positions. Standard instruction advises students to let their hands hang at their sides when not gesturing. Unfortunately, when we are standing in front of people, this natural position makes us feel exposed, and we adopt a number of unnatural stances to cover our discomfort: clasping hands behind our backs; holding hands together at the waistline; plunging hands into pockets (jingling keys and coins unconsciously); dropping one arm while hanging the other in midair just below the rib cage; folding arms across the chest; twisting wedding rings; fiddling with fingernails; grabbing neckties; adjusting cuffs; stroking hair, lips, nose, or face; and a host of habits or fidgets that make us look even more awkward than we feel. These unnatural hand positions not only telegraph our discomfort but so preoccupy our hands that we cannot freely gesture what we need to communicate.

A compromise between the standard advice to let hands hang naturally and these unnatural aberrations is to let your hands rest on the front of the pulpit.[6] This position will make you feel less exposed while keeping your hands free to gesture. Grasping the sides of the pulpit at the upper corners (the greater horns) or the lower corners (the lesser horns) is a common but unnatural stance speakers adopt. This stance not only tends to lock hands into place so that the shoulders and head are forced to bob in the place of hand gestures but also forces a preacher to hunch over. When a preacher wants to project an intense, aggressive, or domineering demeanor, this is appropriate, but otherwise a preacher's body forms a "pulpit shell" that seems to exclude listeners—which is precisely what our bodies are unconsciously doing when nervousness makes us grasp for the pulpit horns.

When we gesture, we need to make sure that the motions appear natural. Natural gestures occur with the hands above the sternum and away (both frontally and laterally) from the body. When gestures stay within the plane of the body and drop to the breadbasket (i.e., below the ribs), a preacher appears constrained. When gestures do not rise above the waist, a preacher projects disinterest or fear. In a lively conversation, our hands naturally come up so that they are within the line of sight of the people we address. When our hands do less in the pulpit, we appear awkward and uncomfortable.

Gesture concepts and sentences, not words and syllables. While many public-speaking courses advise using two gestures per sentence when practicing, no one wants you to gesture this frequently throughout a message. Personality governs the degree of gesturing that is natural for you, but when preachers begin accentuating words and syllables rather than concepts and sentences, they tend to develop repetitive chopping and pointing motions that listeners find distracting and/or annoying. Let your hands indicate the idea you are developing rather than the cadence of your words. Remember also that no gesture at all is better than the halfhearted hand motions that expose distraction or intimidation.

The situation as well as the content of a message will determine the appropriateness of gestures. In a small Sunday school classroom, fully extending your arms may seem pretentious. In a large auditorium, you may have to walk

---

6. In settings without pulpits, a Bible can help preoccupy one hand, while the other does most of the gesturing. This takes away some of the sense of exposure if you absolutely cannot let your hands rest at your sides when they are not gesturing.

the length of the stage to communicate expansiveness. Gestures, like voices, should expand to fill a room but not press the space. When you put one hand in a pocket, you communicate informality—putting both you and your listeners at ease. If this is what you want to communicate, fine. However, if you are trying to impress others with the nobility, importance, or urgency of an idea, a hand in the pocket will undermine your message. Almost any gesture (even those homiletics professors warn against) can be used for specific purposes by skilled speakers. Preachers tend to get into trouble when there is no obvious purpose behind their gestures, they seem too intimidated to gesture, or their gestures seem mechanical rather than natural. The cure for each of these ills is the freedom that experience and familiarity with your message provide. Prepare, prepare, prepare. Greater freedom will come the more you preach, but you can accelerate the process greatly with conscientious preparation.[7]

Posture. The most natural way to speak to others if you have something important to say is to level your chin, place your feet shoulder distance apart, and stand erect with shoulders squared and body slightly inclined toward your listeners. Variations from this posture send other messages.

A preacher who leans on the pulpit initially conveys the desire for intimacy or informality. However, when the leaning continues beyond the expression of a thought or two, the same posture implies fear or sloth—the pulpit seems to have become a shield or a crutch. A common stance for people of all ages experiencing nervousness involves crossing one leg in front of the other below the knee while leaning on the nearest solid object. Inexperienced speakers often unconsciously mimic this stance while placing one or both hands (or even their elbows and forearms) on the lesser horns of the pulpit. This posture automatically and immediately conveys great discomfort to listeners.

When preachers' balance or posture (or lack of it) causes them to lean, rock, sway, bob, or bounce without apparent purpose, listeners lose respect for the words that accompany these eccentricities. Conversely, when preachers lean back, put their chins in the air, and talk down their noses to congregations, people tend to feel that the preachers have no respect for those in the pew.

Do not let concerns for correct posture turn you into a statue. If you say something about great pain, joy, or sorrow, your whole body should express the thought. Most pulpits allow you some degree of movement, and you should feel free to move your feet and body as long as you do not pace. Different congregations have varying degrees of tolerance for the amount of walking a pastor can do outside the pulpit, but when such movements have obvious and definite purposes, few will object. If you do move about freely, keep your shoulders facing your listeners even when you move in different directions. Also,

---

7. My own practice is to go through an entire sermon two to four times out loud before presenting it. I know of no great preacher who did not develop similar habits, particularly in the early stages of his ministry.

beware of trying to express something strongly while taking steps backward. The retreating motion conveys fear or a lack of confidence in your words.

Final Cautions for Delivery

Two cautions should conclude any discussion of effective delivery. First, an appeal for naturalness is not an excuse for slovenliness. While you must be yourself in the pulpit, the majesty of your task and the obligations of your office require you to be the best you can be. Bad grammar, slurred speech, and distracting mannerisms detract from your sermon even if they are true of you. Sometimes colloquial expression in preaching conveys thought and intention better than dictionary precision, but the importance of the spiritual task should preclude mere carelessness. Correct what does not strengthen your message.

Second, no set of delivery dos and don'ts supersedes the power of caring deeply about what you say. Let earnestness be your eloquence. Preaching that is all polish and no fire shines reputations but does not melt hearts. Even if the words you say barely trip over the lip of the pulpit, if you speak with the sincerity of a burdened spirit, others will listen. You communicate this authenticity when your manner and content match. Let your heart show in your work. *Showing genuine enthusiasm for what you deeply believe is the only unbreakable rule of great delivery.*

A Philosophy of Dress

How we present ourselves affects our presentation of the gospel (2 Tim. 2:15). Expounding Scripture is a sacred task. Our dress is one of the cultural gestures we possess to communicate this. We damage the gospel if our presentation of the Word does not honor God's work (Mal. 1:6–12) or becomes a stumbling block for others' reception of it (Rom. 14:13; 1 Cor. 8:9).

We need to be careful that the exercise of our freedom does not indicate disregard for our calling or disrespect for our hearers. No Bible verse indicates what clothing we should wear in every situation, but prudent observation of biblical principles requires us to consider what apparel seems appropriate for particular situations, congregations, and cultures.

Formal preaching situations normally require you to dress in what your community considers formal attire. Usually this does not mean finery. Preachers' garb seems fundamentally at odds with the gospel when it draws attention away from the message (Prov. 25:27; Mal. 2:2; Matt. 23:6). Clothing should be so appropriate for a situation that it simply passes notice. This will not occur if we wear silk shirts in a rural church or frayed blue jeans beneath a suit coat. To the objection that these are but cultural preferences that are beneath the concern of serious expositors (who want fully to embrace their Christian liberties), we must reply that even the apostle Paul did not allow his spiritual privileges to impede the gospel (1 Cor. 9:19–25). As long as a community's standards did not require him to forsake the gospel, he willingly bowed to them to promote it. If we object too strongly to others' expectations for our dress, we should also question whether we are more concerned for our rights than for the effective transmission of the Word (Rom. 12:10; Phil. 2:4).

When informal situations call for informal attire, we will still find it difficult to communicate credibility if our clothes are ill fitted, dirty, rumpled, immodest, out of style, or poorly matched. Poor hygiene and an unkempt appearance can also get in the way of a ready reception of a message (1 Cor. 3:16, 17). Some communities will find certain lengths of hair, facial hair, or some clothing and jewelry styles difficult to accept (cf. 1 Cor. 11:14; 1 Tim. 2:9). Before crying that these standards are unfair and artificial, remember that identification with people is a key aspect of biblical persuasion (1 Cor. 9:22).[8] Those who minister to the poor and the homeless know that dressing in the clothes a thrift shop provides may best communicate their biblical priorities to the community. Pastors called to an urban financial district, however, cannot usually afford to dress so simply and still be heard.

We should not conform to improper cultural standards or reinforce community prejudices, but we gain little for the gospel when we force our own preferences on others. The goal is not to dress for success or to wear camel-hair tunics but to have our clothes and personal appearance be non-issues in our ministries. We have more important matters for people to consider. Congregations will better focus on the more vital issues when we care enough about the people and the gospel to dress so that Christ, not our clothing, preoccupies their thought.

8. Kenneth Burke is the chief twentieth-century figure articulating identification theory as it relates to communication. For a study of identification principles as they relate to preaching, see his "Facing Two Ways: Preaching to Experiential and Doxological Priorities," *Presbyterion* 14, no. 2 (Fall 1988): 98–117; or these book-length treatments: Craig A. Loscalzo, *Preaching Sermons That Connect: Effective Communication through Identification* (Downers Grove, Ill.: InterVarsity, 1992); and Hans Van Der Geest, *Presence in the Pulpit: The Impact of Personality in Preaching,* trans. Douglas W. Stott (Atlanta: John Knox, 1981).

A Philosophy of Style

A Natural Style

The warm, humble dignity most conducive to effective preaching is usually best expressed by those who cultivate a natural and personal style of expression.[1] Natural expression avoids all pretense that makes the gospel seem artificial, high blown, or complex. A personal style communicates care, transparency, and acceptance (of oneself and others), thus exhibiting the reality of grace.

A Plain Style

In our conversational age, complex sentences, multiple syllables, and hundred-dollar words mark poor communicators. Clarity increases as sentence length decreases. Communication improves as words simplify. This is not because people are dumber than they used to be. We simply understand more when others address us plainly. This is why the Bible consistently admonishes preachers to develop a plain style of speaking (1 Cor. 2:4–5; 14:19; 2 Cor. 3:12; 4:2). The Bible does not hesitate to frame its greatest truths in simple words (e.g., Psalm 23; Zacchaeus; the Lord's Prayer; *koine*

---

1. Traditional elements of rhetorical style include clarity, interest, evocation, energy, and emotion. See William H. Kooienga, *Elements of Style for Preaching*, The Craft of Preaching Series (Grand Rapids: Zondervan, 1989), 54.

Greek). Where simple words can be used, we should not detour to more complex terms.

The great preachers of our day all speak in such a way that people can understand. These pulpit experts believe it is better to be understood than to be worshiped. They want to communicate more than impress. Yet people think highly of these preachers. People love to listen to what they can understand. They hate hearing someone talk over their heads even if they are wowed by the intellect that makes them feel so dumb. This does not mean that a minister should talk down to a congregation. Haddon Robinson wisely offers this balance: "Don't overestimate the people's vocabulary or underestimate their intelligence."[2]

Speak plainly and people will listen. These dynamics are not new in our day. Henry Ward Beecher decried the ornate pulpit speech of the established preachers in his age by advising, "A switch with leaves doesn't tingle." Richard Baxter and John Wesley both forbade their disciples to use "church tones" and "stained-glass speech." John Calvin said he constantly "studied to be simple."[3] We err greatly and actually abandon the principles of these faith fathers when we try to import into our age anachronistic, out-of-the-norm speech.[4]

At some point in your preaching career, you must make a decision: Will you preach to people, or will you preach for preachers? The latter may win you acclaim, but the former will far more likely win souls. Deep thought, plainly expressed, most clearly exposes a pastor's heart.

A Genuine Style

Your heart becomes most apparent to people when you are not afraid to share it as you express your faith. This personal transparency occurs not when you make yourself the focus of your sermons but when you are willing to share your feelings, doubts, and fears with others. Some preaching gives the impression that the preacher has no personal contact with the ordinary concerns of life. Such remote commentary offers little comfort. Because it seems unrealistic, this style of preaching possesses little authority for persons of mature thought, even though the preacher may attempt to sound authoritarian.

2. Haddon Robinson, *Biblical Preaching: The Development and Delivery of Expository Messages,* 2nd ed. (Grand Rapids: Baker, 2001), 183.

3. As quoted in John R. W. Stott, *Between Two Worlds: The Art of Preaching in the Twentieth Century* (Grand Rapids: Eerdmans, 1988), 128. Cf. Westminster Larger Catechism, q. 159. See also J. C. Ryle's pastoral classic, "Simplicity in Preaching," in *The Upper Room* (London: Banner of Truth, 1979), 35–55.

4. A hallmark of the Reformers and later Puritans was their commitment to preach in the vernacular of the people.

The pulpit is not a confessional, a cry room, or a sympathy bench, but neither should it become a skybox for addressing people en masse, as if removed from regular existence. It was said of Charles Spurgeon that he "addressed two thousand people as though he were speaking personally to one man."[5] This sort of heart-to-heart preaching demands that a preacher know enough of grace to have no need to hide behind pretenses of perfection. Learning to express your own struggles while heralding without compromise the gospel that gives you hope demands deep soul searching. Still, this type of vulnerability will provide more hope than a thousand exhortations to "be strong and courageous" from one who seems never to have faced a battle.

To be heard, we must show that we can rejoice with those who rejoice and weep with those who weep (Rom. 12:15). In short, we must demonstrate that we are real persons whose warmth, convictions, compassion, commitments, encouragement, and hope have weathered enough storms of life to be genuine. As others have written, it should not appear from the storm-tossed pew that the preacher is the only one who cannot see that the waves are twenty feet high. The apostles told their congregations that the Word progressed so swiftly through the ancient world because "we were delighted to share with you not only the gospel of God but our lives as well" (1 Thess. 2:8). The modern world can be as powerfully impacted if today's preachers are as authentically inclined.

A Creative Style

Genuine care for others can be expressed only with a realistic understanding of their situations and struggles. Despite the fondest wishes of a preacher, most parishioners struggle to pay attention to each word from the pulpit, just as most preachers do when they happen to sit in the pew. As listeners we tend to float with the general thought of a message and dig in our cognitive paddles only when turbulence, a point of particular interest, or the need to progress makes us respond with greater vigor.

Rather than blame listeners for their canoeing tendencies, skilled preachers anticipate the ebb and flow of their listeners' concentration levels. Such pastors use their creative skills to produce delivery, structure, wording, and images that frame a sermon's ideas so as to capture and periodically recapture the thought of those in the pew.[6] Such creativity does not require artifice or entertainment, but it does demand a deep desire to be heard that is reflected in the preacher's evident enthusiasm for the message. Energy, imagination, innovation, intrigue, and insight keyed to a sermon's rhythm

---

5. Woodrow Michael Kroll, *Prescription for Preaching* (Grand Rapids: Baker, 1980), 84.
6. J. Grant Howard, *Creativity in Preaching,* The Craft of Preaching Series (Grand Rapids: Zondervan, 1987), 26–29.

mark a preaching style sympathetic to the needs of listeners and serious about communicating the gospel.

A Courageous Style

The willingness and ability to proclaim the Word of God authentically and authoritatively derives from a deep conviction that when we say what the Bible says, we speak what God desires. Confidence that our words carry a divine imprimatur spares us the need to shield ourselves behind an affected style, cover our feelings in coded pulpit speech, or hide from truths that may bring criticism (2 Tim. 4:1–2). When faithfulness to God becomes the primary aim of our preaching (and the grace of his love our greatest security), we are freed from inordinate concern about personal acceptance, reputation, and offense (Acts 4:29). Self-serving anxieties and self-promoting mannerisms wither before a selfless love for the Word and the souls of those God commends to our care (2 Cor. 10:1–2). The results are boldness produced more by sincerity than by calculation and authority secured by evidence of an intimate familiarity with God rather than projected by a prescribed manner (2 Cor. 3:12).

Our convictions concerning the efficacy of Scripture are most evident not when we strive to make the Word effective by pumping our authority into it but when we have the courage to let it speak for itself. The proper authority of spiritual leaders lies not in a peculiar style or an arrogated manner but solely in the validity of the Word they proclaim. Such authority matches expression to content—neither apologizing for what the Word of God makes plain nor making remote what the Bible designs for intimacy. Thus, courageous preaching does not rely on a bombastic style or an authoritarian manner but instead seeks to express the truth of God in a manner so appropriate for the truth, situation, and personalities involved that the mind, heart, and glory of God shine without hindrance, artifice, or shadow.[7]

---

7. For more study of preaching delivery, dress, and style, see the dated yet excellent work Dwight E. Stevenson and Charles F. Diehl, *Reaching People from the Pulpit: A Guide to Effective Sermon Delivery* (New York: Harper & Row, 1958). See also Charles L. Bartow, *Effective Speech Communication in Leading Worship* (Nashville: Abingdon, 1988); and Calvin Miller, *Spirit, Word, and Story: A Philosophy of Preaching* (Dallas: Word, 1989), 107–225.

Methods of Preparation

The steps preachers take in preparing messages vary according to the personality of the preacher, the time available, the nature of the occasion, the type of sermon, the prior knowledge the preacher has of the text, and many other factors. Still, general guidance is helpful as preachers begin developing their own personal approach to preparing sermons.[1]

Sometimes this guidance comes in colloquial terms: "I read myself full, think myself clear, pray myself hot, and then let myself go." Other times the guidance receives more academic treatment: "Read the text, research the material, then focus everything on a single idea."[2] The following preparation pyramid captures the essence of these formulas while emphasizing ideas central to expository preaching as defined in this book.

---

1. Woodrow Michael Kroll lists the personal preparation habits of a number of well-known preachers in *Prescription for Preaching* (Grand Rapids: Baker, 1980), 138–41.

2. For excellent discussions of formal methods, see Donald E. Demaray, *An Introduction to Homiletics* (Grand Rapids: Baker, 1978), 79–92; and Ian Pitt-Watson, *A Primer for Preachers* (Grand Rapids: Baker, 1986), 37–38.

Figure A3.1

A Sermon Preparation Pyramid

Preach

Pray

Practice

Reduce to Outline

Write Sermon Body

Write Conclusion and Introduction

Place Developmental Matter in Outline

Create a Homiletical Outline

Collect Developmental Matter

Consider Specific Applications

Research the Text

Identify the Fallen Condition Focus

Read and Digest the Thought of the Text

Spiritual Preparation: Piety, Planning, and Prayer

Interchangeable building blocks

Proposition, main points, etc.

Return, if necessary

Quotes, statistics, illustrations, key terms, commentary data, etc.

History, grammar, exegetical outline, issues, etc.

Methods of Presentation

These outlines present the options preachers have for preparing materials (notes, outlines, manuscripts) necessary to present sermons effectively.

  I. Basic options for presenting sermons
    A. Reading
    B. Reciting
    C. Extemporizing
    D. Combinations of the above
 II. Options for fully written sermons
    A. Full manuscript carried into pulpit and read
      1. Chief advantages
        a. Ensured preparation
        b. Precision of expression
      2. Chief disadvantages
        a. Damages eye contact
        b. Limits spontaneity and freedom of expression
        c. Tendency to speak in a "written" style
        d. Extensive preparation time
    B. Full manuscript memorized and recited in pulpit
      1. Chief advantages
        a. Precision of expression
        b. Promotes eye contact

      2. Chief disadvantages

        a. Difficulty (for most persons) of memorizing materials

        b. Woodenness of expression

        c. Extensive preparation time

    C. Full manuscript studied, practiced, and converted to an outline,[1] with the sermon preached from the written or memorized outline[2]

      1. Chief advantages

        a. Ensures complete preparation of thought

        b. Maintains eye contact

        c. Maintains spontaneous style of expression

      2. Chief disadvantage: extensive preparation time

III. Options for partially written sermons

    A. Largely written manuscript: a manuscript with most of its key portions fully written but with some portions outlined
Chief advantages and disadvantages: basically the same as II, C, with some reduced preparation time

    B. Outlined messages (various types)

      1. Extended outline: an outline with main-point and subpoint statements, key features, connecting ideas, and key passages either entirely written out or significantly indicated

        a. Options for using extended outlines

          i. The extended outline is repeatedly extemporized in private so that the message is ultimately memorized and then recited in public.

          ii. The extended outline is practiced for familiarity in private then taken into the pulpit and semi-extemporized there.[3]

          iii. The extended outline is practiced then converted to a bare-bones outline (see below) that is taken into the pulpit and semi-extemporized there.

        b. Chief advantages and disadvantages of extended outlines

---

1. The outline may be transferred to separate pages or, for those who prefer to take the manuscript into the pulpit, highlighted within the manuscript or placed in the margins of the manuscript (for this last option it helps to place the outline in a widened left-hand margin so that the eyes naturally scan it first rather than being forced to read past the manuscript).

2. A. A. Bonar attributes this method to Robert Murray McCheyne, writing in the preacher's biography, "From the beginning of his ministry he reprobated the custom of reading sermons, believing that to do so exceedingly weakens the freedom and natural fervor of the messenger in delivering his message. Neither did he recite what he had written. But his custom was to impress on his memory the substance of what he had beforehand carefully written and then to speak as he found liberty" (*Robert Murray McCheyne: A Biography* [Grand Rapids: Zondervan, 1983], 42).

3. The practice of most preachers most of the time.

      i. The more extensive the outline, the more complete the preparation of thought.

      ii. The more practiced the outline, the more precise the expression of thought.

      iii. The more dependent the preacher is on an extensive outline, the more wooden will be the expression of the sermon and the more limited will be the eye contact.

2. Bare-bones outline: an outline containing only key points, words, phrases, or thoughts—usually compressed onto note-cards, scrap(s) of paper, or impressed on memory alone

  a. Options for using bare-bones outlines

    i. Bare-bones outlines may be used in all the ways that extended outlines are used (Note: Bare-bones outlines are most easily committed to memory for those wanting to preach without notes.).

    ii. Bare-bones outlines are often used to organize thought when there is no time (or need) for more formal preparation of a message.

  b. Chief advantages and disadvantages of bare-bones outlines

    i. Spontaneous expression

    ii. Enforced eye contact

    iii. Rapid preparation

    iv. Likely imprecise expression

    v. May encourage ill-prepared thought

    vi. May cause extreme brevity or length (depending on personality)

C. Hints for preparing partially written and outlined messages

1. Use variations in margins, print size, and boldfacing to indicate differences between major, subordinate, and supporting ideas.

2. Use highlighters (but do not use so many colors that you need a color key to chart your way through the outline).

3. Use large enough print and sufficient spacing so that your eyes can quickly see what you have written from an appropriate pulpit distance.

4. Keep main points separate (e.g., in an extended outline, start new main points at the top of a page rather than having them "bleed" from the end of another point at the bottom of a preceding page. This way your eye never has to guess where to look when you begin each new idea.).

5. Use consistent marking (asterisks, colors, circles, underlining, indentations, boldfacing, number symbolization, etc.), and develop a system for indicating main points, illustrations,

applications, etc. so that you train your eye to recognize at a glance the portion of the outline you need (e.g., for years I have circled illustrations while putting stars by applications so that my eye can almost instantly navigate through an outline).

6. If you will have no pulpit (or yours is small), put your notes on pieces of paper that will easily fit inside your Bible.

7. Remove from view what can confuse. Try to keep before your eyes only the notes that you presently need. When notes that you have finished lie alongside notes you are using or plan to use, you can easily get lost. To avoid this problem (if you are using more than one page of notes), keep your notes stacked, and then as you finish with the material on each page, unobtrusively slide it beneath your Bible or to a shelf beneath the pulpit. (Note: Lifting notes or turning them in the view of listeners shifts their attention from what you are saying to what your notes look like or how many you have left.)

IV. Options for unwritten sermons[4]

A. Mental outline: basic ideas mentally organized (usually in barebones outline form) that take full form only in the pulpit

B. Impromptu presentation: unprepared messages delivered on the spur of the moment due to press of circumstances (hopefully not due to irresponsibility)

V. Hints on preaching from memory

A. Use consistent parallelism and brevity in the wording of main points and subpoints so that memorization of "key words" alone puts the entire outline before the mind.

B. Use the illustration of a "traditionally" developed main point to trigger the memory. The summary of the explanation automatically acts as the introduction to the illustration, and the summary of the illustration acts as the introduction to the application. Thus, the illustration can help remind you of the contents of both the preceding explanation and the following application.

C. Use consistent "eye-catchers" when developing a written outline in order to impress the outline's features on the memory.

D. Go through the sermon several times in private before preaching it in public (Some advise looking it over just before going to sleep and immediately upon waking to "imprint" the message on the memory.).

---

4. These presentation options carry the advantages and disadvantages of bare-bones outlines, only to greater degrees.

Appendix 5

Divisions and Proportions

Conscious of the artistry of expression and freedom of style needed for the crafting of fine sermons, homiletics instructors do not like establishing ironclad rules for the proportions and lengths of sermon divisions.[1] Students, however, often want a general idea of how much time each feature should take. The tables below provide general guidance without intending to impose these specifics on any particular sermon.

The following tables assume that thirty minutes will be allotted for a sermon and that if it were typed (with standard spacing), each page would take approximately three minutes to read aloud at an expressive, moderate pace.

Table A5.1

Sermon Proportions and Divisions
Average Time and Number of Pages for Material
Surrounding the Body of a Thirty-Minute Message

Sermon Component	Average Time	Typed Pages
Text announcement and Scripture introduction	1 minute	⅓

---

1. George E. Sweazey, *Preaching the Good News* (Englewood Cliffs, N.J.: Prentice-Hall, 1976), 80.

Sermon Component	Average Time	Typed Pages
Scripture reading	1–2 minutes	½–⅔
Prayer for illumination	1 minute	⅓
Sermon introduction	2–3 minutes	½–⅔
Sermon conclusion	2 minutes	½–⅔
Closing prayer	1 minute	⅓
Approximate totals:	8–10 minutes	2½–3

*Average Time and Number of Pages for the Body
of a Thirty-Minute Message*
(Note: Twenty minutes remain for the sermon body)

Sermon Component	Average Time	Typed Pages
Each main point in a 3-point message (assuming equal proportions)	6 minutes	2
Each main point component (assuming ⅓, ⅓, ⅓ proportion)		
explanation	2 minutes	⅔ (2–3 paragraphs)
illustration	2 minutes	⅔ (2–3 paragraphs)
application	2 minutes	⅔ (2–3 paragraphs)
Each subpoint (assuming 2–3 subpoints per main point)	⅔–1 minute	⅓ (1 paragraph)
All extemporized comments	2 minutes	⅔

The written content of a thirty-minute sermon that includes a Scripture introduction, sermon introduction, sermon body, and sermon conclusion will usually run 7.5 to 8 pages (excluding the Scripture text and extemporized comments).

Appendix 6

Wedding Messages

I. A common order for a wedding service
   (Books of common worship and denominational directories of
      worship offer dependable orders and forms for the readings
      and prayers below as well as many variations in the order of a
      wedding service.)

Prelude
*

Seating of the Families (If uncertain of the order, consult a
   marriage etiquette book.)
Entrance of Groomsmen, Groom, and Pastor
Bridal Procession
*

Words of Institution
Prayer
*

Presentation of Bride
*

Marriage Vows (In some church traditions, the Scripture reading and wedding message occur before the marriage vows.)
Exchange of Rings (with ring vows, if desired)
*

Unity Candle Lighting (Such ceremony options vary widely by region and era.)
*

Scripture Reading
Wedding Message
*

Prayer of Commitment
*

Benediction
Declaration of Marriage ("I now declare you husband and wife.")
Wedding Kiss ("You may kiss the bride.")
Presentation of the Couple ("I present to you Mr. and Mrs. . . .")

*There are opportunities for special music or a hymn at these points in the service. Not all of these opportunities would be used in a single ceremony.

II. Message guidelines
   A. Preach from an appropriate text (examples below)

Genesis 2	Philippians 2:3–11
Proverbs 31:10ff.	Colossians 3:18–19
1 Corinthians 13	1 John 4:16
Ephesians 5:21–33	1 Peter 3:1–7

   B. Be brief (The average wedding message lasts seven to ten minutes—fifteen minutes is too long unless the couple has requested a formal message. Remember how many people are standing and how nervous they are. Show sensitivity to the nature of the occasion. An entire wedding service, apart from the music, averages only twenty to thirty minutes in length.)

   C. Be personal
- Address the couple, not the crowd (but speak with sufficient projection for the congregation to hear).
- Mentioning something personal about the couple and tying it to a gospel truth bearing on marriage is a good way to begin.
- Do not idealize the couple but realistically honor the institution of marriage.
- Do not reveal matters related to you in confidence, but make the message applicable to the couple.

   D. Develop a theme (based on a key idea or two in the text) rather than preach verse-by-verse exposition
- Exceptions may be made if the couple requests a full, formal sermon.

- Messages based on two or three key concepts in the text with concise explanation, illustration, and application serve well.

E. Be encouraging (most marriage instruction specifics should have been handled in premarital counseling; this is not the time for a course on budgeting, lovemaking, fair fighting, etc.)

- Present the joys of marriage in Christ rather than lecture on marriage pitfalls and problems.
- This is the time to speak *for* Christian marriage, not *against* society's marital ills.
- Do not focus on the couple's failure to follow specifics of premarital advice.

F. Be redemptive

- Present Christ as the marriage-bonder (explain the need for dependence on his strength for building relationships).
- Proclaim God's forgiveness as the model for ours and selfless service to him as the true cement of relationships.
- Make clear the implications of the cross for marriage (e.g., acceptance and acknowledgment of imperfection; necessity of repentance, forgiveness, and reconciliation; value and humility of each person before God; obligations and beauty of holy union). This emphasis is crucial if the wedding message is to avoid being romantic advice and/or patronizing marriage instruction.

Funeral Messages

I. A common order for a funeral service
   (Books of common worship and denominational directories of
      worship offer dependable orders and forms for the readings
      and prayers below as well as many variations for a traditional
      funeral service.)

   *Prelude
   Words of Institution (Often called "Opening Lines" or "Pro-
      cessional Verses" in books of common worship, these are the
      verses that open the service. Traditionally, these verses were
      read as the casket was brought to the front of the church.
      Now they function as a brief call to worship to begin the fu-
      neral service.)
   *Prayer of Consolation (The prayer often leads into a congrega-
      tional recitation of the Lord's Prayer.)
   *Old Testament Readings (Typically a short selection or two.)
   *New Testament Readings (Typically a short selection or two.
      Often these readings conclude with the selection that will be
      used as the text for the message.)
   Personal Biography (Often called the "obituary" but not like a
      newspaper obituary notice. Typically, there are a few optional
      minutes for recounting the person's life endeavors and family
      commitments. Often preachers weave this biography into the

funeral message introduction. This makes the funeral personal without over-eulogizing. If a eulogy is to be given, this is usually the place for it.)

*Funeral Message (Typically brief—five to ten minutes—unless otherwise requested by the family. Before or after the message, the pastor may invite comments from family and friends.)

*Closing Prayer

Benediction (The pastor may choose not to use a benediction if a committal service will follow the funeral service.)

*Special music or a hymn often follows one or more of these components.

II. Principles for funeral messages

    A. Comfort and reach with gospel hope (Do not berate or lecture.)

    B. Be brief (This is a very difficult time for people. Five to ten minutes for a sermon is appropriate unless the family requests a longer, traditional sermon. In some settings, the stature of the deceased and/or particularly tragic circumstances may also require a lengthier address. Messages typically are a logical development of a basic idea or two in a text, *not* verse-by-verse expositions.)

    C. Praise God more than the person (Acknowledge God's grace more than laud human accomplishment. Although it is certainly appropriate to give thanks for the good God worked through the individual's life, care must be taken not to imply that divine acceptance is based on human goodness—the message the world almost inevitably hears.)

    D. Hold the cross high (This is not an evangelistic sermon. However, most pastors will address more nonbelievers at funerals and weddings than at any other time. The truths of the gospel need to be plainly stated because they bear upon every person's ultimate condition.)

    E. Do not damn to hell or preach into heaven (If the person was not known as a believer, state the blessing of the gospel that those who profess Jesus Christ share without saying that it applies to this person.)

    F. Speak simple truths sincerely (This is not the time for theological treatises or exegetical insights. The simple truths of resurrection and reunion based on God's grace alone are the most compelling, meaningful, and comforting things you can say.

The gospel has real power in these moments. Do not be afraid to let the Word do its work.)

III. Contents of funeral messages (Begin personally, then move higher.)

  A. Begin with something personal related to the deceased or the family. (Let the family members know that you care for them and their loved one. Address the family directly and let others listen in by projecting so that all can hear.)

  B. Tie the personal reference to a gospel truth evident in the text(s) you read prior to the message.

  C. Develop the hope Christians have in the face of death based on the theme you introduced and the passage(s) you read. (Funeral messages typically contain references to the joys of heaven, a believer's release from suffering, the ultimate reunion with loved ones, etc. All funeral sermons must include explanations of Christ's victory over sin and death, believers' resurrection hope, and the need of all to claim this gospel by faith alone.)

  D. Explain that the deceased person's hope was in Christ's work, not in human goodness or accomplishment.

  E. Rejoice in the joy that deceased believers now know, but at the same time *affirm* the right for loved ones to grieve for the separation they now experience.

  F. End with hope, the assurance of Christ's victory.

IV. Cautions for funeral messages

  A. Be cautious about references such as "We are gathering here to *celebrate* the passing of Joan Smith into glory." (There are truths in which believers can rejoice, but there is much pain present too. Jesus wept in the face of death. We should not treat the horror of a fallen world's ultimate consequence without hope *or* without regard for the real pain it causes. Do not forbid grief.)

  B. Provide the comfort of your sympathy to the families of those who were not known as believers. (You can say that you are sorry for the family's loss and that you grieve for their hurt. Your sorrow is no more an endorsement of faithlessness than your callousness would be an affirmation of the gospel. Ultimately, you do not know others' hearts. If you have questions about the spiritual state of the deceased, simply preach the gospel treasures of those who *do* have faith without saying that this person does or does not share in them.)

  C. Avoid exaggeration of the deceased person's good life. (At believers' funerals, certainly let the glory of their lives and hope in Jesus fill your message. It is always appropriate to cite the goodness that God has accomplished through a believer's life or to rejoice in the service and testimony such a person provided the kingdom.)

D. Do not use a funeral as a time to "guilt-trip" friends and relatives into heaven. (Although it is legitimate to invite others to share in the gospel hope and even to express the concern the deceased may have had for others' salvation, these appeals should be made with compassion, not with futile, manipulative condemnation.)

E. Your *primary* task is to comfort, not to evangelize. Even though evangelistic truths are presented, this is a funeral sermon. The main purpose is to bring the hope of the gospel to loved ones facing the pain of death.

V. Common texts for funeral messages:

Deuteronomy 33:14	John 11:25–26
Isaiah 40:11	John 14:1–4
Job 19:25	Romans 14:8
Psalm 23	1 Corinthians 15
Psalm 46:1–7	2 Corinthians 1:3–51
Psalm 121	2 Corinthians 4:17–5:1
Psalm 139	Philippians 1:21
	1 Thessalonians 4:13–18
	Revelation 20:11–21:4

Appendix **8**

Evangelistic Messages

In an evangelistic sermon, preachers are not preaching merely to convey facts. They are pleading a case—the Lord's—and calling for a verdict. Martin Luther told Philipp Melanchthon, "Preach so that if the people don't hate their sin, they will hate you." This does not mean that preachers should make their manner offensive, but they must courageously proclaim the eternal consequences and immediate requirements of the gospel.[1]

I. Presuppositions of evangelistic preaching
    A. We are speaking so that people will respond.
    B. We must indicate (and construct a sermon to prompt) a specific response.
    C. We need the following to be truly effective:
        1. Genuine fervor
        2. Prayer for the work of the Holy Spirit
II. General principles of evangelistic preaching
    A. An evangelistic sermon should be biblical.
        Although the sermon need not (and when addressed to the uninformed probably will not) be a verse-by-verse exposition, the message must identify the biblical basis for its claims, appeals, and authority. Every evangelistic sermon must explain

---

1. Cf. Lloyd M. Perry and John Strubhar, *Evangelistic Preaching* (Chicago: Moody, 1979).

the seriousness of sin, the significance of the cross, and the
nature of faith.

B. An evangelistic sermon should be positive.

The gospel is not based on what people should *not* do, nor on
what they *should* do. The gospel is the good news about what
God has done, is doing, and will do for those who place their
hope in the work of Jesus Christ.[2] An evangelistic sermon
often wins a hearing with the identification of a felt need common among unsaved persons. The message then becomes positive as well as biblical by demonstrating that the felt need is
hallowed and indicates that satisfaction of the soul is available
only when true spiritual needs are met by a commitment to
and life in Christ.

C. An evangelistic sermon should be clear.

Today's mass-media experts have determined that they cannot exceed a sixth-grade comprehension level without losing
large segments of their audience. General literacy rates and
still lower biblical literacy rates demand that preachers eliminate theological intricacies and pulpit jargon from messages
designed to reach the unchurched. In our day, the "language of
Zion" creates caricatures, not avenues of communication. The
gospel must be expressed in simple terms. Sin, salvation, and
repentance may be familiar concepts to believers, but preachers must define each simply (or substitute more familiar and
less culturally twisted terms) in evangelistic messages. If this
approach seems too unsophisticated, remember that an understanding of the gospel, not the wisdom of a preacher, is the
power of salvation. I know of no greater barrier to effective
evangelistic preaching than preachers' own deep-seated doubt
that the simple truths of the gospel are capable of turning
modern minds from their idols to the true and living God.

D. An evangelistic sermon should be relatively brief.

No ironclad rules can be enforced regarding the appropriate
length of an evangelistic sermon. The skills of the preacher,
the nature of the message, and the occasion can all influence
the attention spans of modern listeners. Still, reason dictates
that those unaccustomed to a long church sit are likely to have
little tolerance for unrestrained exposition. The Holy Spirit can
change human dynamics, but those who regularly preach evangelistic messages rarely exceed twenty minutes.

---

2. I borrow heavily from the excellent work by V. L. Stanfield, *Effective Evangelistic Preaching* (Grand
Rapids: Baker, 1965), 20–21.

E. An evangelistic sermon should communicate urgency.
An evangelistic sermon without fervor and authentic emotion can hardly communicate the significance of the message. Although "sobbing evangelists" may soil the reputation of those deeply committed to the gospel, we err if we try to eliminate expressions of concern from preaching designed to reach hearts and save souls. Be sincere when you relate the urgent demands of the gospel, and trust God to use what you truly believe along with the truth of his Word to melt skepticism.

III. Summary principles for evangelistic preaching
   A. Be biblical (Provide an authority for the solution you present.)
   B. Be simple (Do not use jargon or theological intricacies.)
   C. Make sure the following are clearly articulated
      1. Christ's work
      2. Human need
      3. Personal response required
   D. Be passionate
   Prepare as though it all depends on you; pray as though it all depends on God.

IV. Distinctives of evangelistic preaching
   A. Practice different approaches for informed and uninformed listeners.
      1. Challenge the uninformed with biblical truths, using felt needs to indicate relevance and initiate points of contact. Quickly move from these issues to more biblical concerns.
      2. Challenge the informed with personal inconsistencies, "nondependables" (e.g., unbiblical matters they are trusting for salvation that are sure to fail, such as baptism, family background, etc.), or the untrustworthiness of other hopes (e.g., "I'm basically a good person.").
      The uninformed must be informed as well as challenged and called to repentance (e.g., Acts 17). The informed must be touched with inconsistencies or nondependables and called to repentance (e.g., the woman at the well). Any sermon that begins with a Fallen Condition Focus[3] has the opportunity to be evangelistic because an FCF requires a Christ-dependent response.
   B. Frame the message to lead to a specific response.
      1. Indicate in the message precisely what commitment or action you will require at the sermon's conclusion *and* what this will involve for listeners. Surprising or manipulating

3. For the definition of Fallen Condition Focus (FCF), see chaps. 2, 10, and 11.

people is inherently unethical and unbiblical.[4] Say precisely what prayer should be prayed. Explain exactly what signing a commitment card means. Tell plainly what one can expect during an invitation or a later private commitment.

2. Make clear the obligations of true repentance.
3. Do not ask people to respond in ways beyond their level of spiritual maturity or biblical understanding, but offer them some concrete way of expressing a commitment (e.g., offering a silent prayer in words the preacher supplies, pledging to learn more, telling a loved one of their decision, meeting with a church leader after the service, coming to the front to receive prayer, raising a hand to affirm a decision, praying on knees at their bedside that night, etc.). The converted heart longs to affirm its faith.

---

4. Leighton Ford, "How to Give an Honest Invitation," in *Preaching to Convince*, ed. James D. Berkley, The Leadership Library, vol. 8 (Carol Stream, Ill.: Christianity Today, 1986), 135–46.

Appendix 9

Study Resources

Table A9.1

Study Bibles

Name	Editor/Author	Status	Nature	Stance	Publisher(s)
Cambridge Annotated Study Bible (NRSV)		CS	NT	HC	Cambridge
New Geneva Study Bible (NKJV)		CS	NT	R	Nelson
The New International Version Study Bible		CS	NT	E	Zondervan
New Open Bible (KJV, NKJV, NAS)		CS	NT	E	Nelson
The Ryrie Study Bible (NIV, NKJV, NAS)	Charles Ryrie	CS	NT	Dsp	Zondervan/ Nelson
Spirit of the Reformation Study Bible (NIV)		CS	NT	R	Zondervan
The Thompson Chain-Reference Bible (KJV, NIV)	Frank Charles Thompson	C	NT	E	Zondervan/ Kirkbride

Status   **Stance**
C = Classic   C = Conservative (generally)
CS = Current Standard   Dsp = Dispensational
D = Dated (still a common reference   E = Evangelical
    but not current and in some cases   HC = Historical Critical
    out of print)   R = Reformed
Nature   RC = Roman Catholic
T = Technical   J = Jewish
NT = Not Technical
HT = Highly Technical

Note: Many works take no specific stance, and these designations indicate emphases that are not necessarily mutually exclusive (e.g., Reformed and evangelical).

Table A9.2

Lexical Aids

Type/Name	Editor/Author	Status*	Nature	Stance	Publisher(s)
Lexicons					
A Hebrew and English Lexicon of the Old Testament (Revised)	William Gesenius, Francis Brown, S. R. Driver, and Charles Briggs	C	HT	HC	Hendrickson/ Oxford
Index to Brown, Driver, and Briggs Lexicon	Bruce Einspahr	CS	T		Moody
A Greek-English Lexicon of the New Testament and Other Early Christian Literature (3rd ed.)	Walter Bauer, Frederick W. Danker, William F. Arndt, F. Wilbur Gingrich	C	HT	HC	University of Chicago Press
Greek-English Lexicon of the New Testament Based on Semantic Domains (2 vols.)	Johannes P. Louw and Eugene A. Nida	CS	T	HC	United Bible Societies

Type/Name	Editor/Author	Status*	Nature	Stance	Publisher(s)
Concise Hebrew and Aramaic Lexicon of the Old Testament	William Halliday	C	T	HC	Eerdmans
Hebrew and Aramaic Lexicon of the Old Testament (4th ed.)	Ludwig Koehler, Walter Baumgartner, Johann J. Stamm	CS	HT	HC	Brill
Word Study Books					
Expository Dictionary of Old and New Testament Words	W. E. Vine	C	NT	E	Revell/Nelson
Theological Dictionary of the Old Testament (20 vols. projected)	G. Johannes Botterweck and Helmer Ringgren	CS	HT	HC	Eerdmans
New International Dictionary of Old Testament Theology	Willem A. VanGemeren	CS	T-HT	E	Zondervan
A Theological Wordbook of the Old Testament (2 vols.)	Gleason Archer, R. Laird Harris, and Bruce Waltke	CS	T	E	Moody
Exegetical Dictionary of the New Testament (3 vols.)	Horst Balz and Gerhard Schneider	CS	T-HT	HC	Eerdmans
A Greek-English Lexicon (broader Greek context from classical era to A.D. 600)	Henry George Liddell and Robert Scott	C	HT	HC	Oxford

Type/Name	Editor/Author	Status*	Nature	Stance	Publisher(s)
The New International Dictionary of New Testament Theology	Colin Brown	CS	T	HC orig.; w/ E rev.	Zondervan
Theological Dictionary of the New Testament (10 vols.)	Gerhard Kittel and Gerhard Friedrich	C	HT	HC	Eerdmans
Theological Dictionary of the New Testament; the "Little Kittel"	Geoffrey W. Bromiley	C	T	HC	Eerdmans
The Vocabulary of the Greek Testament Illustrated from the Papyri and Other Non-Literary Sources	James Hope Moulton and George Milligan	C	HT		Eerdmans
Word Pictures in the New Testament	A. T. Robertson	C-D	NT	C	Baker

Exegetical Analysis

Type/Name	Editor/Author	Status*	Nature	Stance	Publisher(s)
Analytical Key to the Old Testament (4 vols.)	John Joseph Owens	CS	T		Baker
Old Testament Parsing Guide (2 vols.) keyed to Brown, Driver, and Briggs Hebrew Lexicon	Todd Bell, William Banks, and Colin Smith	CS	T		Moody
A Grammatical Analysis of the Greek New Testament (keyed to Zerwick's grammar)	M. Zerwick (trans. M. Zerwick and M. Grosvenor)	CS	T	RC	Pontifical Biblical Institute

Type/Name	Editor/Author	Status*	Nature	Stance	Publisher(s)
Analytical Greek New Testament	Barbara and Timothy Friberg	CS	T		Baker
Linguistic Key to the Greek New Testament	Fritz Reinecker and Cleon Rodgers	CS	T	E	Zondervan
The New Analytical Greek Lexicon	Wesley Perschbacher	CS	T		Hendrickson
Analytical Lexicon to the Greek New Testament	William D. Mounce	CS	T		Zondervan
A Parsing Guide to the Greek New Testament	Nathan E. Han	CS	T		Herald

*Symbol key appears after table A9.1.

Table A9.3

Original Language Grammars

Type/Name	Editor/Author	Status*	Nature	Stance	Publisher
A Grammar of Biblical Hebrew	Paul Joüron; trans. T. Muraoka	CS	HT	HC	Pontifical Biblical Institute
An Introduction to Biblical Hebrew Syntax	Bruce Waltke and M. O'Connor	CS	T	E	Eisenbrauns
Beginning Biblical Hebrew	Mark Futato	CS		E	Eisenbrauns
Hebrew Grammar	William Gesenius; trans. A. E. Cowley and E. Kautzsch	C	HT	HC	Oxford
Greek Grammar Beyond the Basics	Daniel Wallace	CS	T-HT	E	Zondervan
A Practical Grammar for Classical Hebrew	J. Weingreen	CS	T		Oxford

Type/Name	Editor/Author	Status*	Nature	Stance	Publisher
Basics of Biblical Greek	William D. Mounce	CS	T		Zondervan
Biblical Greek	M. Zerwick	CS	T-HT		Pontifical Biblical Institute
A Grammar of the New Testament (4 vols.)	J. H. Moulton, F. W. Howard, and Nigel Turner	CS	HT		T & T Clark
A Greek Grammar of the New Testament	F. W. Blass, A. Debrunner, and R. W. Funk	CS	HT	HC	University of Chicago Press
A Manual Grammar of the Greek New Testament	H. E. Dana and Julius R. Mantey	D	T-HT		Macmillan
Syntax of New Testament Greek	James A. Brooks and Carlton Winbery	CS	T		University Press of America

*Symbol key appears after table A9.1.

Table A9.4

Concordances

Type/Name	Editor/Author	Status*	Nature	Stance	Publisher(s)
Print Concordances					
Analytical Concordance to the Bible (KJV); English keyed to original Hebrew and Greek terms	Robert Young	C	NT		Hendrickson
Crossway Comprehensive Concordance of the Holy Bible	William A. Mounce	CS	NT		Crossway
Exhaustive Concordance of the Bible (KJV) with numerical system keyed to other aids	James Strong	C	NT		Nelson/ Hendrickson

Type/Name	Editor/Author	Status*	Nature	Stance	Publisher(s)
The NIV Exhaustive Concordance with numerical system keyed to Strong's	John R. Kohlenberger III and Edward Goodrick	CS	NT		Zondervan
The NRSV Exhaustive Concordance	Bruce M. Metzger	CS	NT		Nelson
Zondervan NASB Exhaustive Concordance		CS	NT		Zondervan
The Englishman's Hebrew and Chaldee Concordance of the Old Testament	George V. Wigram	C	NT		Hendrickson
A New Concordance of the Bible (Hebrew, OT only)	Abraham Even-Shoshan	CS	HT	J	Baker
The Book Study Concordance of the Greek New Testament	Andreas Kostenberger and Raymond Bouchoc	CS	T		Broadman & Holman
Computer-Konkordanz zum Novum Testamentum graece von Nestle-Aland	H. Bachmann and W. A. Slaby	CS	HT		de Gruyter
A Concordance to the Greek Testament (6th ed.)	W. F. Moulton, A. S. Geden, and I. H. Marshall	CS	HT		T & T Clark
The Englishman's Greek Concordance of the New Testament	George V. Wigram	C	NT		Hendrickson
The Greek-English Concordance of the New Testament	John R. Kohlenberger III	CS	NT		Zondervan

Type/Name	Editor/Author	Status*	Nature	Stance	Publisher(s)
Computer Concordances and Exegesis Tools					
Accordance (for Macintosh users, an interrelated grammar and concordance to the Bible in the original languages with exegetical and parsing aids available)		CS	T-HT		Oak Tree Software
BibleWorks (an integrated grammar and concordance to the Bible with original languages and ties to many exegetical tools listed above)		CS	NT-T	E	BibleWorks
GramCord (an interrelated grammar and concordance to the Bible in the original languages with exegetical and parsing aids available)	Trinity Evangelical Divinity School	CS	T-HT		GramCord Institute
Logos (well-integrated study and commentary for the serious layperson)		CS	NT-T		Logos Research Systems
OnLine Bible (NIV and RSV English versions with original languages and reference helps)		CS	NT-T		OnLine Bible

*Symbol key appears after table A9.1.

Note: Any listing of computer resources will quickly become dated. Rapid advances in computer technology and the proliferation of computer tools require preachers to consult the most current sources before making computer resource purchases. In addition to these computer resources, a burgeoning source of sermon preparation material such as commentaries, illustrations, sermons, and much more exists on the Internet (e.g., desiringgod.com; preachingtoday.com; bible.org; biblestudytools.net; sermons.org; sermonillustrator.org).

Table A9.5

Bible Dictionaries and Encyclopedias

Name	Editor/Author	Status*	Nature	Stance	Publisher(s)
Baker Encyclopedia of the Bible (2 vols.)	Walter A. Elwell	CS	NT	E	Baker
Eerdmans Dictionary of the Bible	David Noel Freedman	CS	NT-T	HC	Eerdmans
Holman Illustrated Bible Dictionary		CS	NT	E	Broadman & Holman
Illustrated Bible Dictionary (3 vols.)	J. D. Douglas	CS	NT	E	InterVarsity/ Tyndale
International Standard Bible Encyclopedia (revised; 4 vols.)	Geoffrey W. Bromiley	CS	T	C	Eerdmans
New Bible Dictionary	J. D. Douglas et al.	CS	NT	E	IVP
New Unger's Bible Dictionary	Merrill F. Unger	CS	NT	E	Moody
Zondervan Pictorial Bible Encyclopedia (5 vols.)	Merrill C. Tenney	CS	NT	E	Zondervan
Anchor Bible Dictionary (6 vols.)	David Noel Freedman	CS	T	HC	Doubleday

*Symbol key appears after table A9.1.

Appendix **10**

Reading Scripture

The first exposition of a text is the reading of Scripture. The way a preacher emphasizes words, characterizes dialogue, and holds the Bible communicates meaning. One preacher's inflection can extol a biblical character's actions, while another preacher's tone when reading the same words can mock those actions. Oral reading requires and expresses interpretation. Thus, the expositor who sets a text before a congregation needs to prepare and present the Scripture reading as responsibly as any other portion of a sermon. The following guidelines will help make your Scripture reading responsible and reliable.[1]

Read meaningfully. Let your voice express the meaning the author intended to convey. Your vocal expression, inflection, and intonation should vary to express the actions, emotions, and truths of the text. You do not convey the meaning of the words *Jesus wept* if your voice makes it sound as though he did not care.

Read expectantly. You believe that "the word of God is living and active ... sharper than any double-edged sword," and that "it penetrates even to dividing soul and spirit" (Heb. 4:12). Read it that way. Preachers who

---

1. For a more thorough discussion of this subject, see Bryan Chapell, "The Incarnate Voice: An Exhortation for Excellence in the Oral Reading of Scripture," *Presbyterion* 15, no. 1 (Spring 1989): 42–57; idem, "A Brief History of Scripture Reading," in *Resources for Music and the Arts,* vol. 4, The Topical Encyclopedia of Christian Worship (Nashville: Abbott-Martyn, 1993); and Thomas Edward McComiskey, *Reading Scripture in Public: A Guide for Preachers and Lay Readers* (Grand Rapids: Baker, 1991).

read a text in a monotone communicate that the Word has no power over them. Preachers who read the Word rapidly imply, "Let's get through this stuff so we can get to the really important things in my sermon." Read a text with the belief that every word carries the power that comes from the mouth of God.

Read naturally. Conveying the import of the Word does not mean that you should read theatrically or in "stained-glass" tones. A dramatic reading draws attention to the preacher rather than to the text. A preacher who tries to make every reading sound as though Moses were speaking from Sinai's heights removes Scripture from the real world of the average person. If a text contains a conversation, speak conversationally. If a text contains a narrative, let your voice tell the story as realistically as the author would have first expressed it. Bring the text into the world of the listeners with such "natural, appropriate, and controlled"[2] speech that the Bible seems readily accessible rather than terribly remote.

Highlight emphatic elements. The best way to make your voice and a text come alive is to emphasize the words and phrases that carry the author's emphases. Typically, biblical authors placed their emphases on *verbs and modifiers.* Your voice should highlight these terms. Sometimes authors expressed their intentions by contrasts, comparisons, repetitions, parallel wording, and so on. Where you spot these techniques, use your voice to underscore them. The introduction of characters, plot turns, new concepts, or unexpected actions or reactions all require such vocal underlining.

Maintain thought units. Sentences, phrases, and combinations of them express thought units. The concepts of an author come unglued when the reader runs one sentence into another, expresses a question as though it were a statement, or cuts a thought short by taking a breath in the middle of a phrase. Observe the punctuation that signals when to pause, breathe so as to keep thought units whole, and use your voice to manage the flow of the author's thought rather than mangle it.

Prepare. Unusual thought turns, unfamiliar terms, and words needing emphasis will elude, confuse, and escape the reader who does not prepare. Nothing so quickly damages a preacher's credibility as stumbling, skipping phrases, and mispronouncing words during a sermon's opening moments. Practice reading the Scripture portion aloud several times so that your tongue, ear, and mind grow familiar with the passage's thoughts, twists, and tones.

Maintain eye contact. Know the text well enough so that when you read it to the congregation you can look up at frequent intervals. In even the most literate congregations, 20 to 30 percent of listeners will be watching you during the Scripture reading rather than following along in their Bibles. Keep minds focused on the Word by maintaining a good deal of eye contact

---

2. McComiskey, *Reading Scripture in Public,* 62.

as you read. The most natural way of reading with eye contact is what I call "ladling." Look down at the text to scoop the wording of a sentence into your mind, and then look up to ladle it out to your listeners with your eyes. Do not break the flow of your reading as you ladle it. Simply recognize that your words will appear lifeless and removed if people see only the top of your head while you read.

Preach from an open Bible. When a preacher bases a message on Scripture, the message's authority comes from God. While keeping the Bible open during a message does not assure a preacher's faithfulness, a preacher who closes the Bible after reading a text inadvertently implies, "Now that we're done with that ritual, let's get to my message." Although no Bible verse commands us to preach from an open Bible, sound communication and theological principles make this the most natural expository stance.

Sample Sermon Evaluation Form

Speaker: _____ Evaluator: _____ Date: _____

Outline and Comment

Scripture introduction and reading:

Sermon introduction:

Proposition (specific wording):

Body (note main points and significant features of each):

General comments:

Content _____ Structure _____ Delivery _____
(S = Superior, E = Excellent, G = Good, N = Needs Work)

Delivery Concerns (circle or comment):

Volume	Eye contact
Vocal variation	Swaying or pacing
Distracting mannerisms	Use of Bible or notes
Gestures	Other_____
Pulpit use	

	Definitely		
	Yes		No
Introduction			
Introduces an FCF derived from *this* text	1 2 3	4 5	
Arouses attention (usually with a human-interest account)	1 2 3	4 5	
Proposition			
Weds principle and application	1 2 3	4 5	
Establishes *this* sermon's main theme	1 2 3	4 5	
Summarizes introduction in concept and terminology	1 2 3	4 5	
Main Points			
Are clear	1 2 3	4 5	

Are universal truths in hortatory statements	1 2 3 4 5	
Are proportional and not coextensive	1 2 3 4 5	
Contain adequate and appropriate:		
Exposition (⅓)	1 2 3 4 5	
Illustration (⅓)	1 2 3 4 5	
Application (⅓)	1 2 3 4 5	
Exegetical Support		
The sermon is what *this* text is about	1 2 3 4 5	
Problems and overall passage content are sufficiently handled	1 2 3 4 5	
Proofs are accurate, understandable, and support the points made	1 2 3 4 5	
The context and genre of the passage are adequately considered	1 2 3 4 5	
The exegesis is not belabored once the points are sufficiently proven	1 2 3 4 5	
The exegesis seems designed to aid rather than to impress	1 2 3 4 5	
Application		
Is clear, helpful, and practical	1 2 3 4 5	
Is redemptive, not legalistic, in focus and motivation	1 2 3 4 5	
Accurately distinguishes a scriptural mandate from a good idea	1 2 3 4 5	
Is supported with sufficient biblical proof from *this* passage	1 2 3 4 5	
Illustrations		
Contain sufficient "lived-body" detail	1 2 3 4 5	
Truly strengthen the points of the sermon	1 2 3 4 5	
Are in appropriate proportion (number and length) to the sermon whole	1 2 3 4 5	
Conclusion Contains		
Summary	1 2 3 4 5	
Clear and compelling exhortation	1 2 3 4 5	
Climax	1 2 3 4 5	
A definite, purposed, pointed end	1 2 3 4 5	

Sample Sermon

Note: Words in brackets are not said out loud when preaching the sermon. They are shown here for instruction and to indicate the various sermon components used.[1] The Fallen Condition Focus (FCF) is italicized in the sermon introduction. Terms signaling main points or subpoints are underlined throughout the sermon. Key terms used in "expositional rain" are in boldface.

[Announce text] Please turn with me to 2 Timothy 4:1–5.

[Scripture introduction] When Paul is writing these lines, he realizes that his death is near, that his race is almost over, and that he must hand the baton of his ministry to Timothy, his faithful but timid young disciple and friend [contextualization]. Most of us understand being timid about the gospel. We want to be faithful but fear messing up the message. The charge that Paul gives to Timothy in this passage will encourage us and help us understand how we are to proclaim the truth of God's Word in the diverse situations that we face every day [creation of longing].

[Reannounce and read text] Read with me from 2 Timothy 4:1–5. . . .

1. I wish to express my thanks to Rev. John Gullet and Rev. Norm Reed, former students and now faithful pastors, for their writing and formatting this instructional sermon in their seminary days. For other sermon and outline examples, see Bryan Chapell, *The Wonder of It All: Rediscovering the Treasures of Your Faith* (Wheaton: Crossway, 1999).

[Prayer for illumination] Pray with me. . . .

[Introduction] As my mother listened to Betty's brazen confession, our worst fears and suspicions were sadly confirmed. Betty had just declared that she was leaving her husband and pursuing a relationship with another man. For some time, my mother had been noticing her longtime friend Betty making frequent trips to visit the owner of the store across the street from her own business. Rumors were flying in the small town where we lived, and my mother had finally decided to find out what was going on. My mother's tentative questions were met with surprising candor from Betty. "It's all right," she said. "God has led me to this new relationship, and besides, I'll be so much happier with him." My mother left their conversation dumbfounded. She was afraid for Betty. She knew that if Betty continued on her present course, God would **judge** her for her **sin**. She knew that Betty needed to hear both the rebuke of God's **Word** and the hope of grace in Jesus Christ from God's **Word**. She wondered, "How can I warn Betty that God **judges sin** and yet provide her with the eternal hope of biblical truth?"

How would you respond in such a situation? My mother's account reminds us that opportunities to proclaim the truths of God's **Word** can arise at any time, often in unexpected circumstances. In his providence, God continually places us in **situation** after **situation** where we can provide hope by carefully and faithfully applying the **Word** of God. But *most of us struggle to speak up with clarity and conviction when God calls us to **proclaim** his truth despite our knowledge that God will judge* [FCF]. What will motivate us to overcome our hesitation and fears and enable us to speak the truth of God's **Word** in the many different circumstances that we face? The apostle Paul's charge in 2 Timothy 4 answers these very questions [Scripture bond]. Paul writes that . . .

[Proposition] Because God will **judge sin**, we must **proclaim** his **Word** in every situation.

Paul tells Timothy plainly, "I charge you therefore before God and the Lord Jesus Christ, who will judge the living and the dead at his appearing and his kingdom." Everything we do is "before God and the Lord Jesus Christ." In light of this divine oversight and future judgment, let us encourage each other to proclaim the Word of God <u>to rescue the needy</u>, <u>to defend the truth</u>, and <u>to fulfill our duty</u>.

[Main point 1] Because God will judge sin, we must proclaim his Word to rescue the needy.

People's needs vary, so Paul's instruction for our proclamation varies accordingly as he addresses the needs of those <u>who do not believe</u> God's Word, those <u>who do not obey</u> God's Word, and those <u>who have lost confidence</u> in God's Word.

[Subpoint 1] How should we approach those who do not believe God's Word? We should **convince** them.

Paul says to Timothy in verse 2, "Preach the word! Be ready in season and out of season. Convince, rebuke, exhort, with all long-suffering and teaching." Paul has just reminded Timothy in verse 16 of chapter 3 that "all Scripture is given by inspiration of God, and is profitable for doctrine, for reproof, for correction, for instruction in righteousness." Scripture has this divine and authoritative character because it is God's own tool to rescue sinful persons from the judgment to come. The God who will judge sin also mercifully provides the gospel whose truths redeem those who believe it. Therefore, Paul gives the highest priority to using Scripture—the Word inspired by God—to convince others to put their trust in him. Such convincing may require us to explain the meaning or defend the credibility of God's Word. These matters almost always require great patience and careful teaching, so Paul further reminds Timothy that he must be prepared to convince others "with all long-suffering and teaching." In other words, convincing others requires our reflecting to them the same patience and care by which God redeemed us. Those who do not believe God's Word must be convinced by those of us to whom he has revealed his truth and in whom his truth now lives.

But not only the unconvinced need the proclamation of the gospel.

[Subpoint 2] How should we approach those who do not obey God's Word? We should **rebuke** them.

There are those who know but do not obey. Those who believe the right things can still fall into error. In verse 2, Paul also tells us how to respond in these situations. There he instructs, "rebuke" with "long-suffering and teaching." There are times we must confront others and tell them directly to stop disobeying or distorting or even denying sound doctrine. As Jesus says in Luke 17:3, "If your brother sins against you, rebuke him, and if he repents, forgive him." When people ignore God's command and the clear teaching of the Word, we must sometimes use a firm rebuke to warn them of the consequences of continuing along the wrong path. If God did not love his children, he would not warn them of the dangers of their sin. Yet because he does love, God uses faithful proclaimers of his Word to warn others through rebuke that is intended to rescue from the horrible consequences of unrepented sin.

[Subpoint 3] How should we approach those who have lost confidence in God's Word? We should **exhort** them.

Paul continues in verse 2 by commanding Timothy to "exhort with all long-suffering and teaching." Sometimes people need urging or encouragement to honor what God requires. Exhorting them means we must help them see the hope that Christ offers for their salvation and strength. Our exhortation should direct others to seek God in his Word for the assurances and "teaching" they need to believe and do what he requires even if it seems difficult. Paul tells us in 2 Corinthians 12:9 that God himself exhorted him (i.e., the apostle himself) by saying, "My grace is sufficient for you, for my strength is made perfect in weakness."

Because God will judge everyone through Christ, we must proclaim God's Word to those who need to be <u>convinced</u>, to those who need to be <u>rebuked</u>, and to those who need to be <u>exhorted</u>.

[Illustration] The Cuban Resettlement Camp in Key Largo, Florida, was abuzz that morning. There were almost eight hundred Cuban refugees in the camp, and they all seemed to be anticipating someone's imminent arrival. As the next bus load of refugees from the Key West site arrived, seven older gentlemen in wheelchairs at last departed from the buses. The crowd, which normally was loud and exuberant at their newfound freedom, was silent and reverent while at the same time extremely attentive to the needs of these seven. These were the seven prisoners of conscience who never denied their faith in God and Jesus Christ. The first three were arrested for street preaching in the main park of Havana in the early 1960s, and the others were arrested for carrying their Bibles openly across that same park as a sign to others that an underground church meeting was about to take place.

These seven were known for their great faith despite brutal torture that had left them crippled and disfigured. They had suffered multiple broken bones after they refused to renounce Christ Jesus and to swear allegiance to the atheist Cuban communist regime. In the coming days, the MPs noticed that these seven would hold religious services every morning, afternoon, and evening in which many would be **convinced** of their sins upon hearing the gospel message for the first time. The seven also openly **rebuked** the sins of individuals with firmness, confidence, and love as they gave instruction on the keys of the Christian life through the study of the Word. But the most impressive acts of these seven involved their **exhortation** in times of weakness. The seven openly **exhorted** other prisoners through their silent suffering and open rejoicing in God's grace. They also openly **exhorted** one another when they felt weak and rejoiced when they felt the strength of God coursing through them.

These seven, who had every right to be bitter, were rejoicing at their being counted among the body of Christ in a Christ-less land and that they were now free to again proclaim the Word of God to a searching people through words and actions that **convinced, rebuked,** and **exhorted**. The devotion of these men to one another and their commitment to proclaiming God's Word to meet one another's needs testify to the beauty of the faithfulness that God desires in his church in order to rescue the needy.

[Application] Just like those men, we who belong to the body of Christ must proclaim God's truth to needy persons in loving **exhortation** and even **rebuke**. If we really want to **convince** others to honor God's Word, then we must faithfully encourage one another to remember that we live in the presence and sight of God and that as his children we are to live by the standards of his Word.

Those of you who are in college have a great need and a great opportunity to be involved in a ministry of proclaiming God's Word. The opposition and temptations you face daily on a college campus are much easier to overcome when you are involved with other Christians who will help you stand firm in your faith and faithfully proclaim the Word of God. You do not have to be on a secular campus long to know that Christianity is rejected by many professors and students. When the truth of God is challenged in your classes, you must seek to **convince** those challengers of their error. If you find yourself puzzled and doubting, you need to seek out fellow believers who can **convincingly** answer the lies and falsehoods with which you are being bombarded. Furthermore, you are constantly surrounded by others whose lifestyles and attitudes are apathetic about everything and every idea. The prevailing relativism and apathy can make your faith stand out like a sore thumb, and sometimes you may feel isolated and even weird because of your beliefs. It is times like that when you need to **exhort** and even **rebuke** one another, **convincing** one another to hold fast to the truth and to live boldly for Jesus Christ on your campus.

But college students aren't the only ones who must proclaim God's Word to meet the needs of their Christian brothers and sisters. All of us, whether we are at home, at church, or at work, are called to the same concern for others. When a friend in your small group falls into sin he or she will not acknowledge, you must be willing lovingly to **rebuke**. Husbands and wives, when your spouse is discouraged and weighed down with children or work or a crazy schedule, you must be there lovingly to **exhort** and encourage with God's Word. When the coworker with whom you have been sharing the gospel expresses doubts about the Christian faith, you must be ready, with the Holy Spirit's help, to **convince** of the reasons for the hope that you have. We have many opportunities to proclaim God's Word to needy persons. Knowing that we live before God and will face judgment before the Lord Jesus Christ should strongly motivate us to proclaim God's Word in every situation.

Just as there are situations in which we must be prepared to **rebuke, convince,** and **exhort** for the sake of those who need the truth, the apostle Paul also challenges us to be prepared to defend God's Word to those who have embraced falsehood.

[Main point 2] Because God will judge sin, we must proclaim his Word to defend the truth.

[Analytical question] When must we defend the truth?

[Subpoint 1] When others **abandon sound doctrine**.

Paul says plainly to Timothy in the beginning of verse 3, "For the time will come when men will not put up with sound doctrine." Paul also addressed this idea in Romans 1 while writing about the sinfulness common among people. He says, "They exchanged the truth of God for a lie." The prophet Isaiah wrote similarly concerning those who abandon the truth. In chapter 30, verse 10, he says, "They say to seers, 'See no more visions!' and to the prophets, 'Give us no more visions of what is right!' Tell us of pleasant things, prophesy illusions." In all ages, there is great temptation to turn from truth to lies that temporarily seem more satisfying. Our day is no different. People still do not put up with sound doctrine. They would often rather listen to lies that make them feel good than honor the sound doctrine found in the Word of God. Because God wants to prepare us to proclaim his Word, he has warned us in advance how many people will respond. We, therefore, must be prepared for people to abandon sound doctrine.

Being prepared for people to abandon what is sound requires us to anticipate others' teaching what is false. Therefore, we must also defend the truth . . .

[Subpoint 2] When others **flock to false teachers**.

Paul continues in verse 3 by saying, "Instead, to suit their own desires, they will gather around them a great number of teachers to say what their itching ears want to hear." In Matthew 24:5, Jesus also indicates this can happen by saying, "For many will come in my name, claiming, 'I am the Christ,' and will deceive many." We all love teachers who tell us what we want to hear and who make us feel good about ourselves by not requiring us to question beliefs or practices with which we have grown comfortable. Many people flock to one type of teacher or another because that person makes them feel happy or satisfied with themselves. Because people are apt to listen to such things, there is never a lack of false teachers.

We must defend the truth not only when others abandon sound doctrine and flock to false teachers but also . . .

[Subpoint 3] When others **will not even listen**.

Paul tells Timothy in verse 4, "They will turn their ears away from the truth." In the midst of this passage, in which Timothy is being encouraged to preach the Word in every situation, Paul honestly writes to him of those who will not listen at all. Yet though they may not even listen, Paul still commands Timothy to preach the Word.

Luke describes a situation in Acts 19 in which Paul goes to a certain city and preaches to the Jews in the synagogue and to others in a public school. In Acts 19:10, Luke records, "This went on for two years, so that all the Jews and Greeks who lived in the province of Asia heard the Word of the Lord." Luke never says that everyone was saved but that they had opportunity to know Christ in their situation because Paul remained faithful in proclaiming God's Word.

Such accounts remind us that though others may **abandon what is sound, flock to what is false,** and "turn their ears away from the truth" so as **not even to listen,** we still have an obligation to preach the Word.

[Illustration] As he stood before the Diet of Worms on the afternoon of April 18, 1521, Martin Luther was asked one question: "Will you recant of your writings and the errors which they contain?" After spending the night in prayer, searching for the right thing to say, he answered, "Unless I am convicted by Scripture and plain reason—I do not accept the authority of popes and councils, for they have contradicted each other—my conscience is captive to the Word of God. I cannot and I will not recant anything, for to go against conscience is neither right nor safe. Here I stand; I cannot do otherwise. God help me. Amen." Martin Luther believed that the Word of God demanded him to stand for the truth even in such a difficult situation. He knew that though others might **abandon sound doctrine,** he must stand firm. While his human judges had the power to excommunicate him, exile him, or even execute him, he said, "My conscience is captive to the Word of God." Martin Luther believed that the church had **flocked to false teachers,** and knowing that they would probably **not even listen,** he answered them by saying, "Here I stand." He viewed himself as ultimately responsible only to a divine judge, and it motivated him to remain faithful to proclaim God's Word in the most challenging of situations. You and I have a similar calling in this day and age in which truth is relative to most persons and tolerance for so many kinds of evils is encouraged. Standing for the truth can be dangerous to our friendships, reputations, and careers.

[Application] Paul wrote this letter to Timothy, who was a young pastor in the city of Ephesus. Yet our situations are very similar. Every day we are faced with challenges, and we must make a decision as to whether we will defend the truth. In the business world, there is pressure from every side to **abandon doctrinally sound** ethics because they are supposedly the old-fashioned way of doing things. "Whatever it takes" is the slogan of the day. Whether dealing with the need to show a profit, the hiring and firing of employees, or simply gaining the approval of peers, believers in the workplace often find themselves in situations in which unethical behavior is not only overlooked but expected. In these situations, we must not succumb to our natural inclinations to follow the crowd and **flock to false teachers** who claim that unethical practices are justifiable because everyone is doing it and/or it is necessary to gain others' approval. For most people in this world, there are few things more important than the favor of men. As a consequence, we all face pressures to compromise. From the student who is encouraged by his peers to cheat on the big exam to the corporate executive who is offered a handsome bonus if she will look the other way regarding an illegal deal, we all face the pressures of the world's false teaching. Consider, then, how many heads would turn and mouths hang wide open if in those situations Christians were to say, "I will not yield to this pressure because to do so would violate the Word of God." I will not tell you that such a proclamation of God's Word will meet with everyone's approval or that it will lead to the salvation of all around you. But God will be honored before those who need him in order to be saved eternally. Knowing this, may you and I be motivated to say with Martin Luther, "'My conscience is captive to the Word of God,' and I will stand for the truth **even when others do not listen**."

The Lord has definitely given us a challenge in the words of Paul by calling us to defend the truth. But he doesn't just stop there. He goes on to tell us how to do this task. The apostle reinforces his commands by reminding us that . . .

[Main point 3] Because God will judge sin, we must proclaim his Word to fulfill our duty.

And how does the apostle Paul say that we are to fulfill our duty? By being watchful, by enduring affliction, and by doing the work of an evangelist.

[Subpoint 1] We must be **watchful**.
In verse 5, Paul commands Timothy to be watchful. The apostle writes, "But you, keep your head in all situations." The literal meaning is "to be sober" or "to be clear minded." Paul commands us not to lose our composure but rather to be watchful for opportunities to proclaim the good news of Jesus Christ. In his letter to the Colossians, Paul writes, "Devote yourselves to prayer, being watchful and thankful. And pray for us, too, that God may open a door for our message, so that we may proclaim the mystery of Christ. . . . Be wise in the way you act toward outsiders; make the most of every opportunity. Let

your conversation be always seasoned with salt, so you may know how to answer everyone."

So be wise, be watchful. God gives his people opportunities to share the gospel. People may ask you questions, such as, "How can you be so joyful? How can you have such hope in the midst of such difficulty?" If you walk with Jesus, you will indeed stand out in this fallen world. So God commands us to be watchful and to be ready to give an explanation for our hope.

[Illustration] About three years ago, God allowed me the opportunity to get to know someone who was indeed always **watchful**, a man who wonderfully fulfilled his duty of proclaiming God's Word to the lost. His name was Chuck. He was an older gentleman in my church who began Bible studies in his home. He would teach anyone who would listen. He taught me many things about God's Word in those studies, but probably the greatest thing he taught me was the importance of **watching** for opportunities to share Jesus Christ with others. He was always **watching** out for someone who did not know about God's grace so that this wonderful witness could be the one to tell them about it. About a year ago Chuck was diagnosed with cancer. It spread quickly, and within a few short months, he found himself lying in a hospital, literally waiting to die. But even in that difficult situation and even in the midst of his pain, he was **watchful** for opportunities. He discovered that the nurses who continually came and checked on him were not believers. So he patiently and lovingly shared God's Word with them. Chuck died just a few weeks later. But two of the nurses who had cared for Chuck and had heard him talk so openly about his faith later came to a saving faith in Jesus Christ. Just as Chuck was always **watchful** for opportunities to share God's Word to those in need, we too must also be **watchful**. But God may require more than watchfulness of us, even as he required more of my friend Chuck.

We must be not only watchful but also . . .

[Subpoint 2] willing to **endure hardship**.

Continuing in verse 5, Paul writes, "Endure afflictions." This is one of Paul's favorite commands. Remember the setting of this letter: The apostle is in prison, bound in chains, and waiting to be executed. Paul knew all about afflictions. In 2 Corinthians 11, Paul writes, "Five times I received from the Jews forty lashes minus one. Three times I was beaten with rods, once I was stoned, three times I was shipwrecked. . . . I have been in danger from rivers, from bandits, from my own countrymen, and from Gentiles. I have known hunger and thirst and have often gone without food and sleep." All for the sake of the gospel!

Now, you may think, "I really don't plan on being stoned or shipwrecked," yet in 2 Timothy 3:12, Paul writes, "In fact, everyone who wants to live a godly life in Christ Jesus will be persecuted." It's a guarantee and a promise. You will suffer hardships and afflictions if you live for Christ. But recall verse 2 in our passage. God has given us the very words of his breath to encourage us. And if you think about it, you will realize that many times the best opportunities we have to share our hope in Jesus Christ come as we are **enduring afflictions**. It was when Chuck was dying of cancer that he was best able to proclaim God's Word to the nurses at the hospital. Therefore, to fulfill our duty, we are to **be watchful**, to **endure affliction**, and also to **do the work of an evangelist**.

[Subpoint 3] We must **work as evangelists**.

In the remainder of verse 5, Paul says, "Do the work of an evangelist, discharge all the duties of your ministry." You may not think of yourself as an evangelist. But when you share with a lost friend the way Jesus encourages you and comforts you in times of trouble, you are indeed engaged in evangelism. When you talk to a coworker while playing racquetball at the gym about how God has radically changed your life and your marriage, you are engaged in evangelism. We are to make the most of every opportunity. People's souls are at stake. Jesus will judge all people, and we know how they may also experience his mercy. God's Word has the amazing power to change eternity for those who believe. We must proclaim it so that it may be heard and believed. This is more than our duty; it is the privilege of being co-laborers with Jesus in the eternal salvation of those who are in danger of hell apart from him.

[Application] Some of you are stay-at-home moms, and your days often seem completely chaotic. Chasing children around the house, running endless errands, doing all sorts of things may not seem like a ministry, but consider what duties you are fulfilling in the apostle Paul's terms. By all the hard work you do to serve your family, friends, and neighbors, you **endure hardship** in service to Christ. By being concerned for their spiritual welfare and taking opportunities to speak of Jesus to friends and to your own children, you **work as an evangelist**. By monitoring the hearts and actions of every person around you to see when a word of testimony, encouragement, or correction should be given, you remain **watchful** for God's opportunities and Satan's challenges. By ministering in these ways to your family, your children, and your neighbors, you fulfill your duty of proclaiming God's Word in every situation.

In so ministering, you also teach others to do the same. By showing children that God's Word is real and exciting and that it comforts us in the midst of afflictions, you teach them to be **watchful**. By thinking of ways to model Christ's servant heart and to show love to those around them—neighbors, the lady who works at the deli counter, or the barber who cuts their hair—your children learn the **work of evangelism**, and they may also learn what it may mean to **endure hardship** in such testimony while you are there to help them through it.

Such opportunities to proclaim our faith exist for us in the myriad situations of life, if we will only remain **watchful**. Moms at home, students at college, those in professional careers all have the opportunities to **work** and to **endure** for Christ's name. God does not isolate us from others, and we should always be considering the evangelistic opportunities given to us. Who admires you and looks to you for guidance? Who rubs elbows with you? Who enjoys your company? Who does business with you? These people are your responsibility—your duty—because God has put them in your life. Consider how you can share Christ with them. Because unbelievers are lost and without hope, we must fulfill all our duties of proclaiming the eternal life that is in Jesus. By God's grace and by the power of his Holy Spirit that dwells in you, let others know of him in every situation!

[Conclusion] The Lord, through Paul, has laid before us a high and holy charge that will require much persistence and much commitment. In his grace, God has called us, motivated us, and enabled us to overcome our fears so that we may proclaim his Word in all situations. God has called you to **fulfill your duty** to speak of him by putting in your heart the concern to proclaim the truth to **rescue the needy** and to **defend the truth** against those who would deny it to the spiritually needy.

The enabling presence of Jesus has been clearly seen in the difficult situation that my mother faced with her friend Betty. Although my mother is not a naturally gifted evangelist, the Lord has used her to faithfully and clearly speak the truth in love to Betty again and again. For weeks on end, my mother patiently but firmly exhorted and rebuked Betty from God's Word, trying to convince her to change her mind and to flee from her sin. Even though Betty continued to abandon the truth and would not listen to my mother's sound and loving admonishing, my mother continued to **fulfill her duty** and to **defend God's truth** in order to **rescue this person in need**.

Although Betty has not yet repented of her sin, my mother knows the joy and blessing of a clear conscience toward Betty. As a result of her obedience in doing the work of an evangelist, she has been strengthened and encouraged to speak God's Word with more confidence than ever before. You and I can also know this confidence, peace, and joy as we faithfully speak of God's judgment and the hope that we have in Jesus. When we consider what God has done for us in Christ by saving us from his judgment, we will have fresh motivation to obey him and to **proclaim his Word in every situation**.

Bibliography

Adams, Jay E. *Preaching with Purpose: A Comprehensive Textbook on Biblical Preaching.* Grand Rapids: Baker, 1982.

———. *Truth Applied: Application in Preaching.* Grand Rapids: Zondervan, 1990.

Allen, Ronald J. *Interpreting the Gospel: An Introduction to Preaching.* St. Louis: Chalice, 1998.

———, and Thomas J. Herrin. "Moving from the Story to Our Story." In *Preaching the Story,* edited by E. Steimle, M. Niedenthal, and C. Rice. Philadelphia: Fortress, 1980.

Barber, Cyril J. *Best Books for Your Bible Study Library.* Neptune, N.J.: Loizeaux, 2000.

———. *The Minister's Library.* 2 vols. Neptune, N.J.: Loizeaux, 1974–89.

———, and Robert M. Krauss Jr. *An Introduction to Theological Research.* Lanham, Md.: University Press of America, 2000.

Bartow, Charles L. *Effective Speech Communication in Leading Worship.* Nashville: Abingdon, 1988.

Baumann, J. Daniel. *An Introduction to Contemporary Preaching.* Grand Rapids: Baker, 1972.

Beale, G. K., ed. *The Right Doctrine from the Wrong Texts? Essays on the Use of the Old Testament in the New.* Grand Rapids: Baker, 1994.

Berkhof, Louis. *Systematic Theology.* Rev. ed. Grand Rapids: Eerdmans, 1953.

Bettler, John F. "Application." In *The Preacher and Preaching,* edited by Samuel T. Logan. Phillipsburg, N.J.: Presbyterian & Reformed, 1986.

Blackwood, Andrew. *Expository Preaching for Today.* Nashville: Abingdon, 1953.

———. *The Fine Art of Preaching.* New York: Macmillan, 1943.

Blomberg, Craig. *Interpreting the Parables.* Downers Grove, Ill.: InterVarsity, 1990.

Bridges, Jerry. *The Discipline of Grace: God's Role and Our Role in the Pursuit of Holiness.* Colorado Springs: NavPress, 1994.

———. *The Joy of Fearing God.* Colorado Springs: Waterbrook, 1997.

Broadus, John A. *On the Preparation and Delivery of Sermons.* Edited by J. B. Weatherspoon. New York: Harper & Row, 1944.

Bryan, Dawson C. *The Art of Illustrating Sermons.* Nashville: Cokesbury, 1938.

Buttrick, David. *Homiletic: Moves and Structures.* Philadelphia: Fortress, 1987.

Carrell, Lori. *The Great American Sermon Survey.* Wheaton: Mainstay Church Resources, 2000.

Carrick, John. *The Imperative of Preaching: A Theology of Sacred Rhetoric.* Carlisle, Pa.: Banner of Truth, 2002.

387

Chapell, Bryan. "Alternative Models: Old Friends in New Clothes." In *A Handbook of Contemporary Preaching*, edited by Michael Duduit. Nashville: Broadman, 1992.

———. *Holiness by Grace: Delighting in the Joy That Is Our Strength*. Wheaton: Crossway, 2001.

———. *In the Grip of Grace*. Grand Rapids: Baker, 1992.

———. *Using Illustrations to Preach with Power*. Rev. ed. Wheaton: Crossway, 2001.

———. *The Wonder of It All: Rediscovering the Treasures of Your Faith*. Wheaton: Crossway, 1999.

Claypool, John R. *The Preaching Event*. San Francisco: Harper & Row, 1989.

Clowney, Edmund. *Preaching and Biblical Theology*. Grand Rapids: Eerdmans, 1961.

———. "Preaching Christ from All the Scriptures." In *The Preacher and Preaching*, edited by Samuel T. Logan. Phillipsburg, N.J.: Presbyterian & Reformed, 1986.

———. *Preaching Christ in All of Scripture*. Wheaton: Crossway, 2003.

———. *The Unfolding Mystery: Discovering Christ in the Old Testament*. Phillipsburg, N.J.: Presbyterian & Reformed, 1988.

"The Controlling Image: One Key to Sermon Unity." *Academy Accents* 7, no. 3 (Winter 1991): 1–2.

Cotterell, Peter, and Max Turner. *Linguistics and Biblical Interpretation*. Downers Grove, Ill.: InterVarsity, 1989.

Craddock, Fred B. *As One without Authority*. 3rd ed. Nashville: Abingdon, 1979.

———. *Preaching*. Nashville: Abingdon, 1985.

Dabney, Robert L. *Lectures on Sacred Rhetoric*. Carlisle, Pa.: Banner of Truth, 1979.

Davis, Henry Grady. *Design for Preaching*. Philadelphia: Fortress, 1958.

De Jong, James A. "Principled Paraenesis: Reading and Preaching the Ethical Material of New Testament Letters." *Pro Rege* 10, no. 4 (June 1982): 26–34.

Demaray, Donald E. *An Introduction to Homiletics*. Grand Rapids: Baker, 1978.

Dillard, Raymond B. *Faith in the Face of Apostasy*. Phillipsburg, N.J.: Presbyterian & Reformed, 1999.

Doriani, Daniel M. *Getting the Message: A Plan for Interpreting and Applying the Bible*. Phillipsburg, N.J.: Presbyterian & Reformed, 1996.

———. *Putting the Truth to Work: The Theory and Practice of Biblical Application*. Phillipsburg, N.J.: Presbyterian & Reformed, 2001.

Duduit, Michael, ed. *A Handbook of Contemporary Preaching*. Nashville: Broadman, 1992.

Duguid, Iain M. *Hero of Heroes: Seeing Christ in the Beatitudes*. Phillipsburg, N.J.: Presbyterian & Reformed, 2001.

———. *Living in the Gap between Promise and Reality: The Gospel according to Abraham*. Phillipsburg, N.J.: Presbyterian & Reformed, 1999.

Eggold, Henry J. *Preaching Is Dialogue: A Concise Introduction to Homiletics*. Grand Rapids: Baker, 1990.

Eslinger, Richard L. *Narrative Imagination: Preaching the Words That Shape Us*. Minneapolis: Fortress, 1995.

———. *A New Hearing: Living Options in Homiletic Method*. Nashville: Abingdon, 1987.

Fabarez, Michael. *Preaching That Changes Lives*. Nashville: Thomas Nelson, 2002.

Farmer, Herbert H. *The Servant of the Word*. New York: Scribner's, 1942.

Fee, Gordon D. *New Testament Exegesis: A Handbook for Students and Pastors*. Philadelphia: Westminster, 1983.

———, and Douglas Stuart. *How to Read the Bible for All Its Worth*. Grand Rapids: Zondervan, 1982.

Fisher, Walter R. "Narration as Human Communication Paradigm: The Case of Public Moral Argument." *Communication Monographs* 51 (1984): 1–22.

———. "The Narrative Paradigm: An Elaboration." *Communication Monographs* 52 (1985): 347–67.

Flynn, Leslie B. *Come Alive with Illustrations: How to Find, Use, and File Good Stories for Sermons and Speeches.* Grand Rapids: Baker, 1987.

Ford, D. W. Cleverley. *The Ministry of the Word.* Grand Rapids: Eerdmans, 1979.

Frame, John. *Doctrine of the Knowledge of God.* Phillipsburg, N.J.: Presbyterian & Reformed, 1987.

Galli, Mark, and Craig Brian Larson. *Preaching That Connects: Using the Techniques of Journalists to Add Impact to Your Sermons.* Grand Rapids: Zondervan, 1994.

Garrison, Webb B. *Creative Imagination in Preaching.* Nashville: Abingdon, 1960.

Giorgi, Amadeo. "The Body: Focal Point of Twentieth-Century Cultural Contradictions." *South Africa Journal of Psychology* 13, no. 2 (1983): 129–69.

Golden, James L., Goodwin F. Berquist, and William Coleman. *The Rhetoric of Western Thought.* 3rd ed. Dubuque: Kendall-Hunt, 1978.

Goldsworthy, Graeme. *Gospel and Kingdom: A Christian Interpretation of the Old Testament.* Carlisle, U.K.: Paternoster, 1994.

———. *Preaching the Whole Bible as Christian Scripture.* Grand Rapids: Eerdmans, 2000.

Grant, Reg, and John Reed. *The Power Sermon: Countdown to Quality Messages for Maximum Impact.* Grand Rapids: Baker, 1993.

Green, Christopher, and David Jackman, eds. *When God's Voice Is Heard: Essays on Preaching Presented to Dick Lucas.* Leicester: Inter-Varsity, 1995.

Greidanus, Sidney. *The Modern Preacher and the Ancient Text: Interpreting and Preaching Biblical Literature.* Grand Rapids: Eerdmans, 1988.

———. *Preaching Christ from the Old Testament.* Grand Rapids: Eerdmans, 1999.

———. "Redemptive History and Preaching." *Pro Rege* 19, no. 2 (December 1990): 9–18.

———. *Sola Scriptura: Problems and Principles in Preaching Historical Texts.* Toronto: Wedge, 1970.

Halvorson, Arndt L. *Authentic Preaching.* Minneapolis: Augsburg, 1982.

Hauerwas, Stanley, and L. Gregory Jones, eds. *Why Narrative? Readings in Narrative Theology.* Grand Rapids: Eerdmans, 1989.

Hodge, Charles. *Systematic Theology.* 3 vols. New York: Scribner, Armstrong, 1875.

Hoekema, Anthony. *Christian Spirituality: Five Views on Sanctification.* Edited by Donald Alexander. Downers Grove, Ill.: InterVarsity, 1988.

Hogan, William L. "It Is My Pleasure to Introduce . . ." *Expositor* 1, no. 3 (August 1987).

———. "Sermons Have Structures." *Expositor* 2, no. 1 (April 1988).

Hostetler, Michael J. *Illustrating the Sermon.* The Craft of Preaching Series. Grand Rapids: Zondervan, 1989.

———. *Introducing the Sermon: The Art of Compelling Beginnings.* The Craft of Preaching Series. Grand Rapids: Zondervan, 1986.

Howard, J. Grant. *Creativity in Preaching.* The Craft of Preaching Series. Grand Rapids: Zondervan, 1987.

Howell, Kenneth J. "How to Preach Christ from the Old Testament." *Presbyterian Journal* 16 (January 1985): 8–10.

Hunter, Barbara, and Brenda Buckley Hunter. *Introductory Speech Communication: Overcoming Obstacles, Reaching Goals.* Dubuque: Kendall-Hunt, 1988.

Jensen, Richard A. *Thinking in Story: Preaching in a Post-literate Age.* Lima, Ohio: CSS, 1995.

Johnson, Byron Val. "A Media Selection Model for Use with a Homiletical Taxonomy." Ph.D. diss., Southern Illinois University at Carbondale, 1982.

Johnson, Dennis E. *The Message of Acts in the History of Redemption.* Phillipsburg, N.J.: Presbyterian & Reformed, 1997.

Jones, Ilion T. *Principles and Practice of Preaching.* Nashville: Abingdon, 1956.

Jones, Thomas F. "Preaching the Cross of Christ." Essay presented at the homiletics lectures, Covenant Theological Seminary, 1976–77.

———. "Truth Has Consequences: Or Balancing the Proposition." In *The Preparation and Delivery of Sermons,* edited by Bryan Chapell. St. Louis: Multi-media Publications, 1992.

Kaiser, Walter C., Jr. *The Messiah in the Old Testament.* Grand Rapids: Zondervan, 1995.

———. *Toward an Exegetical Theology: Biblical Exegesis for Preaching and Teaching.* Grand Rapids: Baker, 1981.

Kemper, Deane A. *Effective Preaching.* Philadelphia: Westminster, 1985.

Killinger, John. *Fundamentals of Preaching.* Philadelphia: Fortress, 1985.

Kinlaw, Dennis F. *Preaching in the Spirit.* Grand Rapids: Francis Asbury, 1985.

Knox, John. *The Integrity of Preaching.* New York: Abingdon, 1957.

Koller, Charles W. *Expository Preaching without Notes.* Grand Rapids: Baker, 1961.

Kooienga, William H. *Elements of Style for Preaching.* The Craft of Preaching Series. Grand Rapids: Zondervan, 1989.

Kraft, Charles H. *Communicating the Gospel God's Way.* Pasadena: William Carey Library, 1979.

Kroll, Woodrow Michael. *Prescription for Preaching.* Grand Rapids: Baker, 1980.

Lane, Beldon C. "Rabbinical Stories: A Primer on Theological Method." *Christian Century* 98 (December 1981): 1306–10.

Larkin, William J. *Culture and Biblical Hermeneutics: Interpreting and Applying the Authoritative Word in a Relativistic Age.* Grand Rapids: Baker, 1988.

Larsen, David L. *The Anatomy of Preaching: Identifying the Issues in Preaching Today.* Grand Rapids: Baker, 1989.

Larson, Craig Brian. *Preaching That Connects: Using the Techniques of Journalists to Add Impact to Your Sermons* (Grand Rapids: Zondervan, 1994).

Lawson, Steven J. *Famine in the Land: A Passionate Call for Expository Preaching.* Chicago: Moody, 2003.

Lehman, Louis Paul. *Put a Door on It.* Grand Rapids: Kregel, 1975.

Lenski, R. C. H. *The Sermon: Its Homiletical Construction.* Grand Rapids: Baker, 1968.

Lewis, Ralph. *Speech for Persuasive Preaching.* Wilmore, Ky.: Asbury Theological Seminary, 1968.

———. "The Triple Brain Test of a Sermon." *Preaching* 1, no. 2 (1985).

Lewis, Ralph L., with Gregg Lewis. *Inductive Preaching: Helping People Listen.* Westchester, Ill.: Crossway, 1983.

Liefeld, Walter L. *New Testament Exposition: From Text to Sermon.* Grand Rapids: Zondervan, 1984.

Liske, Thomas V. *Effective Preaching.* 2nd ed. New York: Macmillan, 1960.

Lloyd-Jones, D. Martyn. *Darkness and Light: An Exposition of Ephesians 4:17–5:17.* Grand Rapids: Baker, 1982.

———. *Preaching and Preachers.* Grand Rapids: Zondervan, 1972.

Longman, Tremper, III. *Literary Approaches to Biblical Interpretation.* Vol. 3. Foundations of Contemporary Interpretation. Grand Rapids: Zondervan, 1987.

———. *Old Testament Commentary Survey.* 3rd ed. Grand Rapids: Baker, 2003.

Loscalzo, Craig A. *Preaching Sermons That Connect: Effective Communication through Identification.* Downers Grove, Ill.: InterVarsity, 1992.

Lovelace, Richard. *Dynamics of Spiritual Life.* Downers Grove, Ill.: InterVarsity, 1979.

Lowry, Eugene L. *Doing Time in the Pulpit: The Relationship between Narrative and Preaching.* Nashville: Abingdon, 1985.

———. *The Homiletical Plot: The Sermon as Narrative Art Form.* Atlanta: John Knox, 1980.

———. *How to Preach a Parable.* Nashville: Abingdon, 1989.

———. *The Sermon: Dancing the Edge of Mystery.* Nashville: Abingdon, 1997.

MacArthur, John, Jr., et al. *Rediscovering Expository Preaching.* Dallas: Word, 1992.

MacPherson, Ian. *The Art of Illustrating Sermons.* Nashville: Abingdon, 1964.

Marquart, Edward F. *Quest for Better Preaching.* Minneapolis: Augsburg, 1985.

Marshall, Walter. *The Gospel Mystery of Sanctification.* Grand Rapids: Reformation Heritage, 1999.

Massey, James Earl. *The Burdensome Joy of Preaching.* Nashville: Abingdon, 1998.

———. *Designing the Sermon: Order and Movement in Preaching.* Edited by William Thompson. Nashville: Abingdon, 1980.

Mawhinney, Bruce. *Preaching with Freshness.* Eugene, Ore.: Harvest House, 1991.

McCartney, Dan, and Charles Clayton. *Let the Reader Understand: A Guide to Interpreting and Applying the Bible.* Wheaton: Victor, 1994.

McComisky, Thomas Edward. *Reading Scripture in Public: A Guide for Preachers and Lay Readers.* Grand Rapids: Baker, 1991.

McGrath, Alister E. "The Biography of God." *Christianity Today* 35 (July 22, 1991): 23–24.

McQuilkin, J. Robertson. *Understanding and Applying the Bible.* Chicago: Moody, 1983.

Meek, Esther Lightcap. *Longing to Know: The Philosophy of Knowledge for Ordinary People.* Grand Rapids: Brazos, 2003.

Merleau-Ponty, Maurice. *The Phenomenology of Perception.* Translated by Colin Smith with revisions by Forrest Williams. Atlantic Highlands, N.J.: Humanitas, 1981.

Miller, C. John. *Outgrowing the Ingrown Church.* Grand Rapids: Zondervan, 1986.

Miller, Calvin. *Marketplace Preaching: How to Return the Sermon to Where It Belongs.* Grand Rapids: Baker, 1995.

———. *Spirit, Word, and Story: A Philosophy of Preaching.* Dallas: Word, 1989.

Miller, Rose Marie. *From Fear to Freedom: Living as Sons and Daughters of God.* Wheaton: Harold Shaw, 1994.

Mitchell, Henry H. *Celebration and Experience in Preaching.* Nashville: Abingdon, 1990.

Mohler, R. Albert, Jr., et al. *Feed My Sheep: A Passionate Plea for Preaching.* Edited by John Kistler. Morgan, Pa.: Soli Deo Gloria, 2002.

Morgan, G. Campbell. *Preaching.* Grand Rapids: Baker, 1974.

Murphy, James J. *Medieval Rhetoric: A Select Bibliography.* Toronto: University of Toronto Press, 1971.

———. *Rhetoric in the Middle Ages: A History of Rhetorical Theory from Saint Augustine to the Renaissance.* Berkeley: University of California Press, 1974.

Old, Hughes Oliphant. *The Reading and Preaching of the Scriptures in the Worship of the Christian Church.* Vol. 1, *The Biblical Period.* Grand Rapids: Eerdmans, 1998.

Osborn, Ronald E. *Folly of God: The Rise of Christian Preaching.* St. Louis: Chalice, 1999.

Packer, J. I. *God Speaks to Man: Revelation and the Bible.* Philadelphia: Westminster, 1965.

———. *Rediscovering Holiness.* Ann Arbor, Mich.: Servant Press, 1992.

Perry, Lloyd M. *Biblical Sermon Guide.* Grand Rapids: Baker, 1970.

———. *A Manual for Biblical Preaching.* Grand Rapids: Baker, 1983.

———, and Charles M. Sell. *Speaking to Life's Problems.* Chicago: Moody, 1983.

Peterson, Eugene, et al. *Weddings, Funerals, and Special Events.* Vol. 10. The Leadership Library. Waco: Word, 1987.

Peterson, Robert A. *Adopted by God: From Wayward Sinners to Cherished Children.* Phillipsburg, N.J.: Presbyterian & Reformed, 2001.

Piper, John. *Future Grace.* Sisters, Ore.: Multnomah, 1995.

———. *The Supremacy of God in Preaching.* Grand Rapids: Baker, 1990.

Pitt-Watson, Ian. *A Primer for Preachers.* Grand Rapids: Baker, 1986.

Postman, Neil. *Amusing Ourselves to Death: Public Discourse in the Age of Show Business.* New York: Viking, 1985.

Poythress, Vern S. *God-Centered Biblical Interpretation.* Phillipsburg, N.J.: Presbyterian & Reformed, 1999.

———. *The Shadow of Christ in the Law of Moses.* Phillipsburg, N.J.: Presbyterian & Reformed, 1991.

Pratt, Richard L., Jr. *He Gave Us Stories: The Bible Student's Guide to Interpreting Old Testament Narratives.* Phillipsburg, N.J.: Presbyterian & Reformed, 1990.

Ramm, Bernard. *Protestant Biblical Interpretation.* 3rd rev. ed. Grand Rapids: Baker, 1970.

Ramsey, Arthur Michael, and Leon-Joseph Suenens. *The Future of the Christian Church.* London: SCM, 1971.

Richard, Ramesh. *Preparing Expository Sermons.* Grand Rapids: Baker, 2001.

Robinson, Haddon. *Biblical Preaching: The Development and Delivery of Expository Messages.* 2nd ed. Grand Rapids: Baker, 2001.

———, and Torrey Robinson. *It's All How You Tell It: Preaching First-Person Expository Messages.* Grand Rapids: Baker, 2003.

Robinson, Wayne Bradley, ed. *Journeys toward Narrative Preaching.* New York: Pilgrim, 1990.

Rogness, Michael. "The Eyes and Ears of the Congregation." *Academy Accents* 8, no. 1 (Spring 1992): 1–2.

Rose, Lucy A. *Speak, Lord, I'm Listening.* Richmond: Printing Services, 1999.

Runia, Klaas. "Experience in the Reformed Tradition." *Theological Forum of the Reformed Ecumenical Synod* 15, nos. 2, 3 (April 1987): 7–13.

Ryken, Leland. *The Word of God in English: Criteria for Excellence in Bible Translation.* Wheaton: Crossway, 2002.

———. *Words of Delight: A Literary Introduction to the Bible.* Grand Rapids: Baker, 1987.

———. *Words of Life: A Literary Introduction to the New Testament.* Grand Rapids: Baker, 1987.

Ryle, J. C. "Simplicity in Preaching." In *The Upper Room.* London: Banner of Truth, 1979.

Salmon, Bruce C. *Storytelling in Preaching.* Nashville: Broadman, 1988.

Sangster, W. E. *The Craft of Sermon Construction.* Grand Rapids: Baker, 1972.

———. *The Craft of Sermon Illustration.* London: Epworth, 1948.

Schaeffer, Francis. *The God Who Is There.* Downers Grove, Ill.: InterVarsity, 1968.

———. "True Spirituality." In *The Complete Works of Francis Schaeffer.* Vol. 3. Wheaton: Crossway, 1982.

Schuringa, H. David. "Hearing the Word in a Visual Age: A Practical Theological Consideration of Preaching within the Contemporary Urge to Visualization." Ph.D. diss., Theologische Universiteit te Kampen, 1995.

Schutz, Alfred. *The Phenomenology of the Social World.* Translated by George Walsh and Frederick Lehnert. Northwestern University Studies in Phenomenology and Existential Philosophy. Evanston, Ill.: Northwestern University Press, 1967.

Shaddix, Jim. *The Passion-Driven Sermon.* Nashville: Broadman & Holman, 2003.

Shaw, John. "The Character of a Pastor according to God's Heart." Ligonier, Pa.: Soli Deo Gloria Publications, 1992.

Silva, Moisés. *Has the Church Misread the Bible? The History of Interpretation in the Light of Current Issues.* Vol. 1. Foundations of Contemporary Interpretation. Grand Rapids: Zondervan, 1987.

Smedes, Lewis B. "Preaching to Ordinary People." *Leadership* 4, no. 4 (Fall 1983): 116.

Spurgeon, Charles Haddon. *An All Round Ministry: Addresses to Ministers and Stu-*

dents. Carlisle, Pa.: Banner of Truth, 1960.

———. *The Art of Illustration.* Lectures to My Students. London: Marshall Brothers, 1922.

———. "Christ Precious to Believers." In *The New Park Street Pulpit.* Vol. 5. London: Passmore & Alabaster, 1860.

———. *Lectures to My Students.* Grand Rapids: Zondervan, 1980.

Steimle, Edmund A., Morris J. Niedenthal, and Charles Rice, eds. *Preaching the Story.* Philadelphia: Fortress, 1980.

Stendahl, Krister. "Preaching from the Pauline Epistles." In *Biblical Preaching: An Expositor's Treasury,* edited by James W. Cox. Philadelphia: Westminster, 1983.

Stevenson, Dwight E., and Charles F. Diehl. *Reaching People from the Pulpit: A Guide to Effective Sermon Delivery.* New York: Harper & Row, 1958.

Stott, John R. W. *Between Two Worlds: The Art of Preaching in the Twentieth Century.* Grand Rapids: Eerdmans, 1988.

———. *The Preacher's Portrait: Some New Testament Word Studies.* Grand Rapids: Eerdmans, 1961.

Stuart, Douglas. *A Guide to Selecting and Using Bible Commentaries.* 5th ed. Dallas: Word, 1990.

———. *Old Testament Exegesis: A Primer for Students and Pastors.* 2nd ed. Philadelphia: Westminster, 1984.

Sweazey, George E. *Preaching the Good News.* Englewood Cliffs, N.J.: Prentice-Hall, 1976.

Thielicke, Helmut. *Encounter with Spurgeon.* Grand Rapids: Baker, 1977.

Thulin, Richard L. *The "I" of the Sermon.* Minneapolis: Fortress, 1989.

Trimp, C. *Preaching and the History of Salvation: Continuing an Unfinished Discussion.* Translated by Nelson D. Kloosterman. Scarsdale, N.Y.: Westminster Discount Book Service, 1996.

———. "The Relevance of Preaching." *Westminster Theological Journal* 36 (1973): 1–30.

Van Der Geest, Hans. *Presence in the Pulpit: The Impact of Personality in Preaching.* Translated by Douglas W. Stott. Atlanta: John Knox, 1981.

Van Groningen, Gerard. *Messianic Revelation in the Old Testament.* Grand Rapids: Baker, 1990.

Van Harn, Roger E. *Pew Rights for People Who Listen to Sermons.* Grand Rapids: Eerdmans, 1992.

Veerman, David. "Sermons: Apply Within." *Leadership* (Spring 1990): 120–25.

Vines, Jerry. *A Practical Guide to Sermon Preparation.* Chicago: Moody, 1985.

von Eckartsberg, Rolf. "The Eco-Psychology of Personal Culture Building: An Existential Hermeneutic Approach." In *Duquesne Studies in Phenomenological Psychology,* edited by Amadeo Giorgi, Richard Knowles, and David L. Smith III. Atlantic Highlands, N.J.: Humanitas/Duquesne University Press, 1979.

Vos, Geerhardus. *Biblical Theology.* Grand Rapids: Eerdmans, 1975.

———. "The Idea of Biblical Theology." Inaugural Address upon Assuming the New Chair of Biblical Theology at Princeton Seminary. N.d. (1895 probable).

White, Hayden. *Tropics of Discourse: Essays in Cultural Criticism.* Baltimore: John Hopkins University Press, 1978.

White, R. E. O. *A Guide to Preachers.* Grand Rapids: Eerdmans, 1973.

Whitesell, Farris D. *Power in Expository Preaching.* Old Tappan, N.J.: Revell, 1963.

Wiersbe, Warren W. *Preaching and Teaching with Imagination: The Quest for Biblical Ministry.* Wheaton: Victor, 1994.

Willhite, Keith, and Scott M. Gibson, eds. *The Big Idea of Biblical Preaching: Connecting the Bible to People.* Grand Rapids: Baker, 1998.

Williams, Michael J. *The Prophet and His Message: Reading Old Testament Prophecy Today.* Phillipsburg, N.J.: Presbyterian & Reformed, 2003.

Willimon, William H. *Peculiar Speech: Preaching to the Baptized.* Grand Rapids: Eerdmans, 1992.

Wilson, Joseph Ruggles. "In What Sense Are Preachers to Preach Themselves?" *Southern Presbyterian Review* 25 (1874): 350–61.

Wilson, Paul Scott. *The Four Pages of the Sermon: A Guide to Biblical Preaching.* Nashville: Abingdon, 1999.

———. *The Practice of Preaching.* Nashville: Abingdon, 1995.

Yohn, David Waite. *The Contemporary Preacher and His Task.* Grand Rapids: Eerdmans, 1969.

York, Hershael W., and Bert Decker. *Preaching with Bold Assurance: A Solid and Enduring Approach to Engaging Exposition.* Nashville: Broadman & Holman, 2003.

Index